A·N·N·U·A·L E·D·I·T·I·O·N·S

American History Volume I

16th Edition

Pre-Colonial through Reconstruction

EDITOR

Robert James Maddox
Pennsylvania State University
University Park

Robert James Maddox, distinguished historian and professor of American history at Pennsylvania State University, received a B.S. from Fairleigh Dickinson University in 1957, an M.S. from the University of Wisconsin in 1958, and a Ph.D. from Rutgers in 1964. He has written, reviewed, and lectured extensively, and is widely respected for his interpretations of presidential character and policy.

McGraw-Hill/Dushkin
530 Old Whitfield Street, Guilford, Connecticut 06437

Visit us on the Internet
http://www.dushkin.com

Credits

1. The New Land
Unit photo—Courtesy of Library of Congress.
2. Revolutionary America
Unit photo—Courtesy of the National Archives.
3. National Consolidation and Expansion
Unit photo—Courtesy of the National Archives.
4. The Civil War and Reconstruction
Unit photo—Courtesy of Library of Congress.

Copyright

Cataloging in Publication Data
Main entry under title: Annual Editions: American History, Vol. One: Pre-Colonial through Reconstruction. 16/E.
  1. United States—History—Periodicals. 2. United States—Historiography—Periodicals. 3. United States—civilization—
Periodicals. I. 1. Maddox, Robert James, comp. II Title: American history, vol. one: Pre-colonial through reconstruction.
ISBN 0–07–242570–9   973'.5   74–187540   ISSN 0733–3560

Sixteenth Edition

Cover image © 2001 PhotoDisc, Inc.

Printed in the United States of America   1234567890BAHBAH54321   Printed on Recycled Paper

Editors/Advisory Board

Staff

To the Reader

In publishing ANNUAL EDITIONS we recognize the enormous role played by the magazines, newspapers, and journals of the public press in providing current, first-rate educational information in a broad spectrum of interest areas. Many of these articles are appropriate for students, researchers, and professionals seeking accurate, current material to help bridge the gap between principles and theories and the real world. These articles, however, become more useful for study when those of lasting value are carefully collected, organized, indexed, and reproduced in a low-cost format, which provides easy and permanent access when the material is needed. That is the role played by ANNUAL EDITIONS.

New to ANNUAL EDITIONS is the inclusion of related World Wide Web sites. These sites have been selected by our editorial staff to represent some of the best resources found on the World Wide Web today. Through our carefully developed topic guide, we have linked these Web resources to the articles covered in this ANNUAL EDITIONS reader. We think that you will find this volume useful, and we hope that you will take a moment to visit us on the Web at *http://www.dushkin.com* to tell us what you think.

Not that long ago, most historical writing fell into identifiable categories: political, economic, diplomatic, and military history, among others. There was, moreover, a tendency to focus on notable leaders and how they helped shape the course of history. Presidents, titans of industry, and generals and admirals who won or lost great battles were interpreted and reinterpreted. This is not surprising. The lives of such men (women did not figure much in traditional accounts, except for a few lines devoted to prominent writers and reformers) seemed inherently more significant and interesting than those of ordinary people. Although attention continues to be paid to such figures, there has been, over the past 30 years, a veritable explosion of interest in individuals and groups that were previously ignored or mentioned only in passing. The roles of women, Native Americans, Hispanics, Asians, and other groups are now introduced and analyzed in an ever-increasing number of books and articles.

These "new" histories can only be applauded for enriching our understanding of the past and for interpreting events through a variety of viewpoints. America's western movement, for example, no longer is presented solely as the "conquering of a continent" by white settlers, but also as a series of tragedies that were experienced by those who stood in its path. Unfortunately, the new historians and the traditionalists all too often push their own agenda, while denouncing the other side's as irrelevant or wrongheaded, at the expense of synthesis. Unfortunately, too, much recent work that appears in professional journals is written in an impenetrable jargon that renders it inaccessible to most readers. The sixteenth edition of *Annual Editions: American History, Volume I*, attempts to present a fair sampling of articles that represent different approaches and that are intelligible.

Annual Editions: American History, Volume I contains a number of features designed to aid students, researchers, and professionals. These include a *topic guide* for locating articles on specific subjects; the *table of contents* abstracts that summarize each essay, with key concepts in bold italics; and a comprehensive *index*. Articles are organized into four units, each preceded by an overview that provides a background for informed reading of the articles, emphasizes critical issues, and presents *key points to consider.*

Again, in this edition *World Wide Web* sites that can be used to further explore the topics are included. Additionally, these sites are cross-referenced by number in the *topic guide.*

Every revision of *Annual Editions: American History, Volume I* replaces about 50 percent of the previous articles with new ones. We try to update and improve the quality of the sections, and we would like to consider alternatives that we may have missed. If you find an article that you think merits inclusion in the next edition, please send it to us (or at least send us the citation, so that the editor can track it down for consideration). We welcome your comments about the readings in this volume, and a postage-paid reader response card is included in the back of the book for your convenience. Your suggestions will be carefully considered and greatly appreciated.

Robert James Maddox

Robert James Maddox
Editor

Contents

UNIT 1

The New Land

Eight selections discuss the
beginnings of America—the new
land—from pre-Columbian times,
early life of the colonists, and
religious intolerance, to the stirrings
of liberty and independence.

The concepts in bold italics are developed in the article. For further expansion please refer to the Topic Guide and the Index.

UNIT 2

Revolutionary America

Seven articles examine the start of the American Revolution. The new land offered opportunities for new ideas that led to the creation of an independent nation.

The concepts in bold italics are developed in the article. For further expansion please refer to the Topic Guide and the Index.

The concepts in bold italics are developed in the article. For further expansion please refer to the Topic Guide and the Index.

UNIT 3

National Consolidation and Expansion

Eleven selections examine the developing United States, the westward movement of people seeking a new life, and the realities of living in early nineteenth-century America.

The concepts in bold italics are developed in the article. For further expansion please refer to the Topic Guide and the Index.

The concepts in bold italics are developed in the article. For further expansion please refer to the Topic Guide and the Index.

UNIT 4

The Civil War and Reconstruction

Eight articles discuss the tremendous effects of the Civil War on America. With the abolishment of slavery, the United States had to reconstruct society.

x

The concepts in bold italics are developed in the article. For further expansion please refer to the Topic Guide and the Index.

The concepts in bold italics are developed in the article. For further expansion please refer to the Topic Guide and the Index.

This topic guide suggests how the selections and World Wide Web sites found in the next section of this book relate to topics of traditional concern to American history students and professionals. It is useful for locating interrelated articles and Web sites for reading and research. The guide is arranged alphabetically according to topic.

The relevant Web sites, which are numbered and annotated on pages 4 and 5, are easily identified by the Web icon (◉) under the topic articles. By linking the articles and the Web sites by topic, this ANNUAL EDITIONS reader becomes a powerful learning and research tool.

TOPIC AREA	TREATED IN	TOPIC AREA	TREATED IN
African Americans	8. Right to Marry 10. Jefferson's Secret Life 15. Founding Fathers, Conditional Antislavery 21. "All We Want Is Make Us Free!" 24. Lives of Slave Women 27. "The Doom of Slavery" 28. Pride and Prejudice in the American Civil War 29. Struggle for Black Freedom before Emancipation ◉ **1, 2, 4, 6, 15, 22, 28, 30**	**Constitution**	14. . . . by the Unanimous Consent of the States 15. Founding Fathers, Conditional Antislavery 19. Chief Justice Marshall Takes the Law in Hand ◉ **1, 4, 5, 14, 15**
Alien and Sedition Acts	17. Order vs. Liberty ◉ **1, 2, 3, 4**	**Culture**	1. Americas 2. Columbus Meets Pocahontas in the American South 4. Laboring in the Fields of the Lord 8. Right to Marry 10. Jefferson's Secret Life 22. "All Men & Women Are Created Equal" 33. Bats, Balls, and Bullets ◉ **1, 2, 4, 5, 6, 7, 8, 9, 10, 11, 18, 23, 25, 26, 27, 28**
American Revolution	9. Flora MacDonald 11. Making Sense of the Fourth of July 12. George Washington, Spymaster ◉ **1, 2, 3, 4, 5, 6, 11, 14, 18**		
Baseball	33. Bats, Balls, and Bullets	**Declaration of Independence**	11. Making Sense of the Fourth of July ◉ **1, 4, 5, 14, 15**
Civil War	27. "Doom of Slavery" 28. Pride and Prejudice in the American Civil War 29. Struggle for Black Freedom before Emancipation 30. Lee's Greatest Victory 31. Yankee Scarlet O'Hara in Atlanta 32. Sherman's War 33. Bats, Balls, and Bullets ◉ **1, 2, 4, 5, 17, 27, 28, 29, 30, 31**	**Environment**	18. Lewis and Clark 25. Eden Ravished ◉ **2, 6, 11, 12, 13, 14, 15, 17, 24**
		Exploration	2. Columbus Meets Pocahontas in the American South 3. "Newfounde Lande" 18. Lewis and Clark ◉ **7, 8, 21, 24**
Clark, George	18. Lewis and Clark ◉ **1, 2, 4, 24**	**Government**	7. Penning a Legacy 11. Making Sense of the Fourth of July 14. . . . by the Unanimous Consent of the States 15. Founding Fathers, Conditional Antislavery 16. Greatness of George Washington 17. Order vs. Liberty 19. Chief Justice Marshall Takes the Law in Hand 23. James K. Polk and the Expansionist Spirit 26. Assault in the Senate 34. New View of Reconstruction ◉ **1, 2, 3, 4, 7, 12, 13, 14, 15, 16, 17, 18, 19, 20, 29**
Colonial America	4. Laboring in the Fields of the Lord 5. Missing Women of Martin's Hundred 6. Bearing the Burden? Puritan Wives 7. Penning a Legacy 8. Right to Marry ◉ **1, 2, 4, 6, 9, 11, 15, 17, 18, 19**		
Commerce	13. Canton War ◉ **19**		

● AE: American History Volume 1

The following World Wide Web sites have been carefully researched and selected to support the articles found in this reader. If you are interested in learning more about specific topics found in this book, these Web sites are a good place to start. The sites are cross-referenced by number and appear in the topic guide on the previous two pages. Also, you can link to these Web sites through our DUSHKIN ONLINE support site at *http://www.dushkin.com/online/*.

The following sites were available at the time of publication. Visit our Web site—we update DUSHKIN ONLINE regularly to reflect any changes.

General Sources

1. American Historical Association (AHA)
http://www.theaha.org
This site is an excellent source for data on just about any topic in American history. All affiliated societies and publications are noted, and AHA and its links provide material related to myriad fields of history.

2. American Studies Web
http://www.georgetown.edu/crossroads/asw/
Links to a wealth of Internet resources for research in American studies, from agriculture and rural development, to government, to race and ethnicity, are provided on this eclectic site.

3. Harvard's John F. Kennedy School of Government
http://www.ksg.harvard.edu
Starting from this home page, you will be able to click on a huge variety of links to information about American history, politics, and government, including material related to debates of enduring issues.

4. History Net
http://www.thehistorynet.com/THNarchives/AmericanHistory/
Supported by the National Historical Society, this site provides information on a wide range of topics. The articles are of excellent quality, and the site has book reviews and even special interviews. It is also frequently updated.

5. Library of Congress
http://www.loc.gov
Examine this Web site to learn about the extensive resource tools, library services/resources, exhibitions, and databases available through the Library of Congress in many different subfields of government studies.

6. Smithsonian Institution
http://www.si.edu
This site provides access to the enormous resources of the Smithsonian, which holds some 140 million artifacts and specimens for "the increase and diffusion of knowledge." Here you can learn about American social, cultural, economic, and political history from a variety of viewpoints.

The New Land

7. Early America
http://earlyamerica.com/earlyamerica/index.html
Explore the "amazing world of early America" through early media data at this site. Topics include Pages of the Past, Lives of Early Americans, Notable Women of Early America, Milestone Events, and many more.

8. 1492: An Ongoing Voyage/Library of Congress
http://lcweb.loc.gov/exhibits/1492/
Displays examining the causes and effects of Columbus's voyages to the Americas can be accessed on this Web site. "An Ongoing Voyage" explores the rich mixture of societies coexisting in five areas of this hemisphere before European arrival. It then surveys the polyglot Mediterranean world at a dynamic turning point in its development.

9. The Mayflower Web Page
http://members.aol.com/calebj/
The Mayflower Web Page represents thousands of hours of research, organization, and typing; it grows daily. Visitors include everyone from kindergarten students to history professors, from beginning genealogists to some of the most noted genealogists in the nation. The site is a merger of two fields: genealogy and history.

10. University of California at Santa Barbara/ Department of Anthropology
http://www.anth.ucsb.edu/projects/index.html
Visit this interesting site to learn about different facets of pre-Columbian America. Click on the Web link for the Great Kiva project, which offers a virtual-reality tour of a major structure of the Anasazi culture of the American southwest. The three-dimensional model provides extraordinary detail.

Revolutionary America

11. The Early America Review
http://www.earlyamerica.com/review/
Explore the Web site of *The Early America Review*, an electronic journal of fact and opinion on the people, issues, and events of eighteenth-century America. The quarterly is of excellent quality.

12. House of Representatives
http://www.house.gov
This home page of the House of Representatives will lead to information about current and past House members and agendas, the legislative process, and so on.

13. National Center for Policy Analysis
http://www.public-policy.org/~ncpa/pd/pdindex.html
Through this site, click onto links to read discussions of an array of topics that are of major interest in the study of American history, from regulatory policy and privatization to economy and income.

14. Supreme Court/Legal Information Institute
http://supct.law.cornell.edu/supct/index.html
Open this site for current and historical information about the Supreme Court. The archive contains a collection of nearly 600 of the most historical decisions of the Court.

15. U.S. Founding Documents/Emory University
http://www.law.emory.edu/FEDERAL/
Through this site you can view scanned originals of the Declaration of Independence, the Constitution, and the Bill of Rights. The transcribed texts are also available, as are *The Federalist Papers*.

16. U.S. Senate
http://www.senate.gov
This home page of the U.S. Senate will lead to information about current and past Senate members and agendas, legislative activities, committees, and so on.

17. The White House
http://www.whitehouse.gov/WH/Welcome.html
Visit the home page of the White House for direct access to information about commonly requested federal services, the White House Briefing Room, and all of the presidents and vice presidents. The "Virtual Library" allows you to search White House documents, listen to speeches, and view photos.

18. The World of Benjamin Franklin
http://www.fi.edu/franklin/
Presented by the Franklin Institute Science Museum, "Benjamin Franklin: Glimpses of the Man" is an excellent multimedia site that lends insight into Revolutionary America.

National Consolidation and Expansion

19. Consortium for Political and Social Research
http://www.icpsr.umich.edu
At this site, the interuniversity Consortium for Political and Social Research offers materials in various categories of historical social, economic, and demographic data. One can view a statistical overview of the United States beginning in the late eighteenth century here.

20. Department of State
http://www.state.gov
View this site for an understanding into the workings of what has become a major U.S. executive branch department. Links explain what the Department does, what services it provides, what it says about U.S. interests around the world, and much more information.

21. The Mexican-American War Memorial Homepage
http://sunsite.unam.mx/revistas/1847/
For a change of pace and culture, visit this site from Mexico's Universidad Nacional Autonoma. It describes, from a Mexican perspective, the Mexican-American War.

22. Mystic Seaport
http://amistad.mysticseaport.org/main/welcome.html
The complex Amistad case is explored in a clear and informative manner on this online educational site. It places the event in the context of the issues of the 1830s and 1840s.

23. Social Influence Website
http://www.influenceatwork.com/intro.html
The nature of persuasion, compliance, and propaganda is the focus of this Web site, with many practical examples and applications. Students of such topics as the roles of public opinion and media influence in policy making should find these discussions of interest.

24. University of Virginia Library
http://www.lib.virginia.edu/exhibits/lewis_clark/
Created by the University of Virginia Library, this site examines the famous Lewis and Clark exploration of the trans-Mississippi west.

25. Women in America
http://xroads.virginia.edu/~HYPER/DETOC/FEM/
Providing the views of women travelers from the British Isles, France, and Germany on the lives of American women, this valuable site covers the years between 1820 and 1842 and is informative, stimulating, and highly original.

26. Women of the West
http://www.wowmuseum.org
The home page of the Women of the West Museum offers several interesting links that include stories, poems, educational resources, and exhibits.

The Civil War and Reconstruction

27. The American Civil War
http://www.janke.washcoll.edu/civilwar/civilwar.htm
Washington College provides this wide-ranging list of data on the Civil War. Some examples of data available are: army life, the British connection, diaries/letters/memos, maps, movies, museums, music, people, photographs, and poetry.

28. Anacostia Museum/Smithsonian Institution
http://www.si.edu/organiza/museums/anacost/
This is the home page of the Center for African American History and Culture of the Smithsonian Institution, which is expected to become a major repository of information. Explore its many avenues.

29. Abraham Lincoln Online
http://www.netins.net/showcase/creative/lincoln.html
A well-organized, high-quality site that will lead you to substantial material about Lincoln and his era. Discussions among Lincoln scholars can be accessed in the Mailbag section.

30. Gilder Lehrman Institute of American History
http://vi.uh.edu/pages/mintz/gilder.htm
Click on the links to the various articles presented through this Web site to read outstanding, first-hand accounts of slavery in America through the period of Reconstruction.

31. Secession Era Editorials Project
http://history.furman.edu/benson/docs/
Newspaper editorials of the 1800s regarding events leading up to secession are presented on this Furman University site. When complete, this distinctive project will offer additional features that include mapping, statistical tools, and text analysis.

We highly recommend that you review our Web site for expanded information and our other product lines. We are continually updating and adding links to our Web site in order to offer you the most usable and useful information that will support and expand the value of your Annual Editions. You can reach us at: *http://www.dushkin.com/annualeditions/.*

www.dushkin.com/online/

Unit Selections

1. **The Americas,** Lewis Lord
2. **Columbus Meets Pocahontas in the American South,** Theda Perdue
3. **A "Newfounde Lande,"** Alan Williams
4. **Laboring in the Fields of the Lord,** Jerald T. Milanich
5. **The Missing Women of Martin's Hundred,** J. Frederick Fausz
6. **Bearing the Burden? Puritan Wives,** Martha Saxton
7. **Penning a Legacy,** Patricia Hudson
8. **The Right to Marry: *Loving v. Virginia,*** Peter Wallenstein

Key Points to Consider

❖ A common perception of Native Americans in the lands north of Mexico is that they lived in relatively small groups who survived independently of one another, and they had self-sustaining, primitive economies based on hunting, fishing, and gathering. In what ways does the article on Cahokia contradict this perception?

❖ The essay on Columbus and Pocahontas is an example of what is called "alternative history." Is it misleading to use an event that did not and could not have taken place to evaluate attitudes and ideas of a bygone era? Or, can such a device shed light on cultural contrasts? Explain.

❖ Spanish friars established missions in what is now southern Georgia and Northern Florida, presumably to save the souls of the native peoples. What practical effects did these missions have on their lives?

❖ In what ways did Puritan men justify the subordination of women? How could women achieve moral authority and influence under such circumstances?

❖ Discuss the constitution that William Penn framed for the colony he wished to establish. What aspects of it were "progressive" for the time?

 **DUSHKIN**ONLINE **Links** **www.dushkin.com/online/**

7. **Early America**
   http://earlyamerica.com/earlyamerica/index.html
8. **1492: An Ongoing Voyage/Library of Congress**
   http://lcweb.loc.gov/exhibits/1492/
9. **The Mayflower Web Page**
   http://members.aol.com/calebj/
10. **University of California at Santa Barbara/ Department of Anthropology**
    http://www.anth.ucsb.edu/projects/index.html

These sites are annotated on pages 4 and 5.

When people say that Columbus "discovered" America, they really mean that he did so for Europeans. There already were between 80 to 100 million inhabitants in the New World who scarcely needed to be discovered. We know that earlier Norse explorers had landed in the New World but they established no permanent settlements and had no lasting effect. Some claim that there were expeditions from the "old" world even before the Norse, but lack of hard evidence consigns these claims to the realm of speculation.

Expeditions mounted first by the Spanish, then the English and French, had profound and often disastrous effects on indigenous peoples. Partly this was due to military operations conducted by the invaders, some of whom deliberately slaughtered anyone who stood in the way of acquiring jewels and precious metals. Even more devastating were the communicable diseases that the Europeans brought with them against which the native peoples had no immunity.

Those we call "native" Americans first came from Asia tens of thousands of years ago across an ancient land bridge to Alaska. Although those who settled in what is now the United States never established powerful empires such as the Aztecs in Mexico or the Incas in Peru, some developed sophisticated social and economic organizations. "The Americas," the first selection in this unit, describes the town of Cahokia that was established near present-day St. Louis, Missouri. At its heydey, about 1050 to 1150 A.D., it was a central trading community for a large region. The essay "Columbus Meets Pocahontas in the American South" uses a symbolic encounter to discuss the ways men and women crossed racial and cultural boundaries, and how such relationships reveal European views of female sexuality. In his report "A 'Newfounde Land'," Alan Williams tells what is known of the Italian explorer, John Cabot, who headed the first European expedition known to have landed in North America. Next, "Laboring in the Fields of the Lord," by Jerald Milanich, examines the establishment of Spanish missions in what is now Georgia and Florida and the disastrous results that followed the highly motivated acts of many of the friars.

The English came relatively late to the New World. Some of them were searching for gold, silver, and jewels, as had their predecessors. Others came to settle permanently, either to escape religious

persecution or merely to build new lives for themselves. J. Frederick Fausz, in "The Missing Women of Martin's Hundred," tells about the "Powhatan uprising" of 1622 that almost destroyed the English settlements along the James River in Virginia. About 20 women were taken captive during this conflict, and they received a mixed reception when they were freed and returned home years later. Women in the English colonies were subordinate to men legally and in a variety of other ways. The essay "Bearing the Burden? Puritan Wives" describes the changing roles of women in Puritan communities. It tells how they were able to attain moral and spiritual authority despite their unequal status.

William Penn's acquisition of a grant of land that would later become Pennsylvania is reviewed in the article "Penning a Legacy." Penn crafted a constitution that provided for religious freedom, voting rights, and penal reform. He also hoped that the Native Americans already in the area would permit the new settlers to live among them "with your love and consent." The last essay in this unit, "The Right to Marry: *Loving v. Virginia*," describes efforts in Virginia to prevent racial mixing of whites and blacks.

The Americas

By Lewis Lord

America was different then. Eagles soared over the oak and poplar forests of Manhattan, where the fragrance of wild roses filled the air and deer, turkeys, and great horned owls inhabited what would become Fifth Avenue. Boston teemed with beavers. Herds of buffalo trod Chicago. And in the heart of the Midwest in that year—A.D. 1000—the first city in what is now the United States was on the verge of becoming an Indian metropolis.

Archaeologists know it as Cahokia, the busiest spot north of the Rio Grande when the new millennium began. At a time when few settlements had even 400 or 500 residents, this 6-square-mile community on the Illinois side of the Mississippi River boasted several thousand. In its 12th-century heyday, Cahokia may have had 20,000 or 25,000 residents, roughly the number in contemporary London. Not until 1800, when Philadelphia counted 30,000, would any U.S. city have more.

Cahokia enjoyed the same advantages that strengthened urban centers of the 19th and 20th centuries: a specialized labor force, an organized government, public construction projects, and a trade network that extended the length of the Mississippi River and reached east to the Atlantic and west to Oklahoma and Nebraska. But it also was bedeviled by problems not unlike those that plague modern cities, especially the

havoc created by too much growth. Five or six centuries after its birth, America's first city, unable to cope with change, was a ghost town.

Yet, while the people vanished, their monuments remained, as can be seen in a visit to Cahokia Mounds State Historical Site, a 2,200-acre tract of open fields and Indian mounds 8 miles east of downtown St. Louis maintained by the state of Illinois. Among the scores of mounds still intact in the rich river bottomland is Monks Mound, towering as high as a 10-story building and covering more ground than the biggest of Egypt's pyramids. From atop this grassy structure—the largest prehistoric earthen mound in the western hemisphere—visitors see in the distance St. Louis's Gateway Arch. Much closer, they hear the whine below of 18-wheelers on an interstate highway built in the 1960s across the ancient city's site.

Corn boom. One millennium ago, Cahokia was emerging from centuries in which people in the region foraged for nuts and berries. Cahokia's rise very likely began with a breakthrough, the introduction around A.D. 800 of a variety of corn suited as much for the Midwest as for Mexico, the land where corn began. New technology also helped: Someone fastened a stone blade to a pole, and farmers in the heartland began cultivating soil with a hoe instead of scratching it with a digging stick. All

around Cahokia, corn-fed villages sprang up on the plain made fertile by floods of the Mississippi and Illinois rivers.

Indians for centuries had built mounds in many shapes—octagons, circles, even the zigzag of a snake. Around A.D. 900, Cahokia developed another form: the four-sided pyramid with a flat top. To this day, no one has shown that a single Mexican ever visited Cahokia. But someone, somehow, had Mexican ideas: Cahokia's earthen mounds were very similar to the stone pyramids built by Mexico's then fading Mayans. And atop Cahokia's mounds stood thatched-roof temples and houses for the privileged, like structures crowning the Mayan platforms.

To build Monks Mound (so named after a local 19th-century Trappist monastery), Cahokians hauled 55-pound basket loads of dirt on their backs from nearby borrow pits. After they did this 14.7 million times over three centuries, constructing one rectangular platform atop another, the 22-million-cubic-foot mound was complete.

Cahokia-style. The French explorers who ventured into the Mississippi Valley in the 1600s found nothing around Cahokia but vine-covered mounds, which they probably mistook for natural hills. But further south along the Mississippi, they came across Indian tribes with lifestyles that scholars believe were

Then: Artist's rendering shows Cahokia in its heyday, 1100-1200.

MICHAEL HAMPSHIRE—CAHOKIA MOUNDS STATE HISTORIC SITE

remarkably like Cahokia's. The Cahokians are considered perhaps the earliest of a people known to anthropologists as "Mississippians"—Indians of the Mississippi Valley and the Southeast who formed villages beside rivers, raised corn, built temple mounds, and worshiped the sun. In the early 1700s, in what is now Mississippi, French colonists settled among perhaps the last Mississippian tribe—the Natchez—and, before annihilating them 30 years later, kept detailed accounts of their habits.

Along with archaeological findings at Cahokia, the Natchez records give scholars plenty of clues about Cahokian life. Evidence suggests, for instance, that each morning at Cahokia a millennium ago likely found a cluster of old men in a house atop Monks Mound raising their arms and emitting frightful howls as a man covered in tattoos arose from his bed. Not once did the Great Sun, as Mississippian chiefs were known, bother to look at them. Instead,

CAHOKIA MOUNDS STATE HISTORIC SITE
Arrowheads were found in one of Cahokia's mounds.

he stepped outside and howled a greeting to his perceived brother, the real sun, as it emerged over the wooded flatlands. Then he lifted a hand above his head and drew a line across the sky, from east to west. That showed the sun which way to go.

Cahokia's great suns apparently expected an eternity of female companionship. Excavation of a small mound a half mile south of Monks Mound revealed the skeleton of an early leader, a

man about 40 years old, resting on a bird-shaped platform of nearly 20,000 marine-shell beads. Nearby lay the remains of more than 100 women between 15 and 25 years old, plus four male skeletons—apparently the chief's attendants—with no heads or hands. When a Natchez sun died, many of his subjects volunteered to be strangled so they could join him in his afterlife. A mass sacrifice, scholars believe, was also precipitated by the death of Cahokia's great sun.

A re-creation of the Cahokia chief's burial, complete with the 20,000 beads, is part of a life-size diorama at the historical site's museum near Collinsville, Ill. Among other scenes: a young woman grinding corn, children playing with a doll made of cattails, a man with tattoos on his face and shoulders (indicating high status) trading salt for a knife, and a boy heating rocks for a sweat lodge, where townspeople expected steam to cleanse their bodies and spirits.

Cahokians could neither read nor write, but they had a knack for astronomy. West of Monks Mound stands a reconstructed circle of 48 wooden posts every day. You could probably smell Cahokia before you saw it."

Most of the trees from the nearby forests, Iseminger suspects, were cut for

Cahokia wrestled daily with challenges that would confront Americans a millennium later: military defense, runaway growth, smog.

that scholars dubbed "Woodhenge" because of its functional similarity to England's Stonehenge. Nearly 10 centuries ago, such a circle apparently served as the Cahokians' calendar: A pole at the center, when aligned with the circle's easternmost post and the front of Monks Mound, marked the equinoxes of spring and fall.

Wall of woe. The original Woodhenge went up when the city was on the rise, and its replica symbolizes Cahokian achievement. Just east of Monks Mound stands another re-creation—a portion of a 20-foot-high wall—that represents the community's decline. "More and more people were settling in Cahokia, and a lot of problems developed," explains archaeologist William Iseminger, the museum curator. "They likely had smog from all the fires that burned

construction and firewood. This damaged the habitat of animals that provided meat for diets not only in Cahokia but also in surrounding communities. Reduction of the forests also probably led to silt buildups in streams, resulting in floods that wrecked croplands. "Cahokia was competing with other people for resources," Iseminger says, "and warfare may have resulted."

What ensued was a defense program that apparently helped spell Cahokia's demise. Around A.D. 1100, the Cahokians enclosed their inner city within a 2-mile-long stockade built from the foot-thick trunks of 20,000 oak and hickory trees. Problems endured, but the wall didn't. Thrice in the next 200 years, the Cahokians rebuilt their wooden perimeter, each time at a cost of 20,000 trees and 130,000 work-hours. Ca-

hokia's forests were being exhausted and so, too, were its people.

By 1200, a gradual exodus from the inner city and its suburbs was underway. The wall still shielded Cahokia from rival chiefdoms, but inside the city, shortages of fuel and food grew steadily worse. No one is sure whether other problems emerged, such as inept leadership, the rise of a more charismatic chief somewhere else, a ruinous change in climate, or diseases brought on by diminished diets and faulty sanitation.

Nor does anyone know where the Cahokians were going. Conceivably they canoed down the Mississippi to Memphis or Natchez, or up the Ohio and the Tennessee to Alabama or Georgia. In all those places, Mississippian communities with platform mounds and a culture akin to Cahokia's would emerge and endure into the 16th century, only to vanish in the wake of Hernando De Soto's epidemic-spreading 1540 trek across the South. Whether Cahokia's refugees inhabited any of the towns is anyone's guess. But the archaeological findings that focus on Cahokia itself are clear: By 1400, it was abandoned.

After a half-millennium run, the country's first city had become its first victim of urban stress.

Columbus Meets Pocahontas in the American South

by Theda Perdue

As icons of the European colonization of the Americas, Columbus and Pocahontas represent opposite sides of the experience—European and Native, invader and defender, man and woman. Biographies and other scholarly writings document their lives and deeds, but these feats pale in comparison to the encounter these two legendary figures symbolize. Columbus embodies European discovery, invasion, and conquest while Pocahontas has become the "mother of us all," a nurturing, beckoning, seductive symbol of New World hospitality and opportunity.[1] The two never actually met in the American South, of course, except metaphorically, but this symbolic encounter involved a sexual dynamic that was inherent to the whole process of European colonization, particularly that of the American South.

John Smith's tale of succor and salvation fixed the Pocahontas image forever in the American mind, and his autobiographical account of peaceful relations with her people, the Powhatans, has exempted Englishmen from the tarring Columbus has received as an international symbol of aggression. The Columbian encounter with Native women seemed, in fact, to be radically different from Smith's. On his initial voyage of discovery, Columbus had relatively little to report about Native women except that they, like men, went "naked as the day

they were born." The loss of one of his ships on this voyage forced Columbus to leave about a third of his crew on Hispaniola. When he returned, he found the burned ruins of his settlement and the decomposing corpses of his men. Local Natives related that "soon after the Admiral's departure those men began to quarrel among themselves, each taking as many women and as much gold as he could." They dispersed throughout the island, and local caciques killed them. The men on Columbus's expedition had their revenge: "Incapable of moderation in their acts of injustice, they carried off the women of the islanders under the very eyes of their brothers and their husbands." Columbus personally presented a young woman to one of his men, Michele de Cuneo, who later wrote that when she resisted him with her fingernails, he "thrashed her well, for which she raised such unheard of screams that you would not have believed your ears." In the accounts of the conquistadores, Spaniards seized women as they seized other spoils of war.[2] Such violence contributed to the "black legend" of Spanish inhumanity to Native peoples and stands in stark contrast to early English descriptions of their encounters with Native women.

John Smith, according to his own account, did not face the kind of resistance from Pocahontas and other Native women

of the Virginia tidewater that the Spanish had met in the Caribbean. When Smith and a delegation from Jamestown called at the primary town of Powhatan, Pocahontas's father, they discovered that he was away, but the chief's daughter and other women invited the Englishmen to a "mascarado." "Thirtie young women," Smith wrote, "came naked out of the woods, only covered behind and before with a few green leaves, their bodies all painted." They sang and danced with "infernal passions" and then invited Smith to their lodgings. By his account, written with uncharacteristic modesty in the third person, "he was no sooner in the house, but all these Nymphes more tormented him then ever, with crowding, pressing, and hanging about him, most tediously crying, Love you not me? Love you not me?"[3]

The Spanish supposedly raped and pillaged while the English nobly resisted seduction.

The contrast is obvious—the Spanish supposedly raped and pillaged while the English nobly resisted seduction. By focusing merely on the colonizing Europeans, however, we lose sight of the Na-

Originally appeared in *Southern Cultures*, Vol. 3, No. 1, 1997, pp. 4-21, a quarterly journal published for the University of North Carolina Center for the Study of the American South. © 1997 by the University of North Carolina Press. Reprinted by permission.

ive women who are central actors in this drama: they are, after all, both the victims of Columbus's barbarity and the seductive sirens luring Smith's party. Despite differences in the ways these women are portrayed in historical sources, their experiences suggest that conquest and colonization had their own sexual dynamic. One of the facts of

Nudity ensured that Native women were never far from the conscious thought of European men.

colonization that rarely surfaces in polite conversation or scholarly writing is sex, yet we know from the written records left by Europeans and from the more obscure cultural traditions of Native people that European men had sexual relations with native American women. What can the Columbian voyages, the Jamestown colonists, and the experiences of subsequent European immigrants to the American South tell us about the ways in which men and women crossed cultural and racial bounds in their sexual relations? What do these relationships reveal about European views of female sexuality? And how did these views shape European expansion?

THE EUROPEAN VIEW OF NATIVE SEXUALITY

One thing seems fairly certain: Native women were never far from the conscious thought of European men, be they Spanish or English. Nudity insured that this was so. Accustomed to enveloping clothes, Europeans marveled at the remarkably scant clothing of the Natives. De Cuneo described the Carib woman whom he raped as "naked according to their custom," and Smith noted that except for a few strategically placed leaves, his hostesses were "naked." De Cuneo and Smith were not alone in commenting on Native women's lack of clothing. The Lord Admiral himself noticed not only that the Caribbean women he encountered wore

little but that they had "very pretty bodies." The Jamestown colonists first encountered the prepubescent Pocahontas frolicking naked with the cabin boys. The combination of her youthful enthusiasm as well as her nudity led William Strachey, official chronicler of the colony, to describe Pocahontas as "a well featured, but wanton young girl." Other Europeans also tended to link the absence of clothing to sexuality: Amerigo Vespucci, for whom America was named, noted that "the women . . . go about naked and are very libidinous."[4]

While Native women frequently exposed breasts, particularly in warm weather, they normally kept pudenda covered. When women did bare all, Europeans had another shock in store: Native women in many societies plucked their pubic hair. While some evidence points to female singeing of pubic hair in ancient Greece and even early modern Spain, most Europeans recoiled from hairless female genitalia. Thomas Jefferson, whose interests extended far beyond politics, attempted to explain hair-plucking among Native Americans: "With them it is disgraceful to be hairy in the body. They say it likens them to hogs. They therefore pluck the hair as fast as it appears." Jefferson revealed both the reaction of non-Native men and the artificiality of the practice: "The traders who marry their women, and prevail on them to discontinue this practice say, that nature is the same with them as with whites."[5] However comfortable Euro-American men may have been with visible penises, depilation left female genitalia far more exposed than most could bear. Because women revealed their private parts intentionally, they seemed to be flaunting their sexuality.

Another cultural modification to the female physique also provoked comment. Among many Native peoples, women as well as men wore tattoos. While some Euro-Americans became so enamored of the practice that they adopted it, others regarded tattooing in the same light as make-up applied to make one more physically attractive. The late eighteenth-century Philadelphia physician Benjamin Rush, for example, compared the body markings of Native peoples to cosmetics used by the

French, a people whom he described as "strangers to what is called delicacy in the intercourse of the sexes with each other."[6] Unnatural markings on the body, to Europeans, signaled an enhanced sexuality.

As contact between Native peoples and Europeans grew, women gave up tattooing and hair plucking, and they adopted the blouses and long skirts common among non-Native women along the colonial frontier. Other features of Native culture, however, perpetuated the view of Native women as sexually uninhibited. Some Europeans found the humor of Native women to be terribly bawdy. Most women enjoyed teasing and joking, and pranks and jokes with sexual overtones were not necessarily taboo. The teasing Smith endured—"Love you not me? Love you not me?"—provides a good example. One Native woman even managed to shock a Frenchman. Louis-Philippe made a tour of the American West at the end of the eighteenth century, and during his visit to the Cherokees, his guide made sexual advances to several women. "They were so little embarrassed," wrote the future French king, "that one of them who was lying on a bed put her hand on his trousers before my very eyes and said scornfully, *Ah sick.*"[7]

Directness characterized courtship as well as rejection. Smith clearly expressed amazement at the forwardness of the "thirtie young women." In *Notes on the State of Virginia,* Thomas Jefferson compared the "frigidity" of Native men with the assertiveness of women: "A celebrated warrior is oftener courted by the females, than he has occasion to court: and this is a point of honor which the men aim at. . . . Custom and manners reconcile them to modes of acting, which, judged by Europeans would be deemed inconsistent with the rules of female decorum and propriety."[8] When the epitome of the American Enlightenment attributed Native women with a more active libido than Native men, who could doubt that it was so?

The arrangement and use of domestic space seemed to confirm a lack of modesty on the part of Native women. Native housing afforded little privacy for bathing, changing what little clothes women did wear, or engaging in sexual intercourse. Several generations, as well as visitors, usually slept in the same lodge. The essayist Samuel Stanhope Smith admitted that Indians were unjustly "represented as licentious because they are seen to lie promiscuously in the same wigwam." Nevertheless, few Natives allowed the lack of privacy in their homes to become a barrier to sexual fulfillment. During early eighteenth-century explorations in Carolina, one of John Lawson's companions took a Native "wife" for the night, and the newlyweds consummated their "marriage" in the same room in which other members of the expedition feasted and slept: "Our happy Couple went to Bed together before us all and with as little Blushing, as if they had been Man and Wife for 7 Years."[9]

Most European accounts of Native women in the South commented on their sexual freedom, particularly before they married. In the late eighteenth century, naturalist Bernard Romans observed: "Their women are handsome, well made, only wanting the colour and cleanliness of our ladies, to make them appear lovely in every eye; . . . they are lascivious, and have no idea of chastity in a girl, but in married women, incontinence is severely punished; a savage never forgives that crime." John Lawson suggested that even married women "sometimes bestow their Favours also to some or others in their Husbands Absence." And the trader James Adair maintained that "the Cherokees are an exception to all civilized or savage nations in having no law against adultery; they have been a considerable while under a petti-coat government, and allow their women full liberty to plant their brows with horns as oft as they please, without fear of punishment."[10]

Women in the Southeast sometimes openly solicited sex from Euro-Americans because sex gave women an opportunity to participate in the emerging market economy. Unlike men, who exchanged deerskins, beaver pelts, and buffalo hides with Europeans for manufactured goods, women often had to rely on "the soft passion" to obtain clothing, kettles, knives, hoes, and trinkets. Among some Native peoples a kind of

specialization developed according to John Lawson, who claimed that coastal Carolina peoples designated "trading girls." Sometimes prostitution was more widespread. Louis-Philippe insisted that "all Cherokee women are public women in the full meaning of the phrase: dollars never fail to melt their hearts."[11]

Selling sex was one thing; the apparent gift of women by their husbands and fathers was quite another. To Europeans, sex was a kind of commodity, purchased from prostitutes with money and from respectable women with marriage. An honorable man protected the chastity of his wife and daughters as he would other property. Native men in many societies, however, seemed to condone or even encourage sexual relations between Europeans and women presumably "belonging" to them. Even husbands who might object to "secret infidelities" sometimes offered their wives to visitors.[12]

Europeans also viewed the widespread practice of polygyny, or a man taking more than one wife, as adulterous because they recognized only the first as the "real" wife. Many Native people favored sororal polygyny, the marriage of sisters to the same man, and the groom often took sisters as brides at the same time. Since this meant, in European terms, that a man married his sister-in-law, sororal polygamy was incest as well as adultery. Jedidiah Morse, in his *Universal Geography,* wrote: "When a man loves his wife, it is considered his duty to marry her sister, if she has one. Incest and bestiality are common among them."[13] Morse apparently regarded marriage to sisters as serious a violation of European sexual mores as human intercourse with animals; in his mind, both constituted perversion.

Polygynous, adulterous, and incestuous or not, marriage meant little to Indians in the estimation of many Euro-Americans. Lawson, for example, described the ease with which the Native peoples of coastal Carolina altered their marital status: "The marriages of these Indians are no further binding than the man and woman agree together. Either of them has the liberty to leave the other upon any frivolous excuse they can make." The trader Alexander Longe relayed a Cherokee priest's view of his people's

lax attitude toward marriage: "They had better be asunder than together if they do not love one another but live for strife and confusion."[14] Europeans would have preferred that they stay together and, despite domestic turmoil, raise their children in an appropriately patriarchal household.[15]

When husband and wife parted, children normally remained with their mothers because Native peoples of the southeast were matrilineal, that is, they traced kinship solely through women. John Lawson attributed this very odd way of reckoning kin, in his view, to "fear of Impostors; the Savages knowing well, how much Frailty possesses *Indian* women, betwixt the Garters and the Girdle." While paternity might be questioned, maternity could not be. Despite the logic of such a system, Europeans had both intellectual and practical objections. Matrilineality seemed too close to the relationship between a cow and calf or a bitch and puppies: it was, the Iroquois historian Cadwallader Colden asserted, "according to the natural course of all animals." "Civilized" man presumably had moved beyond this "natural course" and had adopted laws, civil and religious, that bound fathers to children and husbands to wives. Europeans who married Native women of matrilineal societies nevertheless had difficulty exercising any control over their children and often abandoned them to their mothers' kin because men had no proprietary interest in their offspring. Thomas Nairne wrote of the Creeks: "A Girles Father has not the least hand or concern in matching her. . . . Sons never

European men thought that they had stepped through the looking glass into a sexual wonderland.

enjoy their fathers place and dignity."[16]

Blatant disregard of marital vows and paternal prerogatives was shocking enough, but many Native peoples exhibited little concern for the chastity of their daughters. Jean-Bernard Bossu reported that among Native peoples on the lower Mississippi, "when an unmarried brave passes through a village, he hires a girl for a night or two, as he pleases, and her parents find nothing wrong with this. They are not at all worried about their daughter and explain that her body is hers to do with as she wishes." Furthermore, according to Lawson, "multiplicity of Gallants never [gave] . . . a Stain to a Female's reputation, or the least Hindrance of her Advancement . . . the more *Whorish*, the more *Honourable*."[17]

THE REALITIES OF NATIVE SEXUALITY

European men who traveled through the Native Southeast thought that they had stepped through the looking glass into a sexual wonderland. Actually, they had encountered only a fractured reflection of their own assumptions about appropriate sexual behavior. Native women were not as uninhibited as most whites thought. Europeans failed to realize that Native peoples did have rules regulating marriage and sexual intercourse, although the rules were sometimes quite different from their own. In the Southeast, unmarried people could engage freely in sex, but many factors other than marital status regulated and limited sexuality. A warrior preparing for or returning from battle (sometimes much of the summer), a ball player getting ready for a game, a man on the winter hunt (which could last three to four months), a pregnant woman, or a woman during her menstrual period abstained from sex. In other words, Native southerners had to forego sexual intercourse for a far greater percentage of their lives than Europeans.

Furthermore, there were inappropriate venues for sex. Although a Native couple might engage in sex in a room occupied by others, there were places, such as agricultural fields, where amorous encounters were forbidden. Violation of this rule could have serious consequences. According to the trader James Adair, the Cherokees blamed a devastating smallpox epidemic in 1738 on "the adulterous intercourses of their young married people, who the past year, had in a most notorious manner,

violated their ancient laws of marriage in every thicket, and broke down and polluted many of their honest neighbours bean-plots, by their heinous crimes, which would cost a great deal of trouble to purify again."[18] For many Native southerners, therefore, a "toss in the hay" would have been a very serious offense.

For any given Cherokee, almost one third of all Cherokees were off-limits as sexual partners.

Native peoples also had rules against incest, but they did not define incest in the same way Euro-Americans did. Intercourse or marriage with a member of a person's own clan, for example, was prohibited, and the penalty could be death. Clan membership, which included all individuals who could trace their ancestry back to a remote, perhaps mythical figure, often ran into the thousands and included many people whom Europeans would not have regarded as relatives. Consequently, the number of forbidden partners was far greater than the number under the European definition of incest. The Cherokees, for example, had seven clans. No one could marry into his or her own clan, nor was the father's clan an acceptable marriage pool. The result was that, for any given Cherokee, almost one third of all Cherokees were off-limits as sexual partners.

Each Native people had particular rules regarding marriage and incest. Many societies permitted men to have more than one wife and to marry sisters. The effect was not necessarily the devaluation of women, as European observers often claimed. Some cultural anthropologists suggest, in fact, that sororal polygamy correlates positively with high female status.[19] In the Southeast where husbands lived with their wives, the marriage of sisters to the same man reduced the number of men in the household and strengthened the control of the women over domestic life. As Morse suggested,

sisters often wanted to share a husband just as they shared a house, fields, labor, and children.

Ignorant of Native rules, southern colonials tended to view Native women as wanton woodland nymphs over whose sexuality fathers, brothers, and husbands could exercise little control. Many colonists took full advantage of the situation as they perceived it. Some evidence, however, suggests that southeastern Native women were not as amenable to sexual encounters as Europeans suggested. Louis-Philippe's anecdote reveals a woman, however bold and uninhibited, rejecting a sexual advance. When women did engage in sexual activity, many of them probably succumbed to pressure or force rather than charm.

European culture at this time countenanced considerable violence against women. William Byrd's confidential account of surveying the boundary line between North Carolina and Virginia, for example, describes several episodes of sexual aggression. One young woman, he wrote, "wou'd certainly have been ravish't, if her timely consent had not prevented the violence." This cavalier attitude toward a woman's right to refuse sex characterized much interaction between Native women and Europeans. Race almost certainly exacerbated the situation. The records of the South Carolina Indian trade are replete with Native complaints of sexual abuse at the

---

Some Native peoples came to regard sexual misbehavior as the most distinguishing feature of European cultures.

---

hands of Europeans. One trader "took a young Indian against her Will for his Wife," another severely beat three women including his pregnant wife whom he killed, and a third provided enough rum to a woman to get her drunk and then "used her ill."[20] Obviously, the women in these incidents were not the ones who were lascivious.

Some Native peoples came to regard sexual misbehavior as the most distinguishing feature of European culture. The Cherokee Booger Dance, in which participants imitated various peoples, portrayed Europeans as sexually aggressive, and the men playing that role chased screaming young women around the dance ground. As it turns out, from the Native perspective, the British colonists of the American South may not have been so terribly different from Columbus's men after all.

The people who do stand in stark contrast are Native men. James Adair, a resident of the Chickasaw Nation and a trader throughout the Southeast, perhaps knew the region's Native cultures better than any other European in the eighteenth century. As the husband of a Chickasaw women and an occasional member of Chickasaw war parties against the Choctaws, he wrote with authority that "the Indians will not cohabitate with women while they are out at war; they religiously abstain from every kind of intercourse, even with their own wives." While Adair believed, perhaps correctly, that the reason for a period of abstinence was religious, the implications for female captives was clear. "The French Indians," he wrote, "are said not to have deflowered any of our young women they captivated, while at war with us." Even the most bloodthirsty Native warrior, according to Adair, "did not attempt the virtue of his female captives," although he did not hesitate to torture and kill them. Even the Choctaws, whom Adair described as "libidinous," had taken "several female prisoners without offering the least violence to their virtue, till the time of purgation was expired." Adair could not, however, resist the temptation to slander the Choctaws, the Chickasaws' traditional enemy: "Then some of them forced their captives, notwithstanding their pressing entreaties and tears."[21]

Captivity narratives suggest Indian men raped very few, if any, women victims of colonial wars—"a very agreeable disappointment" in one woman's words.[22] Rules prohibiting intercourse immediately before and after going to war may have contributed to the absence of documented sexual violence, but Native views on female sexuality and autonomy may have been equally responsible. Indians apparently did not view sex as property or as one of the spoils of war.

Columbus's men do seem to have equated sex and material plunder. The accounts of the destruction of the Hispaniola settlement link his men's desire for women with a desire for gold. In perhaps a more subtle way, British colonists also considered women to be a form of property and found the Native men's lack of proprietary interest in their wives and daughters incomprehensible. It called into question the Indians' concept of property in general and paved the way for Europeans to challenge Native people's ownership of land. From the second decade of colonization in the South, wealth depended on the cultivation of land, and southerners found the argument that Indians had no notion of absolute ownership particularly compelling.

People who objectified both land and sex had encountered people who did not.

While Native southerners forcefully maintained their right to inhabit the land of their fathers, they did not, in fact, regard land ownership in quite the same way as the Europeans who challenged their rights to it. They fought for revenge rather than for territory, they held land in common, and they permitted any tribal member to clear and cultivate unused tracts. Land did not represent an investment of capital, and Native southerners did not sell out and move on when other opportunities beckoned. Indeed, the land held such significance for most of them that they suffered severe economic, social, and political disruption rather than part with it. In the 1820s and 1830s, frontiersmen, land speculators, and politicians joined forces to divest Native peoples of their land, and southern state governments and ultimately the federal government took up the aggressors' cause. White southerners made a concerted effort to force their Indian neighbors to surrender their lands and move west of the Mississippi to new territory. What difference did it make, many whites asked, which lands the Indians occupied? With squatters encroaching on them, shysters defrauding them at every turn, and federal and state authorities unwilling to protect them, Native peoples in the South struggled desperately to retain their homelands. They did so for reasons as incomprehensible to Euro-Americans as the sexual behavior of Native women. People who objected both land and sex had encountered people who did not.

Ultimately, Native southerners lost. Representatives of the large southern tribes—the Cherokees, Chickasaws, Choctaws, Creeks, and Seminoles—signed treaties in which they agreed to move west to what is today eastern Oklahoma. Remnants of some of those tribes as well as other isolated Native communities simply retreated into the shadows and eked out a living on marginal land while the cotton kingdom expanded onto the rich soil that Native peoples had surrendered. In the cotton kingdom, land was saleable rather than sacred, and power not parity characterized sexual relationships.

In recent years we have come to admire Native sensitivity to the natural world and to compare ourselves unfavorably to Indians on environmental issues and attitudes toward the land. Columbus and Pocahontas probably thought about sex at least as often as they did ecology, but we seem incapable of recognizing that their views on sex might have been as different as their ideas about land use. Disney's recent movie, *Pocahontas,* merely perpetuates the notion that romantic love is a universal concept that transcends cultural bounds and has little connection with specific aspects of a culture. The film depicts Pocahontas not as the autonomous person she probably was, but as a subservient young woman submissive to her father, betrothed to the warrior Kocoum, and won by Smith. Pocahontas's love for Smith (and vice versa) resolves conflicts with the Indians, and the English presumably set about the task at hand. "Oh, with all ya got in ya, boys,"

Governor Ratcliffe sings, "dig up Virginia, boys." True love, of course, characterized neither the real relationship between Pocahontas and John Smith nor the dealings of Native women and European men. Instead of Disney's John Smith, most Native women really met Columbus. Perhaps in the American South, where Columbus and Pocahontas metaphorically collided so forcefully, we should expand our comparison of Native Americans and Europeans beyond environmental issues and consider the interactions between men and women. Then we might begin to make connections between the materialism and exploitation that have characterized so much of southern history and sexual violence against women.

NOTES

1. Samuel Eliot Morison, *Admiral of the Ocean Sea* (Little Brown and Company, 1942); Grace Steele Woodward, *Pocahontas* (University of Oklahoma Press, 1969); J. A. Leo Lemay, *Did Pocahontas Save Captain John Smith?* (University of Georgia Press, 1993); Philip Young, "The Mother of Us All," *Kenyon Review* 24 (1962): 391–441. See also Rayna Green, "The Pocahontas Perplex: The Image of Indian Women in American Culture," *Massachusetts Review* 16 (1975): 698–714.

2. Marvin Lunenfeld, ed., *1492: Discovery, Invasion, Encounter* (D. C. Heath and Company, 1991), 133, 161–64; S. E. Morison, ed., *Journals and Other Documents in the Life and Voyages of Christopher Columbus* (The Heritage Press, 1963), 212.

3. John Smith, *The Generall Historie of Virginia, New England and the Summer Isles . . .* (London, 1624), Book 3: 67.

4. Woodward, 5; Robert F. Berkhofer, *The White Man's Indian: The History of an Idea from Columbus to the Present* (Knopf, 1978), 7–9.

5. Paul Leicester Ford, ed., *The Writings of Thomas Jefferson*, 10 vols. (G. P. Putnam's Sons, 1892–99), 3: 154–55.

6. George W. Corner, ed., *The Autobiography of Benjamin Rush: His Travels Through Life, Together with His Commonplace Book* [1789–1813], *Memoirs of the American Philosophical Society*, vol. 25 (Princeton University Press, 1948), 71.

7. Louis-Philippe, *Diary of My Travels in America*, tr. Stephen Becker (Delacorte Press, 1977), 84–85.

8. Thomas Jefferson, *Notes on the State of Virginia*, (1787; reprt. Matthew Carey, 1794), 299.

9. Samuel Stanhope Smith, *An Essay on the Causes of the Variety of Complexion and Figure in the Human Species*, ed. Winthrop D. Jordan (1810; reprt. Harvard University Press, 1965), 128; John Lawson, *A New Voyage to Carolina*, ed. Hugh T. Lefler (University of North Carolina Press, 1967), 37–38.

10. Bernard Romans, *A Concise History of East and West Florida* (1775; reprt. University of Florida Press, 1962), 40–43; Lawson, 194; James Adair, *Adair's History of the North American Indians*, ed. Samuel Cole Williams (The Watauga Press, 1930), 1522–53.

11. Lawson, 41; Louis-Philippe, 72.

12. Romans, 40–43.

13. Jedidiah Morse, *The American Universal Geography; or a View of the Present State of All the Kingdoms, States, and Colonies in the Known World* (Thomas and Andrews, 1812), 105.

14. Lawson, 193; Alexander Longe, "A Small Postscript of the Ways and Manners of the Indians Called Charikees," ed. D. H. Corkran, *Southern Indian Studies* 21 (1969): 30.

15. Morse, 575–76; Albert Gallatin, "Synopsis of the Indian Tribes Within the United States East of the Rocky Mountains," vol. 2 of *Archaeologia Americana; Transactions and Collections of the American Antiquarian Society*, (Folson, Wells, and Thurston, 1836), 112–13.

16. Lawson, 57; Cadwallader Colden, *History of the Five Indian Nations of Canada which are Dependent on the Provinces of New York*, 2 vols. (1747; reprt. Allerton Brooks, 1922), 1: xxxiii; Alexander Moore, ed., *Nairne's Muskogean Journals; The 1708 Expedition to the Mississippi River* (University of Mississippi Press, 1988), 33, 45.

17. Seymour Feiler, ed., *Jean-Bernard Bossu's Travels in the Interior of North America, 1751–1762* (University of Oklahoma Press, 1962), 131–32; Lawson, 40.

18. Adair, 244.

19. Alice Schlegel, *Male Dominance and Female Autonomy: Domestic Authority in Matrilineal Societies* (Yale University Press, 1972), 87–88.

20. William K. Boyd, ed., *William Byrd's Histories of the Dividing Line Betwixt Virginia and North Carolina* (The North Carolina Historical Commission, 1929), 147–48; William L. McDowell, ed., *Journals of the Commissioners of the Indian Trade, Sept. 20, 1710–Aug. 29, 1718* (South Carolina Archives Department, 1955), 4, 37; McDowell, *Documents Relating to Indian Affairs, 1754–1765* (University of South Carolina Press, 1970), 231.

21. Adair, 171–72.

22. James Axtell, *The European and the Indian*, (Oxford University Press), 183.

A "Newfounde Lande"

*Five hundred years after John Cabot's 1497 voyage brought
word of the North American continent to Europe, scholars
still hotly debate the exact location of his landfall.*

Alan Williams

IN 1992, THE AMERICAS marked the five-hundredth anniversary of the European discovery of the lands of the Western Hemisphere by Christopher Columbus, a Genoese navigator sailing in the service of Spain's King Ferdinand and Queen Isabella. Considerable controversy surrounded the commemoration of that event, as some disputed the notion that lands already occupied could be "discovered" and others pointed to earlier claims by Europeans of having crossed the Atlantic and visited the Americas long before the arrival of Columbus.

This year the world marks another important quincentennial, and again there is controversy, especially surrounding the exact landfall of the explorer, John Cabot. While the precise location of Columbus's initial landfall has been questioned, it is generally conceded that his discoveries involved first the islands of the Caribbean and later, the mainland of South America. Cabot is honored, especially in England and in Atlantic Canada, as the man who forged the way from Europe to the North American continent, but where in North America remains at issue.

Legends about Atlantic crossings by Carthaginians, Jews, Chinese, and the Welsh place visitors from the Old World in the Western Hemisphere as early as the fifth century B.C. The Irish tell of St. Brendan island-hopping the northern North Atlantic a thousand years later. And the exploits of the Vikings in North America between A.D. 800–1400 are not only recorded in oral Norse sagas, but have been substantiated through modern archaeological investigations in northern Newfoundland, particularly at the Norse settlement uncovered at L'Anse aux Meadows, now recognized as a World Heritage site.

Columbus's four voyages to the New World are well documented. His initial visit to the Caribbean region in 1492–93 was followed the next year by his exploration of the southern coast of Cuba, which he was convinced was the territory of the Grand Khan of China, and Haiti, which he named Hispaniola because it resembled Spain. In 1498, Columbus cruised the Venezuelan coast, believing it to be the coast of Asia. And on his fourth and final voyage to the New World in 1502, Columbus touched what is now known as Central America.

While the "Admiral of the Ocean Sea" was so engaged, John Cabot set sail in 1497 to test his own theories on an all-water route to the Indies and returned to England with the first certain news of the coast of North America. Unlike Columbus, however, Cabot left little documentary information about himself or his voyages to help today's scholars reconstruct his achievements.

It is generally believed that Cabot was really Giovanni Caboto, a native of Gaeta, near Naples, in Italy. Born in or before 1455, he grew up in Genoa and is thus of the same generation and city as Columbus. Cabot later moved to Venice and became a citizen of that city in 1476. He married a Venetian named Mattea, with whom he had three sons, Ludovico, Sancio, and the most famous, Sebastiano.

Cabot made his living as a merchant, trading with Alexandria, in North Africa, from where he acquired Asian spices, dyes, and silks for markets in Europe. Like other seafaring European merchants, Cabot wished for a way to avoid dealing with the Arab "middlemen" who controlled practically all of the land that surrounded the Mediterranean Sea.

An experienced mapmaker and navigator, Cabot believed that it was possible to sail west in order to reach Asia. Hoping to win financial backing that would enable him to prove his theories, Cabot moved to Spain in 1490 and soon after approached officials in Seville with plans for a westward voyage to Cathay (China). When word reached him of the triumph of Christopher Columbus, Cabot knew that there would be little chance of his gaining the patronage of Spain's royalty for his own scheme.

By now obsessed with the idea of finding a western route to Asia, Cabot turned to England for help in his quest. He counted on King Henry VII's desire to outdo his Spanish rival, King Ferdinand II, in the possible acquisition of new territories and the opportunity to tap the wealth that would presumably come to the first nation to reach the shores of Cathay.

In England, Cabot settled with his family in the western port of Bristol, one

Originally intending to seek Spanish backing to test his theory on an all-water route to Asia, Cabot realized the futility of that course when Christopher Columbus returned from his first voyage to the New World in 1493 (above, right). The Italian-born explorer then moved his family from Spain to England, where he proposed his plan—to sail west as Columbus had, but at more northerly latitudes—to the merchants of Bristol and to King Henry VII (above, left).

of the nation's wealthiest cities. The Bristol merchants were a cosmopolitan group, fond of civic pomp, whose city, adorned with fine churches, mimicked London. Their trade in wool, cloth, hides, wine, and fish took their vessels to Iceland, Norway, Iberia, and the Mediterranean. The merchants, like the Norse before them, also sent seamen westward in search of fish and wood. Now Cabot approached them with a new and tantalizing objective.

Confidently asserting that he could reach the East by sailing west, as Columbus had done, Cabot promised to bring back the riches of Asia directly by sea, by-passing the Moslem traders of the eastern Mediterranean. He knew how far Columbus had sailed in southern latitudes without reaching Cathay and he cogently argued that, starting from England's more northerly latitude, he could reach the northeastern part of Cathay by traveling half the distance, just as German cartographer Martin Behaim had indicated on his globe in 1492.* Once they reached land, all that was necessary Cabot told the Englishmen, was to sail southwestward to the

warmer, populated regions of the East, such as Cipango (Japan) and India.

Probably on the basis of his skill as an advanced navigator, Cabot persuaded the merchants of his capability to captain such an expedition. Some of the instruments and charts that he carried were by far the most modern that the merchants had seen. Most of the instruments measured the angle between the stars or the sun and the horizon, so that the ship's position could be calculated. The cross-staff measured the angle of a star in relation to the horizon; the nocturnal figured the position of Ursa Major or Minor in relation to the Pole star; and the indispensable astrolabe determined latitude, the distance north or south of the equator.

After successfully securing the financial backing of the merchants of Bristol, Cabot petitioned the king for permission

---

*Behaim, using the academic geography available at the end of the fifteenth century, produced a terrestrial globe that showed only islands separating Europe from Asia. He grossly underestimated the actual circumference of the earth as well as the distance between Europe and Asia when sailing west.

to sail. He realized that he would not be able to claim any discoveries for England without royal assent, leaving his finds free for the taking by any European country. On March 5, 1496, Cabot and his sons, who do not seem to have accompanied him on his voyage, received letters patent (royal grants of right) from Henry VII authorizing them "to seek out, discover, and find whatsoever isles, countries, regions, or provinces of the heathen and infidels, whatsoever they be, and in what part of the world soever they be. . . ."

A letter written by John Day, an English merchant—"rather a slippery character with many irons in the fire"—who was reporting to Christopher Columbus on John Cabot's voyage, does not indicate exactly when or from where Cabot made his first attempt to cross the ocean, but it appears to have been in 1496, soon after he won his first letters patent from the English king. Day simply noted that Cabot "went with one ship, had a disagreement with his crew, he was short of supplies and ran into weather, and he decided to turn back."

Trying again in 1497, Cabot left Bristol, probably early in May in the *Matthew,* most likely named after his wife, Mattea. He struck out westwards for Cathay somewhere off the Atlantic coast of Ireland. Fifty-three days later, the *Matthew* reached land.

Cabot and his crew went ashore, the first Englishmen, although led by an Italian, to set foot on North American soil. They erected a cross and the banners of England and Venice, claiming all the country for the king. His party being small—Day wrote in a letter soon after Cabot returned home—Cabot "did not dare advance inland beyond the shooting distance of a crossbow and after taking fresh water he returned to his ship." Although they met no inhabitants, Cabot was certain that he had reached the northeastern extremity of Asia. Like Columbus when he coasted Cuba, Cabot expected that populous cities with roofs of gold and sources of silk and spices could not be too far off.

The exact point of Cabot's landing has been the subject of weighty argument. Scholars have so differently reconstructed Cabot's voyage, his known coasting, and his return journey that his North American landfall could have been anywhere between Labrador and Maine, perhaps even the Carolinas, with at least one historian taking him as far south as Florida.

Since no journal kept by Cabot or his crew has survived to indicate precisely where they went, historians have had to rely for documentation on a handful of letters sent from England to Spain and Italy by foreign diplomats. Even the fragmentary information contained in existing chronicles and maps made in the succeeding years, allegedly from Cabot's own globe and charts, may not be reliable.

The problem is further complicated by the fact that Cabot lost his life in 1498, either at sea or in the New World. The great Cabot scholar J. A. William-

MUSEO NAVAL, MADRID

Dating from around 1500, the planisphere of the whole known world drawn by Juan de la Cosa, is the earliest cartographic representation of any part of the North American continent. La Cosa depicted that section of the map (top, right) on a larger scale than the Old World and included references to both Columbus's and Cabot's New World discoveries. Five English flags, thought by some to represent places claimed by Cabot for King Henry VII of England, appear along the northwest Atlantic coast. Because there exists scant documentary information about Cabot's voyage, scholars have for centuries debated exactly what route his ship, the *Matthew*, followed and where in North America he landed. One suggested route takes Cabot directly to the coast of the island of Newfoundland, while the other has him missing Newfoundland on his outbound journey, landing instead on the northern tip of Cape Breton Island (bottom, right).

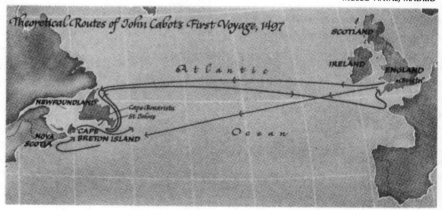

MAP BY JOAN PENNINGTON

son explained the reason why so little of Cabot's discovery is known, saying that while "Columbus had a faithful friend, the Bishop Las Casas [his biographer], and a son who revered his father's memory and saved it from being forgotten, John Cabot . . . had a son Sebastian, who seems to have been jealous of his father's fame and to have done his best to destroy the memory of his achievements."

Nineteenth-century American historiographer Henry Harrisse declared that Sebastian was one of the greatest liars in the history of discovery who, despite his long and generally successful career as a navigator and mapmaker in England and Spain, nevertheless wanted credit for his father's 1497 discovery. Thanks to the younger Cabot's efforts at distortion, the earliest chroniclers referred only to "a Venetian," and if they mentioned a name, it was that of Sebastian, not John.

The "Sebastian supremacy" lasted until the records were carefully searched by a Bristol librarian named Nicholls and an American Cabot scholar, Richard Biddle, in the first half of the nineteenth century. The investigations led historians on both sides of the Atlantic to eventually restore John Cabot to his rightful place in time for the four-hundredth anniversary of the landing in 1897, which saw a flurry of writing on the subject of his voyages.

Discussions concerning Cabot's right to be known as the "first discoverer of North America" and renewed debate on his likely route received added impetus with the uncovering of early cartographic evidence. The earliest find was a world map, made about the year 1500 by Juan de la Cosa, a skilled Biscayan navigator who had sailed with Columbus. Found in 1832, this was the first map to represent any part of the North American continent* and indicates both Columbus's "Indies" and Cabot's "northeastern part of Asia," which forms the western border of the Atlantic Ocean. La Cosa lined these lands with five English

flags, possibly indicating spots at which Cabot claimed territory for the Crown. La Cosa also identifies "Cauo de ynglaterra" (Cape of England) and "mar de descubierta por inglese" (sea discovered by the English).

William Ganong, a great cartographic scholar from New Brunswick, Canada, performed an analysis of the La Cosa map, which has been called "one of the most brilliant 'old map' expositions ever written." Ganong concluded that the La Cosa map could be a simplification of Cabot's own map, the result of successive re-drawings. He further theorized that Cabot missed Newfoundland on the outward voyage, landed on Cape Breton Island, off Nova Scotia, and returned along the southern coast of Newfoundland.

The case can be made that the land below the English flags, heading southward, represents the *whole* coast of North America, from Labrador to the Gulf of Mexico, but with part of the latter hidden by a depiction of St. Christopher. The distinguished historical cartographer R. A. Skelton considered the Cosa map "the only map which unambiguously illustrates John Cabot's voyage of 1497 and—with less certainty—his voyage of 1498."

Ganong's contention that Cabot could have missed Newfoundland on the outward voyage and reached Cape Breton is, naturally enough, disputed by Newfoundlanders, who maintain that it is highly unlikely he would not have sighted the coast of that large island, which is in such close proximity to the eastern shores of Cape Breton Island. However, given the fog-shrouded conditions often existing in that part of the North Atlantic, it is entirely possible that Cabot and his men could have missed observing Newfoundland as they sailed west.

The so-called "Sebastian Cabot" map of 1544, discovered in Germany in 1856, backs Cape Breton as the likely landfall. The words "Prima Tierra Vista" (land first seen) against a promontory obviously meant for Cape North, at the northernmost tip of Cape Breton Island, would seem to indicate that this was the point of land that first met the eyes of Cabot's crew as they looked from the sea.

The notion that Cabot landed on Newfoundland's Bonavista Peninsula

seems to go back only to the 1620s, when Captain John Mason's map of the island included the words "Bona Vista Caboto primum reperta." Many believe that Mason, a governor of the London and Bristol Company who resided in Newfoundland for three years, had either privileged information from an older chart now lost or knew fishermen whose fathers or grandfathers had sailed with Cabot.

But if Sebastian Cabot's claim for Cape Breton was personal, perhaps Mason's was political. Newfoundland author W. A. Munn suggested that Mason printed the Cabot discovery claim over Cape Bonavista in Latin because he wanted every mapmaker in Spain, Portugal, France, and Italy to interpret the meaning clearly: the English "got here first in 1497."

During the quatrocentennial celebrations of Cabot's voyages in 1897, a great rivalry developed between Newfoundlanders and residents of Canada's Maritime provinces, particularly in view of the fact that Newfoundland was not yet a part of Canada.** Both groups celebrated discovery with representatives from Bristol joining the Canadians in Halifax, Nova Scotia, while the Newfoundlanders laid the foundation stone of Cabot Tower, which now sits brooding over The Narrows, at the entrance to the harbor at its capital of St. John's.

The debate continued into the twentieth century. In 1936, Munn scathingly dismissed the "Cape Breton theorists," complaining that the efforts made by L. J. Burpee, editor of the *Canadian Geographical Journal,* and subsequent celebrations in Cape Breton and mainland Nova Scotia in 1934 "created a resentment from Newfoundlanders that Canadians have over-stepped the bounds of courtesy by asserting what they cannot prove."

Great mystery surrounds John Cabot's third and last voyage, undertaken in 1498. Henry VII authorized six ships for Cabot's new venture, but the mariner departed England with five, well-victualed and stocked with trade goods. The expedition encountered a fierce storm that forced one

---

*In 1965, Yale University Press published a privately owned medieval map of the world that included Vinland, a Norse or Viking settlement on the east coast of North America, as detailed by Icelandic navigator Leif Ericson, who visited and named the site in the early eleventh century. However, the authenticity of the New World sections of the Yale map have been sharply disputed.

**The Canadian province of Newfoundland and Labrador was admitted to confederation in March 1949.

of the ships to seek shelter in an Irish port, but "the Genoese kept on his way."

Although one contemporary wrote that it was believed that Cabot "found the new lands nowhere but on the very bottom of the sea," it is generally assumed that Cabot or at least some of his captains reached distant shores, or how else can the unflagged coasts on the La Cosa map be explained? "[W]e know what they found," Williamson commented, "primeval tracts and Indian tribes, no great state or government, no cities, no seaports, ships of trade, no spices and silks for barter—in a word, no Asia. Did any of them come back to tell this? The change in English outlook suggests that they did."

But Cabot was never seen again. Explorer Gaspar Côrte-Real's new world expedition of 1501 obtained a broken gilt sword of Italian manufacture and a pair of silver earrings of Venetian type from Indians somewhere in North America, which could suggest Cabot's fate. But while one story sinks Cabot at Grates Cove on Newfoundland's Avalon Peninsula, another suggests that some of his ships sailed southwestward to Florida and into the Caribbean, where Spaniards, resentful of the encroachment on lands and seas reserved for them by the Treaty of Tordesillas,* overcame and killed him.

---

*The Treaty of Tordesillas, signed on July 7, 1494, settled differences between Spain and Portugal that were brought about after Columbus's first voyage. The treaty divided the lands of the New World between the two Iberian nations.

While Christopher Columbus must be given credit for paving Europe's way to the New World, it does seem safe to say that John Cabot, the uncertainty surrounding his landfall notwithstanding, was the European "discoverer" of North America. The controversy is likely to remain unsettled, at least for the time being, and both Newfoundland and Cape Breton can commemorate this significant anniversary in the history of the "Age of Explorers" without fear of concrete contradiction.

Alan Williams has headed the Department of American and Canadian Studies in the School of History at England's University of Birmingham since 1987.

Laboring in the Fields of the Lord

The Franciscan missions of seventeenth-century Florida enabled Spain to harness the energies of tens of thousands of native people.

Jerald T. Milanich

Jerald T. Milanich is curator of archaeology in the department of anthropology at the Florida Museum of Natural History, Gainesville.

Beginning in the 1590s Franciscan friars established dozens of missions in what is today southern Georgia and northern Florida, but by the time Spain relinquished its Florida colony to Great Britain in 1763 only two missions remained. Spain regained control of the colony in 1783, only to cede it to the United States 38 years later. With the Spaniards gone, memories of

This quartz pendant, nearly three inches long, was found at San Luís, a late seventeenth-century Apalachee mission.

their missions faded. Their wood-and-thatch buildings, like the native peoples they had served, simply disappeared from the landscape.

In the late 1940s archaeologists began searching for the north Florida missions. By the end of the 1970s fieldwork and historical research had, it was thought, closed the book on the history of the settlements. My own research and that of my colleagues has reopened that book, adding new chapters to the history of the Spanish colony.

The missions of La Florida were an integral part of Pedro Menéndez de Avilés' master plan for his colony, whose first town, St. Augustine, was established in 1565. By converting the native peoples to Catholicism, as required by contract between him and his sovereign, Philip II, Menéndez hoped to insure loyal, obedient subjects. He initially arranged for Jesuit friars to establish a handful of missions along the Atlantic and Gulf coasts. The Jesuits, however, failed to build support among the native peoples and returned to Spain in 1572. They were replaced by Franciscans subsidized by the Spanish Crown. At first the hardships of mission work—the rigors of travel, climate, and lack of supplies—sent them packing as well. By 1592 only two friars and one lay brother remained, but three years later 12 new friars arrived, and missionary efforts began in earnest. The friars were assigned to *doctrinas,* missions with churches where native people were instructed in religious doctrine.

The first Franciscan missions were established along the Atlantic coast, from St.

This Guale Indian grasping a cross was interred in a shallow grave on the floor of the church at mission Santa Catalina on Amelia Island, Florida. The piety of the Christian Indians was, in the eyes of the mission friars, extraordinary.

Augustine north to Santa Elena on Parris Island, South Carolina. In 1587, however, raids by unfriendly Indians forced the abandonment of Santa Elena, and the chain of coastal missions serving the Timucuas and their northern neighbors, the Guale, stopped just short of present-day South Carolina. During the next 35 years a second chain of missions was established on the *camino real,* or royal road, that led westward about 350 miles from St. Augustine through the provinces of Timucua and Apalachee in northwestern Florida. Over time, these missions were moved or abandoned and

Reprinted with permission from *Archaeology* magazine, Vol. 49, No. 1, January/February 1996, pp. 60-67. © 1996 by the Archaeological Institute of America.

In this pencil drawing by Edward Jonas, the mission church at San Luís, in modern Tallahassee, Florida, faces a central plaza. Size and construction details—the walls, thatched roof, position of the front door, and presence of two bells—are based on data from excavations by Bonnie McEwan, an archaeologist with the San Luís project, Florida Division of Historic Resources.

new ones founded. Historian John Hann of the Florida Bureau of Archaeological Research estimates that as many as 140 existed at one time or another.

After the British settled Charleston in 1670—in territory that had once been under Spanish control—they began to challenge Spain's hold on La Florida. Through its Carolinian colonists, the British began to chip away at the Spanish presence. One effective way was to destroy the Franciscan missions. In the 1680s Carolinian militia and their native allies raided several missions in north Florida and the Georgia coast. Timucuas and Guale were captured and taken to Charleston where they were sold into slavery to work plantations in the Carolinas and the West Indies. The raids on the Georgia coastal missions grew so intense that by the late 1680s all of the missions north of Amelia Island were abandoned.

In 1702 and 1704 Carolinian raids on the Apalachee and Timucuan missions in northern Florida effectively destroyed the mission system west of the St. Johns River. Churches were burned and their contents smashed. Villagers were scattered, tortured, and killed. Nearly 5,000 Indians were sold into slavery, while others fled west to the Gulf of Mexico. Of some 12,000 original mission Indians fewer than 1,000 remained, and they fled to refugee villages that grew up around St. Augustine. When Spain turned La Florida over to Britain in 1763, only 63 Christian Indians remained, and the retreating Spanish took them to Cuba.

By the early 1980s archaeologists had found the remains of perhaps a dozen missions. In doing so, they had relied on an important document written by a seventeenth-century bishop of Cuba, Gabriel Díaz Vara Calderón. The bishop had vis-

ited La Florida from 1674 to 1675 to witness firsthand what the Franciscan friars had accomplished. His report lists 24 missions along the camino real and provides the distances between them:

Ten leagues [1 league = 3.5 miles] from the city of Saint Augustine, on the bank of the river Corrientes [the St. Johns], is the village and mission of San Diego de Salamototo. It [the river] is very turbulent and almost a league and a half in width. From there to the village and mission of Santa Fe there are some 20 uninhabited leagues. Santa Fe is the principal mission of this province. Off to the side [from Santa Fe] toward the southern border, at a distance of 3 leagues, is the deserted mission and village of San Francisco. Twelve leagues from Santa Fe is the mission of Santa Catalina, with Ajohica 3 leagues away and Santa Cruz de Tarihica 2. Seven leagues away, on

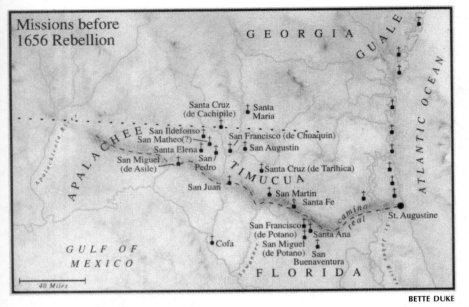

Missions before 1656 Rebellion

BETTE DUKE

Beginning in 1595 Franciscan missions were built along the Atlantic coast from St. Augustine to just short of present-day South Carolina. In 1606 a second chain of missions was started north and south of the camino real, or royal road, that led westward about 350 miles from St. Augustine through the provinces of Timucua and Apalachee in northwestern Florida.

the bank of the large river Guacara [the Suwannee], is the mission of San Juan of the same name. Ten [further on] is that of San Pedro de Potohiriba, 2 that of Santa Helena de Machaba, 4, that of San Matheo, 2, that of San Miguel de Asyle, last in this . . . province.

What made this guide especially valuable was the discovery and publication in 1938 of a map of the camino real drawn by a British surveyor in 1778, when the road was still a major route across northern Florida. Some names of Spanish missions appear on the map. It seemed that it would only be a matter of time until we had discovered all of the sites.

The first clue that the accepted history of the missions needed a major overhaul came in 1976. Excavating a seventeenth-century Spanish-Indian site in north Florida, I had uncovered the burnt remains of a small wooden church and an earth-floored friars' quarters, both adjacent to a Timucuan village. The evidence suggested that the site was one of the missions along the camino real. But which mission was it? Its position on the road did not match any of the locations mentioned in Bishop Calderón's account. It was too far east to be mission San Juan and too far west to be Santa Cruz.

More questions about the geography of the missions surfaced in the late 1980s when I was looking for archaeological traces of the Spanish conquistador Hernando de Soto's 1539 march across northern Florida (see ARCHAEOLOGY, May/June 1989). My field crews did indeed find de Soto-era native villages, but they also discovered two seventeenth-century Spanish missions, both north of the camino real. Again, neither was listed by Bishop Calderón. The good news was that we had an excellent idea of de Soto's route; the bad news was that something was terribly wrong with our understanding of the history and geography of the missions.

I needed dates for the three mysterious sites. One way to get them was to study Spanish majolica pottery, a tin-glazed tableware that is common at Spanish colonial sites in the Americas and abundant at all three missions. Majolicas can be divided into types based on differences in vessel shapes, colors of glazes, and glazed designs. Because some types were popular mainly before ca. 1650 and others mainly after that date, we can date collections to the early or late seventeenth century. Analysis of majolicas from the mystery missions showed that all three were occupied only before 1650. Had something occurred in the mid-seventeenth century that led to their abandonment two decades before Bishop Calderón's visit?

Since the 1930s historians have known of Spanish accounts document-

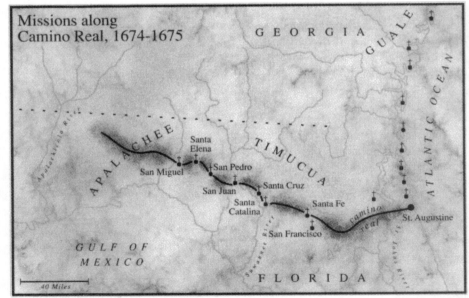

Missions along Camino Real, 1674-1675

BETTE DUKE

After the Timucuan rebellion of 1656, Governor Robolledo relocated the Timucuan missions along the camino real, roughly a day's travel apart, where they functioned as way stations between Apalachee province and St. Augustine. The relocation also reflected the demographic devastation caused by epidemics, especially small pox and measles.

FLORIDA DIVISION OF HISTORICAL RESOURCES

These native ceramics from Apalachee are typical of the mission period. Each Indian culture had its own type of pottery.

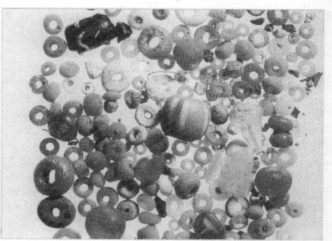

FLORIDA DIVISION OF HISTORICAL RESOURCES

Villagers were paid in glass beads and trinkets, which were exchanged for hides and furs for trading back to the Spanish.

ing a 1656 Indian rebellion at the Timucuan missions. The governor of Spanish Florida, Diego de Rebolledo, sent troops to put down the rebellion. Ten native leaders were rounded up and hanged. The governor was subsequently charged with having displayed great cruelty and was slated to answer for his actions, but he died before a hearing could be held.

What was not known until the early 1990s was that an investigation took place after Rebolledo's death. In the Archivo General de Indias in Seville, Spain, John Worth, then a doctoral student at the University of Florida, found lengthy testimony taken at the hearing and related documents that described the rebellion and its aftermath. They also rewrote what we had known about mission geography.

The documents recount how the rebellion began in the spring of 1656, when Lúcas Menéndez, one of the major chiefs in Timucua, and other chiefs defied Governor Rebolledo's orders. Hearing a report that the British were planning a raid on St. Augustine, the governor had commanded the chiefs of Apalachee and Timucua to assemble 500 men and march to St. Augustine. The Indians were ordered to carry food for a stay of at least a month. Because construction of fortifications was still under way and the number of soldiers stationed in the colony was well below its full complement, the town was poorly prepared to withstand an attack. The governor wanted to reinforce its defenses with Indian warriors.

But the chiefs of Timucua refused to go, a decision that grew out of dissatisfaction with treatment they had received from the governor on previous visits to St. Augustine. Rebolledo had not properly feasted the chiefs, nor had he given them gifts, as was customary. The chiefs also refused to carry their own food and supplies or to provide warriors to defend the town without compensation. The power of native leaders in Timucua had already been threatened by nearly a century of Spanish colonization, and Rebolledo's 1656 order was seen by the Timucuan chiefs as demeaning and an attempt to undercut their authority.

Chief Lúcas Menéndez told his followers and the other chiefs to kill Spaniards, though not the mission friars. The

FLORIDA DIVISION OF HISTORICAL RESOURCES

Painting by John LoCastro depicts the Apalachee Indian council house at San Luís. The 120-foot diameter building was at one end of a central plaza which served as a field for a game in which teams tried to kick a ball into an eagle-nest target atop a pole.

J. T. MILANICH

Remains of 59 villagers buried in a corner of Amelia Island's Santa Catalina church attest the decimation of native people. A 1659 report states that 10,000 people died in one measles epidemic.

first deaths occurred at San Miguel and San Pedro in western Timucua. At each site a Spanish soldier, part of the small military presence in the province, was slain. A Spanish servant and a Mexican Indian who by chance had camped in Timucua while traveling the camino real were the next to die. Warriors led by Lúcas Menéndez then raided a Spanish cattle ranch near modern Gainesville, killing a third Spanish soldier and two African workers. All across northern Florida Timucuas abandoned their missions.

Knowing the Spanish would retaliate, some of the rebellious Timucuas gathered at mission Santa Elena, which they converted into a palisaded fort. Rebolledo sent 60 Spanish infantry and several hundred Apalachee Indians to capture the rebels. After extended negotiations the Timucuas came out. Their leaders were seized along with several Timucuas who had participated in the murders. One man confessed almost immediately and was executed, probably by hanging. Other prisoners were taken to Apalachee and held while word was sent to the governor.

In late November Rebolledo and a small entourage marched from St. Augustine, capturing several chiefs along the way. A trial was held in Apalachee. Ten of the prisoners were sentenced to

forced labor in St. Augustine, while ten others, most of whom were chiefs, were sentenced to death. Rebolledo ordered the men hanged at various places along the camino real as grim reminders of the power of the Spaniards and the fate that awaited those who rebelled against the Crown.

Rebolledo also seized the opportunity to reorganize the province and its missions so they would better serve the needs of the colony and its Spanish overlords. Missions were relocated roughly a day's travel apart so they could function as way stations between Apalachee province and St. Augustine. This arrangement of missions was what Bishop Calderón had observed in 1674 and 1675. That explained two of our three mystery sites. One of the northern two was the pre-1656 mission of Santa Cruz, which was moved south to the camino real after the rebellion. The site we had excavated in 1976 was the mission of San Juan which, after the rebellion, was moved six miles west to a point on the camino real that intersected the Suwannee River. The identity of our third mission remains a mystery, although it seems certain it too was abandoned after the rebellion.

Worth's research led us to believe there were two mission systems in Timucua, one before and one after 1656. What made it necessary for the governor

to reorganize the missions? To answer that question we began to reexamine other Spanish documents discovered by Hann and Worth. They indicated that by 1656 epidemics had devastated the population of Timucua province. Although the occurrence of epidemics—especially smallpox and measles—had long been recognized by scholars, we had no inkling that demographic devastation had occurred so quickly in Timucua. The Spanish sources indicate that by the 1620s Timucuan mission villages had been hard hit, some so reduced in population that their chiefs could not send men to St. Augustine to provide labor for the Spaniards. The documents also indicate that epidemics struck soon after the first missions were founded. In 1595 an unknown epidemic hit the coastal missions. Between 1612 and late 1616 epidemics killed as many as 10,000 mission Indians. Another epidemic struck in 1649–1650, and in 1655 smallpox ravaged Timucua and Guale. In 1657, following the rebellion, Governor Rebolledo wrote that the Indians of Guale and Timucua were few in number "because they have been wiped out with the sickness of the plague [peste] and smallpox which have overtaken them in the past years." Two years later a new governor, Francisco de Corcoles y Martínez, reported that 10,000 mission Indians had died in a measles epidemic.

The decimation of mission Indians is grimly reflected in the archaeological record. The remains of hundreds of native villagers have been found in shallow graves under the floors of more than ten mission churches excavated in Apalachee, Guale, and Timucua. At some churches bodies were found stacked in layers three deep. Many older burials had been pushed aside to make room for new ones. The depopulation of Timucua is what apparently led Rebolledo to convert the missions into way stations on the camino real. With its larger native population, Apalachee province would be the focus of Spanish farming and ranching efforts, the colony's breadbasket, and the main source of labor.

The severity of the epidemics and the geographical reorganization of the Timucuan missions has provided a basis for reinterpreting the role of the missions in

Sick and dying Timucuas are depicted in this sixteenth-century etching by the Flemish engraver Theodor de Bry.

Spanish Florida. Now more than ever we see that missions and colonization were integrally related. Christianized Indians enabled the colony to function. In return for providing religious education for native people, the Spanish could harness them as workers in support of colonial interests. Religious instruction converted villagers to Catholicism and made them obedient, productive members of Spain's empire. One should not underestimate the hold the new beliefs and customs had on these people. The piety of converted Indians was, even in the eyes of the friars, extraordinary. In 1614 Father Francisco Pareja, a Franciscan friar at mission San Juan (north of modern-day Jacksonville), described the intensity of that devotion:

Among them are Indian men who have sufficient knowledge to give instructions while there are Indian women who catechize other Indian women, preparing them for the reception of Christianity. They assist at Masses of obligation on Sundays and feastdays in which they take part and sing; in some districts that have their confraternities and the procession of Holy Thursday, and from the mission stations they come to the principal mission to hear the Salve [the Salve Regina] which is sung on Saturdays. . . . They take holy water and recite their prayers in the morning and evening. They come together in the community house to teach one another singing and reading. . . . Do they confess as Christians? I answer yes. . . . Many persons are found, men and women, who confess and who receive [Holy Communion] with tears, and who show up advantageously with many Spaniards. And I shall make bold and say and sustain my contention by what I have learned by experience that with regard to the mysteries of the faith, many of them answer better than the Spaniards.

Father Pareja also noted the effectiveness of conversion, writing that Catholicism had vanquished many of the native superstitions so effectively that the mission Indians "do not even remember them . . . so much so that the younger generation which has been nourished by the milk of the Gospel derides and laughs at some old men and women. . . ."

Faith was an efficient tool for organizing native people who, now laboring in the fields of the Lord, performed a variety of tasks for the Spaniards. Adult males carried corn from Apalachee and Timucua to the Gulf Coast, where it was shipped to St. Augustine or exported to Cuba or other nearby Spanish colonies. Villagers also drove cattle over the camino real to St. Augustine. Supplies for the missions—lamp and cooking oil for the friars and construction hardware for repairing buildings—were shouldered from St. Augustine back to the missions. Indians tended fields and harvested crops for the soldiers stationed at St. Augustine. They helped build forts

CONDE DE REVILLA GIGEDO AND UNIVERSITY PRESS OF FLORIDA

Pedro Menéndez de Avilés, founder of La Florida, believed convert-ing natives to Catholicism would ensure loyal subjects.

FLORIDA DIVISION OF HISTORICAL RESOURCES

Spanish ceramics, made throughout the seventeenth century, are useful in dating mission sites across northern Florida.

and other fortifications; they cut and transported logs used for lumber; and they quarried coquina stone on Anasta-sia Island to build the town gates and the massive castillo that still dominates St. Augustine's waterfront. As many as 300 Christian Indians were involved in the construction of the castillo when it was begun in the 1670s.

Native laborers were paid in hawks' bells, knives, colorful glass beads, pieces of sheet brass, razors, cloth, and scissors. Some of these items were then traded to non-mission Indians to the north who did not have access to the much sought-after European imports. Mission Indians re-ceived deer hides and, perhaps, furs in ex-change. These could be traded back to the Spaniards for more trinkets. The Span-iards, in turn, exported these hides, which were far more valuable than the trinkets they handed out.

Native people also labored for the Spaniards in the mission provinces. They maintained the camino real, clear-ing brush, repairing creek crossings, and even building bridges. Where roads

crossed rivers too deep to ford, they op-erated ferries, probably little more than rafts or canoes lashed together. At the missions men, women, and children la-bored in support of the friars. They cooked, tended gardens, looked after farm animals, did household chores, hunted and fished, collected firewood, made charcoal, carried burdens, and paddled canoes when the friars traveled. Cornfields were planted, hoed, and har-vested; the corn husked, shelled, ground into meal, and stored. Any surplus was sold by the friars to St. Augustine when times were hard in town, a clever way to generate credit against which Francis-cans, who had taken vows of poverty, could charge items needed to maintain the missions. In Spanish Florida corn was money, whether it was taken to St. Augustine for use there or shipped out of the colony. Mission Indians were en-couraged to increase production, aided by iron tools such as the hoes found at several missions. Increased production of corn for export resulted in huge num-bers of ears being shelled, producing an

equally large number of cobs that were used as fuel. Hundreds of charred corn-cobs have been found at every Spanish mission excavated thus far.

Lifetimes of labor in support of the Spaniards are reflected in bioanthro-pological analyses of the mission Indi-ans themselves. The native workers enjoyed better living conditions than did their Precolumbian ancestors, but the stresses of labor resulted in more broken bones and injuries. Was this a benign system that improved the lot of the na-tive people of Apalachee, Guale, and Timucua? Hardly. Although individual friars went to La Florida to bring a bet-ter life to the native people, in reality the missions provided the means for compelling the Indians to serve the Spanish Empire. In the end the process proved catastrophic. Tens of thousands of Apalachee, Guale, and Timucuas were destroyed by disease and war. By the time the British took over the terri-tory, they had ceased to exist. Archaeol-ogy and history are now giving voice to that forgotten past.

The Missing Women of Martin's Hundred

Indian warriors killed hundreds of Virginia colonists during the Powhatan Uprising of 1622. Also among the victims were 20 women whose stories will never be fully told.

By J. Frederick Fausz

THE SUN HAD been up only a few hours on that fatal spring morning when hundreds of Powhatan warriors descended upon English colonists in Virginia, burning settlements and plantations along the James River in a sudden and fierce attack. So began the Powhatan Uprising of March 22, 1622, which claimed the lives of approximately 347 colonists and came perilously close to extinguishing England's most promising outpost in North America.

Because the Indian uprising had such an important impact on English colonization and Anglo-Powhatan relations, historians have concentrated their research on the larger issues. In the process the more immediate suffering of the colonists has sometimes been obscured. Among the forgotten victims of the attack were the missing women of Martin's Hundred plantation. These female colonists, perhaps 20 in all, were virtually the only captives taken by the Powhatans in the uprising. Few details of their ordeal have survived, and information about their lives is almost nonexistent. In fact, we may never know if they shared the fas-

cinating, if often horrifying, adventures of more well-known Indian captives in American history.

It is certain, however, that these women witnessed the violent deaths of neighbors and loved ones before being abducted; that they lived with their enemies while the English ruthlessly attacked Indian villages in retaliation; and that they received no heroes' welcome upon their return to the colony.

MARTIN'S HUNDRED was one of the largest and most important private plantations in early seventeenth-century Virginia. Founded in 1617 and funded by the Society of Martin's Hundred—a group of investors headed by London attorney Richard Martin—the plantation comprised roughly 20,000 acres flanking the James River. Wolstenholme Towne, named after another of the Society's investors, Sir John Wolstenholme, was the plantation's main population center. In this embryonic settlement, located approximately seven miles downstream from Jamestown, colonists constructed

cottages, a church, a storehouse, and a small fort amid Virginia's tall trees.

The settlement was a disaster almost from the beginning. The Society had dispatched some 250 colonists to the plantation in October 1618 and sent between 30 and 100 additional settlers before March 1622, but by the eve of the Powhatan Uprising, less than 150 remained alive. Disease, malnutrition, poor organization, and ignorance of their new environment all contributed to a high mortality rate. Three months prior to the Indian attack, colony officials described Martin's Hundred as "sorely weakened and . . . in much confusion." The situation was so precarious that the Society informed the Virginia Company of London—whose aim was to establish a Protestant English colony in a land threatened by Spain—that their colonists were physically and financially unable to house, feed, clothe, educate, and convert local Indian children as they had earlier pledged to do.

Since 1614, when Powhatan Chief Wahunsonacock agreed to peace after the English captured his daughter Pocahontas, the former enemies had enjoyed

From *American History*, March 1998, pp. 56-60, 62. © 1998 by Cowles Magazines, Inc. Reprinted through the courtesy of Cowles Magazines, publishers of *American History*.

Although the official number of Virginia colonists killed was recorded at 347, some settlements, such as Bermuda Hundred, did not send in a report, so the number of dead was probably higher. The Indian raids suddenly and shockingly transformed Virginia into a "labyrinth of melancholy," a severely wounded colony struggling to survive. The loss was so great that Martin's Hundred and many other settlements were temporarily abandoned, although England continued to "set forth a verie chargeable supply of people" to Virginia.

Within months of the uprising, Edward Waterhouse, a secretary for the Virginia Company, reported in his official *Declaration of the State of the Colony and . . . a Relation of the Barbarous Massacre* that 77 people—52 men, 16 women, six children, and three unspecified—were killed in the attack at Martin's Hundred alone. However, Waterhouse overestimated the number slain, for he listed as dead several women who were unaccounted for and were *presumed* killed but who were, in fact, captives. At least 58 colonists died at the plantation, and the dazed and despairing survivors had every reason to believe that those missing had either been killed in inaccessible areas, hacked or burned beyond recognition, or captured, which they believed would lead to certain death.

In the weeks and months following the Powhatan onslaught, neither the Virginia Company officials nor the Society of Martin's Hundred attempted to locate and recover the missing settlers. One-sixth of Virginia's colonists had been

When twentieth-century archaeologists excavated Martin's Hundred settlement, they uncovered a wealth of artifacts including a helmet (above), which was part of a shipment of armor and weapons from the Tower of London sent to rearm the survivors of the Indian attack; and a farthing (right), found in a ground slot dug to seat the fort's timbers.

a cordial relationship. However, as more settlers moved in, carving the land up into tobacco plantations and ruining Indian hunting grounds by driving away the game, the Powhatans saw their centuries-old way of life being destroyed. Determined to rid the land of the invaders, Opechancanough ordered the March 22 assault on the Virginia settlements. The warriors struck down the colonists with their own hammers and hatchets. The English were unprepared and surprised, and their attackers burned houses, killed livestock, scattered possessions, and mutilated the dead and dying before fleeing.

Fortunately for the residents of the main settlement of Jamestown, an Indian informant had alerted them to the upcoming attack, and they were on guard, but Wolstenholme Towne was "ruinated and spoyled" by the Indian assault and suffered the highest death toll of any settlement during the uprising.

wiped out in a single day, and for the survivors, staying alive took precedence over a hunt for neighbors they thought were beyond rescue. The devastated colonists spent their time trying to feed

ALL PHOTOS: COLONIAL WILLIAMSBURG FOUNDATION

A recreation of Wolstenholme Towne (above). The site was uncovered by Colonial Williamsburg Foundation archaeologists, headed by Ivor Noël Hume. Among the artifacts discovered in the area was this well-traveled German stoneware jug (below), which crossed the Atlantic Ocean with one of the Martin's Hundred settlers.

and shelter themselves and brace for future attacks by the Indians. In London, Edward Waterhouse published his list of the dead for the purely pragmatic reason "that their lawfull heyres may take speedy order for the inheriting of their lands and estates" in Virginia.

Slowly however, Englishmen on both sides of the Atlantic came to believe that a number of women from Martin's Hundred who had been presumed killed by the Indians were still alive. A year after the uprising, Richard Frethorne, a settler in Wolstenholme Towne, reported that the Powhatans held 15 people from that plantation in their villages, while another source indicated that there were "19 English persons retayned ... in great slavery" among the Indians and that "there were none but women in Captivitie ... for the men they tooke they putt ... to death."

In 1624 Captain John Smith published his *Generall Historie of Virginia* and provided even more detailed information. He reported that an English expe-

dition along the Potomac River had received a message in late June or early July 1622 from Mistress Boyse, "a prisoner with nineteene more" of the Powhatans. Mistress Boyse, who pleaded for the governor to try to secure the captives' release, was the wife of either John Boyse, who had represented Martin's Hundred in the first Virginia legislature of 1619, or his kinsman, Thomas Boyse of the same plantation, who was listed among those killed in the March 1622 attack. With her at the Indian stronghold near present-day West Point, Virginia, were Mistress Jeffries, wife of Nathaniel Jeffries who survived the uprising, and Jane Dickenson, wife of Ralph Dickenson, an indentured servant slain in the assault.

While their former neighbors feared new attacks, the captive women were placed in almost constant jeopardy by the fierce and frequent English raids on

The Powhatan Wars

When the first English colonists landed in Virginia in 1607, they encountered members of the Powhatan Confederacy, an alliance of nine Algonquian nations from the western side of the Chesapeake Bay. Led by Wahunsonacock, called Powhatan by the English after the name of his tribe, the Confederacy numbered between 8,000 and 13,000 people from 30 tribes and covered nearly all of eastern Virginia. Each tribe had its own district chief. One of them was Wahunsonacock's younger brother, Opechancanough, chief of the Pamunkey tribe. After the events of the Powhatan Uprising, the English referred to him as "the bloody monster."

The colonists and their settlement on the James River threatened to end expansion of the Powhatan "empire," and within weeks of their arrival, the settlers were attacked by Powhatan warriors, beginning a conflict that escalated in 1610 and continued for four years, ending only after the English captured Wahunsonacock's daughter, Pocahontas.

In 1617, the aged Wahunsonacock abdicated the Confederacy's leadership, and Openchancanough took his place. He soon turned the revitalized Confederacy into a military force that would claim

LIBRARY OF CONGRESS

John Smith and Opechancanough

thousands of English lives. The uprising that began in 1622 lasted for a decade, until both sides agreed on a peace treaty. But with hostilities halted, a huge colonial expansion began that squeezed the Powhatans into ever smaller sections of their homeland. The Indians again retaliated in the spring of 1644. By then Openchancanough was reported to be more than 100 years old and had to be carried into battle on a litter. This last spasm of violence killed 500 more colonists, but the white population in Virginia was now too large to be defeated. The English captured Openchancanough two years later and imprisoned him in Jamestown, where he was shot and killed by one of his guards. His death brought an end to the Powhatan Confederacy and its resistance to English expansion.

---

the Powhatans. Lodged as they were with Opechancanough, the prime target of retaliation, the English women, like their captors, endured hasty retreats, burning villages, and hunger caused by lost corn harvests.

The colonists' retaliatory raids in the summer and fall of 1622 were so successful that Opechancanough, who had been unprepared for such massive offensives, decided in desperation to negotiate with his enemies, using the captured women as his trump card. In March 1623, he sent a message to Jamestown stating that enough blood had been spilled on both sides, and that because many of his people were starving he desired a truce to allow the Powhatans

to plant corn for the coming year. In exchange for this temporary truce, Opechancanough promised to return the English women. To emphasize his sincerity, he sent Mistress Boyse to Jamestown a week later. When she rejoined her countrymen she was dressed like an Indian "Queen," in attire that probably would have included native pearl necklaces, copper medallions, various furs and feathers, and deerskin dyed red. Boyse was the only woman sent back at this time, and she remained the sole returned captive for many months. For the present, colony officials felt that killing hostile Indians took precedence over saving English prisoners, and they never intended to honor the

truce in good faith. However, the Powhatans were allowed to plant spring corn to lessen their suspicions "that wee may follow their Example in destroying them. . . ."

In May 1623 the colonists arranged a spurious peace parley with Opechancanough through friendly Indian intermediaries. On May 22, Captain William Tucker and a force of musketeers met with Opechancanough and other prominent Powhatans on neutral ground along the Potomac River, allegedly to negotiate the release of the other captives. But Tucker's objective was the slaughter of Powhatan leaders. After the captain and the Indians had exchanged "manye fayned speeches," approximately 200 of the Powhatans who had accompanied their leaders unwittingly drank poisoned wine that Jamestown's resident physician and later governor, Dr. John Pott, had prepared for the occasion. Many of the Indians fell sick or immediately dropped dead, and Tucker's men shot and killed about 50 more. Some important tribal members were slain, but Opechancanough escaped, and with him went any hopes of a quick return for the captured women.

Between May and November of that same year, the colonists ravaged the Powhatans throughout Tidewater Virginia. The "fraudulent peace" had worked, and the Indians had planted corn "in great abundance" only to see Englishmen harvest it for their own use. Successful raids by the settlers not only proved the undoing of the Powhatans but made fortunes for several Jamestown corn profiteers.

These raids against the Indians helped to heal the emotional wounds of the colonists, but victory came at a high price. While the captive women suffered alongside their captors, the Indian war transformed the colony into an even cruder, crueler place than before. The war intensified the social stratification between leaders and laborers and masters and servants, while a handful of powerful men on Virginia Governor Sir Francis Wyatt's council thoroughly dominated the political, economic, and military affairs of the colony.

It soon became clear that the fate of the missing women depended not upon official concern or humanitarian instincts but upon the principle that everything and everybody had a price. Near the end of 1623, more than a year and a half after the uprising, the prosperous Dr. Pott ransomed Jane Dickenson and other women from the Indians for a few pounds of trade beads.

After her release, Dickenson learned that she owed a debt of labor to Dr. Pott for the ransom he had paid and for the three years of service that her deceased husband had left on his contract of servitude at the time of his death. She complained bitterly that her new "servitude . . . differeth not from her slavery with the Indians."

By 1624, no more than seven of the fifteen to twenty hostages had arrived in Jamestown. The majority of them returned with Jane Dickenson. Those who did not come back were presumed killed during the 1622 attack, although one captive, Anne Jackson, was not returned until 1630. Mistress Boyse, the first of the missing women to rejoin the colony was not mentioned in official records following her return. Another of the captives, Mistress Jeffries, died within a few months of her release. Anne Jackson probably returned to the colony badly broken from the consequences of her captivity, for in 1630 the council ordered that she "bee sent for England with the first opportunity," with the stipulation that her brother take care of her until she was on board a ship. Nothing more was heard of Jane Dickenson after she petitioned the council in March 1624 for release from her "slavery" with Dr. Pott

The missing women of Martin's Hundred were uprooted by their enemies, manipulated by their countrymen and mistreated in both societies. No brave frontiersmen stalked their captors, and no romantic legends arose to memorialize them. There were no heroics involved in their return; in the harsh, unforgiving world of Virginia in the early seventeenth century, it was a dispassionate business transaction that brought about their release.

J. Frederick Fausz holds degrees in early American history and has written numerous articles on the subject.

Bearing the Burden? Puritan Wives

Obedience, modesty, taciturnity—all hallmarks of the archetypal 'good woman' in colonial New England. But did suffering in silence invert tradition and give the weaker sex a new moral authority in the community? Martha Saxton investigates, in the first piece from a mini series examining women's social experience in the New World.

Martha Saxton

Martha Saxton teaches Colonial History at Columbia University. She is author of Louisa May Alcott *(Andre Deutsch, 1977) and is currently working on a study of American women's moral standards—those prescribed for them and those they fashioned for themselves.*

Seventeenth-century American Puritans subordinated female to male, wife to husband, and mother to father, insisting on obedience, modesty, and taciturnity for women. They justified this arrangement by emphasising woman's descent from Eve and her innate irrationality, both of which made her more vulnerable to error and corruption than man. Because of this she was to view her husband as God's representative in the family. He would mediate her religious existence and direct her temporal one. She would produce children and care for them, but he would have the ultimate authority over them.

At the same time, the experience of Puritans of both sexes in the second half of the seventeenth century undermined this clearly defined system of authority in which the allocation of secular power flowed from a presumed moral and spiritual hierarchy. After 1660, women began outnumbering men in the churches, and by the end of the century the numerical difference was sufficient to prompt Cotton Mather to attempt to account for the demonstrated female proclivity for spirituality. Mather ascribed enhanced female religiosity precisely to that subordination that Puritan men insisted upon as well as mothers' suffering during childbirth.

Long before Mather published his conclusions at the end of the seventeenth century, other Puritan men anticipated his thinking about female virtue, and many identified its sources in female suffering. Men praised the patient endurance of wives with abusive husbands. Others granted to childbirth pain the power to enhance goodness. Some saw the sacrifices of mothering, rather than childbirth *per se,* as a source of virtue and testified to the moral significance of their mothers in the conduct of their lives. And still others simply acknowledged their mothers, wives, or other female relatives as inspirational or spiritually influential to them.

In the Puritan world then, women could and did earn respect for their moral stature in the family, and this was meaningful to women deprived of public recognition in a society run by men. It would be an important heritage to women of a later era. Pious women would pass on the idea that their principled expressions of conscience could shape morally, both family and society.

Before looking at the way women achieved moral authority, let us look at how Puritan men elaborated beliefs about the propriety of subordinating women to men. John Winthrop, Governor of Massachusetts, who was happily married to three submissive women, writing in the mid-seventeenth century put the ideal case:

> A true wife accounts her subjection her honor and freedom and would not think her condition safe and free but in her subjection to her husband's authority. Such is the liberty of the church under the authority of Christ,

her king and husband; his yoke is so easy and sweet to her as a bride's ornaments; and if through forwardness or wantonness, etc., she shakes it off at any time, she is at no rest in her spirit until she take it up again; and whether her lord smiles upon her and embraceth her in his arms, or whether he frowns and rebukes her, or smites her, she comprehends the sweetness of his love in all, and is refreshed, and instructed by every such dispensation of his authority over her.

While not all American Puritans saw female obedience in such a cheerful light as Winthrop did, all agreed that it was essential to marital satisfaction and should exist regardless of the husband's comportment. John Cotton compared wifely obedience to the excellence and inevitability of the universe, the air we breathe, and the clouds that shower rain upon the earth. Benjamin Wadsworth, in a book published in 1712, wrote that a woman should 'reverence' her husband, as the bible commanded. He was God's representative in the family, and even if he should 'pass the bounds of wisdom and kindness; yet must not she shake off the bond of submission but must bear patiently the burden, which God hath laid upon the daughters of Eve'. And Cotton Mather, writing before his final, tempestuous marriage to Lydia Lee George would give these words a wistful ring, insisted that though the husband be 'ever so much a Churl, yet she treats him considerately'.

An important facet of this unanimous male insistence on female submission was the envy and fascination Puritan men felt for womanly meekness and obedience. Salvation demanded that men, as well as women, submit to God's will in all things. For women, submission to God's will and the will of the men around them made their lives, ideally, a continuum of obedience.

Men, however, enjoyed considerable social power during their lifetime as husbands and, depending upon their status, as community leaders. Submission and the self-suppression that it required, was, therefore, a more prickly and intractable issue for men than for women. Furthermore, as husbands, men determined how heavily or lightly the yoke of marriage would rest on their

wives' shoulders. Men's direct responsibility for the suffering that their domination might cause women was likely to make them particularly alive to the issue.

Cotton Mather, who had openly linked woman's tendency to spiritual excellence with her subordination and suffering, wrote 'But if thou hast an Husband that will do so, [beat his wife] bear it patiently; and know thou shalt have—Rewards—hereafter for it, as well as *Praises* here...'. And Puritan men since the settlement of Plymouth had praised women for remaining uncomplainingly with husbands who were violent and/or unfaithful. Mrs Lyford, of Plymouth endured—and sometimes witnessed—her husband's sexual escapades for years in silence. Eventually, she testified against him. But, wrote the governor of the colony, William Bradford, approvingly, 'being a grave matron, and of good carriage... spoake of those things out of the sorrow of her harte, sparingly'.

The wife of Jared Davis submitted to years of her husband's cruelty, drunkenness, lies, scandalous behaviour, and indolence. He had, according to John Winthrop, neither compassion nor humanity toward his wife, insisted on sex with her when she was pregnant (which Puritans regarded as dangerous) and did not provide for her. The governor admired Mrs Davis who, under all these provocations, continued to try to help her husband. As Winthrop had written elsewhere, Mrs Davis was able to find in her husband's blows, God's love and correction. Winthrop and Bradford believed that the Christlike acceptance of lengthy, undeserved abuse endowed women with a unique moral vantage point from which they might even venture to criticise their victimisers.

Men were also fascinated by—and implicated in—the crisis of child labour and delivery, which combined submission to physical suffering as well as the more difficult task: resignation to the possibility of death. Husbands were awed by their wives' apparent conquest of mortal fear. Puritans believed that pregnancy rendered women more fearful than usual. The Reverend Peter Thacher wrote in his diary in February 1680, that his wife had fallen on a chair, and was

'soe frighted with it that shee had like to have fainted away' because she feared she had hurt the child in her womb. When normally timid women, rendered even more so by pregnancy, triumphed over the terror of death, they reassured the whole community of its ability to conquer its fear of the hereafter through submission to God. As Mather said at the funeral of seventeen-year-old Mrs Rebeckah Burnel in 1724:

But when it pleases Him, to take *children,* and those of that *Sex* which *Fear* is most incident and enslaving to; and make such *Babes and Sucklings* to triumph over the *Enemy,*—Oh! The *Wondrous Power* of our God! . . .

Thirteen years earlier, Cotton Mather's sister, Jerusha, decided when she was five months pregnant that it was time to get herself ready for death. She acknowledged that she was a fearful creature, and especially so because of her pregnancy, and wished to give herself up completely to God. She vowed that if God gave her an easy and short labour that she would dedicate herself to bringing up her child in fear of Him. She petitioned for a 'resigned will' and to be made fit for whatever God demanded for her. When her labour approached she prayed to be delivered from the sin of fear. As it happened, her labour was easy, but she and her baby died a short time later.

Mather, in recording his sister's death, assured his readers that Jerusha, while exceptionally joyous, said 'nothing that look'd at all Delirious', lest they discount the God-given courage with which she had faced her end. He quoted her as saying that when she was healthy 'Death was a Terror to me. But now I know, I shall Dy, I am not at all *afraid of it. This* is a Wonderful *Work of God!* I know *that I am* going to Christ... I *see things that are Unutterable!*'. Her father, Increase Mather, asked her if she were not afraid of death. 'She replied with great Earnestness; "Not in the least! Not in the least! Not in the least!"' Mather ended his memoir with what he said were her last words, 'Eye has not seen, Ear has not heard, neither entered into the Heart of Man, the things which

God has prepared for them that Love Him!' Mather's text pointed out in many ways that if a frail, sickly and frightened (i.e. womanly) woman lived as a Puritan woman should, she would die blissfully; hence, ran the implicit parallel, how much easier would it be for a strong man to do the same.

Similarly, Barbara Ruggles, an inhabitant of Roxburg, was able, according to the Roxburg Church records, to 'shine in her life & death' because of the way she dealt with her afflictions, including a fatal delivery. She had a 'stone chollik in which sicknesse she manifested much patiens, and faith; she dyed in childbed . . . & left a godly savor behind her'.

When a woman lost the mortal battle of birth graciously, she acquired unhesitating male praise. When she won, her husband's admiration might be muted by feelings of competition or guilty ambivalence about the pleasure in which such suffering originated. In journal accounts, husbands often expropriated the religious significance of their wives' brushes with death to themselves. They mingled their admiration with a vision of their *own* sins as the origin of their wives' agonies.

When, in the late 1660s, God visited upon the wife of the Reverend Joseph Thompson of Billerica such a weakness as made the couple fear her pregnancy might end badly, Thompson took a lesson in submission to the Lord's will from his wife's peril. He acknowledged that nothing could happen without God's intervention. The Lord further let him see that he had not been sufficiently grateful for the health, companionship, and work of his wife. He therefore feared that God might punish him by taking her away—although one can imagine that Mrs Thompson probably saw the punishment as hers. He prayed that the Lord would restore his wife's health and vowed perpetual gratitude for her. When his wife recovered, he charged himself with a return to indifference toward his blessings in her and a 'vile hart'. Mrs Thompson's near-death underlined to Thompson the sinful contrast between his unthankful acceptance of his spouse and his brief, divinely-inspired awareness of her value.

And uncertainty and fear gave Thompson an all-too-brief reminder of the level of active, spiritual struggle on which he should be conducting more of his life.

The Reverend Thomas Shepard, in ruminating about the imminent birth of his child in the 1640s, wondered what would happen if the labour did not go well 'and her pains be long and [the] Lord remember my sin? And I began to trouble my heart with fear of the worst'. When he learned that his wife had delivered a baby safely, ' . . . I saw the Lord's mercy and my own folly, to disquiet my heart with fear of what never shall be nor will be, and not rather to submit unto the Lord's will, and, come what can come, to be quiet there'. Like Thompson, Shepard's wife's mortal risk made him acutely conscious of his own sins. When his fears went unrealised he attempted to learn the lesson of peaceful resignation to God's will. He could not avoid seeing that his wife, in giving herself up to the miseries and uncertain outcome of travail, embodied this lesson.

In the same period the Reverend Michael Wigglesworth described his intimate involvement in his wife's labour. When she had pain, he:

> lay sighing, sweating, praying, almost fainting through weakness before morning. The next day, the spleen much enfeebled me, and setting in with grief took away my strength, my heart was smitten within me, and as sleep departed from myne eyes my stomach abhored meat, I was brought very low and knew not how to pass away another night.

He then described feeling hasty and impatient', presumably with the excessive duration of their labour, and he prayed that the Lord make him want to 'stoop to his will'. His wife's endurance taunted him with the patience and submission he lacked. And although he portrayed his wife's labour as his own, it was she who demonstrated uncomplaining fortitude in the face of pains which he likened to 'the pangs of eternal death'.

If women who were courageous in childbirth accrued complicated, competitive admiration from men, energeti-

cally religious mothering produced more straightforward praise. Sons whose mothers had toiled over their salvation knew from their own deep experience of maternal force what such efforts entailed. Unlike husbands who had impregnated their wives but been excluded from the redemptive suffering of labour, sons had been the object of mothers' strenuous efforts and sacrifices. Cotton Mather described a good mother 'travail[ing]' for her children more than once' to save them from the abominable sinfulness with which human birth had infected them. She was to work as hard as she could, instilling the principles of religion in her babies and catechising them as soon as they could speak.

Perhaps the most fearsome aspect of a righteous mother was that she would rather see her children dead than living outside the grace of God. In Michael Wigglesworth's famous epic, *The Day of Doom,* (1662) 'The tender mother will own no other/of all her numerous brood/But such as stand at Christ's right hand/acquitted through his blood'. Mothers with this unique spiritual ferocity, who gave more importance to their children's salvation than to their physical lives, were exhibiting the highest form of human love a Puritan could imagine. And yet, it could engender the starkest fear.

Of all imagery pertaining to females, Puritans had the most positive associations with the lactating breast. In sermons, ministers used metaphors giving God, the father, the capacity to nurse his children. This potent symbol of security, warmth and joy—the union of loving mother and nursing infant stood in stark contrast to the mother who would repudiate her unsaved offspring. In the eyes of a small child, the mother's immense power to give peace and happiness was paired with her ability to destroy forever the ease and hope of the unrepentant child.

These contrasting childhood images of perfect love and total terror persisted in the imaginations of children of such fervent mothers. In childbirth husbands saw wives resigned to God's will to sacrifice their own lives to create life. But the sons of deeply pious women remembered their mothers' seeming willingness to sacrifice *them* if their wickedness demanded it. Such fearsome, Janus-faced mothers undoubtedly contributed to men's admiration for female virtue at the same time that they implanted an abiding fear of powerful women.

Thomas Shepard recalled admiringly that his second wife cried and prayed in secret for her son, requesting that 'if the Lord did not intend to glorify himself by thee, that he would cut thee off by death rather than to live to dishonour him by sin'. His first wife, on the other hand, displayed the other ultimate motherly virtue. In explaining to his son his mother's death, Shepard said that she 'died in the Lord, departing out of this world to another, who did lose her life by being careful to preserve thine, for in the ship thou wert so feeble and froward both in the day and night that hereby she lost her strength and at last her life'. The first Mrs Shepard had sacrificed her life so that her child could live, and the second Mrs Shepard was willing to sacrifice her *son* if his soul became corrupt. A mighty Puritan mother elicited both veneration and terror.

The sons of other spiritually influential women came up with more tranquil memories, formed from less terrifying maternal images. These men recalled prayerful women to whom love meant hawklike watchfulness for their sons' salvation. Thomas Shepard remembered that his own mother, who died when he was still young, bore 'exceeding great love to me and made many prayers for me'. In Increase Mather's *Autobiography* he called his mother, Cotton's grandmother, 'a very Holy, praying woman. She desired two things for him, he remembered: grace and learning. As a boy he learned to read from his mother. His father taught him to write, 'who also instructed me in grammar learning' in Latin and Greek. But, as Cotton later remembered, Increase's mother taught her son, his father, 'all that was Good . . . among her Instructions . . . she mightily Inculcated the lesson of *Diligence*'.

Mather had often heard about his grandmother's potent combination of love and exhortation. He proudly recounted family lore: when Increase was very little his mother told him, that he

was 'very much her *Darling*', and that all she wished for him was to be a good Christian and a good scholar. She pleaded successfully on her deathbed that her fifteen-year-old son go into the ministry. She had been most 'honourable . . . for her *Vertue, . . .* that for which a *Woman* is most of all *to be Praised*'. She was Mather's model for his twice-travailing mother. He wrote, 'She was a Woman of Uncommon Devotion, and in her Importunate Prayers for this her son, she . . . became *Twice a Mother* to him'. Mather's own mother had similar moral structure, challenging the family to live up to her example. Mather remembered her as 'a Godly, an Humble, and a Praying Woman, and one that often set apart *Whole Days* for prayer and Secret Interviews with Heaven'.

Frances Boland arrived in America from Scotland in 1682. In his journal he gave special thanks for the 'pious nurture and example of my godly mother. . . . She was a praying woman and prayed much for her children'. He went on to say what a blessing it was for the young to have parents such as his.

John Dane, a surgeon in Ipswich, Massachusetts, remembered with respect that his mother had been a 'serious woman'. He recalled that she had once had a dream in which she heard a certain minister deliver a sermon; according to Dane's account she accurately foresaw the date, the place, and the text of that preacher's talk. Dane prudently did not praise his mother as a seer and mystic, which would have unsettled New World Puritans. Instead, he portrayed her as a sober student, indifferent to her gift of prophecy and desirous only to make 'good improvement of that sermon', which, thanks to her vision, she was able to enjoy twice.

The zealous mother was an exacting conscience to her children and, by extension, to the community. Embedded in the Puritan notion of community was mutual moral responsibility and the notion that the sin of one member stained the whole society. Boys and girls both grew up cultivating the ability to spot a sin in themselves and others. Cotton Mather wrote approvingly that his sister, Jerusha, recorded in her journal judg-

ments on the activities and behaviour of people in the community. He wrote that in her journal:

> She Remarks on the Dealings of God with Others; Especially if anything either Good or Bad were observable in the condition of the Town; But most of all what occur'd Joyful or Grievous, unto her nearest *Relatives,* and their Families; and she employes agreeable *Meditations* and *Supplications* there-upon.

Wives, in particular, were supposed to watch their husbands' spiritual state. Benjamin Wadsworth had written that 'If Husbands that call themselves Christian, are vain, wicked, ungodly; their pious Wives (if such they have) should by a meek winning Conversation, indeavour their spiritual & eternal Good'. Christopher Lawson sued his wife for divorce in 1669, accusing her of failing in her duty as a converted Puritan to attend to the spiritual needs of her unconverted husband. 'The unbelieving husband', he wrote, 'should be wonn by the good conversation of the believing wife . . .'.

The Reverend John Ward praised his wife for being an 'accusing conscience' and letting him know when he was acting in an ungodly manner. Mather extolled Ward's wife who had lived happily with her husband for forty years:

> Although she would so faithfully tell him of everything that might seem amendable in him . . . yet she ever pleased him wonderfully. And she would oft put him upon the duties of secret fasts, and when she met with anything in reading that she counted singularly agreeable, she would still impart it unto him.

The marriage of the Wards was an active spiritual partnership in which Mrs Ward not infrequently gave her husband direction.

Women often achieved the role of conscience by becoming shadow ministers, absorbing, sometimes writing down (as Jerusha Mather did), and acting upon the weekly sermons of their husbands and/or pastors. Thomas Shepard commended his wife for her 'excellency to reprove for sin and discern the evils of men'. He went on to say that she loved the words of the Lord exceedingly and was, therefore, glad to read his notes for his sermons every week and ponder the thoughts therein.

Cotton Mather memorialised the second Mrs Whiting for her 'singular piety and gravity', who prayed in her closet every day to God. He commended her for writing down the sermons that she heard 'on the Lord's days with much dexterity', while living by their messages all week.

Although Puritan traditions cast doubt on women's capacity for goodness and prohibited them from exercising concrete authority, Puritan women did achieve moral stature from quietly enduring suffering, intense dedication to the salvation of their children, and gentle correction of the behaviour of their spouses and neighbours. The blessing Puritan men bestowed on notably virtuous women registered the conflict in which it was born. Women had to criticise, suggest, and direct others—particularly men—with extreme caution as Puritan men were deeply alarmed when women presumed to judge them. Nonetheless, Puritan women, inclined to religious depth, would find respect and deference in their communities, no small treasures in a male-dominated world. And they would bequeath to later generations of women a tradition of moral criticism and the conviction that zealous effort on behalf of the salvation of others was part of their human responsibility. This belief would empower women to turn their moral energies upon their husbands, families, and, in time, the world around them.

FOR FURTHER READING

Laurel Thacher Ulrich, *Goodwives: Image and Reality in the Lives of Women of Northern New England, 1650–1750* (Knopt, 1982); Carol Karlsen, *The Devil in the Shape of a Woman* (Norton, 1987; David Leverenz, *The Language of Puritan Feeling* (Rutgers University Press, 1980); Perry Miller, *The American Puritan* (Doubleday/Anchor, 1956); Lyle Koehler, *A Search for Power, The "Weaker Sex" in Seventeenth Century New England* (University of Illinois Press, 1980); Kenneth Silverman, *The Life and Times of Cotton Mather* (Harper & Row, 1970).

Penning a Legacy

Imprisoned and vilified for his religious views, William Penn, a member of the Society of Friends, sought to establish a colony in the New World where people of all faiths could live in mutual harmony.

By Patricia Hudson

ON A CHILL WINTER DAY in 1668, 24-year-old William Penn paced back and forth in a cramped chamber in the Tower of London. Arrested for blasphemy after publishing a pamphlet that questioned the doctrine of the Trinity, Penn was being held in close confinement. The Bishop of London had decreed that if Penn didn't recant publicly he would remain imprisoned for the rest of his life. Penn's reply was unequivocal: "My prison shall be my grave before I will budge a jot, for I owe my conscience to no mortal man."

WILLIAM PENN WAS born on October 14, 1644, just a stone's throw from the Tower where he would one day be a prisoner. His father, William, Sr., was an ambitious naval officer who rose to the rank of admiral. Knighted by King Charles II, the elder Penn formed a friendship with the royal family that would play a major role in his son's future.

The Penn family's next-door neighbor on Tower Hill was the diarist Samuel Pepys, who noted in his journal that Admiral Penn was "a merry fellow and pretty good-natured and sings very bawdy songs." Pepys also recorded instances of William, Jr., playing cards with his father, going to the theater, and carelessly leaving his sword in a hired coach and then racing across London to retrieve it.

One incident from Penn's youth foreshadowed his later preoccupation with religious matters—at 17 William was expelled from Oxford University for daring to criticize certain Church of England rituals. Appalled, Admiral Penn packed his overly serious son off to France, hoping that he would grow more worldly amid the glitter of Paris.

When William returned to England after two years abroad, Pepys described him as "a most modish person, grown a fine gentlemen, but [having] a great deal, if not too much, of the vanity of the French garb and affected manner of speech and gait." The admiral, well-pleased with his fashionable son, sent William to Ireland to attend to family business, but it was there, in 1667, that the younger Penn embraced the Quaker faith.

The Society of Friends—dubbed Quakers by their enemies because they admonished listeners to "tremble at the word of the Lord"—had been founded in 1647 by George Fox, a weaver's son-turned-preacher who spoke of the Inner Light and believed that there was "that of God in every man." According to Fox, all people, regardless of their status here on earth, are equal in God's eyes. It was a challenge directed at the very heart of England's class-conscious society, and though all religious dissenters were subject to fines and imprisonments, the establishment singled out Quakers with particular ferocity.

When Penn again returned to London, his family was aghast at the change in him. Not only did young William insist on attending the outlawed Quaker meetings, he also ignored common courtesy by refusing to take off his hat in the presence of his "betters," just one of several methods Friends used to illustrate their belief in equality. In the eyes of acquaintances and family, William had betrayed not only the religious principles of the Church of England but also his social class. Noted Pepys in his diary: "Mr. Will Penn, who is lately come over from Ireland, is a Quaker . . . or some very melancholy thing."

Better educated than most of the early Friends, Penn quickly became one of their most outspoken advocates, taking part in public debates and writing pamphlets that he published at his own expense. One respected London minister, enraged by the conversion of two female members of his congregation to Quakerism, stated that he would "rather lose them to a bawdy house than a Quaker meeting" and then went on to denounce the group's theology.

When Penn responded to the attack in print, the pamphlet became the talk of the city and led to his imprisonment in the Tower. "Hath got me W. Pen's book against the Trinity," Pepys wrote. "I find it so well writ, as I think it too good for him ever to have writ it—and it is a serious sort of book, and not fit for everybody to read."

Despite the threat of life imprisonment, the cold confines of the Tower failed to dampen Penn's crusading spirit. He spent his time there writing a rough draft of *No Cross, No Crown*, one of his most enduring works. After nine months in custody, William was released, perhaps in part as a favor to Admiral Penn, who had loaned the cash-hungry King Charles II a great deal of money over the years.

In 1672, William married Gulielma Maria Springett. During their more than 21 years of marriage, the couple became the parents of seven children. Family responsibilities, however, did not keep Penn from again risking imprisonment by speaking at Friends' meetings, writing political and religious pamphlets, and refusing to take an oath of allegiance.

By the late 1670s, after more than a decade of clashes with the nation's authorities, Penn had grown pessimistic about the likelihood of religious and civil reforms in England and so turned his thoughts to the New World. Although the colonies were heavily populated with dissenters from England, many colonial authorities exercised no more tolerance for Quakers than their English counterparts. In Puritan-controlled Boston, for example, two Quaker women were hanged when they refused to stop preaching in public.

Having experienced firsthand the horrors of forced religious conformity, Penn dreamed of showing the world that peaceful coexistence among diverse religious groups was possible and that a single, state-supported religion was not only unnecessary but undesirable. "There can be no reason to persecute any man in this world about anything that belongs to the next," he wrote.

When Admiral Penn died without collecting the money owed to him by the king, William saw a way to make his dream a reality. In 1680, he petitioned King Charles for a grant of land in America to retire the debt. Acceding to his request, the king conferred upon Penn an enormous tract of land, the largest that had ever been granted to an individual. William proposed calling the colony New Wales, it being "a pretty hilly country," but King Charles insisted on calling it "Pennsylvania"— Penn's Woods—in honor of his old friend, the admiral.

At the age of 36, Penn suddenly faced the enormous task of designing a government from scratch. The constitution he created, with its provisions for religious freedom, extensive voting rights, and penal reform, was remarkably enlightened by seventeenth-century standards. Despite the vast power it conferred on him as proprietor, Penn had been careful to leave "to myself and successors no power of doing mischief, that the will of one man may not hinder the good of an whole country. . . ."

Before he set sail for Pennsylvania himself, Penn appointed three commissioners and charged them with establishing the new colony. While William saw nothing wrong with Europeans settling in the New World, he was among the few colonizers of his time who recognized the prior claims of the indigenous people. Thus, he gave the commissioners a letter, dated October 18, 1681, addressed to the people of the Lenni Lenape tribe who inhabited his proprietorship. The letter stated that King Charles had granted him "a great province; but I desire to enjoy it with your love and consent, that we may always live together as neighbours and friends, else what would the great God say to us, who hath made us not to devour and destroy one another but to live soberly and kindly together in the world?"

When he finally arrived in the colony in October 1682, Penn made a treaty with the Indians, in effect purchasing the land he had already been given by the king. Truly wishing to live in peace, he tried to be fair in his dealings with the Lenni Lenape, unmindful that they—like their Delaware kinsmen who "sold" Manhattan Island to Peter Minuit—did not understand the concept of exclusive ownership of the land and believed that the white men simply sought to share its use.

Penn had intended to settle permanently in Pennsylvania, but within two years a boundary dispute with neighboring Maryland required him to return to London, where a web of troubles awaited him. As a result, nearly 16 years passed before he again set foot in his colony. During his long absence, the colonists had grown resentful of his authority, and in 1701, less than two years after his second voyage to Pennsylvania, a disillusioned Penn sailed back to England, never to return. All told, he spent less than five years in America.

From his return to England until his death 16 years later, Penn continually struggled to stave off financial disaster. Never an astute businessman, he discovered, to his horror, that his trusted business manager had defrauded him, leaving him deeply in debt. At the age of 63, Penn was sent to a debtor's prison. Marveled one friend, "The more he is pressed, the more he rises. He

seems of a spirit to bear and rub through difficulties." Before long, concerned friends raised enough money to satisfy his creditors.

Prior to his death in 1718 at the age of 73, Penn attempted to sell Pennsylvania back to the Crown, hoping to forge at least a modicum of financial security for his six surviving children. In making the offer, Penn sought to extract a promise from the English Crown that the colony's laws and civil rights would be preserved. But while the negotiations were still in progress, Penn suffered a debilitating stroke, and the transaction was never completed. Penn's descendants thus retained control of the colony until the American Revolution.

Despite imprisonment, vilification, and financial ruin, Penn had labored unceasingly to establish the principle of religious freedom in both his homeland and in America. He espoused such "modern" concepts as civil rights, participatory government, interracial brotherhood, and international peace.

Yet, despite the rich legacy that the founder of the colony of Pennsylvania left to Americans, William Penn remains a shadowy figure in our popular consciousness. For most people, his name conjures up little more than a vague picture that is remarkably similar to the bland, beaming face that adorns boxes of Quaker Oats cereal. The reality, however, was quite different; Penn was an extremely complex individual, whose life was filled with triumph and tragedy and was marked by startling contrasts.

In 1984, more than 300 years after the founding of Pennsylvania, the United States Congress posthumously granted Penn U.S. citizenship. "In the history of this Nation," the proclamation read, "there has been a small number of men and women whose contributions to its traditions of freedom, justice, and individual rights have accorded them a special place of honor . . . and to whom all Americans owe a lasting debt." The man who pursued his "Holy Experiment" on the shores of the New World was, indeed, one of those men.

Patricia Hudson is a freelance writer from Tennessee and a former contributing editor of Americana *magazine.*

The Right to Marry:
Loving v. Virginia

Peter Wallenstein

In June 1958, Mildred Jeter and Richard Loving left their native Caroline County, Virginia, for a visit to Washington, D.C., where they got married. They then returned to Virginia and took up residence in the home of the bride's parents. Early in the morning a few weeks later, everyone in the house was asleep—Mr. and Mrs. Loving downstairs, Mr. and Mrs. Jeter upstairs—when the Lovings awoke to find three policemen in their bedroom with flashlights. The intruders arrested and jailed the Lovings. The charge? Their marriage violated state law. He was white, and she was black. By marrying in D.C. to avoid a Virginia law prohibiting interracial marriage, they had committed a serious crime.

In January 1959, Judge Leon M. Bazile sentenced the couple to a year in jail. He suspended the sentences on the condition that "both accused leave Caroline County and the state of Virginia at once and do not return together or at the same time to said county and state for a period of twenty-five years." They moved to Washington, D.C., where they lived with Mrs. Loving's cousin Alex Byrd and his wife Laura. They continued to live in their home away from home, and this is where they raised their three children, Sidney, Donald, and Peggy.

In 1963 they determined to take a stand against the injustice that had forced them into exile. They wrote United States Attorney General Robert F. Kennedy asking for help. He directed their letter to the National Capitol Area Civil Liberties Union, and the ACLU assigned the case to Bernard S. Cohen, a young lawyer practicing in Alexandria, Virginia. Some months later another young lawyer, Philip A. Hirschkop, who had been working in Mississippi assisting civil rights workers, joined Cohen on the case.

The law that the Lovings broke originated in 1691 when the House of Burgesses sought to reduce the number of mixed-race children born in the Virginia colony, particularly mixed-race children whose mothers were white.

The law that the Lovings broke originated in 1691, when the House of Burgesses sought to reduce the number of mixed-race children born in the Virginia colony, particularly mixed-race children whose mothers were white. The Burgesses enacted a measure designed "for prevention of that abominable mixture and spurious issue which hereafter may encrease in this dominion, as well by negroes, mulattoes, and Indians intermarrying with English, or other white woman, as by their unlawfull accompanying with one another." It outlawed interracial marriage for white men and white women alike. While it did not ban the marriage *per se*, it did mandate the banishment of the white partner in any interracial marriage that occurred, at least if that person was not an indentured servant and, thus, did not owe labor to any planter: "Whatsoever English or other white man or women being free shall intermarry with a negroe, mulatto, or Indian man or woman bond or free, shall within three months after such marriage be banished and removed from this dominion forever."

Thus, the white wife of a nonwhite man was forced to have mixed-race children outside of Virginia. If she tried to evade banishment from the colony by skipping the marriage ceremony but then had a mixed-race child in Virginia out of wedlock, she would have to pay a heavy fine. If unable to pay the fine, she would be sold as a servant for five years. Either way, the child would be sold into servitude until he or she reached the age of thirty.

Only the specifics of the law changed in the years that followed. Through the

From *OAH Magazine of History*, Winter 1995, pp. 37-41. © 1995 by the Organization of American Historians. Reprinted by permission.

American Revolution and the Civil War, Virginia law placed a severe penalty on any white person who married a non-white. The law was amended in 1705 to eliminate banishment; the new penalty was a fine and six months in prison. In 1848, the legislature changed the term of imprisonment for the white partner in an interracial marriage to a maximum of twelve months. The Code of 1849 declared interracial marriages "absolutely void."

In 1865, slavery came to an end in Virginia. Interracial marriages remained "absolutely void," but the laws began to take on the more specific shape of those that the Lovings encountered nearly a hundred years later. Both partners in an interracial relationship—the black Virginian and the white—became subject to prosecution. Andrew Kinney, a black man, and Mahala Miller, a white woman, wished to live as husband and wife but could not marry under Virginia law. In 1874, after living together nearly eight years and having three children, they went to Washington, D.C., to get married. When they returned home to Augusta County, authorities brought charges against them for "lewdly associating and cohabiting" together without being married. At his trial, Mr. Kinney urged the judge to instruct the jury that the marriage was "valid and a bar to this prosecution." Instead, the judge instructed the jury that the marriage was "but a vain and futile attempt to evade the laws of Virginia." The question, simply put, was: Did the defendant have a valid marriage that gave him an effective defense against the charge he faced? Or, was his living as though he were married precisely the basis for that charge? Was he married? Or was he guilty?

After being convicted and sentenced to pay the heaviest fine the law allowed, $500, Mr. Kinney appealed to the Virginia Supreme Court. That court upheld the conviction. As to whether the law of Washington, D.C., or that of Virginia governed the case, Judge Joseph Christian, speaking for a unanimous court, declared, "There can be no doubt as to the power of every country to make laws regulating the marriage of its own subjects; to declare who may marry, how they may marry, and what shall be the legal consequences of their marrying." The judge went on to say that "purity of public morals, the moral and physical development of both races, and the highest advancement of our cherished southern civilization, under which two distinct races are to work out and accomplish the destiny to which the Almighty has assigned them on this continent—all require that they should be kept distinct and separate, and that connections and alliances so unnatural that God and nature seem to forbid them, should be prohibited by positive law, and be subject to no evasion." What "God and nature" had sundered, let no man seek to bring together. The law would not allow the marriage of Andrew Kinney and Mahala Miller to persist, at least in Virginia. "If the parties desire to maintain the relations of man and wife, they must change their domicile and go

---

"Mr. Cohen, tell the Court I love my wife, and it is just unfair that I can't live with her in Virginia."

---

to some state or country where the laws recognize the validity of such marriages." Despite their loss in the courts, the couple made their own stand. Five years later, they were still living together and had had five sons. They remained subject to additional prosecution, but local authorities seem to have been content with winning the one case against them.

In 1878, the Virginia General Assembly made two changes—the most significant since the 1691 law. Not only would both partners in an interracial marriage be subject to prosecution but, if convicted, they would also both be sentenced to the state penitentiary for a term of two to five years. And if, like the Kinneys, they sought to evade the law by marrying outside of Virginia, "they shall be as guilty, and be punished as if the marriage had been in this state. The fact of their cohabitation here as man and wife shall be evidence of their marriage." By the time of the Lovings, the legislature had changed the minimum sentence from two years to one year.

But what about the Fourteenth Amendment? Approved in 1868, its first section declared, in part, that no state could "deny to any person within its jurisdiction the equal protection of the laws." Indeed, in 1872 the Alabama Supreme Court ruled Alabama's law against interracial marriages unconstitutional. The court said that the Civil Rights Act of 1866 had conferred "the right to make and enforce contracts, amongst which is that of marriage with any citizen capable of entering into that relation," and that the Fourteenth Amendment had placed the Civil Rights Act's "cardinal principle" in the United States Constitution. Yet, the Alabama Supreme Court itself soon overruled that decision, and no other court adopted its position for many years.

Thus, the Fourteenth Amendment failed to help couples like the Lovings, as a black man in Alabama, Tony Pace, and a white woman, Mary Jane Cox, found out. Convicted of carrying on an interracial relationship, each was sentenced to two years in the Alabama penitentiary, the minimum term the law permitted. They appealed their convictions, but the Alabama Supreme Court ruled against them. Each defendant's punishment, "white and black," was "precisely the same." They appealed again to the nation's highest court, but the United States Supreme Court ruled in 1883 as had the Alabama court. Tony Pace served his sentence in the Alabama penitentiary.

Gradually, laws like Virginia's and Alabama's came under successful attack. In 1948, in *Perez v. Sharp,* the California Supreme Court ruled that a California law against interracial marriage was unconstitutional—the first such ruling since Alabama's short-lived effort in 1872. In the years that followed, states outside the South repealed their laws and left the question of marriage up to individuals regardless of their race. When the Lovings returned to court in the 1960s, however, all southern states retained such laws. As late as 1966, Oklahoma plus every state that had had slavery as late as the Civil War—Texas, Arkansas, Louisiana, Mississippi, Alabama, Tennessee, Georgia, Florida, the Carolinas, Virginia and West Virginia, Maryland, Delaware, Kentucky, and Missouri—still had such laws on the books.

At about the same time, the United States Supreme Court breathed new life into the Fourteenth Amendment's equal protection clause. For example, in 1948 the court ruled in *Shelley v. Kraemer* that state courts could not enforce restrictive covenants in housing documents that prevented nonwhite families from moving into white communities. Several rulings declared against states' banning black students from enrolling in state law schools. And in 1954, the nation's highest court ruled in *Brown v. Board of Education,* on Fourteenth Amendment grounds, that "in the field of public education the doctrine of 'separate but equal' has no place."

The Supreme Court ruled on various cases in the area of privacy at about the same time. How much control should people have over their lives, and how much power should state governments have to restrict people's freedom? What fundamental rights did people have— even if those rights are not explicit in the United States Constitution? The Court declared that people had the right to teach their children a foreign language *(Meyer v. Nebraska,* 1923) and the right to send their children to private schools (*Pierce v. Society of Sisters,* 1925). Married people had the right to have children; the Court voided a law that mandated that people convicted of certain types of crime be sterilized (*Skinner v. Oklahoma*, 1942). In the leading privacy case up to the time of the Loving case, the Court ruled that married people also had the right to decide whether to use birth control information and devices to prevent pregnancy

(*Griswold v. Connecticut,* 1965). In 1973, in *Roe v. Wade,* the Court extended its rulings on matters of privacy when it struck down statutes that prohibited women from obtaining abortions, especially in the first three months of pregnancy. Thus, across a fifty-year period between 1923 and 1973, the Court determined that people had a zone of privacy—the right, at least under certain circumstances, to go about their lives without having authorities intervene and tell them what they must and must not do.

These various developments in twentieth-century American constitutional history came together in the case of the Lovings. There was no reason to assume that the Lovings would be successful. They had not even tried to contest their exile in 1959 but had waited more than four years before contacting the Attorney General's office. Only a few years before their marriage, convictions, and

UPI/Bettman

Mildred and Richard Loving at their news conference on 12 June 1967, the day the U.S. Supreme Court ruled unanimously in their favor.

43

exile, other couples had tried unsuccessfully to get the United States Supreme Court to rule laws like Virginia's unconstitutional. In 1955, a black woman named Linnie Jackson, who had been sentenced to the Alabama penitentiary for an interracial relationship, appealed her conviction to the United States Supreme Court. The Court refused to hear her case. At about the same time, a Chinese man in Virginia, Ham Say Naim, tried to take a case to the United States Supreme Court to have his marriage to a white woman recognized, but the Court turned a deaf ear to him too. That left intact a ruling by the Virginia Supreme Court which had insisted that "regulation of the marriage relation" is "distinctly one of the rights guaranteed to the States and safeguarded by that bastion of States' rights, somewhat battered perhaps but still a sturdy fortress in our fundamental law, the tenth section of the Bill of Rights."

In 1963, despite the obstacles, the Lovings renewed their quest to live together as husband and wife and to raise their three children in Caroline County, Virginia. Their lawyers, Bernard Cohen and Philip Hirschkop, consulted with various ACLU lawyers in preparing the case. They began where the Lovings had finished previously, in Judge Bazile's courtroom. The judge saw no reason to change his mind about anything. The Lovings' marriage, he said, was "absolutely void in Virginia," and they could not "cohabit" there "without incurring repeated prosecutions" for doing so. He declared his convictions on the law in dispute: "Almighty God created the races white, black, yellow, malay and red, and he placed them on separate continents. And but for the interference with his arrangement there would be no cause for such marriages. The fact that he separated the races shows that he did not intend for the races to mix."

The Lovings appealed their case to the Virginia Supreme Court, but that court saw nothing that required change since its ruling in the Naim case ten years earlier. Richard and Mildred Loving then went to the United States Supreme Court to challenge their convictions for having violated Virginia's laws against racial intermarriage.

In the months ahead, the nation's high court faced squarely, for the first time, the question of whether such laws as Virginia's violated the Fourteenth Amendment. Cohen and Hirschkop quoted one judge in the 1948 California decision on interracial marriage: "If the right to marry is a funda-

---

"Under our Constitution, the freedom to marry, or not to marry, a person of another race resides with the individual and cannot be infringed by the State."

---

mental right, then it must be conceded that an infringement of that right by means of a racial restriction is an unlawful infringement of one's liberty." They also asserted that "caprice of the politicians cannot be substituted for the minds of the individual in what is man's most personal and intimate decision. The error of such legislation must immediately be apparent to those in favor of miscegenation statutes, if they stopped to consider their abhorrence to a statute which commanded that 'all marriages must be between persons of different racial backgrounds.'" Such a statute, they contended, would be no more "repugnant to the constitution"— and no less so—than the law under consideration. Something "so personal as the choice of a mate must be left to the individuals involved," they argued; "race limitations are too unreasonable and arbitrary a basis for the State to interfere." They reviewed the history of Virginia's anti-miscegenation statutes— going all the way back to the seventeenth century—to characterize them as "relics of slavery" and, at the same time, "expressions of modern day racism." And, finally, in oral argument, Bernard Cohen conveyed Richard Loving's own words. "Mr. Cohen, tell the Court I love my wife, and it is just unfair that I can't live with her in Virginia."

Speaking for a unanimous Court on 12 June 1967, Chief Justice Earl Warren declared that states' rights had to defer to the Fourteenth Amendment when it came to the claim of "exclusive state control" over the "regulation of marriage." The argument that Virginia's "miscegenation statutes punish equally both the white and the Negro participants in an interracial marriage" could not pass constitutional muster in the 1960s. The burden of proof rested on the state, for "the fact of equal application does not immunize the statute from the heavy burden of justification" required by the Fourteenth Amendment, particularly when racial classifications appeared in criminal statutes. "The fact that Virginia prohibits only interracial marriages involving white persons demonstrates" that those laws were "designed to maintain White Supremacy." Indeed, the statute's original purpose held no interest for the Court; the Chief Justice declared the racial classifications "repugnant to the Fourteenth Amendment, even assuming an even-handed state purpose to protect the 'integrity' of all races." According to Warren the Fourteenth Amendment's clear and central purpose was to "eliminate all official state sources of invidious racial discrimination."

The Chief Justice was sure of the Court's recent history in civil rights cases. He wrote: "We have consistently denied the constitutionality of measures which restrict the rights of citizens on account of race. There can be no doubt that restricting the freedom to marry solely because of racial classifications violates the central meaning of the Equal Protection Clause." As for the Due Process Clause, the Chief Justice noted that "the freedom to marry has long been recognized as one of the vital personal rights essential to the orderly pursuit of happiness by free men. . . . To deny this fundamental freedom on so unsupportable a basis as the racial classifications embodied in these statutes, classifications so directly subversive of the principle of equality at the heart of the Fourteenth Amendment, is surely to deprive all the State's citizens of liberty without due process of law. The Fourteenth Amendment requires that the freedom of choice to marry not be restricted by invidious racial discriminations. Under our Constitution, the freedom to marry, or not marry, a person of another race resides with the individual and cannot be infringed by the State." Chief Justice Warren's final sentence put an end to the Lovings' odyssey through the courts: "These convictions must be reversed."

Richard and Mildred Loving finally won the case ten days after their ninth wedding anniversary. From their temporary farm home in Bowling Green, near Fredericksburg, Mr. and Mrs. Loving drove north to Alexandria for a news conference at their lawyers' office. There Mr. Loving said, "We're just really overjoyed," and Mrs. Loving said, "I feel free now." A photographer snapped a picture, law books in the background, of two happy people sitting close together, his arm around her neck. "My wife and I plan to go ahead and build a new house now," said Richard Loving the construction worker about the permanent new home in Virginia that Richard Loving the husband and father wanted his family to live in. And they did so.

Reporting on the decision, the *New York Times* noted its larger significance. "In writing the opinion that struck down the last group of segregation laws to remain standing—those requiring separation of the races in marriage—Chief Justice Warren completed the process that he set in motion with his opinion in 1954 that declared segregation in public schools to be unconstitutional." Bernard S. Cohen, the Lovings' lawyer, offered a similar benediction on the proceedings. At his clients' press conference, he said: "We hope we have put to rest the last vestiges of racial discrimination that were supported by the law in Virginia and all over the country."

The black-owned newspaper in Virginia's largest city, the *Norfolk Journal and Guide,* led off its front page with the headline "Top Court Junks Marriage Bars" and printed an editorial on "Freedom of Choice at the Altar." It predicted "no noticeable increase in the number of mixed marriages in Virginia." As it explained, "prospective grooms" would continue to enjoy "the privileges of withholding their requests for the bride's hand," and brides would retain "the privilege and authority to prevent mixed marriages simply by saying 'no.'" Nonetheless, the *Journal and Guide* insisted on the importance of the Court's ruling: "What makes this Supreme Court decision so desirable is that it lifts an onerous and brutalizing stigma from Negro Virginians by knocking down that psychological barrier which, in effect, told them and the world that no Negro is good enough to be the husband or wife of a white Virginian." Furthermore, it saluted the Lovings for having taken a stand. "They have done an incalculably great service for their community, their state, and their nation. Had they been less persevering, the legal battle to end Virginia's oppression on the marital front might have been forfeited long ago."

BIBLIOGRAPHY

Garrow, David J. *Liberty and Sexuality: The Right to Privacy and the Making of Roe v. Wade.* New York: Macmillan, 1994.

Grossberg, Michael. *Governing the Hearth: Law and the Family in Nineteenth-Century America.* Chapel Hill: University of North Carolina Press, 1985.

Ross, William G. *Forging New Freedoms: Nativism, Education, and the Constitution, 1917–1927.* Lincoln: University of Nebraska Press, 1994.

Schwartz, Bernard. *Super Chief: Earl Warren and His Supreme Court—A Judicial Biography.* New York: New York University Press, 1983.

Sickels, Robert J. *Race, Marriage, and the Law.* Albuquerque: University of New Mexico Press, 1972.

Wallenstein, Peter. "Race, Marriage, and the Law of Freedom: Alabama and Virginia, 1860s–1960s." *Chicago-Kent Law Review* 70 (1995).

Peter Wallenstein is Associate Professor of History at Virginia Polytechnic Institute and State University.

Unit Selections

Key Points to Consider

❖ Thomas Jefferson remains one of the most popular of the Founding Fathers. Discuss the significance of the new evidence about about his relationship with Sally Hemmings. Does it mean that he was a hypocrite with regard to slavery? Defend your answer.

❖ What purposes was the Declaration of Independence supposed to serve? How have perceptions of this document changed over the years?

❖ Discuss the most significant compromises made at the Constitutional Convention of 1787. How did secrecy help smooth the way for these compromises?

❖ What is meant by "conditional" antislavery? Given the situation at the time, would it have been possible to abolish slavery without splitting the union?

DUSHKIN ONLINE   Links   www.dushkin.com/online/

These sites are annotated on pages 4 and 5.

The American colonies constituted only a portion of the vast British Empires. Economic theory at the time held that the mother country should regulate commercial activity for the benefit of the entire empire. Generally, this meant that the colonies should provide raw materials unavailable in the British Isles in return for manufactured goods. The goal was to ensure a favorable balance of trade between the empire and other nations, and to attain self-sufficiency with regard to strategic materials such as lumber for shipbuilding. The British did not want to have to rely on other countries for such materials because the supply might be cut off in time of war. Whatever made the empire as a whole richer and more powerful, in theory, benefited all its component parts.

The conventional wisdom, known as mercantilism, had mixed effects on the American colonies. Southern producers of rice and corn, for instance, had the advantage of selling in a protected market and of purchasing manufactured goods on British credit. New Englanders gained from selling lumber and from building ships—one of the few industries the British government encouraged for economic and strategic reasons. Others fared less well. People in the middle colonies, especially, often chafed at regulations that prevented them from buying cheaper goods from other countries and from manufacturing products that competed with British companies. For the most part the British government, preoccupied with the myriad problems involved in managing an enormous empire, treated the colonies with a light hand and often failed to enforce its own regulations. What became known as "benign neglect" meant that the colonies in practice enjoyed a great deal of independence in managing their own affairs.

Decades of benign neglect, the passage of time, and the distance from England brought changes in colonists' attitudes. Although regarding themselves as British subjects, they came to assume the autonomy they enjoyed as the natural state of affairs. Few of them had ever visited the mother country, some spent their lives without seeing any visible trappings of the government to which they owed their loyalty. In short, many colonists regarded themselves as "American" as well as subjects of the crown.

The end of what the colonists called the French and Indian War in 1763 brought dramatic changes in the relationship. The war had virtually bankrupted England, and extremely heavy taxes were levied on the British people. The government understandably concluded that colonists should pay their share for a conflict in which they had been involved. After all, one settlement of the war had been removal of the French from North America, which meant they no longer presented a threat to the colonists.

The new taxes and regulations, along with the much more vigorous efforts to enforce the latter, were perceived by the colonists as an unwarranted intrusion on the rights and privileges that they had come to take for granted. These burdens were imposed, moreover, at a time when removal of the French threat made the colonists less dependent upon the crown's protection. Economic disputes quickly spilled over into other areas such as religion and politics. What seemed to the colonists as outrageous behavior by the British government caused more and more of them to conclude that the colonies would be best off if they cut ties with the empire and struck out alone. The British, of course, were determined to hold on to their possessions. Efforts by the government to enforce its will led to armed clashes and then to the Revolutionary War.

The first unit essay, "Flora MacDonald," tells the story of a woman who had become a Scottish heroine in 1746 when she had helped "Bonnie Prince Charlie" escape British authorities. She was received with some fanfare when she moved to North Carolina in 1774, but, when she began recruiting men of Scottish descent to fight for the crown during the revolution, her popularity vanished.

In "Jefferson's Secret Life," the authors discuss new evidence that seems to confirm the old allegation that Thomas Jefferson had sired a number of children with his slave mistress, Sally Hemmings. The article assesses the likely effect of this revelation on the reputation of the author of the Declaration of Independence.

Next, the Declaration of Independence is analyzed in "Making Sense of the Fourth of July." Author Pauline Maier discusses how the meaning and function of the Declaration has changed over the course of time. Then, "George Washington, Spymaster" reviews a less well known aspect of Washington's military leadership during the Revolutionary War.

In 1784 a group of merchants financed a voyage to China on a ship appropriately named The Empress of China. The essay "The Canton War" describes how the first American ship sent to open trade with China quickly became enmeshed in a struggle over human rights.

Ezra Bowen, in ". . . by the Unanimous Consent of the States," presents the numerous compromises made at the Constitutional Convention of 1787. Tight security over the proceedings permitted individuals to take positions that they would have found difficult to defend in public. William Freehling, in the unit's final essay, "The Founding Fathers, Conditional Antislavery, and the Nonradicalism of the American Revolution," argues that although the Founders did not intend to destroy the institution of slavery, they took steps that led to its ultimate demise.

Revolutionary America

Flora MacDonald

By a twist of fate, the Scottish heroine who helped Bonnie Price Charlie escape the British in 1746 immigrated to North Carolina in 1774, only to find herself allied with the Crown during the American Revolution.

By Jean Creznic

" . . . FLORA MACDONALD, a name that will be mentioned in history, and if courage and fidelity be virtues, mentioned with honour," wrote Doctor Samuel Johnson in *Journey to the Western Isles* after he and his friend James Boswell visited her in Scotland in September 1773. As Johnson predicted, her name is honored among her fellow Scots, and her life has become legend, a story that took this eighteenth-century heroine from the islands of Scotland to the colony of North Carolina, on the eve of America's Revolutionary War.

Flora was born in 1722 in Milton, South Uist, one of the Hebrides Islands that lie off the western coast of Scotland. Her father died when she was a child, and her mother remarried in 1728 and moved to the Hebridean Isle of Skye. Ever the independent thinker, six-year-old Flora declared that she would stay in Milton with her older brother, Angus, rather than go to her mother's new home. She said that she would be happier with him there than

in a house that was strange to her. Later, an aunt and uncle took charge and sent her to school in Edinburgh, after which, she lived as a member of a privileged family, spending her time in ladylike pursuits, frequently traveling to visit relatives and friends.

The adventure that brought Flora fame began as she was staying with relatives at Ormaclade, on South Uist. The talk in Scotland was all about Prince Charles Edward Stuart, known by the Scots as Bonnie Prince Charlie, and how he might reestablish the Catholic Stuarts as Great Britain's rightful rulers. The prince was the grandson of the Stuart King James II, who had reigned in Britain during 1685–88. English sentiment against Catholicism ran high during his reign, and James, whose sympathies leaned more and more toward Rome, fled to France in 1688 when the overthrow of the throne appeared imminent. His son, also named James, spent his life in France and Italy, plotting to regain his father's throne.

During the first half of the eighteenth century, the pressure on James's son, Charles Edward, to succeed to the throne was enormous, but England under Protestant King George II had no intention of allowing the Catholic Stuarts to wear the crown. Despite the fact there was no encouragement for Prince Charles Edward from that quarter, agents of the exiled Stuarts traveled the Scottish Highlands, striving to enlist the support of the Highland clans. They succeeded in rallying a small band of Jacobites (supporters of the House of Stuart), most of them MacDonalds, to the cause.

Arriving in Scotland in August 1745, the prince and his followers launched their long awaited campaign. Although well begun, the effort was nevertheless doomed to failure and ended the next year on April 16, 1746, at the Battle of Culloden, where the prince and his five thousand Highland supporters were crushed by some nine thousand infantrymen led by George II's son, William, the Duke of Cumberland.

From *American History,* May/June 1997, pp. 22-24, 65-67. © 1997 by Cowles Magazines, Inc. Reprinted through the courtesy of Cowles Magazines, publishers of *American History.*

The English showed the weakened Scots no mercy, and this defeat sealed the fate of the prince and of the resurgence of the House of Stuart. Charles Edward fled for his life after the battle, hiding from the Duke of Cumberland's soldiers wherever he could, finally making his way to the western isles, and Flora MacDonald.

Some say that Flora's stepfather, Hugh MacDonald—a sympathizer of Prince Charles Edward despite his position as the commander of the government militia in South Uist—suggested her participation in the escape. Others credit the scheme to the prince's comrade and fellow soldier, Captain Felix O'Neill, who

Isle of Skye. Once she succeeded in getting the prince to Skye, he would make his way to mainland Scotland and be picked up by a French naval vessel, which would transport him to safety in Europe.

Hugh MacDonald supplied the passports that Flora needed for the several boatmen, a manservant, and an Irish spinning maid who would help care for his ailing wife. According to the plan, Betty Burke, the Irish maid, would make the crossing bundled up against the wind and sea in a bonnet, cloak, and shawl, making it difficult for anyone to have a close look at her face—all for the best since "Betty," an ignorant and ungainly looking servant girl, would indeed be

Charles Edward and Flora parted, never to meet again.*

Flora spent a few days with her mother, then went to visit her brother at Milton. But word of the adventure got out. The authorities quickly apprehended Flora, and after questioning her, imprisoned her aboard a British sloop-of-war. In July, the ship made for Leith, just beside Edinburgh on the Firth of Forth, where it lay for several weeks.

By this time, all of Scotland seemed to have learned of Flora's part in the prince's escape, and many people, proclaiming her a heroine, came to visit her on the prison ship. November found her in the Tower of London, but she was

---

Flora MacDonald gained renown and the affection of her Scottish Highland countrymen when she helped Prince Charles Edward, the Stuart pretender to the British throne, escape capture in 1746. Her later association with America, though brief, placed her in the thick of the Revolutionary War.

---

was acquainted with Flora and knew her to be a young woman of admirable common sense. Still other accounts say that her actions were entirely spontaneous. Whichever version of the events is accurate, the facts surrounding the plan that Flora devised and carried out have never been disputed.

With a bounty of £30,000 offered for his capture, the Bonnie Prince was hunted by British troops as well as local militia. Every traveler was suspect, and a passport was required of anyone wishing to leave the island or to come ashore. Careful planning would be required to effect the escape of such a notorious fugitive.

Flora, who already had her passport, built a scheme around her intended trip to see her sick mother at Armadale on the

the Bonnie Prince.

Daylight lingers in June in the Hebrides, which increased the risk of the travelers being discovered by government scouts. The prince's party decided to hide themselves on shore until dark, when there would be less chance of being intercepted by British patrol vessels. In spite of high winds and stormy seas, they set out for the Isle of Skye on the night of June 28. En route, they narrowly avoided at least one British boat that passed so close they could hear the sailors' voices.

Landing on Skye the following morning, they made their way to Portree, where friends hid the prince until he could exchange his female attire for kilt and plaid, then sail to the mainland, and on to France. At Portree, Prince

soon paroled to the house of a Mr. Dick, an official Messenger at Arms in whose home prisoners of war who could pay for their keep were permitted to stay. Virtually free, Flora was allowed to visit friends, albeit always accompanied by Mr. Dick's daughters. She became something of a celebrity in London, and wealthy benefactors soon appeared with funds for her support at Mr. Dick's home.

Freed once and for all in July 1747, Flora headed straight for Scotland and home. She went to stay with her mother

*Charles Edward Stuart spent the next twenty years in Europe, devising futile plots to establish his claim to the British throne. He returned to Rome, the city of his birth, at the time of his father's death in 1766. He remained there until he died in 1788. His remains are entombed in the vaults of St. Peter's Basilica in Rome.

2 ◆ REVOLUTIONARY AMERICA

at Armadale, but her adventures had brought her such renown that she was a coveted visitor about Skye.

On November 6, 1750, Flora—reportedly dressed in a gown of Stuart tartan—married Allen MacDonald. But living happily ever after was not to be the lot of Flora and Allen. Hard times for the Highlanders increased after the short-lived campaign that had ended at Culloden, and those who had sided with Prince Charles Edward, especially the few who had given him shelter as he fled, seemed to face the most difficulties.

Over the years, the financial situation of Flora and Allen and their seven children steadily worsened. Feeling they had nothing to look forward to in Scotland but more oppression, the couple decided to leave for America. In 1774, they followed a growing number of their neighbors on Skye, including their married daughter, Anne, to North Carolina.* Leaving their youngest son and daughter with friends in Scotland who would see to the youngsters' education, they took two of their older boys with them.

Flora and Allen were met in North Carolina with great fanfare and ceremony; friends held a ball in her honor at Wilmington. When the festivities subsided after several days, the new immigrants moved on to Cross Creek (now Fayetteville), where Flora stayed while Allen searched for a site on which to establish their new home. Near Rockingham, he found a place that would suit them and named it "Killiegrey." The property already had a dwelling and several outbuildings, so Flora, in her fifties by now, settled in, perhaps thinking she had found peace and security at last.

Their neighbors treated the famous Flora and her husband with great respect, and they came to occupy a prominent position in the community. Aside from one claim that Allen built and operated a grist mill on their land, almost nothing is known of their everyday life. J. P. MacLean's *Flora MacDonald in America*, published in 1909, does say, however, that "their influence was everywhere felt and acknowledged."

The peace that Flora was enjoying proved to be momentary; the American War for Independence erupted, and even remote Killiegrey soon became entangled in the troubles. At first it seemed that the North Carolina Scots would take up the American cause, urged on by a committee of patriots who conferred "with the gentlemen who have lately arrived from the Highlands in Scotland to settle in this province . . . to explain to them the nature of our unhappy controversy with Great Britain, and to advise and urge them to unite with the other inhabitants of America in defense of their rights. . . ."

But Josiah Martin, royal governor of North Carolina, did everything in his power to persuade the Highlanders to remain loyal to the Crown. In view of the treatment they had suffered at home at the hands of the British, it seemed unlikely they would ally themselves with the British cause in America. But threats, propaganda, and coercion from Governor Martin and his agents prevailed, and the Scots, many of them MacDonalds, were won over. They organized a sizable army of volunteers, with Allen as a colonel.

In February 1776, events rushed toward a climax for the Highlanders. Word came that they were to meet a British fleet scheduled to land at Cape Fear and then nip the revolution in North Carolina in the bud. Although they were as secretive as possible, the difficulty inherent in concealing the movements of groups of armed men soon led to the patriots learning what was taking place.

An estimated 1,500 to 3,000 Highlanders assembled for the march, and Flora came out to cheer them on their way. Mounted on a white horse, she reviewed the troops, and then rode along for a short distance with Allen and their son-in-law, Alexander MacLeod, a captain in the regiment. With all attempts at maintaining secrecy apparently forgotten, the marching column made a dramatic departure, "drums beating, pipes playing, flags flying."

The Highlanders headed east to the coast, marching at night and criss-crossing creeks along the way in an attempt to evade opposing forces. They eluded Colonel James Moore, who, with about

650 troops from the First North Carolina Continentals, had been sent to head them off at Corbett's Ferry on the Black River.

When he realized that he had been outmaneuvered, Moore ordered Colonel Richard Caswell, commanding some eight hundred Parisan Rangers from New Bern, to cut the Scots off at Moore's Creek Bridge. Caswell and his men, along with 150 other troops commanded by Colonel Alexander Lillington, reached the bridge and quickly constructed earthworks on the west side of the creek. Deciding to abandon these works and meet the loyalist troops on the other side of the creek, they crossed the bridge, removing a section of flooring behind them as they went. After digging new entrenchments, they waited for the Scots to arrive.

Seeing the abandoned earthworks, the Highlanders assumed that their crossing of the bridge would be unopposed. Nonetheless, Colonel Donald McLeod, the Scots' senior officer, led a charge, shouting "King George and Broadswords" as he ran toward the bridge. Shielded by breastworks, the Americans, who had two cannon to assist them, opened fire, almost immediately shattering the attack.

The first battle of the Revolution fought in North Carolina, "the Insurrection of the MacDonalds" left many Highlanders dead or wounded; a number of the loyalist troops drowned after losing their footing while trying to cross the section of the bridge where the flooring had been removed.* Many of the Highlanders were taken prisoner, among them Allen MacDonald and his son Alexander, a lieutenant in the loyalist regiment, who were jailed in the town of Halifax.

Things went badly for Flora after the Battle of Moore's Creek Bridge. Recognizing the part she had played in recruiting Highlanders and her influential role in the Scottish settlements, the revolutionaries were not about to allow her to escape punishment. She was viewed with suspicion by those who took the patriot side and deeply resented by the

---

*More than 23,000 Highland Scots left their homeland for the American colonies between 1764 and '76.

---

*The surviving loyalist troops claimed that the Americans had greased the wooden girders of the bridge with soft soap and tallow after removing the flooring, causing the attackers to slip while trying to cross.

families who had lost men in the battle at Moore's Creek. Summoned to appear before the local Committee of Safety, Flora answered the charges against her with dignity and courage, defending her activities among her Scottish countrymen. Although the committee permitted her to return to Killiegrey, her property was confiscated a year later.

In August 1777, after having been moved several times by his captors, Allen was permitted to go to New York City to negotiate an exchange for himself and his son, Alexander. He was on his honor "not to convey to the enemy or bring back any intelligence whatever of a political nature, and to return [to Reading, Pennsylvania] in a certain time to be fixed by his parole or when called for, on behalf of the United States."

By November, he had succeeded in his mission and soon joined his battalion in Nova Scotia, where he was stationed at Fort Edward, in Windsor. Flora, having first made her way to British-held New York City with her daughter and grandsons, arrived there the next year. Her health had suffered from her ordeal, and in late 1779, Flora, her daughter, and the children sailed for Scotland.

Home at last, Flora went to stay in a cottage on her brother's property in Milton. In 1784, the war over and his regiment disbanded, Allen returned home to Flora. The couple went back to Kingsburgh House on Skye, where they had started their marriage. Less than six years later, on March 5, 1790, Flora died. One of the bed sheets on which Prince Charles Edward had slept so many years before served as her shroud. She had kept the sheet with her during her North American sojourn and carried it back again to Skye, requesting that she be buried in it when the time came.

By all accounts, Flora's funeral was the grandest ever seen on the Isle of Skye. The procession to the cemetery stretched for more than a mile. People had traveled from all the islands and from the mainland to pay their last respects to the patriotic lady in whose heart Scotland was always first.

Jean Creznic is senior editor of Early American Homes *magazine and a student of Scottish lore.*

Jefferson's Secret Life

*Did the author of the Declaration of Independence take
a slave for his mistress? DNA tests say yes.*

By Barbra Murray and Brian Duffy

It begins in 1802 as an attack on America's high-minded president, the man who declared that all men are created equal. James Callender, a vengeful drunk and disappointed job seeker, accuses Thomas Jefferson of fathering illegitimate children by one of his slaves, Sally Hemings. Jefferson declines even to respond to the charge. But it becomes an unblottable stain. Political opponents and the Federalist press gleefully trumpet the alleged affair.

Decades pass and more evidence surfaces. A young man, descended from the beautiful slave woman in question, tells a newspaper in 1873 that Jefferson was his father. But a year later comes a refutation: A Jefferson biographer suggests that the woman's light-skinned children were sired not by the president but by two nephews. A hundred years on, another bombshell: A national bestseller asserts the Jefferson-Hemings liaison as fact and infers that they were genuinely in love. Defenders ridicule the allegation.

But it was not so easily dismissed. Schoolchildren with only the most casual acquaintance of history can usually be trusted to know only two things about Jefferson: That he authored the Declaration of Independence and that he was alleged to have had a long-running affair with Sally Hemings, the quadroon half-sister of his late wife, Martha.

Popular perceptions aside, the circumstantial case has grown more persuasive in recent years: Jefferson, who traveled widely and often, was found to have been present at Monticello nine months before the birth of each of Hemings's children (except for the first, a son who apparently was conceived in Paris when Jefferson was the minister to France and Sally, at 16, was his daughter's servant). Coincidence? So skeptics would have us believe.

But new evidence appears to set the stage for the final episode of the Jefferson-Hemings epic. This week's issue of the British journal *Nature* presents the results of scientific tests that show a conclusive DNA match between a male descendant of Sally Hemings and another man who can trace his lineage to Thomas Jefferson's paternal uncle. Advances in the mapping of the so-called Y chromosome, which confers maleness on embryos, allow scientists now to consider DNA matches of the type reported by *Nature* as virtual proof positive of genetic linkage. The evidence here, in other words, removes any shadow of a doubt that Thomas Jefferson sired at least one son by Sally Heming (*see* box, "The history that lies in men's genes.")

It would be naive to assume the new evidence will settle the old debate over Jefferson and his legacy. But the confirmation of the Jefferson-Hemings affair could provoke a fresh examination of the American experience of slavery, and of relations between the races. Moreover, it may help reconcile the disparate perceptions of blacks and whites of their common heritage. "America lives in denial," says Clarence Walker, an African-American history professor at the University of California—Davis. "This story has been part of black historical consciousness since the late 18th century." Walker recalls that when the story of Sally and Tom came up in a graduate-school discussion, his white peer dismissed it because Jefferson was a "man of the enlightenment."

The confirmation of the Hemings-Jefferson relationship will also play a pivotal role in dispelling the myth of separation between blacks and whites. "Jefferson's literal embrace of Sally, producing children, becomes almost symbolic of what the South was," notes Orlando Patterson, a professor of sociology at Harvard University and author of the forthcoming book on slavery, *Rituals of Blood.* "What we have now is a powerful, symbolic blurring of the lines, with the most famous of the founding fathers intimately, biologically involved [with his black slave]."

Ultimately it was word of mouth among Hemings family members that kept the story alive. Nearly 50 years after Jefferson's death, Sally Hemings's penultimate child, Madison Hemings, confides in an obscure Ohio newspaper that Jefferson was his father and, in fact, sired all of his mother's other offspring. Another ex-slave from Monticello, Israel Jefferson, backs up the tale in a later account to the same newspaper. But Jefferson defenders will have none of it. Known among critics as an overly protective "Monticello mafia," they seek other explanations for the several children Hemings had that were obviously fathered by white men, some of whom bore a striking resemblance to Jefferson. A year after Madison Hemings's Ohio interview, James Parton's *Life of Thomas Jefferson* purported to solve the Hemings mystery by laying the paternity of her white offspring off on Jefferson's philandering nephew, Peter Carr, son of Jefferson's sister. Others blamed another notorious Carr, Samuel.

> *'Jefferson's embrace of Sally is almost symbolic of what the South was'*

The parentage question. Thus it was that there were two parallel universes of thought on the Jefferson-Hemings question. Among the Jefferson specialists, the question of his parentage of *any* Hemings offspring was answered, almost universally, in the negative. Among the multifarious Hemings heirs and in the wider black community, meanwhile, there was no doubt but that the man from Monticello had fathered children with Hemings. "Those of us who are descendants have 100 percent certainty—you cannot modify 100 percent certainty," says Hemings descendant Michele Cooley-Quille, who comes from the Thomas Woodson branch of the family.

After the 1974 publication of *Thomas Jefferson: An Intimate History* by historian Fawn Brodie, mainstream white America began to buy into the story's veracity. But among the academic elite, the 1974 bestseller ignited a furious debate. Brodie's arguments, while highly persuasive, were not conclusive, and many Jefferson scholars refused to embrace them.

That's pretty much where matters stood. Until now. In fact, had it not been for Gene Foster, that's probably where matters might have stood, period. Dr. Eugene A. Foster, technically retired after a distinguished career as a pathology professor at the Tufts University School of Medicine and the University of Virginia, is a genial bear of a man, 6 foot 4, the strong, silent type. Foster jokes that he is only "technically" retired because he keeps himself busy with a con-

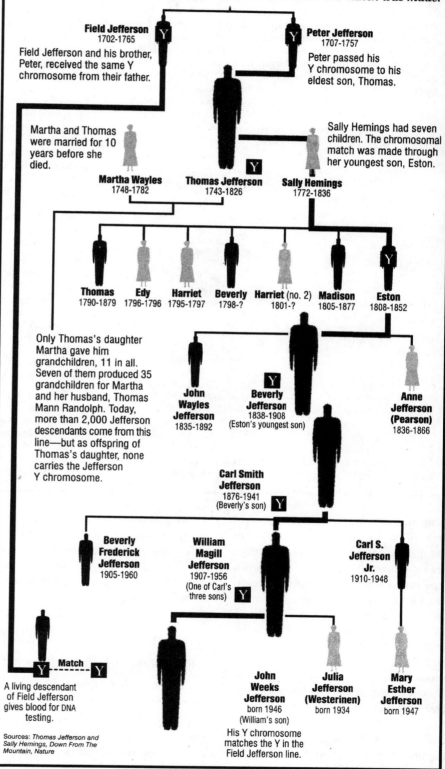

Tracking the Jefferson Y chromosome

Only males carry the Y chromosome. All direct descendants in a line share the same or nearly the same Y chromosome. Here's how the match was made.

Field Jefferson 1702-1765
Field Jefferson and his brother, Peter, received the same Y chromosome from their father.

Peter Jefferson 1707-1757
Peter passed his Y chromosome to his eldest son, Thomas.

Martha and Thomas were married for 10 years before she died.

Sally Hemings had seven children. The chromosomal match was made through her youngest son, Eston.

Martha Wayles 1748-1782

Thomas Jefferson 1743-1826

Sally Hemings 1772-1836

Thomas 1790-1879 · **Edy** 1796-1796 · **Harriet** 1795-1797 · **Beverly** 1798-? · **Harriet** (no. 2) 1801-? · **Madison** 1805-1877 · **Eston** 1808-1852

Only Thomas's daughter Martha gave him grandchildren, 11 in all. Seven of them produced 35 grandchildren for Martha and her husband, Thomas Mann Randolph. Today, more than 2,000 Jefferson descendants come from this line—but as offspring of Thomas's daughter, none carries the Jefferson Y chromosome.

John Wayles Jefferson 1835-1892

Beverly Jefferson 1838-1908 (Eston's youngest son)

Anne Jefferson (Pearson) 1836-1866

Carl Smith Jefferson 1876-1941 (Beverly's son)

Beverly Frederick Jefferson 1905-1960

William Magill Jefferson 1907-1956 (One of Carl's three sons)

Carl S. Jefferson Jr. 1910-1948

Match

A living descendant of Field Jefferson gives blood for DNA testing.

John Weeks Jefferson born 1946 (William's son)
His Y chromosome matches the Y in the Field Jefferson line.

Julia Jefferson (Westerinen) born 1934

Mary Esther Jefferson born 1947

Sources: *Thomas Jefferson and Sally Hemings, Down From The Mountain, Nature*

USN&WR

A FATHER'S GIFT

The History That Lies in Men's Genes

The use of Y chromosome testing to verify the long-debated assertion that Thomas Jefferson fathered at least one slave child is among the more dramatic consequences of a scientific discovery early in this century, one that helped gain a 1933 Nobel Prize for American geneticist Thomas Hunt Morgan. By studying fruit flies, Morgan found that recognizably different bundles of genes, which he called X and Y chromosomes, determine whether the insects are male or female. He soon recognized that the pattern holds in higher organisms, including humans. Inheritance of two X's, one from each parent, confers femaleness, while an X from mother and a Y from father produce a male.

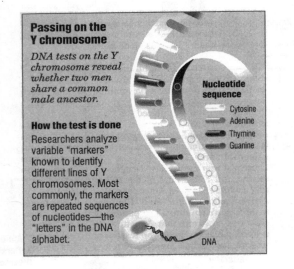

Passing on the Y chromosome

DNA tests on the Y chromosome reveal whether two men share a common male ancestor.

How the test is done

Researchers analyze variable "markers" known to identify different lines of Y chromosomes. Most commonly, the markers are repeated sequences of nucleotides—the "letters" in the DNA alphabet.

Nucleotide sequence
- Cytosine
- Adenine
- Thymine
- Guanine

DNA

In people, the sex chromosomes are but one pair among 23 pairs of chromosomes in all, each packed with genes. Most chromosomes get shuffled in succeeding generations. By contrast, Y chromosomes carry a unique set of genes and, ex-

cept for rare, random mutations, pass down unchanged through generations. They thus provide a deep view into the string of males in any man's ancestry.

Perfect match. The methods used to identify individual Y chromosomes have arisen only in the past 10 years or so. The key is identification of distinct genetic markers, sometimes called polymorphisms, which are typically stretches of "nonsense" DNA between the actual genes. They can vary widely from one man to the next. One or two markers can be identical purely by coincidence, but if many (scores are known) are identical, chances mount that two men have a recent, common ancestor. The British labs that performed the Jefferson tests compared 19 markers, all matched exactly those found in a descendant of Field Jefferson, the president's uncle, and a descendant of Eston Hemings Jefferson, Sally Hemings's youngest son. The researchers, who published their results in *Nature [see Nov. 1998 issue],* put the odds of a non-Jefferson match at less than 0.1 percent, based on their failure to find any Y chromosome that came close to matching the Jefferson pattern in 1,200 samples from unrelated men.

Even if no match were found among living men in the Hemings and Jefferson lines, or between some but not all subbranches of those lines, that would not exclude unions between Thomas Jefferson and Sally Hemings. The genetic trail could have been broken in subsequent generations if any of the mothers in the presumed chain actually had her son by a man outside the Jefferson line. Similarly, while people linked to Jefferson via a maternal link would probably carry some of his genes on other chromosomes, the Y chromosome test cannot show that.

Study of Y chromosomes has brought other big payoffs for genealogists and geneticists. Members of a Jewish priesthood, the Cohanim, who by tradition must be sons of a priest and who date their ancestry back 3,300 years to Aaron, older brother of Moses, found their Y chromosomes to be so similar that they must indeed share a common ancestor from about that long ago.—*Charles W. Petit*

stant stream of "projects of interest." One of those, as it happened, was Thomas Jefferson. Which is not altogether surprising, since Jefferson's presence is felt everywhere in Charlottesville, where Foster lives with his wife, Jane, a retired instructor of French. But Foster got onto Jefferson in a roundabout way. At dinner one evening back in 1996 with a family friend, the conversation turned to the subject of Anastasia, the daughter of the last Romanov czar, Nicholas. Specifically, the talk centered on how DNA had been used to determine whether a deceased Charlottesville woman, Anna Anderson, was the Romanov daughter Anastasia, as she claimed. Winifred Bennett, the Fosters'

friend, proposed that the same methodology might be used to resolve the Jefferson-Hemings mystery. The reverberations from Fawn Brodie's book were still echoing in Charlottesville. Gene Foster was intrigued.

'There arose two parallel universes of thought, one white, the other black'

He started poking around. A biology professor at the university passed along word of recent advances in mapping techniques for the Y chromosome. That was fine, but where to get samples to

test? Foster would have to find male-line Jefferson descendants. But Jefferson's only legitimate son died in infancy. (Jefferson's wife, Martha, gave birth to six children, but only two lived to adulthood.) That left Foster with only two Jefferson male lines to research: that of the president's brother, Randolph, and of their paternal uncle, Field Jefferson. The Randolph line looked promising at first. But it turned out that the line of direct male descendants had expired sometime in either the 1920s or 1930s.

Foster turned to the Field line. First he sought out Herbert Barger, a respected Jefferson family genealogist. Barger agreed to help. By early 1997,

Holding out for an Icon

Character counts, the historians insisted

By Lewis Lord

For the black Americans who 44 years ago read and believed an article in *Ebony* magazine—the one headlined "Thomas Jefferson's Negro Grandchildren"—the revelations from the DNA labs come as no surprise. *Ebony,* circulated in those days to nearly a half-million African-Americans, profiled several "elderly Negroes" who had placed a third president atop their family tree. "Many reputable historians," the magazine said, "concede that Jefferson fathered at least five Negro children."

Those historians must have been black. Until the civil rights days of the 1960s, hardly a white scholar in America was on record as believing that Sally Hemings bore Jefferson's children. The pattern of denials was so strong that Annette Gordon-Reed, a black woman who teaches at New York Law School, recently wrote a much-acclaimed book— *Thomas Jefferson and Sally Hemings: An American Controversy*—meticulously dissecting the historians' conclusions and the ways in which they were reached and articulated. The DNA results, she says, barely concern her. "It's the historiography that's offensive. You can't use arguments that are dehumanizing to blacks to turn around a story."

Foremost among the historical naysayers was Dumas Malone, a Mississippi-born and Georgia-raised Pulitzer winner who dismissed "the miscegenation legend" as "filth." Malone placed Jefferson with Washington and Lincoln in "our Trinity of immortals." The possibility of a "vulgar liaison," he wrote, was "virtually unthinkable in a man of Jefferson's moral standards."

For nearly a century, the prime evidence of an affair was an account by Madison Hemings, Sally's next-to-last child, who settled in Ohio. In an 1873 interview in Ohio's *Pike County Republican,* Hemings reported that his mother told him that Jefferson fathered all of her children. Another former Monticello slave, interviewed by the same paper, agreed with Heming's richly detailed account.

But the ex-slaves' memoirs hardly got outside Pike County. What kept the Tom-and-Sally story alive was a tradition of oral history in a scattering of black families across America, as one generation quietly and, in many instances, secretly told the next what had happened. Occasionally, as in the 1954 *Ebony* article, the story would emerge, then recede into the closet.

The few historians who addressed the subject seemed determined to keep it there. In 1960, Merrill Peterson, in *The Jefferson Image in the American Mind,* found the Sally story sustained in part by the "Negroes' pathetic wish for a little pride and their subtle ways of confounding the white folks." Dumas Malone cautioned, "'There is material here for the tragedian, but the historian must recognize

---

'Amalgamation,' Jefferson said, 'produces a degradation'

---

that oral tradition is not established fact."

Black vs. white. Malone, while discounting oral accounts by blacks, welcomed the testimony of Jefferson's aristocratic white kin. He even embraced a pair of stories that conflicted with each other. Explaining why the Hemings children looked like Jefferson, the historian recalled that a grandson of the president once told an interviewer that their father was Peter Carr, a Jefferson nephew. A granddaughter, Malone also noted, identified Sally's lover as Peter's brother Samuel. (DNA tests... indicate that neither nephew was involved.)

For their chief argument, Jefferson's defenders invariably turned to his character. Sex with a slave would be an abuse of power, one historian contended, and Jefferson was not an "abusive" person. To show that sex with a black was unlikely, scholars trotted out Jefferson's pseudo-scientific views on race, among them: "Amalgamation produces a degradation to which no one . . . can innocently consent." Still

others concluded that the Sage of Monticello, once he was widowed at 39, had no interest in sex and was content to devote his remaining 44 years to architecture, laws, and literature.

The first white historian to suggest that a Hemings-Jefferson affair just might have happened was Winthrop Jordan, now at the University of Mississippi, whose 1968 book *White Over Black* made a relevant biological point. Taking a fresh look at Malone's Monticello data, Jordan reported that "Jefferson was at home nine months prior to each birth."

That helped clear the way for an event that transformed how millions of Americans viewed Jefferson. In a 1974 bestseller, UCLA historian Fawn Brodie used a blend of history and psychoanalysis to shape an argument that Jefferson and Hemings had a long and caring sexual relationship. Jefferson's "slave family," she suggested, represented "not a flaw in the hero but a flaw in society."

Five years later, Brodie's book, *Thomas Jefferson: An Intimate History,* inspired a piece of Barbara Chase-Riboud fiction, *Sally Hemings: A Novel,* which, in turn, prompted programmers at CBS to envision a Tom-and-Sally television miniseries. Several Virginia historians, led by Malone, were outraged. The basis for such a miniseries, Malone wrote CBS, was a "tawdry and unverifiable story." The network scrapped the project after Jefferson's Virginia descendants joined the campaign to protect his name.

But the notion that Jefferson had a slave mistress no longer could be brushed aside. Even Malone, who had worked 43 years on a six-volume biography of the president, seemed to sense where the story was going. In 1984, two years before he died at age 94, the historian told the *New York Times* that what struck him as most speculative about Brodie's account was not that Jefferson might have slept with Hemings but rather that he had carried on a love affair with her in Paris and later as president for years on end. A sexual encounter, on the other hand, Malone said, could be neither proved nor disproved: "It might have happened once or twice."

When a Saint Becomes a Sinner

Public affection for Jefferson is so strong that his legacy seems secure

By Joseph J. Ellis

Well, now we know. More fastidious minds may linger over scientific details and statistical probabilities, and a few die-hard Jefferson worshipers will surely mount a spirited assault on the reliability of DNA evidence. The fact that there is not a match with the first of Sally Hemings's children, Thomas, may deflect some attention from the match with her last child, Eston.

But the Eston match is really all that matters because, in conjunction with the circumstantial evidence that already existed, it proves beyond any reasonable doubt that Jefferson had a long-term sexual relationship with his mulatto slave. As one of those students of Jefferson who had previously questioned that possibility, I think it is important that this near certain conclusion be announced to what Jefferson called "a candid world." Over its long history, the story of "Tom and Sally" has achieved the status of America's most enduring soap opera. We have now reached the final episode.

The salient question now seems to be: What difference does it make? For the several hundred Hemings descendants who have maintained that their oral tradition was more reliable than the oral tradition of the white members of the Jefferson family, and also more historically accurate than a substantial group of Jefferson scholars was prepared to acknowledge, this news is deliverance. It confirms the stories they have been passing along from generation to generation. Robert Cooley, one of the most outspoken Hemings descendants, once said he looked forward to a long talk with Mr. Jefferson in the hereafter. Cooley, who died last July, must be enjoying that conversation now.

President William Jefferson Clinton also has a vested interest in this revelation. He launched his first-term inaugural parade at Monticello and hosted at the White House a special screening of the Ken Burns documentary on Jefferson. I happened to be present at the reception afterward when Clinton asked the assembled historical consultants: "Do you think the story of a sexual liaison with Sally Hemings is true?" When one of the historians responded in the negative, a look of disappointment streaked across the president's face. He was, we now know, at that very time involved in his own sexual liaison with Monica Lewinsky.

And he is now, of course, under scrutiny by the House Judiciary Committee for this dalliance and the subsequent coverup, and DNA evidence (i.e., the famous blue dress) also played a clinching role. The Foster study seems impeccably timed to arrive like a comet that has been winging through space for 200 years before landing squarely in the middle of the Clinton impeachment inquiry.

Witness for Clinton. Jefferson has always been Clinton's favorite Founding Father. Now, a sexually active, all-too-human Jefferson appears alongside his embattled protégé. It is as if Clinton had called one of the most respected character witnesses in all of U.S. history to testify that the primal urge has a most distinguished presidential pedigree. The dominant effect of this news will be to make Clinton's sins seem less aberrant and more palatable. If a vote against Clinton is also a vote against Jefferson, the prospects for impeachment become even more remote.

Within the scholarly world, the acceptance of a Jefferson-Hemings liaison had been gaining ground over recent years. Now that it is proven beyond any reasonable doubt, the net effect is to reinforce the critical picture of Jefferson as an inherently elusive and deeply duplicitous character. We already knew that he lived the great paradox of American history. Which is to say he could walk past the slave quarters at Monticello thinking grand thoughts about human equality and never notice the disjunction. Now it would seem that his oft-stated belief in black inferiority and his palpable fear of racial amalgamation somehow coexisted alongside his intimate relationship with an attractive black woman. His public announcements and his private behavior apparently occupied wholly different and mutually exclusive compartments in his soul. The man who wrote "A Dialogue Between My Head and My Heart" in a letter to Maria Cosway, with whom he was intensely infatuated during his Paris years, apparently did not permit those different parts of his own personality to speak to one another.

If the scholarly portrait of Jefferson had already begun to depict him as inherently hypocritical, the popular perception has remained resolutely reverential. If the scholarly Jefferson has become a more controversial and problematic icon, the vast majority of ordinary Americans continue to regard him as the most potent symbol of

'Tom and Sally,' America's most enduring soap opera, has reached its finale

American values in the entire gallery of national greats. He is on Mount Rushmore, the Tidal Basin, the nickel, and the $2 bill. He is somehow central to our national sense of self. Lincoln said that America was founded on a proposition. Well, Jefferson wrote the proposition in 1776, in 35 magical words: *We hold these Truths to be self-evident, that all Men are created equal, that they are endowed by their Creator with certain unalienable Rights, that among these are Life, Liberty, and the pursuit of Happiness.*

As one of his earnest biographers put it: "If America is right, Jefferson was right." Since his enshrinement in the Jefferson Memorial in 1943, he has levitated out of the historical muck and into a midair location that hovers over the political landscape like a dirigible at the Super Bowl, flashing inspirational messages to both teams. Not just an essential ingredient in the American political tradition, he has become the essence itself.

American symbol. This mythological Jefferson has also become the one American hero who is also at home abroad. The values Jefferson has come to embody were the values of Polish dissidents in the Gdansk shipyards; the Chinese youths in Tiananmen Square; the Buddhist monks in Tibet. Wherever there is a struggle between the forces of light and the forces of darkness,

(Box continued on next page)

Jefferson is America's most accessible and effective ambassador. He translates more resonantly than any other American symbol.

Will these new revelations about his sexual connection to Sally Hemings undermine this apparently bottomless affection? Will Jefferson be knocked off the elevated pedestal on which we have placed him? My best guess is that he will survive this trial even more successfully than Clinton survives his. Jefferson's reputation, to be sure, has had its ups and downs. But his legacy, or what we take to be his legacy, has so thoroughly infiltrated the national ethos, has so fully insinuated itself into the creedal convictions of America's promise to itself and the world, that a diminution of Jefferson will be regarded, as he put it, as "treason against the hopes of mankind." If the American past were a gambling casino, everyone who has bet against Jefferson has eventually lost. There is no reason to believe it will be different this time.

Indeed, Jefferson's legacy might appear more lustrous than ever before. For he is now thoroughly human, the American demigod made flesh who dwelt among us, the saint who sinned, the great man with ordinary weaknesses. As we approach the end of the "American Century," he has metamorphosed into the new role model for our postmodern temperament, if you will, a '90s kind of guy.

This new chapter in the Jefferson saga of renewed relevance can also develop quite naturally by spinning the Sally and Tom story as a tragic romance between two besmitten lovers prohibited from declaring their mutual affection by the racial strictures of the day. There is no historical evidence to support such an interpretation. But then there is no historical evidence to refute it, either. Several biographers, most famously Fawn Brodie, along with a larger group of novelists and poets, have already introduced this imaginative version of the story into the mainstream American culture, with considerable success. Given the strong pro-Jefferson

Inherently elusive, Jefferson, we now know, lived the great paradox of American history

currents that run relentlessly beneath the surface of our national mythology, the urge to make Jefferson and Hemings America's premier biracial couple could prove irresistible.

Finally, some of Jefferson's most severe critics in recent years—Michael Lind and Conor Cruise O'Brien come to mind—have argued that the man from Monticello is an inappropriate icon for our more racially diverse and multicultural American society. From a strictly logical point of view, this makes eminent sense, since Jefferson's writings clearly reveal a prevailing presumption that America must remain a white man's country.

Now, however, Jefferson's life and his most intimate personal choices just as clearly reveal an interracial commitment that probably endured for 38 years. The Hemings descendants have sustained the story of their lineage for many generations because they are proud of their biological connection to Jefferson. While it will require a rather large stretch to transform Jefferson from a thinking man's racist to a multi-cultural hero, some commentators are sure to make the leap.

Perhaps a more historically responsible way to make a similar if slightly different case is to suggest that advancing technology has at least allowed us to open a window onto the covert and concealed interracial intimacies that have always been there but that many white Americans have preferred to deny. So now Jefferson surfaces again, not only offering aid and comfort to an embattled President Clinton but also making himself useful as a most potent guide into a fresh round of more candid conversations about the way we truly were and are one people.

Joseph J. Ellis, a professor of history at Mount Holyoke College, won a 1997 National Book Award for American Sphinx: The Character of Thomas Jefferson.

Foster had the names and phone numbers of seven living descendants of Field Jefferson. He fired off letters to all of them. Only one wrote back. So Barger intervened on Foster's behalf, and five of Field's descendants agreed to cooperate, allowing Foster to draw blood samples.

That was one part of the equation. But if he were to obtain a definitive Y chromosome match, Foster would need DNA from a male who had good reason to believe he was a descendant of Jefferson and Hemings. There was one obvious place to look: among the 1,400 members of the Thomas Woodson Family Association, an organization of African-Americans scattered across the country. The group is named for Hemings's first son, Tom, the child apparently conceived in Paris. Byron Woodson agreed to cooperate with Foster. But then his

father, Col. John Woodson, put a stop to it. He didn't want to be messing around with subjects like illegitimacy, he said.

The Woodsons had maintained for nearly two centuries that they were descendants of Jefferson, but other branches of the family pooh-poohed the claim. Foster pressed. If they were to come up without any evidence linking the Woodson line to Jefferson, he told the colonel, "they'll say you knew that all along. But if we come up with evidence that, in fact, Jefferson was the father. . . ." Foster let the sentence drop. The colonel relented. The Woodsons, he said, would cooperate with Foster's study. Five Woodsons eventually gave blood.

Closing loopholes. But there was more to be done. The philandering Carr boys could not be dismissed out of hand. Jefferson's distinguished defenders would dismiss any paternity evi-

dence that didn't address that question. Foster tracked down three male descendants of the Carrs. They, too, gave blood. There remained one other line of male descendants to track down, and here Foster got lucky. Eston Hemings was Sally Hemings seventh and last child and Foster identified a lone male descendant. The man readily agreed to participate. Next Foster wanted some "control" samples. These were drawn from male descendants of several old-line Virginia families. The idea was to eliminate potential similarities in the Y chromosome tests due to geographic proximity. Foster was amazed by the cooperation. These were people, he said, "who had nothing to gain." And yet they welcomed him into their homes. One even had fresh-baked brownies waiting for him when he turned up to draw blood.

Now it was time to test. Foster had 19 samples in all. A fellow pathologist at the University of Virginia extracted the DNA from the blood samples. Foster numbered and coded them, then stowed them in a bubble-wrapped envelope. Researchers at Oxford had agreed to test the samples. Foster flew to London, the samples secure in his carry-on. A bus from Heathrow airport deposited him at the ancient university town, and Foster delivered the samples to researcher Chris Tyler-Smith, whom Foster describes as his "main collaborator." First the two men placed the materials in a refrigerator. Then they toddled off to a pub for lunch.

The rest, as the saying goes, is history, albeit of a peculiar sort. According to Hemings's heirs, Jefferson fathered seven children by her, four boys and three girls. Foster's meticulously collected samples were tested by three different Oxford labs using different procedures. The results fail to match the Field Jefferson line with the Woodson line, Hemings, or, interestingly, with the heirs of the Carr brothers. But the tests did establish a definite Y chromosome match on Eston Hemings, who was born in the second term of Jefferson's presidency.

What does that mean? That one can say with certainty that Sally Hemings bore Thomas Jefferson at least one son. But the tests do not preclude the possibility that there were other offspring. Indeed, abundant historical evidence suggests that this is so.

Beverly and Harriet Hemings very likely had Jefferson blood. After being allowed to run away—a privilege granted only to Hemings's children—the two blended into white society in the Washington, D.C., area. Today, they may have hundreds of descendants who have never suspected that their ancestry is either African or presidential.

Madison Hemings cannot be ruled out. Freed by Jefferson's will, he settled among blacks in Ohio, where he told an interviewer that his mother was Jefferson's "concubine" and he and his siblings were the president's children. But Madison's Y chromosome line cannot be tested; one of his three sons vanished into white society and the other two had no children. (But one daughter had a son who became California's first black state legislator.)

Tom, the boy conceived in Paris, still may have been Jefferson's son, even though there was no DNA match in his family line. The negative may have resulted from an unknown male—an illegitimate father—breaking the Y chromosome chain.

The link with Eston Hemings could easily have been missed. Freed with his brother Madison, he moved to Wisconsin, changed his name to Eston Jefferson, and gave everyone the impression he was white. One of his sons, John Jefferson—redheaded like the third president—was wounded at Vicksburg while serving as a lieutenant colonel in the Union Army. A century later, descendants working on the family tree kept hitting a dead end, running up against the name "Hemings." Not until they read Fawn Brodie's book did they sense they were kin to a slave and a president.

With Gerald Parshall and Lewis Lord

Making Sense of the Fourth of July

The DECLARATION OF INDEPENDENCE is not what Thomas Jefferson thought it was when he wrote it—and that is why we celebrate it

By Pauline Maier

JOHN ADAMS THOUGHT AMERICANS would commemorate their Independence Day on the second of July. Future generations, he confidently predicted, would remember July 2, 1776, as "the most memorable Epocha, in the History of America" and celebrate it as their "Day of Deliverance by solemn Acts of Devotion to God Almighty. It ought to be solemnized with Pomp and Parade, with Shews, Games, Sports, Guns, Bells, Bonfires and Illuminations from one End of this Continent to the other from this Time forward forever more."

His proposal, however odd it seems today, was perfectly reasonable when he made it in a letter to his wife, Abigail. On the previous day, July 2, 1776, the Second Continental Congress had finally resolved "That these United Colonies are, and of right ought to be, free and independent States, that they are absolved from all allegiance to the British Crown, and that all political connection between them and the State of Great Britain is, and ought to be, totally dissolved." The thought that Americans might instead commemorate July 4, the day Congress adopted a "Declaration on Independency" that he had helped prepare, did not apparently occur to Adams in 1776. The Declaration of Inde-

pendence was one of those congressional statements that he later described as "dress and ornament rather than Body, Soul, or Substance," a way of announcing to the world the fact of American independence, which was for Adams the thing worth celebrating.

In fact, holding our great national festival on the Fourth makes no sense at all—unless we are actually celebrating not just independence but the Declaration of Independence. And the declaration we celebrate, what Abraham Lincoln called "the charter of our liberties," is a document whose meaning and function today are different from what they were in 1776. In short, during the nineteenth century the Declaration of Independence became not just a way of announcing and justifying the end of Britain's power over the Thirteen Colonies and the emergence of the United States as an independent nation but a statement of principles to guide stable, established governments. Indeed, it came to usurp in fact if not in law a role that Americans normally delegated to bills of rights. How did that happen? And why?

According to notes kept by Thomas Jefferson, the Second Continental Congress did not discuss the resolution on

independence when it was first proposed by Virginia's Richard Henry Lee, on Friday, June 7, 1776, because it was "obliged to attend at that time to some other business." However, on the eighth, Congress resolved itself into a Committee of the Whole and "passed that day & Monday the 10th in debating on the subject." By then all contenders admitted that it had become impossible for the colonies ever again to be united with Britain. The issue was one of timing.

John and Samuel Adams, along with others such as Virginia's George Wythe, wanted Congress to declare independence right away and start negotiating foreign alliances and forming a more lasting confederation (which Lee also proposed). Others, including Pennsylvania's James Wilson, Edward Rutledge of South Carolina, and Robert R. Livingston of New York, argued for delay. They noted that the delegates of several colonies, including Maryland, Pennsylvania, Delaware, New Jersey, and New York, had not been "impowered" by their home governments to vote for independence. If a vote was taken immediately, those delegates would have to "retire" from Congress, and their states might secede from the union, which would seriously weaken the Americans'

This article originally appeared in *American Heritage,* July/August 1997, pp. 54-65. Adapted from *American Scripture: Making the Declaration of Independence,* by Pauline Maier. © 1998 by Alfred A. Knopf, Inc. Reprinted by permission.

chance of realizing their independence. In the past, they said, members of Congress had followed the "wise & proper" policy of putting off major decisions "till the voice of the people drove us into it," since "they were our power, & without them our declarations could not be carried into effect." Moreover, opinion on independence in the critical middle colonies was "fast ripening & in a short time," they predicted, the people there would "join in the general voice of America."

CONGRESS DECIDED TO GIVE THE laggard colonies time and so delayed its decision for three weeks. But it also appointed a Committee of Five to draft a declaration of independence so that such a document could be issued quickly once Lee's motion passed. the committee's members included Jefferson, Livingston, John Adams, Roger Sherman of Connecticut, and Pennsylvania's Benjamin Franklin. the drafting committee met, decided what the declaration should say and how it would be organized, then asked Jefferson to prepare a draft.

Meanwhile, Adams—who did more to win Congress's consent to independence than any other delegate—worked feverishly to bring popular pressure on the governments of recalcitrant colonies so they would change the instructions issued to their congressional delegates. By June 28, when the Committee of Five submitted to Congress a draft declaration, only Maryland and New York had failed to allow their delegates to vote for independence. That night Maryland fell into line.

Even so, when the Committee of the Whole again took up Lee's resolution, on July 1, only nine colonies voted in favor (the four New England states, New Jersey, Maryland, Virginia, North Carolina, and Georgia). South Carolina and Pennsylvania opposed the proposition, Delaware's two delegates split, and New York's abstained because their twelve-month-old instructions precluded them from approving anything that impeded reconciliation with the mother country. Edward Rutledge now asked that Congress put off its decision until the next day, since he thought that the South

Carolina delegation would then vote in favor "for the sake of unanimity." When Congress took its final tally on July 2, the nine affirmative votes of the day before had grown to twelve: Not only South Carolina voted in favor, but so did Delaware—the arrival of Caesar Rodney broke the tie in that delegation's vote—and Pennsylvania. Only New York held out. Then on July 9 it, too, allowed its delegates to add their approval to that of delegates from the other twelve colonies, lamenting still the "cruel necessity" that made independence "unavoidable."

Once independence had been adopted, Congress again formed itself into a Committee of the Whole. It then spent the better part of two days editing the draft declaration submitted by its Committee of Five, rewriting or chopping off large sections of text. Finally, on July 4, Congress approved the revised Declaration and ordered it to be printed and sent to the several states and to the commanding officers of the Continental Army. By formally announcing and justifying the end of British rule, that document, as letters from Congress's president, John Hancock, explained, laid "the Ground & Foundation" of American self-government. As a result, it had to be proclaimed not only before American troops in the hope that it would inspire them to fight more ardently for what was now the cause of both liberty and national independence but throughout the country, and "in such a Manner, that the People may be universally informed of it."

Not until four days later did a committee of Congress—not Congress itself—get around to sending a copy of the Declaration to its emissary in Paris, Silas Deane, with orders to present it to the court of France and send copies to "the other Courts of Europe." Unfortunately the original letter was lost, and the next failed to reach Deane until November, when news of American independence had circulated for months. To make matters worse, it arrived with only a brief note from the committee and in an envelope that lacked a seal, an unfortunately slipshod way, complained Deane, to announce the arrival of the United States among the powers of the

earth to "old and powerfull states." Despite the Declaration's reference to the "opinions of mankind," it was obviously meant first and foremost for a home audience.

As copies of the Declaration spread through the states and were publicly read at town meetings, religious services, court days, or wherever else people assembled, Americans marked the occasion with appropriate rituals. They lit great bonfires, "illuminated" their windows with candles, fired guns, rang bells, tore down and destroyed the symbols of monarchy on public buildings, churches, or tavern signs, and "fixed up" on the walls of their homes broadside or newspaper copies of the Declaration of Independence.

BUT WHAT EXACTLY WERE THEY celebrating? The news, not the vehicle that brought it; independence and the assumption of self-government, not the document that announced Congress's decision to break with Britain. Considering how revered a position the Declaration of Independence later won in the minds and hearts of the people, Americans' disregard for it in the first years of the new nation verges on the unbelievable. One colonial newspaper dismissed the Declaration's extensive charges against the king as just another "recapitulation of injuries," one, it seems, in a series, and not particularly remarkable compared with earlier "catalogues of grievances." Citations of the Declaration were usually drawn from its final paragraph, which said that the united colonies "are and of Right ought to be Free and Independent states" and were "Absolved of all Allegiance to the British Crown"—words from the Lee resolution that Congress had inserted into the committee draft. Independence was new; the rest of the Declaration seemed all too familiar to Americans, a restatement of what they and their representatives had already said time and again.

The adoption of independence was, however, from the beginning confused with its declaration. Differences in the meaning of the word *declare* contributed to the confusion. Before the Declaration of Independence was issued—while, in fact, Congress was still editing Jefferson's draft—Pennsylvania newspapers announced that on July 2 the Continental Congress had "declared the United Colonies Free and Independent States," by which it meant simply that it had officially accepted that status. Newspapers in other colonies repeated the story. In later years the "Anniversary of the United States of America" came to be celebrated on the date Congress had approved the Declaration of Independence. That began, it seems, by accident. In 1777 no member of Congress thought of marking the anniversary of independence at all until July 3, when it was too late to honor July 2. As a result, the celebration took place on the Fourth, and that became the tradition. At least one delegate spoke of "celebrating the Anniversary of the Declaration of Independence," but over the next few years references to the anniversary of independence and of the Declaration seem to have been virtually interchangeable.

The Fourth of July was rarely celebrated during the Revolution and seems actually to have declined in popularity once the war was over.

Accounts of the events at Philadelphia on July 4, 1777, say quite a bit about the music played by a band of Hessian soldiers who had been captured at the Battle of Trenton the previous December, and the "splendid illumination" of houses, but little about the Declaration. Thereafter, in the late 1770s and 1780s, the Fourth of July was not regularly celebrated; indeed, the holiday seems to have declined in popularity once the Revolutionary War ended. When it was remembered, however, festivities seldom, if ever—to judge by newspaper accounts—involved a public

reading of the Declaration of Independence. It was as if that document had done its work in carrying news of independence to the people, and it neither needed nor deserved further commemoration. No mention was made of Thomas Jefferson's role in composing the document, since that was not yet public knowledge, and no suggestion appeared that the Declaration itself was, as posterity would have it, unusually eloquent or powerful.

I
N FACT, ONE OF THE VERY FEW PUBlic comments on the document's literary qualities came in a Virginia newspaper's account of a 1777 speech by John Wilkes, an English radical and a long-time supporter of the Americans, in the House of Commons. Wilkes set out to answer a fellow member of Parliament who had attacked the Declaration of Independence as "a wretched composition, very ill written, drawn up with a view to captivate the people." Curiously, Wilkes seemed to agree with that description. The purpose of the document, he said, was indeed to captivate the American people, who were not much impressed by "the polished periods, the harmonious, happy expressions, with all the grace, ease, and elegance of a beautiful diction" that Englishmen valued. What they liked was "manly, nervous sense . . . even in the most awkward and uncouth dress of language."

A
LL THAT BEGAN TO CHANGE IN the 1790s, when, in the midst of bitter partisan conflict, the modern understanding and reputation of the Declaration of Independence first emerged. Until that time celebrations of the Fourth were controlled by nationalists who found a home in the Federalist party, and their earlier inattention to the Declaration hardened into a rigid hostility after 1790. The document's anti-British character was an embarrassment to Federalists who sought economic and diplomatic rapprochement with Britain. The language of equality and rights in the Declaration was different from that of the Declaration of the Rights of Man issued by the French National Assembly in 1789, but it still seemed too

"French" for the comfort of Federalists, who, after the execution of Louis XVI and the onset of the Terror, lost whatever sympathy for the French Revolution they had once felt. Moreover, they understandably found it best to say as little as possible about a fundamental American text that had been drafted by a leader of the opposing Republican party.

It was, then, the Republicans who began to celebrate the Declaration of Independence as a "deathless instrument" written by "the immortal Jefferson." The Republicans saw themselves as the defenders of the American Republic of 1776 against subversion by pro-British "monarchists," and they hoped that by recalling the causes of independence, they would make their countrymen wary of further dealings with Great Britain. They were also delighted to identify the founding principles of the American Revolution with those of America's sister republic in France. At their Fourth of July celebrations, Republicans read the Declaration of Independence, and their newspapers reprinted it. Moreover, in their hands the attention that had at first focused on the last part of the Declaration shifted toward its opening paragraphs and the "self-evident truths" they stated. The Declaration, as a Republican newspaper said on July 7, 1792, was not to be celebrated merely "as affecting the separation of one country from the jurisdiction of another"; it had an enduring significance for established governments because it provided a "definition of the rights of man, and the end of civil government."

The Federalists responded that Jefferson had not written the Declaration alone. The drafting committee—including John Adams, a Federalist—had also contributed to its creation. And Jefferson's role as "the scribe who penned the declaration" had not been so distinguished as his followers suggested. Federalists rediscovered similarities between the Declaration and Locke's *Second Treatise of Government* that Richard Henry Lee had noticed long before and used them to argue that even the "small part of that memorable instrument" that could be attributed to Jefferson "he stole from *Locke's Essays*." But after the War of 1812, the Federalist party slipped from sight, and with it, efforts to disparage the Declaration of Independence.

When a new party system formed in the late 1820s and 1830s, both Whigs and Jacksonians claimed descent from Jefferson and his party and so accepted the old Republican position on the Declaration and Jefferson's glorious role in its creation. By then, too, a new generation of Americans had come of age and made preservation of the nation's revolutionary history its particular mission. Its efforts, and its reverential attitude toward the revolutionaries and their works, also helped establish the Declaration of Independence as an important icon of American identity.

THE CHANGE CAME SUDDENLY. As late as January 1817 John Adams said that his country had no interest in its past. "I see no disposition to celebrate or remember, or even Curiosity to enquire into the Characters, Actions, or Events of the Revolution," he wrote the artist John Trumbull. But a little more than a month later Congress commissioned Trumbull to produce four large paintings commemorating the Revolution, which were to hang in the rotunda of the new American Capitol. For Trumbull, the most important of the series, and the one to which he first turned, was the Declaration of Independence. He based that work on a smaller painting he had done between 1786 and 1793 that showed the drafting committee presenting its work to Congress. When the new twelve-by-eighteen-foot canvas was completed in 1818, Trumbull exhibited it to large crowds in Boston, Philadelphia, and Baltimore before delivering it to Washington; indeed, *The Declaration of Independence* was the most popular of all the paintings Trumbull did for the Capitol.

Soon copies of the document were being published and sold briskly, which perhaps was what inspired Secretary of State John Quincy Adams to have an exact facsimile of the Declaration, the only one ever produced, made in 1823. Congress had it distributed throughout the country. Books also started to appear: the collected biographies of those who signed the Declaration in nine volumes by Joseph M. Sanderson (1823–27) or one

volume by Charles A. Goodrich (1831), full biographies of individual revolutionaries that were often written by descendants who used family papers, and collections of revolutionary documents edited by such notable figures as Hezekiah Niles, Jared Sparks, and Peter Force.

Jefferson forgot, as the years went by, how substantial a role other members of the committee had played in framing the Declaration's text.

Postwar efforts to preserve the memories and records of the Revolution were undertaken in a mood of near panic. Many documents remained in private hands, where they were gradually separated from one another and lost. Even worse, many revolutionaries had died, taking with them precious memories that were gone forever. The presence of living remnants of the revolutionary generation seemed so important in preserving its tradition that Americans watched anxiously as their numbers declined. These attitudes first appeared in the decade before 1826, the fiftieth anniversary of independence, but they persisted on into the Civil War. In 1864 the Reverend Elias Brewster Hillard noted that only seven of those who had fought in the Revolutionary War still survived, and he hurried to interview and photograph those "venerable and now sacred men" for the benefit of posterity. "The present is the last generation that will be connected by living link with the great period in which our national independence was achieved," he wrote in the introduction to his book *The Last Men of the Revolution.* "Our own are the last eyes that will look on men who looked on Washington; our ears the last that will hear the living voices of those who heard his words. Henceforth the American Revolution

will be known among men by the silent record of history alone."

Most of the men Hillard interviewed had played modest roles in the Revolution. In the early 1820s, however, John Adams and Thomas Jefferson were still alive, and as the only surviving members of the committee that had drafted the Declaration of Independence, they attracted an extraordinary outpouring of attention. Pilgrims, invited and uninvited, flocked particularly to Monticello, hoping to catch a glimpse of the author of the Declaration and making nuisances of themselves. One woman, it is said, even smashed a window to get a better view of the old man. As a eulogist noted after the deaths of both Adams and Jefferson on, miraculously, July 4, 1826, the world had not waited for death to "sanctify" their names. Even while they remained alive, their homes became "shrines" to which lovers of liberty and admirers of genius flocked "from every land."

ADAMS, IN TRUTH, WAS MIFFED by Jefferson's celebrity as the penman of Independence. The drafting of the Declaration of Independence, he thought, had assumed an exaggerated importance. Jefferson perhaps agreed; he, too, cautioned a correspondent against giving too much emphasis to "mere composition." The Declaration, he said, had not and had not been meant to be an original or novel creation; his assignment had been to produce "an expression of the American mind, and to give that expression the proper tone and spirit called for by the occasion."

Jefferson, however, played an important role in rescuing the Declaration from obscurity and making it a defining event of the revolutionary "heroic age." It was he who first suggested that the young John Trumbull paint *The Declaration of Independence.* And Trumbull's first sketch of his famous painting shares a piece of drawing paper with a sketch by Jefferson, executed in Paris sometime in 1786, of the assembly room in the Old Pennsylvania State House, now known as Independence Hall. Trumbull's painting of the scene carefully followed Jefferson's sketch, which unfortunately included architectural inaccuracies, as Trumbull later learned to his dismay.

Jefferson also spent hour after hour answering, in longhand, letters that he said numbered 1,267 in 1820, many of which asked questions about the Declaration and its creation. Unfortunately, his responses, like the sketch he made for Trumbull, were inaccurate in many details. Even his account of the drafting process, retold in an important letter to James Madison of 1823 that has been accepted by one authority after another, conflicts with a note he sent Benjamin Franklin in June 1776. Jefferson forgot, in short, how substantial a role other members of the drafting committee had played in framing the Declaration and adjusting its text before it was submitted to Congress.

INDEED, IN OLD AGE JEFFERSON found enormous consolation in the fact that he was, as he ordered inscribed on his tomb, "Author of the Declaration of American Independence." More than anything else he had done, that role came to justify his life. It saved him from a despair that he suffered at the time of the Missouri crisis, when everything the Revolution had accomplished seemed to him in jeopardy, and that was later fed by problems at the University of Virginia, his own deteriorating health, and personal financial troubles so severe that he feared the loss of his beloved home, Monticello (those troubles, incidentally, virtually precluded him from freeing more than a handful of slaves at his death). The Declaration, as he told Madison, was "the fundamental act of union of these States," a document that should be recalled "to cherish the principles of the instrument in the bosoms of our own citizens." Again in 1824 he interpreted the government's re-publication of the Declaration as "a pledge of adhesion to its principles and of a sacred determination to maintain and perpetuate them," which he described as a "holy purpose."

But just which principles did he mean? Those in the Declaration's second paragraph, which he understood exactly as they had been understood in 1776—as an assertion primarily of the right of revolution. Jefferson composed the long sentence beginning "We hold these truths to be self-evident" in a well-known eighteenth-century rhetorical style by which one phrase was piled on another and the meaning of the whole became clear only at the end. The sequence ended with an assertion of the "Right of the People to alter or to abolish" any government that failed to secure their inalienable rights and to institute a new form of government more likely "to effect their Safety and Happiness." That was the right Americans were exercising in July 1776, and it seemed no less relevant in the 1820s, when revolutionary movements were sweeping through Europe and Latin America. The American example would be, as Jefferson said in the last letter of his life, a "signal arousing men to burst the chains under which monkish ignorance and superstition had persuaded them to bind themselves, and to assume the blessings and security of self-government."

Others, however, emphasized the opening phrases of the sentence that began the Declaration's second paragraph, particularly "the memorable assertion, that 'all men are created equal, that they are endowed by their Creator with certain unalienable rights, and that to secure these rights, governments are instituted among men, deriving their just powers from the consent of the governed.' " That passage, the eulogist John Sergeant said at Philadelphia in July 1826, was the "text of the revolution," the "ruling vital principle" that had inspired the men of the 1770s, who "looked forward through succeeding generations, and saw stamped upon all their institutions, the great principles set forth in the Declaration of Independence." In Hallowell, Maine, another eulogist, Peleg Sprague, similarly described the Declaration of Independence as an assertion *by a whole people,* of ... *the native equality of the human race,* as the true foundation of all political, of all human institutions."

AND SO AN INTERPRETATION OF the declaration that had emerged in the 1790s became ever more widely repeated. The equality that Sergeant and Sprague emphasized was not, however, asserted for the first time in the Declaration of Independence.

Even before Congress published its Declaration, one revolutionary document after another had associated equality with a new American republic and suggested enough different meanings of that term—equal rights, equal access to office, equal voting power—to keep Americans busy sorting them out and fighting over inegalitarian practices far into the future. Jefferson, in fact, adapted those most remembered opening lines of the Declaration's second paragraph from a draft Declaration of Rights for Virginia, written by George Mason and revised by a committee of the Virginia convention, which appeared in the *Pennsylvania Gazette* on June 12, 1776, the day after the Committee of Five was appointed and perhaps the day it first met. Whether on his own inspiration or under instructions from the committee, Jefferson began with the Mason draft, which he gradually tightened into a more compressed and eloquent statement. He took, for example, Mason's statement that "all men are born equally free and independent," rewrote it to say they were "created equal & independent," and then cut out the "& independent."

Jefferson was not alone in adapting the Mason text for his purposes. The Virginia convention revised the Mason draft before enacting Virginia's Declaration of Rights, which said that all men were "by nature" equally free and independent. Several other states—including Pennsylvania (1776), Vermont (1777), Massachusetts (1780), and New Hampshire (1784)—remained closer to Mason's wording, including in their state bill of rights the assertions that men were "born free and equal" or "born equally free and independent." Unlike the Declaration of Independence, moreover, the state bills or "declarations" of rights became (after an initial period of confusion) legally binding. Americans' first efforts to work out the meaning of the equality written into their founding documents therefore occurred on the state level.

IN MASSACHUSETTS, FOR EXAMPLE, several slaves won their freedom in the 1780s by arguing before the state's Supreme Judicial Court that the provision in the state's bill of rights that all men were born free and equal made slavery unlawful. Later, in the famous case of *Commonwealth* v. *Aves* (1836), Justice Lemuel Shaw ruled that those words were sufficient to end slavery in Massachusetts, indeed that it would be difficult to find others "more precisely adapted to the abolition of negro slavery." White Americans also found the equality provisions in their state bills of rights useful. In the Virginia constitutional convention of 1829–30, for example, a delegate from the trans-Appalachian West, John R. Cooke, cited that "sacred instrument" the Virginia Declaration of Rights against the state's system of representing all counties equally in the legislature regardless of their populations and its imposition of a property qualification for the vote, both of which gave disproportional power to men in the eastern part of the state. The framers of Virginia's 1776 constitution allowed those practices to persist despite their violation of the equality affirmed in the Declaration of Rights, Cooke said, because there were limits on how much they dared change "in the midst of war." They therefore left it for posterity to resolve the inconsistency "as soon as leisure should be afforded them." In the hands of men like Cooke, the Virginia Declaration of Rights became a practical program of reform to be realized over time, as the Declaration of Independence would later be for Abraham Lincoln.

But why, if the states had legally binding statements of men's equality, should anyone turn to the Declaration of Independence? Because not all states had bills of rights, and not all the bills of rights that did exist included statements on equality. Moreover, neither the federal Constitution nor the federal Bill of Rights asserted men's natural equality or their possession of inalienable rights or the right of the people to reject or change their government. As a result, contenders in national politics who found those old revolutionary principles useful had to cite the Declaration of Independence. It was all they had.

THE SACRED STATURE GIVEN THE Declaration after 1815 made it extremely useful for causes attempting to seize the moral high ground in public debate. Beginning about 1820, workers, farmers, women's rights advocates, and other groups persistently used the Declaration of Independence to justify their quest for equality and their opposition to the "tyranny" of factory owners or railroads or great corporations or the male power structure. It remained, however, especially easy for the opponents of slavery to cite the Declaration on behalf of their cause. Eighteenth-century statements of equality referred to men in a state of nature, before governments were created, and asserted that no persons acquired legitimate authority over others without their consent. If so, a system of slavery in which men were born the subjects and indeed the property of others was profoundly wrong. In short, the same principle that denied kings a right to rule by inheritance alone undercut the right of masters to own slaves whose status was determined by birth, not consent. The kinship of the Declaration of Independence with the cause of antislavery was understood from the beginning—which explains why gradual emancipation acts, such as those in New York and New Jersey, took effect on July 4 in 1799 and 1804 and why Nat Turner's rebellion was originally planned for July 4, 1831.

Even in the eighteenth century, however, assertions of men's equal birth provoked dissent. As slavery became an increasingly divisive issue, denials that men were naturally equal multiplied. Men were not created equal in Virginia, John Tyler insisted during the Missouri debates of 1820: "No, sir, the principle, although lovely and beautiful, cannot obliterate those distinctions in society which society itself engenders and gives birth to." Six years later the acerbic, self-styled Virginia aristocrat John Randolph called the notion of man's equal creation "a falsehood, and a most pernicious falsehood, even though I find it in the Declaration of Independence." Man was born in a state of "perfect helplessness and ignorance" and so was from the start dependent on others. There was "not a word of truth" in the notion that men were created equal, repeated South Carolina's John C. Calhoun in 1848. Men could not survive, much less de-

velop their talents, alone; the political state, in which some exercised authority and others obeyed, was in fact man's "natural state," that in which he "is born, lives and dies." For a long time the "false and dangerous" doctrine that men were created equal had lain "dormant," but by the late 1840s Americans had begun "to experience the danger of admitting so great an error . . . in the Declaration of Independence," where it had been inserted needlessly, Calhoun said, since separation from Britain could have been justified without it.

FIVE YEARS LATER, IN SENATE DEbates over the Kansas-Nebraska Act, Indiana's John Pettit pronounced his widely quoted statement that the supposed "self-evident truth" of man's equal creation was in fact "a self-evident lie." Ohio's senator Benjamin Franklin Wade, an outspoken opponent of slavery known for his vituperative style and intense patriotism, rose to reply. Perhaps Wade's first and middle names gave him a special bond with the Declaration and its creators. The "great declaration cost our forefathers too dear," he said, to be so "lightly thrown away by their children." Without its inspiring principles the Americans could not have won their independence; for the revolutionary generation the "great truths" in that "immortal instrument," the Declaration of Independence, were "worth the sacrifice of all else on earth, even life itself." How, then, were men equal? Not, surely, in physical power or intellect. The "good old Declaration" said "that all men are equal, and have inalienable rights; that is, [they are] equal in point of right; that no man has a right to trample on another." Where those rights were wrested from men through force or fraud, justice demanded that they be "restored without delay."

Abraham Lincoln, a little-known forty-four-year-old lawyer in Springfield, Illinois, who had served one term in Congress before being turned out of office, read these debates, was aroused as by nothing before, and began to pick up the dropped threads of his political career. Like Wade, Lincoln idealized the men of the American Revolution, who were for him "a forest of giant oaks," "a fortress of strength," "iron men." He also shared the deep concern of his contemporaries as the "silent artillery of time" removed them and the *"living history"* they embodied from this world. Before the 1850s, however, Lincoln seems to have had relatively little interest in the Declaration of Independence. Then, suddenly, that document and its assertion that all men were created equal became his "ancient faith," the "father of all moral principles," an "axiom" of free society. He was provoked by the attacks of men such as Pettit and Calhoun. And he made the arguments of those who defended the Declaration his own, much as Jefferson had done with Mason's text, reworking the ideas from speech to speech, pushing their logic, and eventually, at Gettysburg in 1863, arriving at a simple statement of profound eloquence. In time his understanding of the Declaration of Independence would become that of the nation.

Lincoln believed the Declaration "contemplated the progressive improvement in the condition of all men everywhere." Otherwise, it was "mere rubbish."

Lincoln's position emerged fully and powerfully during his debates with Illinois's senator Stephen Douglas, a Democrat who had proposed the Kansas-Nebraska Act and whose seat Lincoln sought in 1858. They were an odd couple, Douglas and Lincoln, as different physically—at full height Douglas came only to Lincoln's shoulders—as they were in style. Douglas wore well-tailored clothes; Lincoln's barely covered his limbs. Douglas was in general the more polished speaker; Lincoln sometimes rambled on, losing his point and his audience, although he could also, especially with a prepared text, be

a powerful orator. The greatest difference between them was, however, in the positions they took on the future of slavery and the meaning of the Declaration of Independence.

Douglas defended the Kansas-Nebraska Act, which allowed the people of those states to permit slavery within their borders, as consistent with the revolutionary heritage. After all, in instructing their delegates to vote for independence, one state after another had explicitly retained the exclusive right of defining its domestic institutions. Moreover, the Declaration of Independence carried no implications for slavery, since its statement on equality referred to white men only. In fact, Douglas said, it simply meant that American colonists of European descent had equal rights with the King's subjects in Great Britain. The signers were not thinking of "the negro or . . . savage Indians, or the Feejee, or the Malay, or any other inferior or degraded race." Otherwise they would have been honor bound to free their own slaves, which not even Thomas Jefferson did. The Declaration had only one purpose: to explain and justify American independence.

To LINCOLN, DOUGLAS'S ARGUMENT left only a "mangled ruin" of the Declaration of Independence, whose "plain, unmistakable language" said *"all"* men were created equal. In affirming that government derived its "just powers from the consent of the governed," the Declaration also said that no man could rightly govern others without their consent. If, then, "the negro is a man," was it not a "total destruction of self-government, to say that he too shall not govern *himself?"* To govern a man without his consent was "despotism." Moreover, to confine the Declaration's significance to the British peoples of 1776 denied its meaning, Lincoln charged, not only for Douglas's "inferior races" but for the French, Irish, German, Scandinavian, and other immigrants who had come to America after the Revolution. For them the promise of equality linked new Americans with the founding generation; it was an "electric cord" that bound them into the nation

"as though they were blood of the blood, and flesh of the flesh of the men who wrote that Declaration," and so made one people out of many. Lincoln believed that the Declaration "contemplated the progressive improvement in the condition of all men everywhere." If instead it was only a justification of independence "without the *germ,* or even the *suggestion* of the individual rights of man in it," the document was "of no practical use now—mere rubbish—old wadding left to rot on the battlefield after the victory is won," an "interesting memorial of the dead past . . . shorn of its vitality, and practical value."

LIKE WADE, LINCOLN DENIED THAT the signers meant that men were equal in *"all respects,"* including "color, size, intellect, moral developments, or social capacity." He, too, made sense of the Declaration's assertion of man's equal creation by eliding it with the next, separate statement on rights. The signers, he insisted, said men were equal in having " 'certain inalienable rights. . . .' This they said, and this they meant." Like John Cooke in Virginia three decades before, Lincoln thought the Founders allowed the persistence of practices at odds with their principles for reasons of necessity: to establish the Constitution demanded that slavery continue in those original states that chose to keep it. "We could not secure the good we did if we grasped for more," but that did not "destroy the principle that is the charter of our liberties." Nor did it mean that slavery had to be allowed in states not yet organized in 1776, such as Kansas and Nebraska.

Again like Cooke, Lincoln claimed that the authors of the Declaration understood its second paragraph as setting a standard for free men whose principles should be realized "as fast as circumstances . . . permit." They wanted that standard to be "familiar to all, and revered by all; constantly looked to, and constantly labored for, and even though never perfectly attained, constantly approximated and thereby constantly spreading and deepening its influence, and augmenting the happiness and value of life to all people of all colors everywhere." And if, as Calhoun said, American independence could have been declared without any assertion of human equality and inalienable rights, that made its inclusion all the more wonderful. "All honor to Jefferson," Lincoln said in a letter of 1859, "to the man who . . . had the coolness, forecast, and capacity to introduce into a merely revolutionary document, an abstract truth, applicable to all men and all times, and to embalm it there," where it would remain "a rebuke and a stumbling-block to the very harbingers of re-appearing tyranny and oppression."

JEFFERSON AND THE MEMBERS OF THE second continental Congress did not understand what they were doing in quite that way on July 4, 1776. For them, it was enough for the Declaration to be "merely revolutionary." But if Douglas's history was more accurate, Lincoln's reading of the Declaration was better suited to the needs of the Republic in the mid-nineteenth century, when the standard of revolution had passed to Southern secessionists and to radical abolitionists who also called for disunion. In his hands the Declaration became first and foremost a living document for an established society, a set of goals to be realized over time, the dream of "something better, than a mere change of masters" that explained why "our fathers" fought and endured until they won the Revolutionary War. In the Civil War, too, Lincoln told Congress on July 4, 1861, the North fought not only to save the Union but to preserve a form of government "whose leading object is to elevate the condition of men—to lift artificial weights from all shoulders—to clear the paths of laudable pursuit for all." The rebellion it opposed was at base an effort "to overthrow the principle that all men were created equal."

And so the Union victory at Gettysburg in 1863 became for him a vindication of that proposition, to which the nation's fathers had committed it in 1776, and a challenge to complete the "unfinished work" of the Union dead and bring to "this nation, under God, a new birth of freedom."

Lincoln's Gettysburg Address stated briefly and eloquently convictions he had developed over the previous decade, convictions that on point after point echoed earlier Americans: Republicans

---

The Declaration Lincoln left was not Jefferson's Declaration, although Jefferson and other revolutionaries shared the values Lincoln stressed.

---

of the 1790s, the eulogists Peleg Sprague and John Sergeant in 1826, John Cooke in the Virginia convention a few years later, Benjamin Wade in 1853. Some of those men he knew; others were unfamiliar to him, but they had also struggled to understand the practical implications of their revolutionary heritage and followed the same logic to the same conclusions. The Declaration of Independence Lincoln left was not Jefferson's Declaration, although Jefferson and other revolutionaries shared the values Lincoln and others stressed: equality, human rights, government by consent. Nor was Lincoln's Declaration of Independence solely his creation. It remained an "expression of the American mind," not, of course, what all

Americans thought but what many had come to accept. And its implications continued to evolve after Lincoln's death. In 1858 he had written a correspondent that the language of the Declaration of Independence was at odds with slavery but did not require political and social equality for free black Americans. Few disagreed then. How many would agree today?

The Declaration of Independence is in fact a curious document. After the Civil War members of Lincoln's party tried to write its principles into the Constitution by enacting the Thirteenth, Fourteenth, and Fifteenth Amendments, which is why issues of racial or age or gender equality are now so often fought out in the courts. But the Declaration of Independence itself is not and has never been legally binding. Its power comes from its capacity to inspire and move the hearts of living Americans, and its meaning lies in what they choose to make of it. It has been at once a cause of controversy, pushing as it does against established habits and conventions, and a unifying national icon, a legacy and a new creation that binds the revolutionaries to descendants who confronted and continue to confront issues the Founders did not know or failed to resolve. On Independence Day, then, Americans celebrate not simply the birth of their nation or the legacy of a few great men. They also commemorate a Declaration of Independence that is their own collective work now and through time. And that, finally, makes sense of the Fourth of July.

Pauline Maier is William Rand Kenan, Jr., Professor of American History at the Massachusetts Institute of Technology.

George Washington, Spymaster

Without his brilliance at espionage the Revolution could not have been won

By Thomas Fleming

GEORGE WASHINGTON A MASTER of espionage? It is commonly understood that without the Commander in Chief's quick mind and cool judgment the American Revolution would have almost certainly expired in 1776. It is less well known that his brilliance extended to overseeing, directly and indirectly, extensive and very sophisticated intelligence activities against the British.

Washington had wanted to be a soldier almost from the cradle and seems to have acquired the ability to think in military terms virtually by instinct. In the chaos of mid-1776, with half his army deserting and the other half in a funk and all his generals rattled, he kept his head and reversed his strategy. The Americans had started with the idea that a general action, as an all-out battle was called, could end the conflict overnight, trusting that their superior numbers would overwhelm the presumably small army the British could afford to send to our shores. But the British sent a very big, well-trained army, which routed the Americans in the first several battles in New York. Washington sat down in his tent on Harlem Heights and informed the Continental Congress that he was going to fight an entirely different war. From now on, he wrote, he would "avoid a general action." Instead he would "protract the war."

HE WAS involved in figuring out how to burn down New York City despite orders not to.

In his 1975 study of Washington's generalship, *The Way of the Fox,* Lt. Col. Dave Richard Palmer has called this reversal "a masterpiece of strategic thought, a brilliant blueprint permitting a weak force to combat a powerful opponent." It soon became apparent that for the blueprint to be followed, Washington would have to know what the British were planning to do, and he would have to be able to prevent them from finding out what he was doing. In short, espionage was built into the system.

Washington had been acquainted with British colonial officials and generals and colonels since his early youth, and he knew how intricately espionage was woven into the entire British military and political enterprise. Any Englishman's mail could be opened and read if a secretary of state requested it. Throughout Europe every British embassy had its intelligence network.

Thus Washington was not entirely surprised to discover, shortly after he took command of the American army in 1775, that his surgeon general, Dr. Benjamin Church, was telling the British everything that went on in the American camp at Cambridge, Massachusetts. He *was* surprised to find out, not long after he had transferred his operations to New York in the spring of 1776, that one of his Life Guard, a soldier named Thomas Hickey, was rumored to be involved in a plot to kill him.

By that time Washington had pulled off his own opening gambit in a form of intelligence at which he soon displayed something close to genius: disinformation. Shortly after he took command in Cambridge, he asked someone how much powder the embryo American army had in reserve. Everyone thought it had three hundred barrels, but a check of the Cambridge magazine revealed most of that had been fired away at Bunker Hill. There were only thirty-six barrels—fewer than nine rounds per man. For half an hour, according to one witness, Washington was too stunned to speak. But he recovered and sent people into British-held Boston to spread the story that he had eighteen hundred barrels, and he spread the same rumor throughout the American camp.

In chaotic New York, grappling with a large and aggressive British army, deserting militia, and an inapplicable strategy, Washington temporarily lost control

From *American Heritage,* February/March 2000, pp. 45-51. © 2000 by Forbes, Inc. Reprinted by permission of *American Heritage* magazine, a division of Forbes, Inc.

of the intelligence situation. That explains the dolorous failure of Capt. Nathan Hale's mission in September 1776. Hale, sent to gather information behind British lines, was doomed almost from the moment he volunteered. He had little or no contact with the American high command, no training as a spy, no disguise worthy of the name, and an amorphous mission: to find out whatever he could wherever he went.

There is little evidence that Washington was even aware of Hale's existence. He was involved in something far more serious: figuring out how to burn down New York City in order to deprive the British of their winter quarters, despite orders from the Continental Congress strictly forbidding him to harm the place. He looked the other way while members of Hale's regiment slipped into the city; they were experts at starting conflagrations thanks to a tour of duty on fire ships—vessels carrying explosives to burn enemy craft—on the Hudson.

ON SEPTEMBER 21 A THIRD OF New York went up in flames. The timing was disastrous for Hale, who was captured the very same day. Anyone with a Connecticut accent became highly suspect, and the British caught several incendiaries and hanged them on the spot. They gave Hale the same treatment: no trial, just a swift, humiliating death. Hale's friends were so mortified by his fate, which they considered shameful, that no one mentioned his now-famous farewell speech for another fifty years. Then an old man told his daughter about it, and Yale College, seeking Revolutionary War heroes among its graduates, quickly immortalized him.

Washington never said a word about Hale. His only intelligence comment at the time concerned New York. The fire had destroyed Trinity Church and about six hundred houses, causing no little discomfort for the British and the thousands of Loyalist refugees who had crowded into the city. In a letter, Washington remarked that "Providence, or some good honest fellow, has done more for us than we were disposed to do for ourselves."

HONEYMAN TOLD Rall about his narrow "escape" and assured him the Americans were half-naked and freezing.

One of Hale's best friends, Maj. Benjamin Tallmadge, never got over his death. He probably talked about it to Washington, who assured him that once they got the protracted war under control, all espionage would be handled from Army headquarters, and no spy's life would be wasted the way Hale's had been.

Surviving long enough to fight an extended conflict was no small matter. In the weeks after Hale's death, disaster after disaster befell the American army. Washington was forced to abandon first New York and then New Jersey. On the other side of the Delaware, with only the shadow of an army left to him, he issued orders in December 1776 to all his generals to find "some person who can be engaged to cross the river as a spy" and added that "expense must not be spared" in securing a volunteer.

He also rushed a letter to Robert Morris, the financier of the Revolution, asking for hard money to "pay a certain set of people who are of particular use to us." He meant spies, and he had no illusion that any spy would risk hanging for the paper money the Continental Congress was printing. Morris sent from Philadelphia two canvas bags filled with what hard cash he could scrape together on an hour's notice: 410 Spanish dollars, 2 English crowns, 10 shillings, and 2 sixpence.

The search soon turned up a former British soldier named John Honeyman, who was living in nearby Griggstown, New Jersey. On Washington's orders Honeyman rediscovered his loyalty to the king and began selling cattle to several British garrisons along the Delaware. He had no trouble gaining the confidence of Col. Johann Rall, who was in command of three German regiments in Trenton. Honeyman listened admiringly as Rall described his heroic role in the fighting around New York and agreed with him that the Americans were hopeless soldiers.

On December 22, 1776, having spent about a week in Trenton, Honeyman wandered into the countryside, supposedly in search of cattle, and got himself captured by an American patrol and hustled to Washington's headquarters. There he was publicly denounced by the Commander in Chief as a "notorious" turncoat. Washington insisted on interrogating him personally and said he would give the traitor a chance to save his skin if he recanted his loyalty to the Crown.

A half-hour later the general ordered his aides to throw Honeyman into the guardhouse. Tomorrow morning, he stated, the Tory would be hanged. That night Honeyman escaped from the guardhouse with a key supplied by Washington and dashed past American sentries, who fired on him. Sometime on December 24 he turned up in Trenton and told Colonel Rall the story of his narrow escape.

The German naturally wanted to know what Honeyman had seen in Washington's camp, and the spy assured him that the Americans were falling apart. They were half-naked and freezing, and they lacked the food and basic equipment, such as shoes, to make a winter march. Colonel Rall, delighted, prepared to celebrate Christmas with no military worries to interrupt the feasting and drinking that were traditional in his country. He never dreamed that Honeyman had given Washington a professional soldier's detailed description of the routine of the Trenton garrison, the location of the picket guards, and everything else an assaulting force would need to know.

AT DAWN ON DECEMBER 26 WASHington's ragged Continentals charged through swirling snow and sleet to kill the besotted Colonel Rall and capture most of his troops. New Jersey had been on the brink of surrender; now local patriots began shooting up British patrols, and the rest of the country, in the words of a Briton in Virginia, "went liberty mad again."

Washington set up a winter camp in Morristown and went to work organizing American intelligence. He made Tallmadge his second-in-command, though he was ostensibly still a major in the 2d Continental Dragoons. That regiment was stationed in outposts all around the perimeter of British-held New York, and Tallmadge visited these units regularly, supposedly to make sure that all was in order but actually working as a patient spider setting up spy networks inside the British lines. His methods, thanks to Washington's tutelage, could not have been more sophisticated. He equipped his spies with cipher codes, invisible ink, and aliases that concealed their real identities. The invisible ink, which the Americans called "the stain," had been invented by Dr. James Jay, a brother of the prominent patriot John Jay, living in England. It was always in short supply.

Two of the most important American agents operating inside British-held New York were Robert Townsend, a Quaker merchant, and Abraham Woodhull, a Setauket, Long Island, farmer. Their code names were Culper Jr. and Culper Sr. As a cover, Townsend wrote violently Loyalist articles for the New York *Royal Gazette;* this enabled him to pick up information from British officers and their mistresses, and he sent it on to Woodhull via a courier named Austin Roe.

Woodhull would then have a coded signal hung on a Setauket clothesline that was visible through a spyglass to Americans on the Connecticut shore. A crew of oarsmen would row across Long Island Sound by night, collect Townsend's letters, and carry them to Tallmadge's dragoons, who would hurry them to Washington. The general applied a "sympathetic fluid" to reveal the secret messages written in Dr. Jay's "stain."

When the British occupied Philadelphia, in 1777, Washington salted the city with spies. His chief assistant there was Maj. John Clark, a cavalryman who became expert at passing false information about American strength at Valley Forge to a spy for the British commander General Howe. Washington laboriously wrote out muster reports of the Conti-

WASHINGTON had Tallmadge equip all his spies with cipher codes, invisible ink, and aliases.

nental Army, making it four or five times its actual size; the British, recognizing the handwriting, accepted the information as fact and gave the spy who had obtained it a bonus. Washington must have enjoyed this disinformation game; at one point, describing a particularly successful deception, Clark wrote, "This will give you a laugh."

The most effective American spy in Philadelphia was Lydia Darragh, an Irish-born Quaker midwife and undertaker. The British requisitioned a room in her house to serve as a "council chamber" and discussed their war plans there. By lying with her ear to a crack in the floor in the room above, Mrs. Darragh could hear much of what they said. Her husband wrote the information in minute shorthand on scraps of paper that she hid in large cloth-covered buttons. Wearing these, her fourteen-year-old son would walk into the countryside to meet his brother, a lieutenant in the American army. He snipped off the buttons, and the intelligence was soon in Washington's hands.

Mrs. Darragh's biggest coup was getting word to Washington that the British were about to make a surprise attack on his ragged army as it marched to Valley Forge in early December 1777. When the attack came, the Continentals were waiting with loaded muskets and cannon, and the king's forces withdrew.

T HE BRITISH RETURNED TO PHILA-delphia determined to find whoever had leaked their plan. Staff officers went to Mrs. Darragh's house and demanded to know exactly when everyone had gone to bed the previous night—except one person. "I won't ask you, Mrs. Darragh, because I know you retire each night exactly at nine," the chief interrogator said. Lydia Darragh smiled and said nothing. After the war

she remarked that she was pleased that as a spy she had never had to tell a lie.

The British, of course, had a small army of spies working for them as well, and they constantly struggled to penetrate Washington's operations. Toward the end of 1779, one of their Philadelphia spies wrote to Maj. John André, the charming, witty, artistically talented director of British intelligence: "Do you wish to have a useful hand in their army and to pay what you find his services worth? The exchange is 44 to 1." The numbers refer to the vertiginous depreciation of the Continental dollar; British spies, too, wanted to be paid in hard money.

The Americans did their best to make trouble for André by spreading around Philadelphia and New York the rumor that he was given to molesting boys. It is not clear whether Washington was involved in these particular smears, and they hardly chime with André's reputation for charming women, notably a Philadelphia belle named Peggy Shippen, who eventually married Gen. Benedict Arnold.

In any event, André was very successful at keeping tabs on the Americans. Surviving letters from his spies show him obtaining good estimates of American army strength in 1779. At one point Gen. Philip Schuyler made a motion in the Continental Congress that it leave Philadelphia because "they could do no business that was not instantly communicated" to the British.

André's most successful agent was a woman named Ann Bates, a former schoolteacher who married a British soldier while the army was in Philadelphia. Disguised as a peddler, she wandered through the American camp, counted the cannon there, overheard conversations at Washington's headquarters, and accu-

HIS AGENTS WERE so good he had to appeal for the lives of three arrested for communicating with the enemy.

ately predicted the American attack on the British base in Newport, Rhode Island, in 1778.

The intelligence war reached a climax, or something very close to one, between 1779 and 1781. American morale was sinking with the Continental currency, and trusting anyone became harder and harder. Washington could never be sure when a spy had been "turned" by British hard money, and the British tried to accelerate the decline of the paper dollar by printing and circulating millions of counterfeit bills.

Soon an astonished American was writing, "An ordinary horse is worth twenty thousand dollars." In despair Congress stopped producing money; this brought the army's commissary department to a halt. The Continental desertion rate rose, with veterans and sergeants among the chief fugitives.

Washington struggled to keep the British at bay with more disinformation about his dwindling strength. His spies had achieved such professionalism that he had to appeal to Gov. William Livingston of New Jersey to spare three men arrested in Elizabethtown for carrying on an illegal correspondence with the enemy. That was exactly what they had been doing—as double agents feeding the British disinformation.

The three spies stood heroically silent. Washington told Livingston they were willing to "bear the suspicion of being thought inimical." But realism could not be carried too far; the Continental Army could not hang its own agents. Would the governor please do something? Livingston allowed the spies to escape, and intelligence documents show that three years later they were still at work.

By June 1780 agents had given the British high command accurate reports of the American army's weakness in its Morristown camp. The main force had diminished to four thousand men; because of a shortage of fodder, there were no horses, which meant the artillery was immobilized. The British had just captured Charleston, South Carolina, and its garrison of five thousand, demoralizing the South. They decided a strike at Washington's force could end the war,

WITHOUT Washington's warning from a spy, the British might have ended the war at Morristown.

and they marshaled six thousand troops on Staten Island to deliver the blow.

A few hours before the attack, a furtive figure slipped ashore into New Jersey from Staten Island to warn the Continentals of the enemy buildup. He reached the officer in command in Elizabethtown, Col. Elias Dayton, and Dayton sent a rider off to Morristown with the news. Dayton and other members of the New Jersey Continental line, backed by local militia, were able to slow the British advance for the better part of a day, enabling Washington to get his army in motion and seize the high ground in the Short Hills, aborting the British plan.

It was a very close call. Without the warning from that spy, the British army would certainly have come over the Short Hills, overwhelmed Washington's four thousand men in Morristown, and captured their artillery. This probably would have ended the war.

After the royal army retreated to New York, word reached them that a French expeditionary force was landing in Newport, Rhode Island, to reinforce the struggling Americans. The British commander, Sir Henry Clinton, decided to attack before the French had a chance to recover from the rigors of the voyage and fortify.

This was the Culper network's greatest moment. Robert Townsend, alias Culper Jr., discovered the plan shortly after Clinton put six thousand men aboard transports and sailed them to Huntington Bay on the north shore of Long Island. They waited there while British frigates scouted Newport Harbor to assess the size of the French squadron.

Townsend's warning sent Washington's disinformation machine into overdrive. Within twenty-four hours a double agent was in New York, handing

the British top-secret papers, supposedly dropped by a careless courier, detailing a Washington plan to attack the city with every Continental soldier and militiaman in the middle states.

The British sent horsemen racing off to urge Sir Henry Clinton in Huntington Bay to return to New York with his six thousand men. Clinton, already discouraged by the British admiral's lack of enthusiasm for his plan to take Newport, glumly agreed and sailed his soldiers back to their fortifications. There they waited for weeks for an assault that never materialized.

When Clinton was in Huntington Bay, he and two aides were made violently ill by tainted wine they drank with dinner aboard the flagship. He ordered the bottle seized and asked the physician general of the British army to examine the dregs in the glasses. The doctor said the wine was "strongly impregnated with arsenic." During the night the bottle mysteriously disappeared, and Clinton was never able to confirm the assassination attempt or find the perpetrator. This may have been Washington's way of getting even for the Hickey plot.

The main event in the later years of the intelligence war was the treason of Benedict Arnold in 1780. However, the American discovery of Arnold's plot to sell the fortress at West Point to the British for six thousand pounds—about half a million dollars in modern money—was mostly luck. There was little that Benjamin Tallmadge or his agents could claim to their credit except having passed along a hint of a plot involving an American general a few weeks before.

There is no doubt that West Point would have been handed over and Benedict Arnold and John André given knighthoods if three wandering militiamen in Westchester County had not stopped André on his return to New York with the incriminating plans in his boot. The motive of these soldiers was not patriotism but robbery; Westchester was known as "the neutral ground," and Loyalists and rebels alike wandered there in search of plunder.

Hanging John André was one of the most difficult things Washington had to do in the intelligence war. The major was the object of universal affection, and Alexander Hamilton and others on Washington's staff urged him to find a way to commute the sentence. Washington grimly replied that he would do so only if the British handed over Arnold. That of course did not happen, and André died on the gallows. In the next twelve months, Washington made repeated attempts to capture Arnold. He ordered an American sergeant named Champe to desert and volunteer to join an American legion that Arnold was trying to create. To give Champe a convincing sendoff, Washington ordered a half a dozen cavalrymen to pursue him, without telling them he was a fake deserter. Champe arrived in the British lines with bullets chasing him.

WASHINGTON WOULD SEEM TO have liked these little touches of realism. Unusually fearless himself, he had once said as a young man that whistling bullets had "a charming sound." One wonders if spies such as Honeyman and Champe agreed.

Soon Champe was a member of Arnold's staff, living in the former general's house on the Hudson River in New York. Through cooperating agents, Champe communicated a plan to knock Arnold unconscious when he went into his riverside garden to relieve himself one moonless night. A boatload of Americans would be waiting to carry him back to New Jersey and harsh justice.

On the appointed night the boat was there, and Arnold went to the garden as usual, but Champe was on a troopship in New York Harbor. Clinton had ordered two thousand men, including Arnold's American legion, south to raid Virginia. Champe had to watch for an opportunity and deserted back to the American side.

Arnold's defection badly upset American intelligence operations for months. He told the British what he knew of Washington's spies in New York, and they made several arrests. Townsend quit spying for six months, to the great distress of Washington and Tallmadge.

The intelligence war continued during the year remaining until Yorktown.

HANGING John André was one of the most difficult things he had to do in the intelligence war.

Washington's reluctant decision to march south with the French army to try to trap a British army in that small Virginia tobacco port was accompanied by strenuous disinformation efforts intended to tie the British army to New York for as long as possible. In the line of march as the allied force moved south through New Jersey were some thirty large flatboats. British spies reported that the Americans were constructing large cooking ovens at several points near New York. Both seemed evidence of a plan to attack the city.

Benedict Arnold, now a British brigadier, begged Sir Henry Clinton to ignore this deception and give him six thousand men to attack the long, vulnerable American line of march. Clinton said no. He wanted to husband every available man in New York. By the time the British commander's Philadelphia spies told him where Washington was actually going, it was too late. The royal army under Charles Lord Cornwallis surrendered after three weeks of pounding by heavy guns, the blow that finally ended the protracted war.

EVEN AFTER THE FIGHTING WOUND down, intelligence activity went on. In the fall of 1782, a year after Yorktown, a French officer stationed in Morristown wrote, "Not a day has passed since we have drawn near the enemy that we have not had some news of them from our spies in New York." For a final irony, the last British commander in America, Sir Guy Carleton, sent Washington a report from a British agent warning about a rebel plot to plunder New York and abuse Loyalists as the British army withdrew, and Washington sent in Major Tallmadge and a column of troops—not only to keep order but

also to protect their agents, many of whom had earned enmity for appearing to be loyal to George III.

Among the American spies in New York was a huge Irish-American tailor named Hercules Mulligan who had sent Washington invaluable information. His greatest coup was a warning that the British planned to try to kidnap the American commander in 1780. Mulligan reported directly to Washington's aide Col. Alexander Hamilton.

Another of the deepest agents was James Rivington, editor of the unctuously loyal New York *Royal Gazette*. He is believed to have stolen the top-secret signals of the British fleet, which the Americans passed on to the French in 1781. The knowledge may have helped the latter win the crucial naval battle off the Virginia capes that September, sealing Cornwallis's fate at Yorktown.

The day after the British evacuated New York, Washington had breakfast with Hercules Mulligan—a way of announcing that he had been a patriot. He also paid a visit to James Rivington and apparently gave him a bag of gold coins. When he was composing his final expense account for submission to the Continental Congress with his resignation as Commander in Chief, Washington included from memory the contents of the bag of coins Robert Morris had rushed to him in late December 1776; 410 Spanish dollars, 2 English crowns, 10 shillings, and 2 sixpence. The circumstances under which he received it, Washington remarked, made it impossible for him ever to forget the exact amount of that crucial transfusion of hard money. It is another piece of evidence, barely needed at this point, that intelligence was a centerpiece of the strategy of protracted war—and that George Washington was a master of the game.

Thomas Fleming writes often for American Heritage. *His most recent book is* Duel: Alexander Hamilton, Aaron Burr, and the Future of America (*Basic Books, 1999*).

The Canton War

In addition to opening up trade with China, the first visit ever by an American ship to the port of Canton in 1784 also led to the first human-rights struggle between the Asian giant and the United States.

By Robert W. Drexler

IN THE LATE eighteenth century, the lure of the Orient and the promise of great wealth began to attract American seamen and traders to China's port of Canton, which had been open to Europeans since an early sixteenth-century Portuguese vessel offered its cargo of spices in exchange for silk and camphor. During the next 250 years, Dutch, Danish, French, and British traders had also traveled to China, buying tea, silk, porcelain, and other goods that brought great wealth to investors in such enterprises as the Dutch and the British East India companies.

Relative latecomers, the newly independent Americans made their first foray into China in 1784. Revolutionary War veteran Samuel Shaw of Boston arrived in Canton (now Guangzhou) on August 30 of that year, having spent two days at Whampoa, the city's anchorage, some 12 miles downriver. The United States had just won its independence from Great Britain, and Shaw had come to one of the world's oldest nations as a representative of its youngest.

The New Englander recorded his momentous meeting with local mandarins in his journal, noting that "Ours being the first American ship that had ever visited China, it was some time before the Chinese could fully comprehend the distinction between Englishmen and us. They styled us the *New People*, and when, by the map, we conveyed to them an idea of the extent of our country . . .

they were not a little pleased at the prospect of so considerable a market for the productions of their own empire."

And so this first American venture into commercial trade with China was off to a promising start. Three months later, however, an incident involving human rights violations caused Shaw to reconsider whether he should continue the relationship. His decision led to the Americans becoming embroiled in what became known as the "Canton War."

As the commercial agent of a group of American investors, Samuel Shaw—shown above in a portrait by John Johnston—sailed to Canton, China, in 1784 aboard the *Empress of China,* which thus became the first merchant ship from the new United States to do business with the Asian giant.

America's war for independence from Great Britain had only recently ended, when a group of merchants from New York and Philadelphia, intent on trading with China, offered Shaw the position of factor and commercial agent for a voyage that would take him from the United States to the mercantile center of Canton. He undertook the 188-day voyage from New York aboard the *Empress of China,* which thus became the first American vessel to reach East Asia. As the ship's business agent, Shaw planned to obtain a large cargo of Chinese tea in exchange for more than 28 tons of ginseng, a tuberous root highly fancied in China as an aphrodisiac, which had been found growing wild on the slopes of the Appalachian Mountains in New York and New England.

Because foreign ships were not allowed to sail upriver from Whampoa, Shaw and his colleagues left the *Empress of China* there and boarded Chinese boats for Canton, where all Westerners were required to live and trade in a confined area on the outskirts of the city. Shaw's first meetings with both Chinese and European merchants was a cordial one. "On the day of our arrival," he wrote, "we were visited by the principal Chinese merchants, and by the chiefs and gentlemen of the Danish and Dutch factories; the next day, by several English gentlemen. . . ." When Shaw paid return calls on those who had

From *American History,* April 1997, pp. 42-45, 63. © 1997 by Cowles Magazine, Inc. Reprinted through the courtesy of Cowles Magazines, publishers of *American History.*

Foreign traders were required to live and conduct business outside the walls of the city of Canton. Not long after Shaw's 1784 voyage to China, the Americans followed the example of the Danish, Spanish, Swedish, British, French, and other nationalities who had established compounds or *Hongs* on the banks of the Pearl River.

visited him, his arrival was heralded by the firing of no fewer than 150 salutes from the guns of the European ships. It was a traditional courtesy, but one that was practiced excessively in those waters. The local Chinese usually tolerated such Western toying with the gunpowder that their ancestors had invented some thousand years earlier. A similar salute by a British ship, however, soon threatened to destroy the Western trading system in Canton.

On the evening of November 24, 1784, Captain Williams of the British ship *Lady Hughes* entertained dinner guests on board his vessel. As the visitors prepared to return ashore, one of the ship's guns fired the customary salute. The force of this blast inadvertently killed a Chinese

fisherman and wounded two others in a sampan that was alongside, but out of view of the *Lady Hughes.* Aware that under Chinese law the only atonement for a killing was the execution of the one responsible, Captain Williams immediately sent the offending gunner into hiding. He knew that the Chinese authorities would not care that the death had been accidental; execution would be mandatory.

Despite the harshness of their law, the Chinese did make a fine distinction regarding the method of execution. Intentional killings saw the murderer decapitated; accidents carried a sentence of strangulation, which the Chinese considered preferable because the victim's body was not disfigured. Often, the condemned were brought to the public exe-

cution ground in an opium-induced daze—not so much out of compassion as from a Chinese desire to avoid a loss of decorum at the event.

Unable to discover where the gunner of the *Lady Hughes* was hiding, the Chinese authorities kidnapped an English merchant, George Smith, who was employed by the ship's owners. They intended to hold Smith hostage in an effort to force Captain Williams to hand over the gunner for execution. Lured into the quarters of a Chinese associate, Smith was seized, forced into a sedan chair, and carried off to within the walled city of Canton, where he was confined inside a prison that featured all the horrors that the Chinese had been refining for ages.

foreign trader in Canton, whose property or person could now no longer be considered secure." Shaw was among those who went to the meeting, which was held at a pagoda in an area normally closed to foreigners. Upon arrival, he and the other merchants were made to pass between ranks of guards armed with drawn broadswords.

The mandarin warned the nervous merchants against becoming involved in a dispute caused by the British, who, he reminded them, were their commercial competitors. He thereupon benignly offered tea, served in fine porcelain ware, and seemed unperturbed when the merchants declined the refreshment. He then presented two bolts of exquisite silk to each of them as a token of "friendship." None of the men could resist taking the gift, including Shaw, who dutifully gave it to the American Congress when he returned home.

The Chinese official informed the assembled merchants that all but the British would now be "permitted" to send their boats and armed men back to their merchant vessels anchored downriver, but he insisted that the boats fly a Chinese banner, instead of their national flags, for "protection." Most of the merchants were ready to yield to the Chinese demands, but Shaw, disgusted by their attitude, vowed that he and his

Tea, shipped in boxes such as the one below, was the mainstay of the China trade. In 1785, New York City newspapers announced the availability of a shipment of tea and other desirable commodities, recently arrived aboard the *Empress of China*.

In addition to seizing Smith, the Chinese authorities halted all business transactions with Westerners in Canton and ordered their Chinese servants and staff to withdraw behind the city's walls. The foreign merchants, including Shaw, found themselves isolated on the narrow strip of land between the walls and the Pearl River, where the Western traders had built their business and living quarters.

The Chinese drew up some forty gunboats on the river to intimidate the Westerners, who in those early years had no warships of their own to summon for protection. Most of the commercial vessels mounted only a few guns for defense against pirates, as well as for saluting, and carried some small arms for the crew. The besieged merchants got word to their ships anchored at Whampoa to send small boats with armed crewmen up the river to defend them in their quarters. The Chinese fired on the boats, but all got through safely, including one from the *Empress of China* which was transporting, in effect, the first American armed force in Asia.

After a few days, Chinese officials began parleys with the Westerners, warning them that all the province's armed forces were being readied to suppress the foreigners' resistance to the implementation of imperial law. Although the Chinese had only vague, confused ideas about the merchants' countries of origin, they were already adept at playing one nationality off against another. In this case, the officials aimed to isolate the British by ordering each of the other foreign contingents to send a representative to meet with a senior mandarin.

Before attending the meeting, the group conversed with the Englishmen and agreed that they would be united in conveying the message "that the seizing of Mr. Smith was considered, not as a matter affecting the English only, but as nearly concerning every

shipmates would stay and support the British, come what may.

The forces the Chinese had deployed to threaten the merchants had not intimidated the American. Their arms, Shaw observed, consisted mostly of swords, matchlock muskets, and bows and arrows. Although the Westerners would not have been able to defend their quarters against a horde of attackers, Shaw estimated that together, with the British included, they could fight their way back to the safety of their ships.

Until a year before this affair, Shaw had devoted his entire adult life to fighting against the British, not for them. Having enlisted in the Continental Army outside Boston in 1775 as soon as he turned 21, he had endured the winter at Valley Forge, Pennsylvania; crossed the Delaware River with George Washington; and, as a major in the artillery, helped defeat the British at Yorktown, Virginia, in 1781. After the war ended, however, Shaw had favored reconciliation with Great Britain and its Tory sympathizers in America. Now, at Canton, he was defending British merchants and ships belonging to the gigantic East India Company, the same firm whose tea Shaw's compatriots had dumped into Boston harbor in 1773.

Shaw argued with the European merchants that the kidnapping of Smith was not just a British concern but a threat to the interests of all foreign merchants, and he urged that they form a united front against the Chinese. In addition, he declared himself astonished that no provisions had been made jointly by the merchants for such an eventuality. Shaw insisted that minutes be taken during their meetings so that each would be obliged to state for the record his willingness to join the others in defense of their mutual interests.

The American's resistance to Chinese brutality and threats was all the more remarkable because he had more to lose if the Chinese suspended his right to trade at Canton. The European merchants were backed by powerful trading companies that had enormous resources to help them weather a suspension. Some, like the British and the Dutch, had colonial bases in India or Southeast Asia to which they could conveniently withdraw. By contrast, Shaw and his colleagues aboard the *Empress of China* were gambling on a single, thinly stretched voyage that, if it were to fail, would incur serious personal losses for all involved, including financial ruin for Shaw himself.

But it was obvious from Shaw's conduct in Canton that he had lost none of the youthful idealism and physical courage he had displayed during the Revolutionary War. Unfortunately, these qualities were in short supply among his fellow merchants. Rejecting Shaw's arguments, the Europeans deserted the British and, even worse, the British themselves finally brought back their ship's gunner and exchanged him for the hostage. But they thanked Shaw for his support and told him there was no longer need for his boatload of armed Americans at the merchants' quarters.

Shaw sent his men back downriver to the *Empress of China*. He made certain, however, that their boat "was not disgraced by the Chinese flag" and that it returned proudly flying the flag of the new United States.

This incident resolved, trading was resumed in Canton, and Shaw purchased the cargo of tea he had sought. Some months later he learned that the hapless gunner of the *Lady Hughes* had been executed by strangulation. Westerners thereafter did not fire salutes in the waters around Canton.

When Shaw returned to the United States, his cargo of tea fetched a handsome profit for all those who had invested in the venture. He wrote a formal account of his historic voyage for John Jay, who was then serving as secretary for foreign affairs of the government under the Articles of Confederation. Describing the *Lady Hughes* incident as the "Canton War," Shaw reported to Jay, with considerable understatement, that it had placed "the Americans in a more conspicuous point of view than has commonly attended the introduction of other nations into that ancient and extensive empire."

In his personal journal, however, Shaw recorded much stronger sentiments: "Thus ended a very troublesome affair, which commenced in confusion, was carried out without order and terminated disgracefully. Had the spirit of union among the Europeans taken place which the rights of humanity demanded, and could private interest have been for a moment sacrificed to the general good, the conclusion of the matter must have been honorable, and probably some additional privileges would have been obtained. But as it did terminate, we can only apply to it the observation of the Chinese themselves, "Truly, all Fanquois* have much lose his face in this business."

Shaw made three more voyages to China and other parts of East Asia without serious incident. In 1786, the Confederation Congress named him the first American Consul in Canton, an appointment that was renewed four years later by President George Washington. Shaw also established the first American business firm based in Canton, which was actively involved with commerce in the China and Indian seas.

On a voyage to Canton in 1793, Shaw contracted liver disease during a stopover in Bombay, India. Arriving in Canton, he remained confined to his house; then, finding no relief, he sailed back to the United States on March 17, 1794, aboard the Washington. The disease worsened, and ten weeks into the voyage, Shaw died at the age of 39. He was buried at sea off the Cape of Good Hope.

Shaw's business knowledge contributed to the early economic success of the United States, but more than that, this highly principled man and his successive journeys into the Orient gave the proud, new nation a secure position among the world's established countries.

Robert W. Drexler is a former American Consul to Hong Kong. His biography of Samuel Shaw, Pathfinder to China, *was published by University Press of America.*

---

*"Fanquois" was a contemptuous term applied indiscriminately to Europeans.

Constitutional Convention, Philadelphia, 1787:

...by the Unanimous Consent of the States

*'Something must be done, or we shall disappoint
not only America, but the whole world.'*

Elbridge Gerry

By Ezra Bowen

*The author, Ezra Bowen, a Senior Writer
at* Time *magazine, is the son of historian
Catherine Drinker Bowen.*

On Wednesday, June 27, a muggy afternoon pressed down upon Philadelphia. It was the summer of 1787. Flies droned through the high-ceilinged room of the State House where more than 40 Convention delegates from the quarrelsome American confederation of states, the New England men sweltering in their woolen suits, braced for yet another round of contention. They got it, this time from Maryland's Luther Martin, who enhanced a reputation for tiresome bombast with a three-hour speech. His subject was the rights of the thirteen sovereign states with which this Convention, said he ad infinitum, had neither legal power nor fair reason to tamper.

Already restive from five weeks of debate, his listeners could hardly bear it: Oliver Ellsworth of Connecticut later chided Martin, saying that the speech "might have continued two months, but for those marks of fatigue and disgust... strongly expressed on whichever side of the house you turned your mortified eyes."

Two days later brilliant Alexander Hamilton, one of the men who at various times left the Convention to return or not, walked out. He might come back, he said, but only if persuaded it would not be a "mere waste of time." Hamilton's position was clear. His discourses, described by some as "logic on fire," presented the case for strong, central government—a near kin to the British monarchy, in fact—that the states felt most threatening.

And as it happened, Hamilton's vote didn't matter much to the Convention just then. He was one of three New York delegates and the other two hated the idea of federal government. Since Convention rules permitted each state only a single vote, they steadily overrode him. But soon it would be very much worth Hamilton's while to return. For during the first two weeks in July the proceedings dramatically neared complete collapse. And then, perhaps frightened by the possibility of total failure, the Convention finally hammered out a deal that not only held the delegates to the end but ultimately produced a daring blueprint for a federal constitution. It would, in time, substantially govern the most powerful nation on Earth.

From the viewpoint of high statesmanship, the pressure for compromise was strong. All the delegates knew they were laboring under the critical eye of history in the cause of as yet untried liberties. "What a triumph for our enemies. ... to find that we are incapable of governing ourselves," George Washington wrote, "and that systems founded on the basis of equal liberty are merely ideal and fallacious." No delegate doubted that stronger government of some sort was needed to replace the toothless Articles of Confederation. After the Revolution, national authority had become almost a joke. The Congress had no real power to tax, regulate commerce, enforce foreign treaties; and criminals who crossed state lines were likely to go scot-free, since extradition was almost unheard of.

Worse still, the beggar government had gone virtually broke. Seven of the states, and the Congress as well, had been churning out paper money until, as pamphleteer Tom Paine once memorably put it, their paper was worth less than hobnails and wampum. Delegates to the Philadelphia Convention, some of whom had to ride or sail as much as 600 miles through spring mud or tides to get there, were obliged to change money into Pennsylvania shillings, the local coinage, as though entering a foreign country. Shipping states in the North wanted more laws to help them compete for world commerce against cut-rate British cargo rates. But most of the agricultural South was opposed to any protective ordinance that would drive up costs for its comfortable export trade in tobacco, indigo and rice.

Division and danger were everywhere. Beyond their economic squeeze the British were still a clear potential threat to American nationhood. The Union Jack still flew over the western posts where fur traders gathered pelts for London glove and hat makers. Former ally France desperately wanted to collect its wartime loans. Spain, another wartime friend, still controlled Florida, and was conniving for control of trade in the wild, fast-growing western reaches that stretched to the Mississippi, America's border under the terms of the 1783 Treaty of Paris. Spain had closed the Mississippi to American trade at New Orleans, and the river was the only shipping route from much of the western wilderness. Indeed, Georgia, which claimed land running from Savannah clear to the Mississippi, had just declared martial law in fear of Indians and Spaniards.

For more than a decade settlers had been flooding west over the mountains. Since early February 1787 alone, more than 1,000 flatboats had headed west on the Ohio carrying 18,000 pioneers, with 12,000 horses, cattle and sheep. These rude frontiersmen did not see eye to eye with the rich planters of Virginia or with the Eastern seaboard traders of New York, Philadelphia and Boston. Not at all. Would these immigrants to the west form into new states or, God forbid, new countries under the protection of some foreign power? If as states, would their votes be equal to those of the original thirteen? Would, say, Virginia's laws and contracts under the Confederation hold up in a separate, sovereign Kentucky, or separate, sovereign anywhere else, such as "Transylvania," part of what is now Kentucky and Tennessee, to name just one other would-be western state then

taking shape? And might these new states hold slaves or be free? "I dread the cold and sower temper of the back countries," said peg-legged, urbane lawyer and Pennsylvania delegate Gouverneur Morris, sounding very like any sober Briton contemplating the surly, separatist mood of colonial immigrants 15 years earlier.

Here was a set of time bombs that a young nation with huge, unorganized territories, whatever government it chose, must try to defuse as quickly as possible.

Some central control was crucial, but how much would be enough and yet not too much? Fear of an executive, or any central government for that matter, was strong in most delegates. They had fought for more than six years to throw off the distant, and not too onerous, rule of George III and his ministry. That helped explain both the toothlessness of the Articles of Confederation, and why they now defined each former colony represented at this Convention as a "sovereign and independent" state. James Madison, idealistic, politically relentless, the man who more than any other had brought the Convention into existence, spoke for all of them when he observed that "all men having power ought to be distrusted to a certain degree."

Almost as much, though, they feared the tyranny of the majority, any majority. And they knew that earlier attempts at creating anything like a democratic republic had failed. They had it from the much-admired Montesquieu, the world's leading authority on stable government, that democracies were unstable, that anything like a large republic was impossible to govern. Trying to regulate so vast and diverse a land as the United States (if there ever were to be a United States), as one Yankee wit put it, would be a bit like attempting "to rule Hell by prayer."

Besides, the small states wanted to know, what would happen to them when they were at the mercy of their large and populous neighbors? The same was true of the Southern states vis-à-vis the North. Beyond that lay the question of slavery, mentioned by name at the Convention as little as possible because the

delegates knew from the beginning that confrontation over it might wreck any chance they had of agreeing on *any* effective central power. They were there, after all, not to abolish slavery but to shape, against great odds, a stable government that could maintain democratic order as freedom evolved. Though slavery's existence contradicted the terms of the Declaration of Independence they did not seriously discuss abolition. However hotly individual delegates might inveigh against it, slavery was still legally practiced in all but one of the sovereign states; the obnoxious slave trade itself had been outlawed, or sharply discouraged, by only seven. Every delegate understood that slaves were legally private property and, in the South, worth millions. Every delegate understood that under English common law, the protection of property had served as the foundation of all political rights.

Yet at first the Convention moved swiftly, far faster than anyone had expected. Even when disagreements and contentious vote taking occurred (over the course of nearly four months there would be more than 569 votes taken), the proceedings, early on at least, did not bog down.

Mostly this was due to the advance lobbying and planning of Madison, a Virginia planter by birth, but by trade perhaps the most farsighted and perceptive politician and political analyst alive. From 1780 to 1783 he served as a hardworking delegate in the Continental Congress, and from bitter experience while confronting petty state rivalry as he tried to get the states to pay for the war against Britain, Madison had come to the conclusion that the country might not survive at all without a drastic change in the "partition of power" between the states and the nation. To save the tottering Union he had studied past attempts at democracy; made himself an expert economist; helped enlist the reluctant Washington's support for this Convention; and nurtured an outline, condensed into 15 "resolves," officially known as the Virginia Plan, for totally overhauling the Articles of Confederation.

Madison was small, some said no more than five feet tall, with a voice that could scarcely carry across a crowded room. So a friend and fellow Virginian, Edmund Randolph, was chosen to speak for the resolves—to be, as Madison later put it, the "organ on the occasion." Six feet tall, handsome, a man "of distinguished talents, and in the habit of public speaking," Randolph was already, at 33, the Governor of Virginia, the most important state for any such Convention, being as it was both large and at the same time Southern and agricultural and so able to influence states least likely to favor strong central government. Hardly had the Convention opened than Randolph had the floor, and variously shocked and delighted the delegates with Madison's distilled ideas.

The rough structure of what Madison (and Randolph) urged is familiar to us today—indeed, at the time, six of the states had constitutions roughly similar in shape. A government divided into three parts: executive, legislative and judicial, variously elected and appointed. And as a rough form the Convention swiftly agreed to it. Easy passage was also given to the idea of a bicameral legislature, a fixture everywhere but Georgia and Pennsylvania. The Virginia Plan's provision for popular election of the lower house also was accepted, though it would come up again for bitter dispute. So, in fact, would virtually everything else. The real trouble, though, lay in the proposals for what sort of power each house would have, and on what numerical (and voting) basis representatives would be chosen.

"An individual independence of the States," Madison had written, "is utterly irreconcilable. . . . Let national Government be armed with positive and complete authority." He wanted to extend his "national supremacy" to the judiciary as well, and noted that in order "to give the new system its proper energy," all this executive power should be "ratified by the authority of the people."

The words "national" and "supreme" exploded through the hall when Randolph read them, imperiling sacred creeds. During the war with Britain, New Jersey troops had refused to swear allegiance to the Confederation, declaring "New Jersey is our country." New York delegate John Lansing, dead set against a new constitution anyway, promptly

scalded this "triple-headed monster, as deep and wicked a conspiracy as ever was invented in the darkest ages against the liberties of a free people." Rising to challenge Randolph, South Carolina's Charles Pinckney, a dandy and later a Congressman, demanded: I wish to know if you "mean to abolish the State Governments altogether."

With characteristic mildness and courtesy, Randolph explained that he had merely "meant to introduce" some general propositions. And indeed, to others, this nationalist concept seemed exactly what anarchic America needed. Among them, Pennsylvania's James Wilson declared: "We must bury all local interests and distinctions."

The Convention might have broken down right there, except for two procedural devices that the delegates wisely adopted. The first was that no vote on any matter would be binding until a final vote was taken on a full, finished text of the Constitution. That way, no delegate would feel he was being pressured, and collectively, with a chance to reflect and reexamine, they all might produce a better document to place before the judgment of their countrymen.

Through another bit of cautious wisdom, they decided to keep the debates secret. Thomas Jefferson, in France as American Minister, protested in a letter "so abominable a precedent," yet not a single delegate objected. Guards were posted every day at the door. And at one point Washington, who hardly spoke in his role as President of the Convention, rose with a piece of paper in his hand. It was, he said sternly, a copy of their proceedings someone had dropped on the State House floor. If the newspapers ever got hold of such documents, the General scolded, their revelations could "disturb the public repose by premature speculations. I know not whose Paper it is," he continued, "but there it is." He tossed the paper on a table with the comment "let him who owns it take it," then bowed and walked out.

"It is something remarkable," delegate William Pierce of Georgia recalled, "that no Person ever owned that Paper."

As a result of what was essentially a gentleman's agreement about tight secu-

rity, no one but the delegates really knew what was said in the hall until 53 years later when Madison's widow released the meticulous notes he had copied out each night, a record of the debate that, translated into direct dialogue, has been used ever since in dramatic accounts of the Convention. Madison was convinced to the end that secrecy had given delegates freedom to speak with nearly complete candor, and even to change their minds, often several times, as they never would have done if each word had been shared with the press or with their volatile constituencies. "If the debates had been public," Madison later wrote, "no constitution would ever have been adopted."

Indeed the public might have erupted early over some of the arguments about the power and structure of the proposed executive branch. When Wilson put forward a motion for a single President, even Randolph boggled; he preferred an executive council. Of special concern, too, was the proposition that the President have veto power over laws written by the proposed National Legislature. "But why might not a Catiline or a Cromwell arise in this Country as well as in others?" South Carolina's Pierce Butler wanted to know. George Mason spoke darkly about "hereditary Monarchy."

Benjamin Franklin was worried too. Pennsylvania, after all, had an 11-man Executive Council. But everyone knew that if a national government were devised, George Washington would be elected the first President of the United States. They knew, too, that he had once been offered virtual dictatorship of the troubled country and steadfastly refused. With that in mind, though still distrustful of human nature, Franklin concluded, "The first man put at the helm will be a good one," but then added, "Nobody knows what sort may come afterwards." It took 60 different votes before the Convention finally agreed to a single President with a legislative veto—albeit a veto that two-thirds of the Congress could, as it still can, override.

Many men who arrived in Philadelphia fearful of executive power, and seeing states' rights as the best bulwark against an overreaching central government with a tendency to fall under the control of powerful interests, were impressed by Madison's reassurances. In a startling speech that contradicted Montesquieu's political theories, Madison refuted the argument that huge size and a large, diverse population were a hazard to stable democratic government. Quite the reverse. The unified Virginia Plan, he said, would so "enlarge the sphere and thereby divide the community into so great a number of interests . . . that . . . a majority will not be likely at the same moment to have a common interest . . . and . . . in case they should have such an interest, they may not be apt to unite in the pursuit of it."

Numerous standards were put forward as qualifications for serving as a national senator or representative. Many remain in the Constitution today. One that does not is the possession of property. If a man held property, it was estimated, the more substantial a citizen his interest would make him; he was likely to have a thoughtful, sober stake in stable government. After all, the delegates in the State House were mostly lawyers, bankers, merchants or plantation owners. Twenty-one of them had fought in the Revolution, 24 had served in the Continental Congress and, together with the leading figures from smaller states, they felt they had created the nation.

In June, debate began more and more to home in on the question over which the Convention soon almost foundered. Not only who would elect the representatives to the National Legislature, whatever their quality, but above all, how those representatives might be apportioned. According to the steadily evolving Virginia Plan, members of the first house (what we now call the House of Representatives) were to be chosen by the people for terms of three years.

For the other house (or Senate) representatives were to be chosen by the state legislatures for seven years. The aim was to create a lower house directly answerable to the people on a short-term basis, balanced by a less volatile, more elite body (a "House of Lords," opponents were to brand it) that did not need to worry about quick, popular complaint. Representation in both chambers would be portioned out roughly according to the number of people in each state, the slaves included, but with each slave to be counted as three-fifths of a person—a bizarre bit of arithmetic that the Continental Congress had first settled on in 1783.

Many delegates were still a long way from swallowing such a radical direct-election principle. "[I am] opposed to the election by the people," said Roger Sherman of Connecticut bluntly. A lean, sharp-nosed man, "cunning as the devil" (even his friends put it that way), Sherman was born poor but had risen by shrewd industry as a farmer and lawyer. The people, he continued, "want information and are constantly liable to be misled." Delaware's John Dickinson scornfully defined the people as "those multitudes without property and without principle, with which our Country like all others, will in time abound."

Present-day politicians would not dare say such things, even if they believed them. But in 1787 these views were widespread. The debates were secret, and to many men interested in stable government they seemed the essence of common sense. It was a time, after all, when not a single government in the world received its power directly from the people; two years later, in the name of "the people," the uncontrolled power of the mob in France would eventually lead to a bloodbath, followed by an emperor. Elbridge Gerry, the man who would one day give his name to the word gerrymander, had been a firebrand during America's struggle against George III. Now, he told the delegates, he was convinced that "The evils we experience flow from the excess of democracy."

Many delegates disagreed. Whatever they may have felt about the mob, it was clear to them that the power of any just government must derive from the people, however much they and all other contending political forces needed to be hedged around with checks and balances. Along with Madison, one apparently surprising proponent of power to the people turned out to be James Wilson of Philadelphia, a rich businessman and lawyer to the monied interests, including, during the Revolution, men accused of still being loyal to George III. George Mason of Virginia was another. Born to the privilege and responsibility of a 5,000-acre plantation, with more slaves than any delegate, he not only espoused abolition but now observed that since the "people will be represented; they ought therefore to choose the Representatives."

Gouverneur Morris, of course, disagreed. Other tempers were rising, along with the thermometer, as delegates fixed on points of conflict. Gunning Bedford of Delaware continued to denounce population-based representation as disastrous to the interest of small states. Virginia's population of 750,000 was almost 13 times that of Delaware; Pennsylvania, second largest of the original thirteen, had 430,000. How could the rights of a small state survive in such a government? "It seems as if Pennsylvania and Virginia . . . wished to provide a system in which they would have an enormous and monstrous influence," Bedford asserted. And later he thundered at the large-state delegates, "*I do not, gentlemen, trust you.*"

But the Delaware delegate really jolted the Convention when he said, the "small [states] will find some foreign ally of more honor and good faith, who will take them by the hand and do them justice."

This dangerous turn in the arguments, raising the specter of a separate American confederacy under the thumb of Britain, Spain or France, brought the proceedings to their most desperate impasse. Madison said that the small states could depart if so inclined; they would have to join later, anyway. Wilson, equally out of patience, derided states, large and small, as "imaginary creatures," divisive, obsolescent. George Read, of Bedford's own delegation, grandly declared, "The State Governments must be swept away."

Small wonder, in the face of such wrangling, that delegates were all but ready to give up. Hamilton's conscience later brought him back. Mason, who stayed through to the end, declared that if he were doing this for money, a thousand pounds a day would not be enough pay. Even George Washington admitted, "I *almost* despair of seeing a favourable issue to the proceedings of the Convention, and do therefore repent having had any agency in the business."

Yet those days in early July, the worst times for the delegates, turned out to be the best times for the future United States of America. From them came a political compromise that saved the Convention and led to a Constitution that could be presented to the country with more than a fighting chance of ratification.

As the hot words flew, and proposals and counterproposals were voted on, one of the blows struck in the direction of possible compromise came from an unexpected quarter, Roger Sherman, who seemed to be changing his mind about the direct vote of the people.

According to Madison's notes, "Mr. Sherman proposed that the proportion of suffrage in the 1st branch should be according to the respective number of free inhabitants [a clear advantage for the large states]; and that in the second branch or Senate, each State should have one vote and no more." Thus could small states retain power beyond the size of their electorates. Like most useful ideas, the one Sherman presented was both simple and functional. But like all compromises it contained elements that each major faction—small states, large states, nationalists and states-righters—regarded either as imperfect or outright distasteful.

Also proposed by John Dickinson of Delaware and Oliver Ellsworth of Connecticut, the compromise was voted down. But the idea that "in *one* branch the *people,* ought to be represented; in the *other,* the *States*" did not disappear. Wilson and most other nationalists still wanted as little significant residue of state sovereignty as possible. Some delegates were outraged by the very idea that, say, tiny Rhode Island, which had boycotted the Convention and had been heavily engaged in smuggling before the Revolution, could vote with the august weight of Virginia or Massachusetts.

Like Wilson and Read, Madison was out of patience with state rivalries and petty fears of being dominated by neighbors. Such things seemed likely to destroy the dream of shaping the birth of a great republic. In his direct and prescient way he now let the delegates know where the real historic peril lay. "The great danger to our general government," said Madison, "is the great southern and northern interests of the continent being opposed to each other." The states, he also pointed out, are "divided into different interests not by their difference of size . . . but principally from their having or not having slaves."

It was true. Even with the help of a three-fifths count on slaves, if a National Congress based on proportional representation were put together right now, the North would have 31 votes to 25 for the South. Furthermore, during the same summer up in New York, the Confederation Congress was trying to put the finishing touches on an ordinance for the newly won Northwest Territories (previously claimed by Virginia, among others, and extending to the headwaters of the Mississippi) by which slavery was forbidden, currently and in the future, when these territories might become states.

Pierce Butler of South Carolina now offered an astonishing proposal—to add to the South's voting power by counting slaves equally with whites in apportioning the number of national delegates each state had. Gouverneur Morris riposted that Pennsylvanians, anyway, would not stand for "being put on a footing with slaves." Crusty Elbridge Gerry had already observed that property should not be involved in rules for political representation. Otherwise why should not horses and cattle in the North, like slaves in the South, count toward voting totals.

As the floor debate sank to the level of bitter farce, Wilson turned the discussion skillfully, in a slightly different direction. He spoke of taxation, but, as had been proposed earlier, taxation used as a way of measuring voting powers. Taxes came from property. Slaves were property. America had been founded on the principle that there be no taxation without representation.

The argument moved the debate forward. Delegates began working on various ratios whereby representatives of the South in the legislature would not be at the immediate mercy of the North. They sought ways of expanding the number of representatives in the future so as to preserve political balance as the country grew—and populous western states came in. And it was, indeed, this vision of a threatening future, when the large and powerful Eastern states might find themselves in the minority, that made them see there was merit in having at least one house in which all states had the same number of representatives regardless of population.

And at last, with the main issue so clearly defined, but with the regional voting blocks now slightly divided among themselves, the Convention gained momentum once more under the rising banner of compromise. When the strongest nationalists, including Madison and Wilson, clung to their objections about the proposed arrangement for the Senate, delegates thought of something Ben Franklin, ever the conciliator, had raised earlier—an idea made to order for propertied men. Why not have the first house control all money bills?

For the populous states this appeared to be a nice trade-off—dollars, and the power of appropriating public funds, against a loss of political clout in the Senate—and it became part of a package that was moving toward a floor vote.

Madison still did not like it. The dispute "ended in the compromise," Madison later wrote Jefferson, "but very much to the dissatisfaction of several members from the large States." The deal left the national government far weaker than Hamilton would have wanted, too, but he took a non-utopian view. It was not hard, he would suggest, to choose "between anarchy and Convulsion on one side," and the chance of good on the other. South Carolina's John Rutledge eventually voiced the changing mood toward accommodation when, noting that the delegates could not do what they all thought best, he added, "we ought to do something."

And they did. On Monday, July 16, by the narrow vote of five states to four, with one state divided, the Convention passed the Connecticut delegation's much-amended measure, which would soon become known as the Great Compromise. A strong, central government had been agreed upon, but the small states were protected from the large in the Senate, while in the House, the South, with slaves counted as part of population, could not easily be over-borne by the North. It was clear that no other arrangement would be acceptable to a majority. Even so, Madison was openly angry. He had always insisted the supremacy of the central government in the proposed federation must be un-equivocal. Beyond that the idea of Dela-ware as Virginia's equal in the Senate seemed antirepublican to him. But what could he do? The very fact of the Com-promise seemed to prove his perception that in an enormous country only the free play of diverse and contending in-terests could lead to an acceptably bal-anced decision.

As a final concession, Southerners agreed that, after 1808, the slave trade could be prohibited by Congress. Sher-man had noted that the "abolition of slavery seemed to be going on in the United States, and that the good sense of the several States would probably by degrees compleat it." Some conscience-troubled northern Southerns, like Wash-ington, who hated slavery but lived off its production, agreed. They hoped that in 20 years the practice might fade away, a hope made somewhat more reasonable to them because their kind of mixed farming depended less on slaves than did the deep South's. Southerners may have been somewhat reassured by a clause in the Northwest Ordinances mandating the return of fugitive slaves who entered free territory.

Two more exhausting months would pass before their work was finished, but after July 16 the delegates were clearly minded to get the job done. Members of the House, they agreed, would serve two years, not three. There would be two Senators per state, with six-year terms. And they would, indeed, be elected by the state legislators. It was not until 1913 that the 17th Amendment conveyed their elec-tion directly to the people.

Though the Convention established a national judiciary, it never gave the courts specific authority to review leg-islative acts, or to strike them down as unconstitutional. That famous precedent was set in 1803, with the celebrated

Marbury v. Madison case, when arch-federalist John Marshall, Chief Justice during the presidency of anti-federalist Thomas Jefferson, broadly interpreted the new Constitution's breadth and power by declaring an act of Congress unconstitutional. So doing, he balanced for all time the three branches of gov-ernment. He also opened the debate that rages today on how far judges may properly go in interpreting the original text and intent of the Constitution.

In 1787 some delegates believed they had done well to lay down broad prin-ciples rather than an interminable list of strict instructions. Others felt the docu-ment they were completing was far too vague and would fail to be ratified. "I'll be hanged if ever the people of Maryland agree to it," declared Luther Martin.

Martin had company. George Mason had become seriously alienated. Now at the elev-enth hour he chose to ask why the docu-ment had no Bill of Rights. Mason was the spokesman on the point, though he surely had taken his sweet time about bringing it up. He would sooner chop off his right hand, Mason said, "than put it to the Constitution as it now stands." If some things were not changed or added, he wanted "to bring the whole subject before another general Conven-tion." Eager to be finished, the other delegates disagreed and the Convention hurried on.

On September 17, 1787, the day the document was signed, Gouverneur Mor-ris, a master of style to whom the final polishing of prose had been assigned, listened proudly as the finished work was read aloud to the 41 delegates who had stayed for the last act. It began with the ringing phrase, "We the People." With Franklin's special blessing, Morris had also fashioned a particular ending to the Constitution: "Done in Conven-tion by the Unanimous Consent of the States present this Seventeenth Day of September."

It was a neat device, with a double purpose. Once signed, the Constitution would go to the Congress and then to state ratifying conventions. To carry the country, it needed all the help it could get and preferably should emerge from

the State House with unanimous ap-proval. For, as one Philadelphian, not in the Convention but clearly in the know, had lately noted, "no sooner will the chicken be hatch'd, but every one will be for plucking a feather." Franklin hoped the insertion of the words "the States" would keep the bird whole. As state delegates, he purred, gentlemen could approve the Constitution with their signatures while as individuals they retained personal reservations.

The artful measure nearly succeeded. Delegate after delegate stepped forward to sign. But some, most notably George Mason and Randolph, refused their sig-natures. They held firm though warned both of the "infinite mischief" the lack of their names might do at the ratifying conventions, where nine of the thirteen states would have to approve the docu-ment, and of the "anarchy and Convul-sions" that might well ensue if the Constitution were rejected.

Predictably, it was in Virginia that one key ratification fight took place. In Richmond, Madison spearheaded one side, Mason and states' rightist Patrick ("give me liberty or give me death") Henry the other. "Who authorized them to speak the language of *We the People*," Henry roared, "instead of, *We the States*?"

If a bare majority of Congress could make laws, he argued, the "situation of our western citizens is dreadful. You have a bill of rights to defend you against state government [yet] you have none against Congress. . . . May they not pronounce all slaves free . . . ?" The tor-rent of Henry's words, steadily rebutted by Madison, lasted 23 days. Sometimes he made five speeches a day, and his list of proposed rights and amendments that must be added to the Constitution grew to 40. But eventually, though he didn't vote aye, he ceased fire, partly yielding to the promise that a Bill of Rights would be added after ratification.

Within two years, the national Con-gress under the new Constitution proposed the first ten amendments that make up the present Bill of Rights. But the historic is-sue of whether a young nation, so dedi-cated and so constituted, could long endure, was anything but settled.

The Founding Fathers, Conditional Antislavery, and the Nonradicalism of the American Revolution

William W. Freehling

By 1972, two years after publishing "The Editorial Revolution," I more clearly understood that the story of the events of 1860 must begin with the Founding Fathers. But I still hoped that my narrative of disunion could begin in 1850. I thus decided to publish my thoughts on the earlier history separately. The resulting first version of this essay, entitled "The Founding Fathers and Slavery," appeared in American Historical Review in 1972.[1] "Founding Fathers" has been widely republished. I nevertheless regret its overemphasis on antislavery accomplishment. My changed title reflects my partial disenchantment. I am grateful to the American Historical Review for permission to republish some of the previous essay in this much-altered form.

When I wrote the original essay, historians were increasingly scoffing that the Founding Fathers ignored the Declaration of Independence's antislavery imperatives.[2] That denunciation has continued to swell despite my countervailing emphasis, indeed partly because of my overstated argument.[3] My original essay, as David Brion Davis pointed out, too much conflated Thomas Jefferson

and the Founding Fathers.[4] The essay also erroneously portrayed the Founding Fathers as pragmatic reformers, eager to assault slavery whenever political realities permitted. They were in truth skittish abolitionists, chary of pouncing on antislavery opportunity. The Founding Fathers freed some slaves but erected obstacles against freeing others. They also sometimes moved past those obstacles for crass rather than ideological reasons. Thus historians who dismissed the Founding Fathers as antislavery reformers could easily dismiss my argument.

I have come to be more unhappy about the historians who appropriated "Founding Fathers." They have used my contention that the Founding Fathers chipped away at slavery to support their contention that the Declaration of Independence inspired a true American social revolution.[5] I find that argument unpersuasive, even about the white male minority. The notion is still less persuasive about African Americans and about other members of the nonwhite and nonmale majority, which means that the contention mischaracterizes American society writ large. Neither women nor African Americans nor Native Ameri-

cans conceived that the American Revolution revolutionized their lives. Their position is relevant if we are to widen American history beyond Anglo-Saxon males, to write the story of a multicultural civilization.

Some historians answer that the majority's definition of a proper social revolution is irrelevant for judging the American Revolution, since only the white male minority had the power to define the event and the society. Such positions tend to narrow American history into solely a history of the white male power structure. But in the specific case of slavery, the elite's standard for judgment widens perspectives. Wealthy revolutionaries' criterion, no less than poorer Americans' criterion and posterity's criterion, required a proper American Revolution to include the slaves. By that universal yardstick, the Founding Fathers achieved no social revolution.

The Founding Fathers instead set us on our nonrevolutionary social history. Despite their dismay at slavery, America's worst multicultural dislocation, they both timidly reformed and established towering bulwarks against reform, not least because many of them *preferred a monoracial America. I have revised this essay to include more of the bulwarks against antislavery, in company with those who think the Founding Fathers did nothing to further abolition. But I hope the revision will yield more tolerance for my continued belief, and latter-day slaveholders' worried conviction, that the Founding Fathers also did a most nonrevolutionary something to weaken slaveholders' defenses. For without that ambivalent perspective on the nation's founders, we can understand neither the subsequent meandering road toward emancipation nor America's persistently nonradical road toward a radically new multicultural social order, based on the ethics of the Declaration of Independence.*

The American Revolutionaries intended to achieve a political revolution. They brilliantly succeeded. They split the British Empire, mightiest of the world's powers. They destroyed monarchical government in what became the United States. They recast the nature of republican ideology and structure with the federal Constitution of 1787. Over the next generation, their revolution helped undermine their own aristocratic conception of republicanism, leading to Andrew Jackson's very different egalitarian republicanism.

With a single exception, the men of 1776 intended no parallel revolution in the culture's social institutions. The Founders had no desire to confiscate property from the rich and give it to the poor. They gave no thought to appropriating familial power from males and giving it to females, or seizing land from whites and returning it to Native Americans. They embraced the entire colonial white male system of social power—except for slave holders' despotism over slaves. That they would abolish. To judge them by their standards, posterity must ask whether this, their sole desired social revolution, was secured.

The Founding Fathers partially lived up to their revolutionary imperative: They barred the African slave trade from American ports; they banned slavery from midwestern territories; they dis-

solved the institution in northern states; and they diluted slavery in the Border South. Yet the Founding Fathers also backed away from their revolutionary imperative: They delayed emancipation in the North; they left antislavery half accomplished in the Border South; they rejected abolition in the Middle South; and they expanded slaveholder power in the Lower South. These retreats both inhibited final emancipation where slavery had been damaged and augmented slave holders' resources where slavery had been untouched. The advances and retreats set off both an antislavery process and a proslavery counteroffensive. Slavery would eventually be abolished, partly because the Founding Fathers shackled the slaveholders. But emancipation would be so long delayed—partly because the Founders rearmed the slavocracy—that the slavery issue would epitomize the social nonradicalism of the American Revolution.

1

Since every generation rewrites history, most historians achieve only fading influence. One twentieth-century American historical insight, however, seems unlikely to fade. In his multivolume history of slavery as a recognized problem, David Brion Davis demonstrated that throughout most of history, humankind failed to recognize any problem in slavery.[6] Then around the time of the American Revolution, Americans suddenly, almost universally, saw the institution as a distressing problem. Davis showed that throughout the Western world, a changed Enlightenment mentality and a changing industrial order helped revolutionize sensibility about slavery. The American political revolution quickened the pace of ideological revolution. Slavery, as the world's most antirepublican social system, seemed particularly hypocritical in the world's most republican nation. Most American Revolutionaries called King George's enslavement of colonists and whites' enslavement of blacks parallel tyrannies. "Let us either cease to enslave our fellow-men," wrote the New England cleric Nathaniel Niles,

"or else let us cease to complain of those that would enslave us."[7]

Yet the Founding Fathers' awareness of slavery as a problem never deepened into the perception that slavery's foundations were a problem. A slaveholder's claim to slaves was first of all founded on property rights; and the men of 1776 never conceived of redistributing private property or private power to ensure that all men (or women!) were created equal. They believed that governments, to secure slaves' natural right to liberty, must pay slaveholders to surrender the natural right to property. That conviction put a forbidding price tag on emancipation.

The price escalated because these discoverers of slavery as a problem (and nondiscoverers of maldistributed property as a problem) also failed to see that other foundation of slavery, racism, as problematic.[8] Thomas Jefferson, like most of his countrymen, suspected that blacks were created different, inferior in intellectual talents and excessive in sexual ardency. Jefferson also worried that freed blacks would precipitate racial warfare. He shrank from abolition, as did most Americans who lived amidst significant concentrations of slaves, unless the freedmen could be resettled outside the republic.[9]

That race removal condition, like the condition that seized property required compensation, placed roadblocks before emancipation. To colonize blacks in foreign lands would have added 25 percent to the already heavy cost of compensated abolition. To coerce a million enslaved humans to leave a republic as a condition for ending coercive slavery could also seem to be a dubious step toward government by consent.

The Founding Fathers' conditional aspiration to free black slaves furthermore had to compete with their unconditional aspiration to build white republics. It was no contest. The American Revolutionaries appreciated all the problems in establishing free government; but that appreciation energized them, inspired them, led to sustained bursts of imaginative remedies. In contrast, these propertied racists exaggerated all the problems in freeing blacks; and that exaggeration paralyzed them, turned them into procrastinators, led to infrequent stabs at limited reforms.

The inhibitions built into the conditional antislavery mentality could be seen even in the Virginia abolitionist who scorned the supposedly necessary conditions. Edward Coles, James Madison's occasional secretary, intruded on Thomas Jefferson's mailbox with demands that the ex-President crusade for emancipation without waiting for slaveholder opposition to relent. Coles himself acted on antislavery imperatives without waiting for action on deportation imperatives. He migrated with his Virginia slaves to almost entirely free-soil Illinois, manumitted all of them, gave each family a 160-acre farm, and provided for the education of those who were underage. After that rare demonstration of how to turn conditional antislavery into unconditional freedom, Coles advised his ex-slaves to return to Africa! The black race, said Coles, might never prosper in the bigoted white republic. That message, coming from that messenger, well conveyed the national mentality that rendered an antislavery revolution impossible.[10]

2

In conditionally antislavery post-Revolutionary America, the more blacks in a local area, the less possibility of emancipation. Where blacks formed a high percentage of the labor force, as in the original Middle South states of North Carolina and Virginia (35 percent enslaved in 1790) and in the original Lower South states of Georgia and South Carolina (41 percent enslaved in 1970), whites' economic aspirations and race phobias overwhelmed conditional antislavery.[11] In contrast, where blacks were less dense and the slavebased economy was noncrucial, as in the original northern states (all under 5 percent enslaved in 1790) and in the original Border South states of Delaware and Maryland (25 percent enslaved in 1790), the inhibiting conditions for antislavery could be overcome—but after revealing difficulties.

In northern states, the sparse numbers of blacks made slavery seem especially unimportant, both economically and racially, to the huge majority of nonslaveholders. The low percentage of blacks, however, made abolition equally unimportant, economically and racially, to most northern citizens. For the Founders to secure emancipation in the North, an unimportant set of economic/racial antislavery imperatives and a conditional strategy for solving the newly perceived slavery problem had to supplement each other, for neither tepid crass motives nor a compromised ideological awakening could, by itself, overwhelm a vigorous proslavery minority.[12]

That vigor will come as a shock to those who think slavery was peculiar to the South. Yet northern slaveholders fought long and hard to save the institution in temperate climes. Although neither slavery nor emancipation significantly influenced the northern economy, the ownership of humans vitally influenced northern slaveholders' cash flow. Slaveholders made money using slavery up North, and they could always sell slaves for several hundred dollars down South. These crass motives of a few could never have held back an ideological surge of the many had a disinterested majority passionately believed that illegitimate property in humans must be unconditionally seized. But since northern nonslaveholders conceded that this morally suspect property had legal sanction, the struggle for emancipation in the North was long a stalemate.

The only exception was far northward, in New Hampshire, Vermont, and Massachusetts. In those upper parts of New England, the extreme paucity of blacks, a few hundred in each state, led to the phenomenon conspicuously absent elsewhere: total abolition, achieved with revolutionary swiftness, soon after the Revolution. But in the more southerly New England states of Connecticut and Rhode Island, and in the mid-Atlantic states of Pennsylvania, New Jersey, and New York, where percentages of blacks were in the 1 to 5 percent range, emancipation came exceedingly gradually, with antirevolutionary evasions.

Blacks' creeping path to northern freedom commenced in Pennsylvania in 1780, where the Western Hemisphere's first so-called post-nati emancipation law was passed.[13] Post-nati abolition meant freedom for only those born after the law was enacted and only many years after their birth. The formula enabled liberty-loving property holders to split the difference between property rights and human rights. A post-nati law required that no then-held slave property be seized. Only a property not yet on earth was to be freed, and only on some distant day. Accordingly, under the Pennsylvania formula, emancipation would eventually arrive only for slaves thereafter born and only when they reached twenty-eight years of age. Slaveholders thus could keep their previously born slaves forever and their future-born slaves throughout the best years for physical labor. That compromised emancipation was the best a conditional abolition mentality could secure, even in a northern Quaker state where only 2.4 percent of the population was enslaved.

Connecticut and Rhode Island passed post-nati edicts soon after Pennsylvania set the precedent. New York and New Jersey, the northern states with the most slaves, delayed decades longer. New York slaveholders managed to stave off laws freeing the future-born until 1799, and New Jersey slaveholders, until 1804. So it took a quarter century after the revolution for these northern states to enact post-nati antislavery—in decrees that would free no one for another quarter century.

Slaves themselves injected a little revolutionary speed into this nonrevolutionary process. Everywhere in the Americas, slaves sensed when mastery was waning and shrewdly stepped up their resistance, especially by running away. An increase of fugitive slaves often led to informal bargains between northern masters and slaves. Many northern slaveholders promised their slaves liberty sooner than post-nati laws required if slaves provided good service in the interim. Thus did perpetual servitude sometimes shade gradually into fixed-time servitude and more gradually still into wage labor, with masters retaining years of forced labor and slaves gaining liberty at a snail's pace. In 1817, New York's legislature declared that the weakening system must end by 1827.[14]

Although New Jersey and Pennsylvania never followed suit, by 1840 only a few slaves remained in the North. By 1860, thirteen New Jersey slaves were the last vestige of northern slavery.

For thousands of northern slaves, however, the incremental post-nati process led not to postponed freedom in the North but to perpetual servitude in the South. When New York and New Jersey masters faced state laws that would free slaves on a future date, they could beat the deadline. They could sell a victimized black to a state down south, which had no post-nati law. One historian estimates that as many as two-thirds of New York slaves may never have been freed.[15]

Despite this reactionary outcome for some northern slaves and the long delay in liberation of others, the post-nati tradition might still be seen as a quasi-revolutionary movement if it had spread to the South. But every southern state rejected post-nati conceptions, even Delaware, and even when President Abraham Lincoln offered extra federal inducements in 1861. Instead of state-imposed gradual reform, the two original Border South states, Delaware and Maryland, experimented with an even less revolutionary process: voluntary manumission by individual masters. Delaware, which contained 9,000 slaves and 4,000 free blacks in 1790, contained 1,800 slaves and 20,000 free blacks in 1860. Maryland, with 103,000 slaves and 8,000 free blacks in 1790, contained 87,000 slaves and 84,000 free blacks in 1860. The two states' proportions of black freedmen to black slaves came to exceed those of Brazil and Cuba, countries that supposedly had a monopoly on Western Hemisphere voluntary emancipation.

Just as fugitive slaves accelerated post-nati emancipation in Pennsylvania, New York, and New Jersey, so the threat of runaways sometimes speeded manumissions in Delaware and Maryland. Especially in border cities such as Baltimore and Wilmington, masters could profitably agree to liberate slaves at some future date if good labor was thereby secured before manumission. A hard-working slave for seven years was a bargain compared to a slave who might run

away the next day, especially since the slavemaster as republican, upon offering a favorite bondsman future freedom, won himself a good conscience as well as a better short-term worker. This combination of altruism and greed, however, ultimately lost the slaveholder a long-term slave. That result, portending a day when no slaves would remain in northern Maryland, was deplored in southern Maryland tobacco belts, where manumission slowed and blacks usually remained enslaved.[16]

The Maryland-Delaware never-completed manumission movement failed to spread south of the Border South, just as the long-delayed northern post-nati movement never spread south of the mid-Atlantic. True, in Virginia, George Washington freed all his many slaves. But that uncharacteristically extensive Middle South manumission came at a characteristic time. President Washington profited from his slaves while living and then freed them in his last will and testament. President Thomas Jefferson freed a more characteristic proportion of his many Middle South slaves—10 percent. Meanwhile, Jefferson's luxurious life-style piled up huge debts, which prevented the rest of his slaves from being manumitted even after his death.

South of Virginia, Jefferson's 10 percent manumission rate exceeded the norm. A master who worked huge gangs of slaves in the pestilential Georgia and South Carolina lowlands rarely freed his bondsmen before or after he died. By 1830, only 2 percent of the South Carolina/Georgia blacks were free, compared to 8.5 percent of the Virginia/North Carolina blacks and 39 percent of the Maryland/Delaware blacks. The revolutionary U.S. sensibility about slavery had, with nonrevolutionary speed, emancipated the North over a half century and compromised slavery in the original two Border South states. But the institution remained stubbornly persistent in the Border South and largely intact in the Middle South; and Lower South states had been left unharmed, defiant, and determined to confine the Founding Fathers' only desired social revolution to the American locales with the lowest percentages of slaves.

3

National considerations of slavery in the Age of the Founding Fathers repeated the pattern of the various states' considerations. During national debates on slavery, many South Carolina and Georgia Revolutionary leaders denounced the new conception that slavery was a problem. Their arguments included every element of the later proslavery polemic: that the Bible sanctioned slavery, that blacks needed a master, that antislavery invited social chaos. They warned that they would not join or continue in an antislavery Union. They sought to retain the option of reopening the African slave trade. In the first Congress after the Constitution was ratified, they demanded that Congress never debate abolition, even if silence meant that representatives must gag their constituents' antislavery petitions.[17]

The Georgians and South Carolinians achieved congressional silence, even though other Southerners and all Northerners winced at such antirepublican intransigence. North of South Carolina, almost every Founding Father called slavery a deplorable problem, an evil necessary only until the conditions for abolition could be secured. The conditions included perpetuating the Union (and thus appeasing the Lower South), protecting property rights (and thus not seizing presently owned slave property), and removing freed blacks (and thus keeping blacks enslaved until they could be deported). The first step in removing blacks from the United States was to stop Africans from coming, and the last step was to deport those already in the nation. In between, conditional antislavery steps were more debatable, and the Upper South's position changed.

The change involved whether slavery should be allowed to spread from old states to new territories. In the eighteenth century, Virginians presumed, to the displeasure of South Carolinians and Georgians, that the evil should be barred from new territories. In 1784, Thomas Jefferson's proposed Southwest Ordinance would have banned slavery from Alabama and Mississippi Territories after 1800. The bill would theoretically have prevented much of the nineteenth-century Cotton Kingdom from importing slaves. The proposal lost in the Continental Congress by a single vote, that of a New Jerseyite who lay ill at home. "The fate of millions unborn," Jefferson later wrote, was "hanging on the tongue of one man, and heaven was silent in that awful moment."[18]

The bill, however, would not necessarily have been awful for future Mississippi and Alabama cotton planters. Jefferson's bill would have allowed planters in these areas to import slaves until 1800. The proposed delay in banning imports into Mississippi and Alabama stemmed from the same mentality, North and South, that delayed emancipation in Pennsylvania, New York, and New Jersey for decades. In Mississippi and Alabama, delay would have likely killed antislavery. Eli Whitney invented the cotton gin in 1793. By 1800, thousands of slaves would likely have been picking cotton in these southwestern areas. Then the property-respecting Founding Fathers probably would not have passed the administrative laws to confiscate Mississippi and Alabama slaves, since the conditional antislavery mentality always backed away from seizing slaves who were legally on the ground. Probabilities aside, the certainty about the proposed Southwestern Ordinance of 1784 remains. The Founding Fathers defeated its antislavery provisions. Nationally no less than locally, they preserved slavery in Lower South climes.

They also retained their perfect record, nationally no less than locally, in very gradually removing slavery from northern habitats. Just as state legislators abolished slavery in northern states, with nonrevolutionary slowness, so congressmen prevented the institution from spreading into the nation's Northwest Territories, with yet more nonradical caution. Although the Continental Congress removed Jefferson's antislavery provisions from the Southwest Ordinance of 1784, congressmen attached antislavery clauses to the Northwest Ordinance of 1787. Slavery was declared barred from the area of the future states of Illinois, Indiana, Michigan, Wisconsin, and Ohio. Antislavery consciousness helped inspire the ban, as did capitalistic consciousness. Upper South tobacco planters in the Continental Congress explicitly declared that they did not wish rival tobacco planters to develop the Northwest.[19]

The history of the Northwest Ordinance exemplified not only the usual combination of selfishness and selflessness, always present whenever the Founders passed an antislavery reform, but also the usual limited and slow antislavery action whenever conditional antislavery scored a triumph. Just as northern post-nati laws freed slaves born in the future, so the national Northwest Ordinance barred the *future* spread of slavery into the Midwest. But had the Northwest Ordinance emancipated the few slaves who presently lived in the area? Only if congressmen passed a supplemental law providing administrative mechanisms to seize present property. That a property-protecting Congress, led by James Madison, conspicuously failed to do, just as property-protecting northern legislatures usually freed only future-born slaves. Congressmen's failure to enforce seizure of the few midwestern slaves indicates again the probability that they would have shunned mechanisms to confiscate the many slaves in Alabama and Mississippi in 1800 had the Southwest Ordinance of 1784 passed.

The few midwestern slaveholders, their human property intact, proceeded to demonstrate, as did New York slaveholders, that slavery could be profitably used on northern farms. Slaveholding farmers soon found allies in midwestern land speculators, who thought more farmers would come to the prairies if more slaves could be brought along. These land speculators, led by the future president William Henry Harrison of Indiana, repeatedly petitioned Congress in the early nineteenth century to repeal the Northwest Ordinance's prohibition on slave imports. But though congressmen would not confiscate present slave property, they refused to remove the ban on future slaves.

Although frustrated, a few stubborn Illinois slaveholders imported black so-called indentured servants who were slaves in all but name. Once again, Congress did nothing to remove these de facto slaves, despite the de jure declaration of the Northwest Ordinance. So when Illinois entered the Union in 1818, Congress had massively discouraged slavery but had not totally ended it. The congressional discouragement kept the number of indentured black servants in Illinois to about nine hundred, compared to the over ten thousand slaves in neighboring Missouri Territory, where Congress had not barred slavery. But those nine hundred victims of the loopholes in the Northwest Ordinance kept the reality of slavery alive in the Midwest until Illinois was admitted to the Union and Congress no longer had jurisdiction over the midwestern labor system.

Then slaveholders sought to make Illinois an official slave state. In 1824, a historic battle occurred in the prairies over a statewide referendum on legalizing slavery. The leader of Illinois's antislavery forces was none other than now-Governor Edward Coles, that ex-Virginian who had moved northward to free his slaves. Coles emphasized that slavery was antithetical to republicanism, while some of his compatriots pointed out that enforced servitude was antithetical to free laborers' economic interests. Once again, as in the Baltimore masters' decisions to manumit slaves and in the congressional decision to ban slavery from the Midwest, economic and moral motives fused. The fusion of selfish and unselfish antislavery sentiments secured 58 percent of Illinois electorate. That too-close-for-comfort margin indicated how much conditional antislavery congressmen had risked when they failed to close those indentured servant loopholes. But in the Midwest as in the North, the new vision of slavery as a problem had finally helped secure abolition—half a century after the American Revolution.

4

While the Founding Fathers belatedly contained slavery from expanding into the Midwest, Thomas Jefferson and his fellow Virginians ultimately abandoned the principle of containment. In 1819–20, when Northerners sought to impose post-nati antislavery on the proposed new slave state of Missouri, Jefferson called the containment of slavery wrong. Slaves should not be restricted to old areas, he explained, for whites would never free thickly concentrated slaves. Only if slaves were thinly spread over new areas would racist whites free them.[20]

Given many Founding Fathers' conviction that emancipation must be conditional on the removal of concentrations of blacks, their latter-day argument that slaves should be diffusely scattered made more sense than their earlier argument that slaves must be prevented from diffusing. Still, the Upper South's retreat from containment of slavery illuminates the forbidding power of that race removal condition. If Upper South Founding Fathers had opted for diffusion of blacks rather than containment in 1787, as they did in 1819–20, even the diluted antislavery provision in the Northwest Ordinance probably would not have passed. Then the already almost-triumphant Illinois slaveholders probably would have prevailed, and slavery would have had a permanent toehold in the North. On the subject of the expansion of slavery into new areas, as in the matter of the abolition of slavery in old states, the Founding Fathers had suffered a total loss in the South, had scored a difficult victory in the North, and had everywhere displayed the tentativeness of so conditional a reform mentality.

5

To posterity, the Virginians' switch from containing slavery in old American areas to diffusing slavery over new American areas adds up to a sellout of antislavery. The Thomas Jeffersons, however, considered the question of whether slavery should be contained or diffused in America to be a relatively minor matter. The major issues were whether blacks should be prevented from coming to America and whether slaves should be deported from America. On these matters, conditional antislavery men never wavered.

In the letter Jefferson wrote at the time of the Missouri Controversy in which he first urged diffusion of blacks within America, he repeated that blacks should eventually be diffused outside the white

republic. Four years later, in his final statement on antislavery, Jefferson stressed again his persistent conditional antislavery solution. His "reflections on the subject" of emancipation, Jefferson wrote a northern Federalist, had not changed for "five and forty years." He would emancipate the "afterborn" and deport them at "a proper age," with the federal government selling federal lands to pay for the deportations. Federal emancipation/colonization raises "some constitutional scruples," conceded this advocate of strict construction of the government's constitutional powers. "But a liberal construction of the Constitution," he affirmed, may go "the whole length."[21]

Jefferson's "whole length" required not only federal funding but also an organization that would resettle blacks outside the United States. That need found fruition in the Upper South's favorite conditional antislavery institution, the American Colonization Society, founded in 1817.[22] William Lloyd Garrison would soon denounce the society as not antislavery at all. But to Jefferson's entire Virginia generation, and to most mainstream Americans in all parts of the country in the 1817–60 period, the American Colonization Society was the best hope to secure an altogether liberated (and lily-white) American populace.

The only significant southern opponent of the society concurred that colonization of blacks could undermine slavery. South Carolinians doubted that the American Colonization Society would remove millions of blacks to its Liberian colony. (The society, in fact, rarely resettled a thousand in one year and only ten thousand in forty-five years.) But South Carolina extremists conceded that an Upper South-North national majority coalition could be rallied for colonization. They also realized that once Congress voted for an emancipation plan, whatever the absurdity of the scheme, abolition might be near. Capitalists would never invest in the property. Slaves would sense that liberation was imminent. Only a suicidal slaveholding class, warned the Carolinians, would take such a chance. Carolinians threatened to secede if Congress so much as discussed the heresy. So con-

gressional colonization discussion halted in the late 1820s, just as South Carolina's disunion threats had halted antislavery discussions in the First Congress.[23]

A few historians have pronounced these South Carolinians to be but bluffers, cynical blusterers who never meant to carry out their early disunion threats.[24] The charge, based solely on the opinion of the few Founding Fathers who wished to defy the Carolinians, does not ring true. Many South Carolina coastal planters lived among 8:1 concentrations of blacks to whites, a racial concentration unheard of elsewhere. The Carolinians farmed expensive miasmic swamplands, unlike the cheaper, healthier slaveholding areas everywhere else. Unless black slaves could be forced to endure the pestilential Carolina jungle, the lushest area for entrepreneurial profits in North America would become economically useless. So enormous a percentage of blacks might also be racially dangerous if freed. South Carolinians' special stake in slavery engendered understandable worry when Northerners and Southerners called slavery an evil that must be removed.

So South Carolinians threatened disunion. Posterity cannot say whether they would have had the nerve to secede if an early national Congress had enacted, for example, Jefferson's conditional antislavery plan of using federal land proceeds to deport slaves. South Carolinians might have early found, as they later discovered, that their nerves were not up to the requirements of bringing off a revolution against every other state. But though they might not have been able to carry out their threats, that hardly means they were bluffing. Their threats were credible because these sincere warriors intended to act, if the nation defied their non-bluff.

Still, the larger point is that so conditional an antislavery mentality was not equipped to test South Carolinians' capacity to carry out their threats, any more than that mentality's compromised worldview was equipped to seize presently owned property from recalcitrant slaveholders. The master spirit of the age was a passion to build white republics, not an inclination to deport black slaves; and South Carolinians threatened to splinter the Union unless congressmen ceased to talk of deporting blacks. The Founding Fathers' priorities prevailed. South Carolina's threats effectively shut off congressional speculation about removing slaves from America. That left only the other major conditional antislavery aspiration still viable: shutting off the flow of Africans to America.

6

South Carolinians long opposed closure of the African slave trade, too. But their opposition to stopping future slaves from traveling to America was mild compared to their opposition to deporting slaves from America. Like the northern slaveholders who could accept emancipation if they had fifty more years to use slaves, South Carolinians could accept the end of the African slave trade if they had twenty more years to import Africans.

Their potential interest in more African imports first surfaced at the beginning of the American national experience. When drafting the Declaration of Independence and cataloging King George's sins, Thomas Jefferson proposed condemning the tyrant for supposedly foisting Africans on his allegedly slavery-hating colonies. South Carolinians bridled at the language. Jefferson deleted the draft paragraph. Although Jefferson was not present at the 1787 Philadelphia Constitutional Convention, history repeated itself. When northern and Upper South delegates proposed that Congress be empowered to end the African slave trade immediately, South Carolinians warned that they would then refuse to join the Union. The issue was compromised. Congress was given authority to close the overseas trade only after 1807. South Carolinians had a guaranteed twenty-year-long opportunity to import African slaves.

In the early nineteenth century, with the emerging Cotton Kingdom avid for more slaves, Carolinians seized their expiring opportunity. In 1803, the state officially opened its ports for the importation of Africans. Some 40,000 Africans landed in the next four years. Assuming the normal course of black natural increase in the Old South, these latest arrivals in the land of liberty multiplied to 150,000 slaves by 1860, or almost 4 percent of the southern total.

Jefferson was President at the moment when Congress could shutter South Carolina's twenty-year window of opportunity. "I congratulate you, fellow-citizens," Jefferson wrote in his annual message of December 2, 1806, "on the approach of the period when you may interpose your authority constitutionally" to stop Americans "from all further participation in those violations of human rights which have been so long continued on the unoffending inhabitants of Africa, and which the morality, the reputation, and the best interests of our country have long been eager to proscribe.[25] Closure of the African slave trade could not take effect until January 1, 1808, conceded Jefferson. Yet the reform, if passed in 1807, could ensure that no extra African could legally land in a U.S. port. In 1807 Congress enacted Jefferson's proposal.

Prompt enactment came in part because almost all Americans beyond South Carolina shared Jefferson's ideological distaste for slavery. The African slave trade seemed especially loathsome to most white republicans. But neither the loathing nor the enactment came wholly because of disinterested republican ideology. Jefferson and fellow racists hated the African slave trade partly because it brought more *blacks* to America. So too South Carolina planters were now willing to acquiesce in the prohibition partly because they considered their forty thousand imports to be enough so-called African barbarians. So too Upper South slave sellers could gain more dollars for their slaves if Cotton South purchasers could buy no more blacks from Africa. With the closure of the African slave trade—as with the Northwest Ordinance and as with the abolition of northern slavery and as with the manumission of Baltimore slaves—republican selflessness came entwined with racist selfishness; and no historian can say whether the beautiful or the ugly contributed the stronger strand.

The closure of the African slave trade emerges in the textbooks as a nonevent, worthy of no more than a sentence. Whole books have been written on the Founding Fathers and slavery without a word devoted to the reform.[26] Yet this law was the jewel of the Founding Fathers' antislavery effort, and no viable assessment of that effort can ignore this far-reaching accomplishment. The federal closure's impact reached as far as Africa. Brazil and Cuba imported over 1.5 million Africans between 1815 and 1860, largely to stock sugar and coffee plantations.[27] Slaveholders in the United States could have productively paid the then-prevailing price for at least that many black imports to stock southwestern sugar and cotton plantations.

The effect of the closure of the African slave trade also reached deep into the slaves' huts and the masters' Big Houses. If the South had contained a million newly landed "raw Africans," as Southerners called those human folk, southern slaveholders would have deployed more savage terror and less caring paternalism to control the strangers. The contest between the United States, where the nineteenth-century overseas slave trade was closed, and Cuba and Brazil, where it was wide open, makes the point. Wherever Latin Americans imported cheap Africans, they drove down slave life expectancies. In the United States, alone among the large nineteenth-century slavocracies, slaves naturally increased in numbers, thanks to less fearful, more kindly masters and to more acculturated, more irreplaceable blacks.

The closure of the African trade also changed the demographical configuration of the South and the nation, to the detriment of slaveholders' political power. When white immigrants shunned the Slave South and voyaged to the free-labor North, the South could not import Africans to compensate. The North grew faster in population, faster in labor supply, faster in industrialization, faster in the ability to seize agricultural territories such as Kansas, and faster in the ability to control congressional majorities. Worse, after African slave trade closure, the Cotton South could race after the free-labor North only by draining slaves from the Border South. The combination of manumissions and African slave trade closure doubly hindered slavery in the most geographically northern slave states. In 1790 almost 20 percent of

American slaves had lived in this Border South tier. By 1860 the figure was down to 11 percent. On the other hand, in 1790 the Lower South states had 21 percent of American slaves, but by 1860, the figure was up to 59 percent. From 1830 to 1860 the percentage of slaves in the total population declined in Delaware from 4 to 1 percent; in Maryland from 23 to 13 percent; in Kentucky from 24 to 19 percent; in Missouri from 18 to 10 percent; and in the counties that would become West Virginia from 10 to 5 percent. By 1860 Delaware, Maryland, Missouri, and the area that would become West Virginia had a lower percentage of slaves than New York had possessed at the time of the Revolution, and Kentucky did not have a much higher percentage. The goal of abolition had become almost as practicable in these border states as it had been in New York in 1776, twenty-five years before the state passed a post-nati law and fifty years before the New York slave was freed. Had no Civil War occurred, fifty years after 1860 is a good estimate for when the last Border South slave might have been freed. Then slavery would have remained in only eleven of the fifteen slave states.

To sum up the antislavery accomplishments in the first American age that considered slavery a problem: When the Founding Fathers were growing up, slavery existed throughout Great Britain's North American colonies. The African slave trade was open. Even in the North, as John Jay of New York reported, "very few . . . doubted the propriety and rectitude" of slavery.[28] When the Founders left the national stage, slavery had been abolished in the North, kept out of the Midwest, and placed on the defensive in the South. A conditional antislavery mentality, looking for ways to ease slavery and blacks out of the country, prevailed everywhere except in the Lower South. If the Founders had done none of this—if slavery had continued in the North and expanded into the Northwest; if a million Africans had been imported to strengthen slavery in the Lower South, to retain it in New York and Illinois, to spread it to Kansas, and to preserve it in the Border South; if no free black population had devel-

oped in Delaware and Maryland; if no conditional antislavery ideology had left Southerners on shaky moral grounds; if, in short, Jefferson and his contemporaries had lifted not one antislavery finger—everything would have been different and far less worrisome for the Lower South slavocracy.

7

But the Founding Fathers also inadvertently empowered a worried Low South to wage its coming struggle. "Inadvertent" is the word, for most American Revolutionaries did not wish to strengthen an intransigent slavocracy, any more than they wished to delay African slave trade closure or to silence congressional consideration of colonization. The problem, again, was that these architects of republicanism cared more about building white republics than about securing antislavery. So opportunities to consolidate a republican Union counted for much and the side effects on slavery counted for little—when side effects on slavery where even noticed.

Thus at the Constitutional Convention, Lower South slaveholders, by threatening not to join the Union unless their power was strengthened, secured another Union-saving compromise. Slaves were to be counted as three-fifths of a white man, when the national House of Representatives was apportioned. This constitutional clause gave Southerners around 20 percent more congressmen than their white numbers justified. Since the numbers of members in the president-electing electoral college were based on the numbers of congressmen, the South also gained 20 percent more power over the choice of chief executive. An unappetizing number illustrates the point. The South received one extra congressman and presidential elector throughout the antebellum years as a result of South Carolina's 1803–07 importation of Africans.

The Founding Fathers also augmented Lower South territory. In 1803, Thomas Jefferson's Louisiana Purchase from France added the areas of Louisiana, Arkansas, and Missouri to the Union. In 1819, James Monroe's treaty with Spain secured the areas of Florida,

Southern Alabama, and Southern Mississippi. A desire to protect slavery was only marginally involved in the Florida purchase and not at all involved in the Louisiana Purchase. Presidents Jefferson and Monroe primarily sought to protect national frontiers. But they were so determined to bolster national power and gave so little thought to the consequences for slaveholder power that their calculations about blacks could not offset their diplomatic imperatives. Their successful diplomacy yielded territories already containing slaves. Then their antislavery mentality was too conditional to conceive of confiscating slave property. The net result: The Founding Fathers contributed four new slave states and parts of two others to the eventual fifteen slave states in the Union. That increased the South's power in the U.S. Senate 27 percent and the Lower South's economic power enormously.

If the Founding Fathers had done none of this—if they had not awarded the South the extra congressmen and presidential electors garnered from the three-fifths clause; if they had not allowed South Carolina to import forty thousand more Africans; if they had not acquired Florida, Louisiana, Arkansas, Missouri, southern Mississippi, and southern Alabama; if in short they had restricted the slavocracy to its pre-1787 power and possessions—the situation would have been far bleaker for the Cotton Kingdom. Indeed, without the Founding Fathers' bolstering of slaveholder power, their antislavery reforms, however guarded, might have been lethal. As it was, the American Revolutionaries made the slave system stronger in the South, where it was already strongest, and weaker in the North, where it was weakest. That contradictory amalgam of increased slaveholder vulnerabilities and increased slaveholder armor established the pattern for everything that was to come.

8

In the 1820–60 period, and on the 1861–65 battlefields, the slaveholders fought their added vulnerabilities with their added power. By 1860, the slaveholders had fifteen states against the North's sixteen. But if the four Border South states fell away, the North's margin would widen to twenty against eleven. Then all sorts of dangers would loom for a once-national institution, which in the wake of the Founding Fathers was slowly becoming more defensively and peculiarly southern.

Southern proslavery campaigns, ideological and political, could be summed up as one long campaign to reverse the Founding Fathers' conditional antislavery drift. The conditional antislavery ideology, declaring emancipation desirable *if* blacks could be removed and *if* the Union could be preserved, persisted in the North and the Upper South throughout the antebellum period. That predominant national apologetic attitude toward slavery, Lower South zealots persistently feared, could inspire a national political movement aimed at removing blacks and slaves from the nation unless the Lower South deterred it.

Deterrence began with a determined proslavery campaign aimed at showing Southerners that slavery was no problem after all. In its extreme manifestations in the 1850s, proslavery visionaries, led by Virginia's George Fitzhugh, called wage slavery the unrecognized problem. The impolitic implication (although Fitzhugh disavowed it): Even white wage earners should be enslaved.[29] Proslavery polemicists more commonly called freedom for blacks the unrecognized problem. The common message: Black slaves should never be freed to starve as free workers in or out of America.

While proslavery intellectuals took aim at the Founding Fathers' revolutionary awareness that slavery was a problem, proslavery politicians sought to counter the waning of slavery in the Border South. With the Fugitive Slave Law of 1850, particularly aimed at stopping border slaves from fleeing to permanent liberty in the North, and the Kansas-Nebraska Act of 1854, originally urged by its southern advocates to protect slavery in Missouri, Southerners endeavored to fortify the border regime which the Fathers had somewhat weakened. So too the most dramatic (although unsuccessful) Lower South political movement of the 1850s, the

campaign to reopen the African slave trade, sought to reverse the Fathers' greatest debilitation of the slavocracy.

The minority's persistent proslavery campaigns and frequent congressional victories eventually convinced most Northerners that appeasement of a slaveholding minority damaged rather than saved white men's highest priority: majority rule in a white men's republic. That determination to rescue majority rule from the Slavepower minority underrode Abraham Lincoln's election in 1860; and with Lincoln's election came the secession of the Lower South minority. Secessionists feared not least that the President-elect might build that long-feared North-Upper South movement to end slavery by deporting blacks, especially from the compromised Border South.

The ensuing Civil War would prove that latter-day Southerners had been right to worry about slavery's incremental erosion in the borderlands. The four Border South states would fight for the Union, tipping the balance of power against the Confederacy. Abraham Lincoln would allegedly say that though he hoped to have God on his side, he *had* to have Kentucky. He would retain his native Kentucky and all the borderlands, including his adopted Illinois, which the Founders had at long last emancipated.

He would also obtain, against his initial objections, black soldiers, who would again sense an opportunity to read themselves into the Declaration of Independence. Just as fugitive slaves had pushed reluctant Pennsylvania, New York, and Maryland slaveholders into faster manumissions, so fugitive blacks should push a reluctant Great Emancipator to let them in his army and thereby make his victory theirs. Black soldiers would help win the war, secure emancipation, and thus finally defeat the slaveholders' long attempt to reverse the Founding Fathers' conditional antislavery drift.

To omit the Fathers' guarded contributions to America's drift toward the Civil War and emancipation in the name of condemning them as hypocrites is to miss the tortuous way black freedom came to the United States. But to omit the Fathers' contributions to Lower

South proslavery power in the name of calling them social revolutionaries is to deny the very meaning of the word *revolution*.

9

More broadly and more significantly, the American Revolutionaries' stance on blacks illuminated their ambivalent approach to the one truly radical social implication of the Revolution. As the historian Jack P. Greene has brilliantly shown, nothing was radical about the Declaration's affirmation of an American right to life, liberty, and the pursuit of happiness, so long as only white males' pursuits counted as American.[30] Whatever the poverty in urban slums and tenants' shacks, American colonials had long since developed a radically modern social order, dedicated to white males' pursuit of happiness and rooted in unprecedented capitalist opportunity. The Revolution, while expanding political opportunity and political mobility, only a little further widened an economic doorway already unprecedentedly open—but labeled "white males only."

For the others who peopled America—the women, the Native Americans, the blacks, in short, the majority—opportunity was closed. To include these dispossessed groups in the American Revolution—to open up a world where all men and women were at liberty to pursue their happiness—was the Declaration's truly radical social implication. No such color-blind, ethnically blind, gender-blind social order had ever existed, not on these shores, not anywhere else.

The Founding Fathers caught an uneasy glimpse of this potential social revolution. Despite their obsession with white republics and white property, they recognized that the Declaration applied to blacks, too. But their racism led them to take a step backward from the revolutionary promise of the Declaration of Independence. Most of them were no advocates of an egalitarian multicultural society *in* America. The Virginia Dynasty especially would extend quality to black Americans by moving them *out* of America. That reactionary black-removal foundation of antislavery statecraft, peculiar among all the New World slavocracies to these North Americans, did not a progressive social revolution portend.

Thomas Jefferson had captured the nonradicalism of the American Revolution in one of the great American phrases. "We have the wolf by the ears," he wrote at the time of the Missouri Controversy, "and we can neither hold him, nor safely let him go."[31] The Founding Fathers had more wolves by the ears than Jefferson had in mind: blacks, slaves, their own antislavery hopes, their implication, that *all* people must be included in the Declaration of Independence. They propounded those ideals, but they quailed before their own creation. Someday, the ideals may prevail and Americans may cease to recoil from the Declaration's implications. But it would not happen to the Founders, not with revolutionary speed, not to men who equipped a nation to hang on to slavery's slippery ears for almost a century.

Notes

1. William W. Freehling, "The Founding Fathers and Slavery," *American Historical Review, 77* (1972): 81–93.
2. See, for example, Robert McColley, *Slavery and Jeffersonian Virginia* (Urbana, Ill., 1964); Donald L. Robinson, *Slavery in the Structure of American Politics, 1765–1820* (New York, 1971); William Cohen, "Thomas Jefferson and the Problem of Slavery," *Journal of American History, 56* (1969): 503–26.
3. Later writers have also extended the blame for failure to emancipate to encompass Northerners as well as Southerners. See, for example, Larry E. Tise, *Proslavery: A History of the Defense of Slavery in America, 1701–1840* (Athens, Ga., 1987), and Gary B. Nash, *Race and Revolution* (Madison, Wisc., 1990).
4. David Brion Davis, *The Problem of Slavery in the Age of Revolution, 177–1823* (Ithaca, N.Y., 1975), 168.
5. Most recently and notably in Gordon S. Wood, *The Radicalism of the American Revolution* (New York, 1992), 186–87, 401 *n* 43. For an estimate of this matter very close to my own,

see Drew R. McCoy in *Journal of American History,* 79 (1993): 1563–64.
6. David Brion Davis, *The Problem of Slavery in Western Culture* (Ithaca, N.Y., 1966), and Davis, *The Problem of Slavery in the Age of Revolution.*
7. Quoted in ibid., 292.
8. A phenomenon splendidly illustrated in Winthrop D. Jordan, *White over Black: American Attitudes toward the Negro, 1550–1812* (Chapel Hill, N.C., 1968).
9. For further discussion of Jefferson's conditional antislavery position, see William W. Freehling, *The Road to Disunion,* Vol. 1, *Secessionists at Bay, 1776–1854* (New York, 1990), 123–31. For further discussion of the black-removal condition, see below, ch. 7.
10. For an excellent discussion of this episode, see Drew R. McCoy, *The Last of the Fathers: James Madison and the Republican Legacy* (New York, 1989), 310–16.
11. All demographic statistics in this essay derive from *The Statistics of the Population of the United Sates,* comp. Francis A. Walker (Washington, D.C., 1872), 11–74, and U.S. Bureau of the Census, *A Century of Population Growth; From the First Census of the United States to the Twelfth, 1790–1900* (Washington, D.C., 1909).
12. The classic study of emancipation in the North is Arthur Zilversmit, *The First Emancipation: The Abolition of Slavery in the North* (Chicago, 1967).
13. For an excellent discussion of the Pennsylvania episode, see Gary B. Nash and Jean R. Soderlund, *Freedom by Degrees: Emancipation and Its Aftermath in Pennsylvania* (New York, 1991).
14. For a fine recent study of the New York phase, see Shane White, *Somewhat More Independent: the End of Slavery in New York City, 1770–1810* (Athens, Ga., 1991).
15. Claudia Dale Golden, "The Economics of Emancipation," *Journal of Economic History, 33* (1973): 70.
16. Torrey Stephen Whitman, "Slavery, Manumission, and Free Black Workers in Early National Baltimore," Ph.D. diss., Johns Hopkins University, 1993, expertly develops these themes. On the broader Maryland milieu, see Barbara J. Fields, *Slavery and Freedom on the Middle Ground: Maryland during the Nineteenth Century* (New Haven, Conn., 1985).
17. Joseph C. Burke, "The Pro-Slavery Argument in the First Congress," *Duquesne Review, 16* (1969): 3–15; Howard Ohline, "Slavery, Economics, and Congressional Politics," *Journal of Southern History, 46* (1980): 335–60; Richard Newman, "The First Gag Rule," forthcoming. I am grateful to Mr. Newman for allowing me to use his excellent essay before its publication.

18. Quoted in Merrill D. Peterson, *Thomas Jefferson and the New Nation: A Biography* (New York, 1970), 283.
19. William Grayson to James Monroe, August 8, 1787, in *Letters of Members of the Continental Congress,* ed. Edmund C. Burnett, 8 vols. (Washington, D.C., 1921–36), 8:631–33. The following account of the Northwest Ordinance and its Illinois aftermath has been much influenced by the salutary notes of cynicism in Peter Onuf's fine *Statehood and Union: A History of the Northwest Ordinance* (Indianapolis, Ind., 1987) and in Paul Finkelman's several illuminating essays, especially "Slavery and the Northwest Ordinance: A Study in Ambiguity," *Journal of the Early Republic, 6* (1986): 343–70, and "Evading the Ordinance: The Persistence of Bondage in Indiana and Illinois," *Journal of the Early Republic, 9* (1989): 21–51. But for a cautionary note, see David Brion Davis's judicious "The Significance of Excluding Slavery from the Old Northwest in 1787," *Indiana Magazine of History, 84* (1988); 75–89.
20. Jefferson to John Holmes, April 22, 1820, in *The Writings of Thomas Jefferson,* ed. Paul Leicester Ford, 10 vols. (New York, 1892–99), 10:157–58.
21. Jefferson to Jared Sparks, February 24, 1824, ibid., 10:289–92.
22. Phillip J. Staudenraus, *The African Colonization Movement, 1816–1865* (New York, 1961).
23. The theme is discussed at length in William W. Freehling, *Prelude to Civil War: The Nullification Controversy in South Carolina, 1816–1836* (New York, 1966).
24. See, for example, Paul Finkelman's otherwise illuminating "Slavery and the Constitutional Convention: Making a Covenant with Death," in *Beyond Confederation: Origins of the Constitution and National Identity,* ed. Richard Beeman et al. (Chapel Hill, N.C., 1987), 188–225.
25. A *Compilation of the Messages and Papers of the Presidents,* comp. James D. Richardson, 10 vols. (Washington, D.C., 1900), 1:408.
26. See, for example, Nash, *Race and Revolution.*
27. David Eltis, *Economic Growth and the Ending of the Transatlantic Slave Trade* (New York, 1987).
28. John Jay to the English Anti-Slavery Society, [1788], in *The Correspondence and Public Papers of John Jay,* ed. Henry P. Johnston, 4 vols. (New York, 1890–93), 3:342.
29. See below, pp. 98–100.
30. Jack P. Greene, *Pursuits of Happiness: The Social Development of Early Modern British Colonies and the Formation of American Culture* (Chapel Hill, N.C., 1988).
31. Jefferson to John Holmes, April 22, 1820, in *Jefferson's Writings,* ed. Ford, 10:157–58.

Unit Selections

Key Points to Consider

❖ George Washington presided over the formative years of government under the new Constitution. What were his strengths? His weaknesses? In what ways did the election of 1796 mark the beginning of a new era?

❖ Discuss the Alien and Sedition Acts. What effects did they have with regard to freedom of the press?

❖ What were the women who attented the Seneca Falls conference trying to accomplish? Why was the question of suffrage so controversial?

❖ The question of slavery bedeviled Americans from the debates during the Constitutional Convention to the Civil War and came to have an impact on practically every question. How did the *Amistad* mutiny become a national issue? What effect did the acquisition of the new territory following the Mexican war have on the debate? Why did the Brooks-Sumner affair cause so much furor?

❖ Why were non-Indian Americans so exploitative of the environment? In what ways did they degrade natural resources?

DUSHKINONLINE **Links**   **www.dushkin.com/online/**

These sites are annotated on pages 4 and 5.

The Articles of Confederation had granted relatively few powers to the national government, which was one of the reasons why the Federalists wanted to scrap them. The Consitution drawn up in Philadelphia in 1787 was designed to provide a more powerful federal system. Following elections in 1788, the new government got underway in 1789. Much of what was done during the first years, everyone knew, would establish precedents for the future. There was much debate, for instance, over how one should address the president, and the precise relationship between his office and the congress. When differences emerged over interpreting specific articles in the Constitution, who or which branch should decide which was correct? And perhaps most important, should the document be interpreted stricly or loosely? That is, should governmental powers be limited to those expressly granted, or were there "implied" powers that could be utilized as long as they were not expressly prohibited? Various individuals and groups argued on principle, but the truth is that they were largely interested in promoting programs that would benefit the interests they represented.

There were no provisions in the Constitution for political parties. Although President George Washington believed he served the nation as a whole, what he disdainfully referred to as "factions" arose fairly early during his first administration. Secretary of the Treasury Alexander Hamilton usually argued in behalf of measures that would benefit commercial and manufacturing interests located mostly in the Northeast. Secretary of State Thomas Jefferson and his able ally James Madison represented rural and agricultural interests that were concentrated in the West and South. These two groups clashed frequently over what the Constitution did or did not permit, which sources of revenue should be tapped, and a host of other matters. Washington contributed to the development of political parties because he sided with Hamilton most of the time.

The first essay in this section, "The Greatness of George Washington," evaluates his conduct as president and as an individual. Historian Gordon Wood gives Washington high marks for his conduct of the presidency and for the moral character he brought to the office. Washington played a key role in founding a system that, with the exception of the Civil War, has endured to this day. Larry Gragg, in "Order vs. Liberty," discusses the Alien and Sedition Acts, passed during the tenure of Washington's sucessor, John Adams. These laws were designed in part to stifle the freedoms of those who opposed the administration. The third article having to do with the development of government is "Chief Justice Marshall Takes the Law in Hand." Marshall served as the fourth chief justice of the Supreme Court, and more than anyone else he helped ensure that federal law would prevail over states' rights.

In the early 1800s, Americans knew little about the vast, uncharted territories that extended from the Mississippi River to the Pacific Ocean. Thomas Jefferson had for years shown an interest in exploring this area, and when he became president he requested funds from congress to form an expeditionary group that became known as The Corps of Discovery. Headed by Meriwether Lewis and William Clark, in 1804 the corps embarked on an arduous journey that eventually brought it to the shores of the Pacific. The essay "Lewis and Clark: Trailblazers Who Opened the Continent" describes this expedition from its beginning to its return home and the performance of its two leaders.

Floyd Largent, in "The Florida Quagmire," treats efforts by the federal government to remove Indian tribes from Florida to make room for white settlements. This touched off the Second Seminole war in 1835, which cost a great many lives on both sides. The Indians' tenacity in fighting to retain their lands eventually caused the federal government to back off from further efforts.

As the unit continues, three essays address the efforts of subjugated groups to gain freedoms or at least some control over their daily lives. " 'All We Want Is Make Us Free!' " describes the outcome of a slave mutiny aboard the Spanish ship *Amistad* in 1839. This event gained wide attention and ultimately led to the case being heard before the Supreme Court of the United States. Next, Constance Rynder in " 'All Men & Women Are Created Equal' " tells of the first womens' rights convention, held in Seneca Falls, New York, in 1848. Within the convention, most of the resolutions gained wide acceptance—all except the one on suffrage, which caused much controversy. Press coverage of the meeting often was harsh and sarcastic. The essay "The Lives of Slave Women" is about the conditions under which these women lived and worked, and their efforts to achieve some measure of influence on those conditions.

There are two articles on the growing sectionalism that eventually would tear the nation apart. Harlan Hague, in "James K. Polk and the Expansionist Spirit," analyzes Polk's efforts to acquire Texas and the Oregon territory. Polk compromised with the British over Oregon but went to war with Mexico over Texas. Most Northerners favored the acquisition of Oregon; most Southerners were more interested in Texas in order to expand the realm of slavery. Polk left to his successors the question of how to deal with slavery in the newly acquired territories. "Assault in the Senate," by David Johnson, discusses the impact of "Bully" Brooks's vicious assault on Senator Charles Sumner on the senate floor. Brooks attacked the senator for a speech he had given in which he condemned Southerners in general and some by name, one of whom was Brooks's uncle. Northerners used the incident to depict Southerners as brutal and uncivilized; Southerners tended to think Sumner had gotten what he deserved.

The article "Eden Ravished" concerns the environment. Despite warnings to the contrary, Americans tended to treat the lands, rivers, and forests as though they were inexhaustible resources that could be exploited without regard for the future. Later generations would have to pay the bills for wasteful uses of these national assets.

The Greatness of George Washington

By Gordon S. Wood

George Washington may still be first in war and first in peace, but he no longer seems to be first in the hearts of his countrymen. Or at least in the hearts of American historians. A recent poll of 900 American historians shows that Washington has dropped to third place in presidential greatness behind Lincoln and FDR. Which only goes to show how little American historians know about American history.

Polls of historians about presidential greatness are probably silly things, but, if they are to be taken seriously, then Washington fully deserved the first place he has traditionally held. He certainly deserved the accolades his contemporaries gave him. And as long as this republic endures he ought to be first in the hearts of his countrymen. Washington was truly a great man and the greatest president we have ever had.

But he was a great man who is not easy to understand. He became very quickly, as has often been pointed out, more a monument than a man, statuesque and impenetrable. Even his contemporaries realized that he was not an ordinary accessible human being. He was deified in his own lifetime. "O Washington," declared Ezra Stiles, president of Yale, in 1783. "How I do love thy name! How have I often adored and blessed thy God, for creating and forming thee, the great ornament of human kind! . . . Thy fame is of sweeter perfume than Arabian spices. Listening angels shall catch the odor, waft it to heaven and perfume the universe!"

One scholar has said that Washington has been "the object of the most intense display of hero worship this nation has ever seen." Which helps explain the continuing efforts to humanize him—even at the beginning of our history. Parson Mason Weems, his most famous biographer, was less of a churchman than he was a hustling entrepreneur. He was ready when Washington died in 1799: "I've something to whisper in your lug," Weems wrote to his publisher Matthew Carey a month after the great man's death. "Washington you know, is gone! Millions are gaping to read something about him. I am very nearly primed and cocked for 'em." Weems had his book out within the year.

The most famous anecdotes about Washington's early life come from Weems. He wanted to capture the inner private man—to show the early events that shaped Washington's character, even if he had to make them up. Weems presumed that the source of Washington's reputation for truthfulness lay in his youth. He tells a story that he said he had heard from Washington's nurse. It was, he says, "too valuable to be lost, too true to be doubted." This was, of course, the story of the cherry tree about whose chopping down Washington could not tell a lie.

Despite the continued popularity of Parson Weems' attempt to humanize him, Washington remained distant and unapproachable, almost unreal and unhuman. There have been periodic efforts to bring him down to earth, to expose his foibles, to debunk his fame, but he remained, and remains, massively monumental. By our time in the late 20th century he seems so far removed from us as to be virtually incomprehensible. He seems to come from another time and another place—from another world.

And that's the whole point about him: he does come from another world. And his countrymen realized it even before he died in 1799. He is the only truly classical hero we have ever had. He acquired at once a world-wide reputation as a great patriot-hero.

And he knew it. He was well aware of his reputation and his fame earned as the commander-in-chief of the American revolutionary forces. That awareness of his heroic stature and his character as a republican leader was crucial to Wash-

From *Virginia Quarterly Review*, Spring 1992. © 1992 by Virginia Quarterly Review. Reprinted by permission.

ington. It affected nearly everything he did for the rest of his life.

Washington was a thoroughly 18th-century figure. So much so, that he quickly became an anachronism. He belonged to the pre-democratic and pre-egalitarian world of the 18th century, to a world very different from the world that would follow. No wonder then that he seems to us so remote and so distant. He really is. He belonged to a world we have lost and we were losing even as Washington lived.

II

In many respects Washington was a very unlikely hero. To be sure, he had all the physical attributes of a classical hero. He was very tall by contemporary standards, and was heavily built and a superb athlete. Physically he had what both men and women admired. He was both a splendid horseman at a time when that skill really counted and an extraordinarily graceful dancer. And naturally he loved both riding and dancing. He always moved with dignity and looked the leader.

Yet those who knew him well and talked with him were often disappointed. He never seemed to have very much to say. He was most certainly *not* what we would today call an "intellectual." We cannot imagine him, say, expressing his views on Plato in the way Jefferson and John Adams did in their old age. Adams was especially contemptuous of Washington's intellectual abilities. It was certain, said Adams, that Washington was not a scholar. "That he was too illiterate, unread for his station and reputation is equally past dispute."

Adam's judgment is surely too harsh. Great men in the 18th century did not have to be scholars or intellectuals. But there is no doubt that Washington was not a learned man, especially in comparison with the other Founding Fathers. He was very ill at ease in abstract discussions. Even Jefferson, who was usually generous in his estimates of his friends, said that Washington's "colloquial talents were not above mediocrity." He had "neither copiousness of ideas nor fluency of words."

Washington was not an intellectual, but he was a man of affairs. He knew how to run his plantation and make it pay. He certainly ran Mount Vernon better than Jefferson ran Monticello. Washington's heart was always at Mount Vernon. He thought about it all the time. Even when he was president he devoted a great amount of his energy worrying about the fence posts of his plantation, and his letters dealing with the details of running Mount Vernon were longer than those dealing with the running of the federal government.

But being a man of affairs and running his plantation or even the federal government efficiently were not what made him a world-renowned hero. What was it that lay behind his extraordinary reputation, his greatness?

His military exploits were of course crucial. But Washington was not really a traditional military hero. He did not resemble Alexander, Caesar, Cromwell, or Marlborough; his military achievements were nothing compared to those Napoleon would soon have. Washington had no smashing, stunning victories. He was not a military genius, and his tactical and strategic maneuvers were not the sort that awed men. Military glory was *not* the source of his reputation. Something else was involved.

Washington's genius, his greatness, lay in his character. He was, as Chateaubriand said, a "hero of an unprecedented kind." There had never been a great man quite like Washington before. Washington became a great man and was acclaimed as a classical hero because of the way he conducted himself during times of temptation. It was his moral character that set him off from other men.

Washington fit the 18th-century image of a great man, of a man of virtue. This virtue was not given to him by nature. He had to work for it, to cultivate it, and everyone sensed that. Washington was a self-made hero, and this impressed an 18th-century enlightened world that put great stock in men controlling both their passions and their destinies. Washington seemed to possess a self-cultivated nobility.

He was in fact a child of the 18th-century Enlightenment. He was very much a man of his age, and he took its

moral standards more seriously than most of his contemporaries. Washington's Enlightenment, however, was not quite that of Jefferson or Franklin. Although he was conventionally enlightened about religion, "being no bigot myself to any mode of worship," he had no passionate dislike of the clergy and organized Christianity, as Jefferson did. And although he admired learning, he was not a man of science like Franklin. Like many other 18th-century Englishmen, he did *not* believe, as he put it, that "becoming a mere scholar is a desirable education for a gentleman."

Washington's Enlightenment was a much more down-to-earth affair, concerned with behavior and with living in the everyday-world of people. His Enlightenment involved what eventually came to be called cultivation and civilization. He lived his life by the book—not the book of military rules but the book of gentility. He was as keenly aware as any of his fellow Americans of the 18th-century conventions that defined what a proper gentleman was.

Such conventions were expressed in much of the writing of the Enlightenment. The thousands of etiquette books, didactic stories, *Spectator* papers, Hogarth prints, gentlemanly magazines, classical histories—all were designed to teach Englishmen manners, civility, politeness, and virtue. Out of all this writing and art emerged an ideal of what it was to be both enlightened and civilized, and a virtuous leader. Our perpetuation of a liberal arts education in our colleges and universities is a present-day reminder of the origins of this ideal; for the English conception of a liberally educated gentleman had its modern beginnings in the 18th century.

An enlightened, civilized man was disinterested and impartial, not swayed by self-interest and self-profit. He was cosmopolitan; he stood above all local and parochial considerations and was willing to sacrifice his personal desires for the greater good of his community or his country. He was a man of reason who resisted the passions most likely to afflict great men, that is, ambition and avarice. Such a liberal, enlightened gentleman avoided enthusiasms and fanaticisms of all sorts, especially those of religion. Tolerance and liberality were his watchwords. Politeness and compassion toward his fellow man were his manners. Behaving in this way was what constituted being civilized.

Washington was thoroughly caught up in this enlightened promotion of gentility and civility, this rational rolling back of parochialism, fanaticism, and barbarism. He may have gone to church regularly, but he was not an emotionally religious person. In all of his writings there is no mention of Christ, and God is generally referred to as "the great disposer of human events." Washington loved Addison's play *Cato* and saw it over and over and incorporated its lines into his correspondence. The play, very much an Enlightenment tract, helped to teach him what it meant to be liberal and virtuous, what it meant to be a stoical classical hero. He had the play put on for his troops during the terrible winter at Valley Forge in 1778.

One of the key documents of Washington's life is his "Rules of Civility and Decent Behaviour in Company and Conversation," a collection of 110 maxims that Washington wrote down sometime before his 16th birthday. The maxims were originally drawn from a 17th-century etiquette book and were copied by the young autodidact. They dealt with everything from how to treat one's betters ("In speaking to men of Quality do not lean nor Look them full in the Face") to how the present one's countenance ("Do not Puff up the Cheeks, Do not Loll out the tongue, rub the Hands, or beard, thrust out the lips, or bite them or keep the Lips too open or too Close").

All the Founding Fathers were aware of these enlightened conventions, and all in varying degrees tried to live up to them. But no one was more serious in following them than Washington. It is this purposefulness that gave his behavior such a copybook character. He was obsessed with having things in fashion and was fastidious about his appearance to the world. It was as if he were always on stage, acting a part. He was very desirous not to offend, and he exquisitely shaped his remarks to fit the person to whom he was writing—so much so that some historians have accused him of deceit. "So anxious was he to appear neat and correct in his letters," recalled Benjamin Rush, that he was known to "copy over a letter of 2 or 3 sheets of paper because there were a few erasures on it." He wanted desperately to know what were the proper rules of behavior for a liberal gentleman, and when he discovered those rules he stuck by them with an earnestness that awed his contemporaries. His remarkable formality and stiffness in company came from his very self-conscious cultivation of what he considered proper, genteel, classical behavior.

Washington and Franklin, both children of the Enlightenment, had very different personalities, but among the Founding Fathers they shared one important thing. Neither of them went to college; neither had a formal liberal arts education. This deficiency deeply affected both of them, but Washington let it show. Washington always remained profoundly respectful of formal education. Colleges like William and Mary were always an "Object of Veneration" to him. His lack of a formal liberal arts education gave him a modesty he never lost. He repeatedly expressed his "consciousness of a defective education," and he remained quiet in the presence of sharp and sparkling minds. He was forever embarrassed that he had never learned any foreign languages. In the 1780's he refused invitations to visit France because he felt it would be humiliating for someone of his standing to have to converse through an interpreter. He said that it was his lack of a formal education that kept him from setting down on paper his recollections of the Revolution. It was widely rumored that his aides composed his best letters as commander-in-chief. If so, it is not surprising that he was diffident in company. Some even called it "shyness," but whatever the source, this reticence was certainly not the usual characteristic of a great man. "His modesty is astonishing, particularly to a Frenchman," noted Brissot de Warville. "He speaks of the American War as if he had *not* been its leader." This modesty only added to his gravity and severity. "Most people say and do too much," one friend recalled. "Washington . . . never fell into this common error."

III

Yet it was in the political world that Washington made his most theatrical gesture, his most moral mark, and there the results were monumental. The greatest act of his life, the one that made him famous, was his resignation as commander-in-chief of the American forces. This act, together with his 1783 circular letter to the states in which he promised to retire from public life, was his "legacy" to his countrymen. No American leader has ever left a more important legacy.

Following the signing of the peace treaty and British recognition of American independence, Washington stunned the world when he surrendered his sword to the Congress on Dec. 23, 1783 and retired to his farm at Mount Vernon. This was a highly symbolic act, a very self-conscious and unconditional withdrawal from the world of politics. Here was the commander in chief of the victorious army putting down his sword and promising not to take "any share in public business hereafter." Washington even resigned from his local vestry in Virginia in order to make his separation from the political world complete.

His retirement from power had a profound effect everywhere in the Western world. It was extraordinary, it was unprecedented in modern times—a victorious general surrendering his arms and returning to his farm. Cromwell, William of Orange, Marlborough—all had sought political rewards commensurate with their military achievements. Though it was widely thought that Washington could have become king or dictator, he wanted nothing of the kind. He was sincere in his desire for all the soldiers "to return to our Private Stations in the bosom of a free, peaceful and happy Country," and everyone recognized his sincerity. It filled them with awe. Washington's retirement, said the painter John Trumbull writing from London in 1784, "excites the astonishment and admiration of this part of the world. 'Tis a Conduct so novel, so unconceivable to People, who, far from giving up powers they possess, are willing to convulse the empire to acquire more." King George III supposedly predicted that if

Washington retired from public life and returned to his farm, "he will be the greatest man in the world."

Washington was not naïve. He was well aware of the effect his resignation would have. He was trying to live up to the age's image of a classical disinterested patriot who devotes his life to his country, and he knew at once that he had acquired instant fame as a modern Cincinnatus. His reputation in the 1780's as a great classical hero was international, and it was virtually unrivaled. Franklin was his only competitor, but Franklin's greatness still lay in his being a scientist, not a man of public affairs. Washington was a living embodiment of all that classical republican virtue the age was eagerly striving to recover.

Despite his outward modesty, Washington realized he was an extraordinary man, and he was not ashamed of it. He lived in an era where distinctions of rank and talent were not only accepted but celebrated. He took for granted the differences between himself and more ordinary men. And when he could not take those differences for granted he cultivated them. He used his natural reticence to reinforce the image of a stern and forbidding classical hero. His aloofness was notorious, and he worked at it. When the painter Gilbert Stuart had uncharacteristic difficulty in putting Washington at ease during a sitting for a portrait, Stuart in exasperation finally pleaded, "Now sir, you must let me forget that you are General Washington and that I am Stuart, the painter," Washington's reply chilled the air: "Mr. Stuart need never feel the need of forgetting who he is or who General Washington is." No wonder the portraits look stiff.

Washington had earned his reputation, his "character," as a moral hero, and he did not want to dissipate it. He spent the rest of his life guarding and protecting his reputation, and worrying about it. He believed Franklin made a mistake going back into public life in Pennsylvania in the 1780's. Such involvement in politics, he thought, could only endanger Franklin's already achieved international standing. In modern eyes Washington's concern for his reputation is embarrassing; it seems obsessive and egotistical. But his contemporaries understood. All gentlemen tried scrupulously to guard their reputations, which is what they meant by their honor. Honor was the esteem in which they were held, and they prized it. To have honor across space and time was to have fame, and fame, "the ruling passion of the noblest minds," was what the Founding Fathers were after, Washington above all. And he got it, sooner and in greater degree than any other of his contemporaries. And naturally, having achieved what all his fellow Revolutionaries still anxiously sought, he was reluctant to risk it.

Many of his actions after 1783 can be understood only in terms of this deep concern for his reputation as a virtuous leader. He was constantly on guard and very sensitive to any criticism. Jefferson said no one was more sensitive. He judged all his actions by what people might think of them. This sometimes makes him seem silly to modern minds, but not to those of the 18th century. In that very suspicious age where people were acutely "jealous" of what great men were up to, Washington thought it important that people understand his motives. The reality was not enough; he had to *appear* virtuous. He was obsessed that he not seem base, mean, avaricious, or unduly ambitious. No one, said Jefferson, worked harder than Washington in keeping "motives of interest of consanguinity, of friendship or hatred" from influencing him. He had a lifelong preoccupation with his reputation for "disinterestedness" and how best to use that reputation for the good of his country. This preoccupation explains the seemingly odd fastidiousness and the caution of his behavior in the 1780's.

One of the most revealing incidents occurred in the winter of 1784–85. Washington was led into temptation, and it was agony. The Virginia General Assembly presented him with 150 shares in the James River and Potomac canal companies in recognition of his services to the state and the cause of canal-building. What should he do? He did not feel he could accept the shares. Acceptance might be "considered in the same light as a pension" and might compromise his reputation for virtue. Yet he believed passionately in what the canal compa-nies were doing and had long dreamed of making a fortune from such canals. Moreover, he did not want to show "disrespect" to the Assembly or to appear "ostentatiously disinterested" by refusing this gift.

Few decisions in Washington's career caused more distress than this one. He wrote to everyone he knew—to Jefferson, to Governor Patrick Henry, to William Grayson, to Benjamin Harrison, to George William Fairfax, to Nathanael Greene, even to Lafayette—seeking "the best information and advice" on the disposition of the shares. "How would this matter be viewed by the eyes of the world?" he asked. Would not his reputation for virtue be harmed? Would not accepting the shares "deprive me of the principal thing which is laudable in my conduct?"

The situation is humorous today, but it was not to Washington. He suffered real anguish. Jefferson eventually found the key to Washington's anxieties and told him that declining to accept the shares would only add to his reputation for disinterestedness. So Washington gave them away to the college that eventually became Washington and Lee.

Washington suffered even more anguish over the decision to attend the Philadelphia Convention in 1787. Many believed that his presence was absolutely necessary for the effectiveness of the Convention, but the situation was tricky. He wrote to friends imploring them to tell him "confidentially what the public expectation is on this head, that is, whether I will or ought to be there?" How would his presence be seen, how would his motives be viewed? If he attended, would he be thought to have violated his pledge to withdraw from public life? But, if he did not attend, would his staying away be thought to be a "dereliction to Republicanism"? Should he squander his reputation on something that might not work?

What if the Convention should fail? The delegates would have to return home, he said, "chagrined at their ill success and disappointment. This would be a disagreeable circumstance for any one of them to be in; but more particularly so, for a person in my situation." Even James Madison had second thoughts about the possibility of misusing such a precious asset as Washington's reputation. What finally convinced Washington to attend the Convention was the fear that people might think he wanted the federal government to fail so that he could manage a miliary takeover. So in the end he decided, as Madison put it, "to forsake the honorable retreat to which he had retired, and risk the reputation he had so deservedly acquired." No action could be more virtuous. "Secure as he was in his fame," wrote Henry Knox with some awe, "he has again committed it to the mercy of events. Nothing but the critical situation of his country would have induced him to so hazardous a conduct."

IV

When the Convention met, Washington was at once elected its president. His presence and his leadership undoubtedly gave the Convention and the proposed Constitution a prestige that they otherwise could not have had. His backing of the Constitution was essential to its eventual ratification. "Be assured," James Monroe told Jefferson, "his influence carried this government." Washington, once committed to the Constitution, worked hard for its acceptance. He wrote letters to friends and let his enthusiasm for the new federal government be known. Once he had identified himself publicly with the new Constitution he became very anxious to have it accepted. Its ratification was a kind of ratification of himself.

After the Constitution was established, Washington still thought he could retire to the domestic tranquility of Mount Vernon. But everyone else expected that he would become president of the new national government. He was already identified with the country. People said he was denied children in his private life so he could be the father of his country. He had to be the president. Indeed, the Convention had made the new chief executive so strong, so kinglike, precisely because the delegates expected Washington to be the first president.

Once again this widespread expectation aroused all his old anxieties about his reputation for disinterestedness and the proper role for a former military leader. Had he not promised the country that he would permanently retire from public life? How could he then now assume the presidency without being "chargeable with levity and inconsistency; if not with rashness and ambition?" His protests were sincere. He had so much to lose, yet he did not want to appear "too solicitous for my reputation."

Washington's apparent egotism and his excessive coyness, his extreme reluctance to get involved in public affairs and endanger his reputation, have not usually been well received by historians. Douglas Southall Freeman, his great biographer, thought that Washington in the late 1780's was "too zealously attentive to his prestige, his reputation and his popularity—too much the self-conscious national hero and too little the daring patriot." Historians might not understand his behavior, but his contemporaries certainly did. They rarely doubted that Washington was trying *always* to act in a disinterested and patriotic way. His anxious queries about how this or that would look to the world, his hesitations about serving or not serving, his expressions of scruples and qualms—all were part of his strenuous effort to live up to the classical idea of a virtuous leader.

He seemed to epitomize public virtue and the proper character of a republican ruler. Even if John Adams was not all that impressed with George Washington, Adam's wife Abigail was certainly taken with him. She admired his restraint and trusted him. "If he was not really one of the best-intentioned men in the world," she wrote, "he might be a very dangerous one." As Gary Wills has so nicely put it, Washington gained his power by his readiness to give it up.

As president he continued to try to play the role he thought circumstances demanded. He knew that the new government was fragile and needed dignity. People found that dignity in his person. Madison believed that Washington was the only part of the new government that captured the minds of the people. He fleshed out the executive, established its independence, and gave the new government the pomp and ceremony many thought it needed.

Sometimes it had more pomp than even he enjoyed. His formal levees, complete with silver buckles and powdered hair, were painful affairs for everyone. These receptions, held at first on Tuesday and Friday afternoons and later on only Tuesdays, were an opportunity for prominent men to meet the president. The invited guests, all men, entered the president's residence at three o'clock, where they found the president standing before the fireplace. Fifteen minutes were allowed for the guests to assemble in a circle. As each guest entered the room he walked to the President, bowed, and without speaking backed to his place in the circle. The only voice heard was that of a presidential aide softly announcing the names. Promptly on the quarter hour the doors were shut; the President then walked around the circle, addressed each man by name, and made some brief remark to him. He bowed but never shook hands. Washington thought that handshaking was much too familiar for the president to engage in; consequently he kept one hand occupied holding a fake hat and the other resting on his dress sword. When the president had rounded the circle, he returned to the fireplace and stood until, at a signal from an aide, each guest one by one went to him, bowed without saying anything, and left the room. However excruciatingly formal these levees were, Washington thought they would continue. He thus designed the bowed shaped of the Blue Room to accommodate them.

Although many critics thought that the levees smacked of the court life of kings of Europe, Washington was not a crypto-monarchist. He was a devoted republican, at heart just a country gentleman. Martha used to break up tea parties at 9:30 p.m. by saying that it was past the President's bedtime.

As president he tried to refuse accepting any salary just as he had as commander-in-chief. Still, he wanted to make the presidency "respectable," and he spared few expenses in doing so; he spent 7 percent of his $25,000 salary on liquor and wine for entertaining. He was especially interested in the size and character of the White House and of the capital city that was named after him. The scale and grandeur of Washington, D.C., owe much to his vision and his backing of Pierre L'Enfant as architect. If Secretary of State Thomas Jefferson had had his way, L'Enfant would never have kept his job as long as he did, and the capital would have been smaller and less magnificent—perhaps something on the order of a college campus, like Jefferson's University of Virginia.

V

Washington was keenly aware that everything he did would set precedents for the future. "We are a young nation," he said, "and have a character to establish. It behoves us therefore to set out right, for first impressions will be lasting." It was an awesome responsibility. More than any of his contemporaries, he thought constantly of future generations, of "millions unborn," as he called them.

He created an independent role for the president and made the chief executive the dominant figure in the government.

He established crucial precedents, especially in limiting the Senate's role in advising the president in the making of treaties and the appointing of officials. In August 1789 he went to the Senate to get its advice and consent to a treaty he was negotiating with the Creek Indians. Vice President John Adams who presided read each section of the treaty and then asked the senators, How do you advise and consent? After a long silence, the senators, being senators, began debating each section, with Washington impatiently glaring down at them. Finally, one senator moved that the treaty and all the accompanying documents that the president had brought with him be submitted to a committee for study. Washington started up in what one senator called "a violent fret." In exasperation he cried, "This defeats every purpose of my coming here." He calmed down, but when he finally left the Senate chamber, he was overheard to say he would "be damned if he ever went there again." He never did. The advice part of the Senate's role in treaty making was dropped.

The presidency is the powerful office it is in large part because of Washington's initial behavior. He understood power and how to use it. But as in the case of his career as commander-in-chief, his most important act as president was his giving up of the office.

The significance of his retirement from the presidency is easy for us to overlook, but his contemporaries knew what it meant. Most people assumed that Washington might be president as long as he lived, that he would be a kind of elective monarch—something not out of the question in the 18th century. Some people even expressed relief that he had no heirs. Thus his persistent efforts to retire from the presidency enhanced his moral authority and helped fix the republican character of the Constitution.

He very much wanted to retire in 1792, but his advisors and friends talked him into staying on for a second term. Madison admitted that when he had first urged Washington to accept the presidency he had told him that he could protect himself from accusations of overweening ambition by "a voluntary return to public life as soon as the state of the Government would permit." But the state of the government, said Madison, was not yet secure. So Washington reluctantly stayed on.

But in 1796 he was so determined to retire that no one could dissuade him, and his voluntary leaving of the office set a precedent that was not broken until FDR secured a third term in 1940. So strong was the sentiment for a two-term limit, however, that the tradition was written into the Constitution in the 22nd amendment in 1951. Washington's action in 1796 was of great significance. That the chief executive of a state should willingly relinquish his office was an object lesson in republicanism at a time when the republican experiment throughout the Atlantic world was very much in doubt.

Washington's final years in retirement were not happy ones. The American political world was changing, becoming more partisan, and Washington struggled to comprehend these changes. During President Adams' administration he watched with dismay what he believed was the growing inter-

ference of the French government in American politics. For him the Jeffersonian Republican party had become "the French Party." It was, he said, "the curse of this country," threatening the stability and independence of the United States. He saw plots and enemies everywhere and became as much of a high-toned Federalist as Hamilton.

His fear was real; his sense of crisis was deep. He and other Federalists thought that the French might invade the country and together with "the French Party" overthrow the government. "Having Struggled for Eight or nine Years against the invasion of our rights by one power, and to establish an Independence of it," he wrote in 1798, "I could not remain an unconcerned spectator of the attempt of another Power to accomplish the same object, though in a different way." He thus listened attentively to all the urgent Federalist calls that he come out of retirement and head the army that the Congress had created to meet the French invasion.

Again he expressed reluctance, and asked whether becoming commander-in-chief would not be considered "a restless Act—evidence of my discontent in retirement." Yet in 1798 he was far more eager to step back into the breach and do his duty than he ever had been before. It was a measure of his despair with this "Age of Wonders"!

Before he could actually commit himself, however, President John Adams acted and, without his permission, appointed him commander of all the military forces of the United States. He accepted, but scarcely comprehended how it had all come about. The next thing he knew he was on his way to Philadelphia to organize the army. Events were outrunning his ability to control them or even to comprehend them, and he more and more saw himself caught up in "the designs of Providence." His command was a disaster. He wrangled over the appointments of the second in command, intrigued against Adams, and interfered with his cabinet. When neither the French invasion nor the American army materialized, Washington crept back to Mount Vernon thoroughly disillusioned with the new ways of American politics.

In July 1799 Governor Jonathan Trumbull of Connecticut with the backing of many Federalists urged Washington once again to stand for the presidency in 1800. Only Washington, Trumbull said, could unite the Federalists and save the country from "a French President." Finally Washington had had enough. In his reply he no longer bothered with references to his reputation for disinterestedness and his desire to play the role of Cincinnatus. Instead he talked about the new political conditions that made his candidacy irrelevant. In this new democratic era of party politics, he said, "personal influence," distinctions of character, no longer mattered. If the members of the Jeffersonian Republican party "set up a broomstick" as candidate and called it "a true son of Liberty" or "a Democrat" or "any other epithet that will suit their purpose," it still would "command their votes in toto!" But, even worse, he said,

the same was true of the Federalists. Party spirit now ruled all, and people voted only for their party candidate. Even if he were the Federalist candidate, Washington was "thoroughly convinced I should not draw a *single* vote from the anti-Federal side." Therefore his standing for election made no sense; he would "stand upon no stronger ground than any other Federal character well supported."

Washington wrote all this in anger and despair, but, though he exaggerated, he was essentially right. The political world was changing, becoming democratic, and parties, not great men, would soon become the objects of contention. To be sure, the American people continued to long for great heroes as leaders, and from Jackson through Eisenhower they have periodically elected Washington-*manqués* to the presidency.

But democracy made such great heroes no longer essential to the workings of American government. And Washington, more than any other single individual, was the one who made that democracy possible. As Jefferson said "the moderation and virtue of a single character . . . probably prevented this revolution from being closed, as most others have been, by a subversion of that liberty it was intended to establish."

Washington was an extraordinary heroic man who made rule by more ordinary mortals possible. He virtually created the presidency, and gave it a dignity that through the years it has never lost. But, more important, he established the standard by which all subsequent presidents have been ultimately measured—not by the size of their electoral victories, not by their legislative programs, and not by the number of their vetoes, but by their moral character. Although we live in another world than his, his great legacy is still with us.

Order vs. Liberty

When Congress passed the Alien and Sedition Acts in 1798, it opened a heated debate about the limits of freedom in a free society.

By Larry Gragg

On July 4, 1798, the citizens of the capital city of Philadelphia turned out in large numbers to celebrate the nation's independence day. While militia companies marched through the streets, church bells rang, and artillery units fired salutes, members of the United States Senate were trying to conduct a debate on a critical bill. One senator noted "the military parade so attracted the attention of the majority that much the greater part of them stood with their bodies out of the windows and could not be kept to order." Once they resumed their deliberations, however, the Federalist majority succeeded in gaining passage of an implausible bill, one quickly approved by the House of Representatives and signed on July 14 by President John Adams.

Ironically, as senators celebrated the freedom they had won from Britain, they approved a sedition bill that made it illegal to publish or utter any statements about the government that were "false, scandalous and malicious" with the "intent to defame" or to bring Congress or the president into "contempt or disrepute." This bill, seemingly a violation of the Constitution's First Amendment free speech protections, had a chilling effect on members of the Republican Party and its leader, Thomas Jefferson, who admitted that he feared "to write what I think." Support for this restrictive legislation had grown out of Federalist belief that the young nation was facing its gravest crisis yet, in the possibility of war with France and the spread of anti-immigrant feeling. The new law violated the beliefs of many Republicans, who regarded Federalists as reactionary defenders of privilege intent on bringing

THE GRANGER COLLECTION

A 1798 American cartoon depicts the XYZ Affair, when French officials demanded a bribe before negotiating with a commission from the United States. Subsequent outrage helped passage of the Alien and Sedition Acts.

From *American History,* October 1998, pp. 24-28, 56-59. © 1998 by Cowles Magazines, Inc. Reprinted through the courtesy of Cowles Magazines, publishers of *American History.*

back the monarchy. Federalists saw their Republican opposites as irresponsible radicals eager to incite a social revolution as democratic as the one that had torn through France.

Nothing divided Federalist from Republican more than their response to the French Revolution. Republicans applauded the revolutionaries' destruction of aristocratic privileges, the overthrow of the monarchy, and the implementation of constitutional government. Yet, Federalists saw the same dramatic changes as the degeneration of legitimate government into mob rule, particularly during the 1793 and 1794 bloody "Reign of Terror" when "counterrevolutionaries" lost their lives on the guillotine.

Federalist fears deepened as they watched the new French republican government encourage wars of liberation and conquest in Belgium, Switzerland, Holland, and the Italian peninsula. Rumors were rampant in 1798 about a possible French invasion of America, one that allegedly would be supported by American traitors and a population of French émigrés that had grown to more than 20,000.

The United States' rapidly growing immigrant population deeply troubled Federalists. One Pennsylvania newspaper argued that "none but the most vile and worthless" were inundating the country. William Shaw, the president's nephew, arguing that "all our present difficulties may be traced" to the "hordes of Foreigners" in the land, contended America should "no longer" be "an asylum to all nations." Federalists worried about the 50,000 Irish immigrants in the new nation, some of whom had been exiled for plotting against British rule. These malcontents, they argued—along with French immigrants, and a sprinkling of British radicals like the liberal theologian and scientist Joseph Priestley—presented a grave challenge to the nation. The Federalists feared that the extremist ideas of the dissenters would corrupt and mobilize the destitute.

The British government, even more terrified than the Americans that ideas from the radical French regime might spread, had been at war with France for five years, trying to contain it. Both nations had seized neutral American ships headed to their enemy's ports. President Adams initiated a two-pronged plan to stop the French from seizing any further ships. He sent three emissaries to negotiate with the French government, and he worked to push bills through Congress to increase the size of the navy and army. Federalist revulsion at anything associated with France reached a peak in spring 1798 when word arrived in Philadelphia that three French agents, identified only as X, Y, and Z, had demanded a bribe from the American diplomats before they would begin negotiations.

One Pennsylvania newspaper argued that "none but the most vile and worthless" were inundating the country.

Insulted by the French government, convinced that war was inevitable, and anxious over a "dangerous" alien population in their midst, Federalists in Philadelphia were ready to believe any rumor. They saw no reason to doubt the warning in a letter found outside the president's residence in late April. It supposedly contained information about a plot by a group of Frenchmen "to sit [sic] fire to the City in various parts, and to Massacre the inhabitants." Hundreds of militiamen patrolled the city streets as a precaution, and a special guard was assigned to the president's home. John Adams ordered "chests of arms from the war-office," as he was "determined to defend my house at the expense of my life."

In such a crisis atmosphere, Federalists took action to prevent domestic subversion. They supported four laws passed in June and July 1798 to control the threats they believed foreigners posed to the security of the nation and to punish the opposition party for its seditious libel.

Two of these laws represented the Federalist effort to address perceived threats from the nation's immigrant groups. The Alien Enemies Act permitted the deportation of aliens who hailed from a nation with which the United States was at war, while the Alien Friends Act empowered the president, during peacetime, to deport any alien whom he considered dangerous.

Although some historians acknowledge that there were legitimate national security concerns involved in the passage of the two alien acts, others conclude that the two additional pieces of legislation were blatant efforts to destroy the Republican Party, which had gained many immigrant supporters.

The Naturalization Act extended the residency requirement for citizenship from five to 14 years. For a few politicians, such as Congressmen Robert Goodloe Harper and Harrison Gray Otis, even this act was insufficient. They believed that citizenship should be limited to those born in the United States.

Apart from its limitations on speech, the Sedition Act, the last of the four laws, made it illegal to "unlawfully combine or conspire together, with intent to oppose any measure or measures of the government." While the First Amendment to the U.S. Constitution established that Congress couldn't pass laws "abridging the freedom of speech, or of the press; or the right of the people peaceably to assemble," there had been little discussion about the amendment's precise meaning since its adoption seven years earlier.

In 1798 many Federalists drew upon *Commentaries on the Laws of England* written by Sir William Blackstone—the man considered by the framers of the Constitution to be the oracle of the common law—for their definition of liberty of the press. Blackstone wrote, "liberty of the press . . . consists in laying no previous restraints upon publications." However, if a person "publishes what is improper, mischievous, or illegal, he must take the consequences of his own temerity." In other words, if a person spoke or wrote remarks that could be construed as seditious libel, they weren't entitled to free speech protection.

According to the Federalists, if seditious libel meant any effort to malign or weaken the government, then the Republican press was repeatedly guilty. Republican papers, claimed the Federalists, such as the Philadelphia *Aurora,* the New York *Argus,* the Richmond *Examiner,* and Boston's *Independent Chronicle* printed the most scurrilous statements, lies, and misrepresentations about President Adams and the Federalist Party.

The president's wife, Abigail, complained bitterly about journalistic "abuse, deception and falsehood." Particularly galling to her were the characterizations of her husband in editor Benjamin Bache's *Aurora.* In April 1798 Bache called the president "old, querulous, Bald, blind, crippled, Toothless Adams." Bache, she argued, was a "lying wretch" given to the "most insolent and abusive" language. He wrote with the "malice" of Satan. The First Lady repeatedly demanded that something be done to stop this "wicked and base, violent and calumniating abuse" being "leveled against the Government." She argued that if journalists like Bache weren't stopped, the nation would be plunged into a "civil war."

At the same time, Federalists were hardly models of decorum when describing Republicans. Their opponents were, one Federalist wrote, "democrats,

In the 200 years since the passage of the Alien and Sedition Acts, each generation of Americans has struggled to determine the limits of free speech and freedom of the press.

mobocrats and all other kinds of rats." Federalist Noah Webster characterized Republicans as "the refuse, the sweepings of the most depraved part of mankind from the most corrupt nations on earth." Although President Adams neither framed the Sedition Act nor encouraged its introduction, he certainly supported it. He issued many public statements about the evils of the opposition press. Adams believed that journalists who deliberately distorted the news to mislead the people could cause great harm to a representative democracy.

Letters and remarks of John and Abigail Adams made passage of a sedition bill easier, but the task of pushing it through Congress fell to Senator James Lloyd of Maryland and Congressmen Robert Goodloe Harper and Harrison Gray Otis. Although it passed by a wide margin in the Senate, the bill

barely gained approval in the House of Representatives, where the vote was 44 to 41. To win even that small majority, Harper and Otis had to change the original bill in significant ways. Prosecutors would have to prove malicious intent, and truth would be permitted as a defense. Juries, not judges, would determine whether a statement was libelous. To underscore its political purpose, the act was to expire on March 3, 1801, the last day of President Adams' term of office.

PROSECUTIONS BEGAN QUICKLY. On June 26, even before the Sedition Act was passed, Supreme Court Justice Richard Peters issued a warrant for the arrest of Benjamin Bache. Bache, the most powerful of all the Republican newspaper editors, was charged with "libeling the President and the Executive Government in a manner tending to excite sedition and opposition to the laws." Less than two weeks later, federal marshals arrested John Daly Burk, editor of the New York newspaper *Time Piece,* for making "seditious and libelous" statements against the president. Neither faced trial, however. Bache died in Philadelphia during the yellow fever epidemic of September 1798, and Burk, who wasn't a citizen, agreed to deportation if charges were dropped. He then fled to Virginia to live under an assumed name.

During the next two years 17 people were indicted under the Sedition Act, and 10 were convicted. Most were journalists. Included among them were William Duane, who had succeeded Benjamin Bache as editor of the *Aurora;* Thomas Cooper, a British radical who edited a small Pennsylvania newspaper; Charles Holt, editor of a New London, Connecticut, newspaper; and James Callender, who had worked on the

THE GRANGER COLLECTION

Congressional debate on the alien and sedition bills caused fierce arguments between Federalists and Republicans. An 1808 cartoon depicts a fight that took place on the House floor between Federalist Roger Griswold (wielding the cane) and Republican Matthew Lyon.

Aurora before moving to Virginia's Richmond *Examiner.* Like Benjamin Bache, Callender delighted in condemning the president.

The Federalists didn't target only journalists. They went after other individuals, including David Brown of Dedham, Massachusetts, who spouted anti-government rhetoric wherever a crowd gathered. Brown was arrested in April 1799, charged with "uttering seditious pieces" and helping to erect a liberty pole with a placard that read "A Speedy Retirement to the President. No Sedition bill, No Alien bill, Downfall to the Tyrants of America."

Incredibly, even an inebriated Republican, Luther Baldwin of Newark, New Jersey, became a victim. Following the adjournment of Congress in July 1798, President Adams and his wife were traveling through Newark on their way to their home in Quincy, Massachusetts. Residents lined the streets as church bells rang, and ceremonial cannon fire greeted the party. As the procession made its way past a local tavern owned by John Burnet, one of the patrons remarked, "There goes the President and they are firing at his a__." According to the Newark *Centinel of Freedom,* Baldwin added that, "he did not care if they fired thro' his a__." Burnet overheard the exchange and exclaimed, "That is seditious." Baldwin was arrested and later convicted of speaking "seditious words tending to defame the President and Government of the United States." He was fined $150, assessed court costs and expenses, and sent to jail until he paid the fine and fees.

The most outrageous case, however, involved Congressman Matthew Lyon, a Republican from Vermont. This fiery Irishman was one of the sharpest critics of President Adams and the Federalists. He had even engaged in a brawl on the House floor with Federalist Roger Griswold. Convinced that the Federalists intended to use the Sedition Act to silence their congressional opposition, Lyon confided to a colleague that it "most probably would be brought to bear upon himself first victim of all."

While not the initial victim, Lyon quickly felt the wrath of the majority party. In the summer of 1798, he wrote an article criticizing President Adams' "continual grasp for power" and his "unbounded thirst for ridiculous pomp, foolish adulation, and selfish avarice." During his fall re-election campaign, Lyon also quoted from a letter that suggested Congress should dispatch the president to a "mad house" for his handling of the French crisis. In October, a federal grand jury indicted Lyon for stirring up sedition and bringing "the President and government of the United States into contempt."

United States Supreme Court justices, sitting as circuit court judges, presided in the sedition trials. These judges, all Federalists, rejected the efforts of defendants and their counsel to challenge the law's constitutionality. Samuel Chase, who sat in three of the cases, clearly was on a mission. "There is nothing we should more dread," he argued, "than the licentiousness of the press."

Chase and the other judges handed down tough sentences. While none imposed the statute's maximum penalties of a $2,000 fine or a jail sentence of two years, they often sent the guilty to jail. Most of the convicted endured three- or four-month sentences. James Callender, however, served nine months, and David Brown twice as long. The average fines were about $300, although Luther Baldwin's fine was $150 and Matthew Lyon's was $1,000.

As the trials progressed, two Republican Party leaders, Thomas Jefferson and James Madison, tried to overturn the Sedition Act. Concluding that the Bill of Rights couldn't prevent abuses of power by the federal government, the two men collaborated on a set of protest resolutions asserting that the government was a compact created by the states and that citizens, speaking through their state legislatures, had the right to judge the constitutionality of actions taken by the government. In this instance, they called upon the states to join them in declaring the Alien and Sedition Acts to be "void, and of no force."

While only Kentucky and Virginia endorsed the resolutions, the efforts of Jefferson and Madison encouraged Republicans to make the Alien and Sedition Acts major issues in the campaign of 1800. Voter anger over these bills, along with higher taxes and the escalating federal debt resulting from increased defense spending, gave Republicans a majority in the House of Representatives. The Federalists lost almost 40 seats, leaving the new Congress with 66 Republicans and only 40 Federalists.

There were other unexpected results from the passage of the Sedition Act. Clearly, Federalists had hoped to stifle the influence of the fewer than 20 Republican newspapers published in 1798. Some, like John Daly Burk's *Time Piece,* did cease publication; others suspended operation while their editors were in jail. However, circulation increased for the majority of the periodicals. Most discouraging to the Federalists, particularly as the campaigns for the 1800 election got under way, was the fact that more than 30 new Republican newspapers began operation following passage of the Sedition Act.

Not even prison stopped Republican Congressman Matthew Lyon. The most visible target of the Federalists, Lyon conducted his re-election campaign from his jail cell in Vergennes, Vermont. Considered a martyr by his supporters, Lyon regularly contributed to this image through letters and newspaper articles. "It is quite a new kind of jargon to call a Representative of the People an Opposer of the Government because he does not, as a legislator, advocate and acquiesce in every proposition that comes from the Executive," he wrote. In a December run-off election, Lyon won easily.

By 1802, in the wake of the Federalist election defeat, the Alien Friends Act, the Sedition Act, and the Naturalization Act had expired or been repealed. The Alien Enemies Act remained in effect, but no one had been prosecuted under its provisions because the United States hadn't declared war on France, a necessary condition for the law's implementation. After winning the presidency in the 1800 election, Thomas Jefferson pardoned all those convicted of violating the Sedition Act who remained in prison.

By virtually every measure, the Federalist effort to impose a one-party press and a one-party government on the fledgling nation had failed. Ironically, the Sedition Act prompted the opposition to expand its view of free speech and freedom of the press. In a series of essays, tracts, and books, Republicans began to argue that the First Amendment protected citizens from any federal restraint on the press or speech. Notable among them was a pamphlet entitled *An Essay on the Liberty of the Press,* published in 1799 by George Hay, a member of the Virginia House of Delegates. Hay argued "that if the words freedom of the press have any meaning at all they mean a total exemption from any law making any publication whatever criminal." In his 1801 inaugural address, Thomas Jefferson echoed Hay's sentiments, stressing the necessity of preserving the right of citizens "to think freely and to speak and to write what they think."

For most, the arguments of Hay and Jefferson have prevailed, although even the Republicans were willing to acknowledge that states could and should impose speech restrictions under certain conditions. Moreover, there have been occasions, most notably during World War I, when the federal government declared that free expression was secondary to military necessity. In an effort to suppress dissent and anti-war activity in 1917, Congress passed the Espionage Act, a law that made it a felony to try to cause insubordination in the armed forces or to convey false statements with intent to interfere with military operations. It was followed by the Sedition Act of 1918, which banned treasonable or seditious material from the mail. Under this provision the mailing of many publications, including the *New York Times* as well as radical and dissident newspapers, was temporarily halted.

In the 200 years since the passage of the Alien and Sedition Acts, each generation of Americans has struggled to determine the limits of free speech and freedom of the press. In large part, it has been a dilemma of reconciling freedom and security with liberty and order. For the Federalist Party in 1798, however, the answer was simple; order and security had to prevail.

Larry Gragg, professor of history at the University of Missouri-Rolla, is the author of two books on the Virginia Quakers and the Salem witch crisis.

Lewis and Clark

Trailblazers Who Opened the Continent

Few Americans better embodied the spirit of adventure and dedication that led 19th-century explorers to brave the perils of an unknown land.

By Gerald F. Kreyche

EVERY SOCIETY has a need for heroes who serve as role models. The U.S. is no exception and has produced its share of them—Pres. Abraham Lincoln, aviator Charles Lindbergh, civil rights leader Martin Luther King, Jr., and the astronauts, to name a few. Heroes belong to the ages, and we can refresh our pride and patriotism by recalling their deeds.

In the early 19th century, two relatively unsung heroes, Meriwether Lewis and William Clark, braved the perils of a vast unknown territory to enlarge knowledge, increase commerce, and establish a relationship with unknown Indians. Their journals produced eight detailed volumes of data ranging from maps, climate, geography, and ethnic observations to the discovery of new species of plants and animals.

In the late 18th century, America's western border was constituted first by the Allegheny Mountains and later the Mississippi River. Little was known of the geography immediately beyond the Father of Waters, and less yet of what lay west of the Missouri River. This was to change, however, for Pres. Thomas Jefferson had an unquenchable yearning for such knowledge and did something about it.

Dr. Kreyche, American Thought Editor of USA Today, is emeritus professor of philosophy, DePaul University, Chicago, Ill.

As early as 1784, he conferred with George Rogers Clark about exploring this uncharted area. In 1786 he hired John Ledyard, a former marine associate of British explorer James Cook, to walk from west to east, beginning in Stockholm, Sweden. The intent was to traverse Russia, Alaska, the western Canadian coast, and thence across the Louisiana Territory. Ledyard walked from Stockholm to St. Petersburg, Russia, in two weeks. The Russians stopped him at Irkutsk, Siberia, and Jefferson was disappointed again. Undaunted, Jefferson made plans for Andre Michael to explore the area, but this, too, failed.

After being inaugurated in 1801, Jefferson had the power to make his pet project a reality. He appointed as his private secretary Meriwether Lewis, a well-born young army captain. In January, 1803, in a secret message to Congress, the President asked for funding to realize his exploratory project of what lay between the Missouri River and the Pacific Ocean. The sum of $2,500 was appropriated. (The project eventually was to cost $38,000, an early case of a governmental cost overrun.)

Jefferson asked Lewis to head the project. Lewis had served under William Clark (younger brother of George Rogers Clark) in earlier times and offered him co-leadership of the expedition, designated The Corps of Discovery. Clark accepted Lewis' offer to "partici-

pate with him in its fatiegues its dangers and its honors." Clark, no longer on active army status, was told he would receive a regular army captaincy, but Congress refused to grant it. Nevertheless, Lewis designated Clark as captain and co-commander; the expedition's men so regarded him and the journals so record it.

Lewis and Clark were scientist-explorers and singularly complementary. Although both were leaders of men and strict disciplinarians, Lewis was somewhat aloof, with a family background of bouts of despondency; Clark was more the extrovert and father figure. Lewis had great scientific interests in flora, fauna, and minerals, and Clark's surveying and engineering skills fit well with the demands of the expedition. While Lewis tended to view Indians fundamentally as savages, Clark, like Jefferson, saw the Indian as a full member of the human race and child of nature. At all times, the two soldiers were a team, each leading the expedition every other day. No known quarrel between them ever was recorded, although on a few occasions they thought it expedient to separate, probably to cool off and get out of each other's hair.

To prepare for their journey into the unknown, Lewis stayed in the East to study astronomy, plant taxonomy, practical medicine, etc., and to gather equipment from the armory at Harper's Ferry,

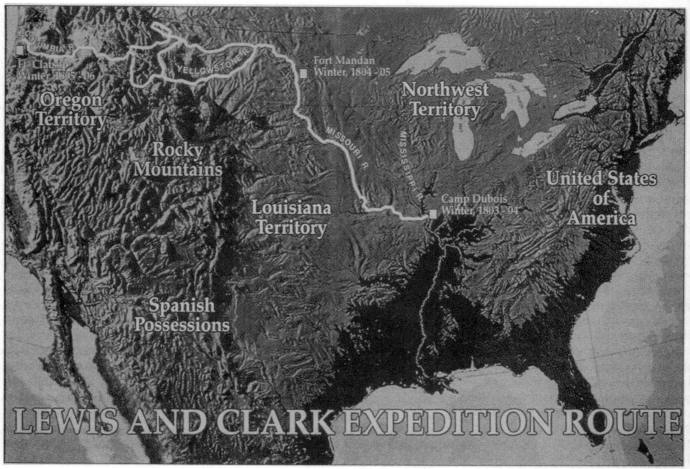

LEWIS AND CLARK EXPEDITION ROUTE

MAP COURTESY OF NATIONAL PARK SERVICE, DEPARTMENT OF THE INTERIOR

The Lewis and Clark expedition started off from Wood River, Ill., opposite St. Louis, and headed northwest, concluding at Fort Clatsop at the mouth of the Columbia River in Oregon.

Va. The supplies would include trading goods such as awls, fishhooks, paints, tobacco twists, Jefferson medals, whiskey, and a generous amount of laudanum (a morphine-like drug). Lewis supervised the building of a 22-foot keelboat needed to take them up the Missouri to a winter quartering place. Additionally, he had his eye out for recruits for the expedition.

Clark went to St. Louis to recruit "robust, helthy, hardy" young, experienced, and versatile backwoodsmen. All were single. The captains needed interpreters, river experts, and hunters able to live under the most demanding conditions. Also sought were men with multiple skills who could do carpentry and blacksmith work and follow orders. With the exception of a hunter-interpreter, George Drouillard, if they were not already in the army, they enrolled in it. Privates re-

ceived five dollars a month; sergeants, eight dollars. Both leaders and the sergeants kept journals.

On May 14, 1804, the regular group of 29 men, plus a temporary complement of 16 others, set off from the St. Louis area for Mandan, in what is now North Dakota, the site of their winter quarters. With them came Lewis' Newfoundland dog, Scannon, and Clark's body-servant, a black man named York. Clark's journal entry reads, "I set out at 4 o'clock P.M. in the presence of many of the neighboring inhabitants, and proceeded under a jentle brease up the Missourie." Little did they know it would be some 7,200 miles and nearly two and a half years before their return.

The trip upriver was backbreaking, as spring floods pushed the water downstream in torrents. Hunters walked the shores, while the keelboat men alter-

nately rowed, poled, sailed, and rope-pulled the boat against the current. Wind, rain, and hail seemed to meet them at every turn in the serpentine Missouri. Snags and sandbars were everywhere. Bloated, gangrenous buffalo carcasses floated downstream, witnesses to the treachery of thin ice ahead. Often, for security reasons, the expedition party docked at night on small islands, some of which floated away as they embarked in the morning.

Ambassadors of goodwill, they stopped at major Indian villages, counseling peace instead of internecine warfare as well as distributing gifts. At the same time, they questioned the Indians about what lay ahead. Generally, such information was reliable. Tragedy struck at Council Bluffs (now Iowa), where Sgt. Charles Floyd died, probably of a ruptured appendix. He was the only member of the Corps to lose his life. After a proper eulogy, the captains wrote in their journals, as they were to do many times, "We proceeded on." Today, an obelisk marks the general location.

THE MYTH OF SACAJAWEA

On Nov. 2, 1804, they reached a river confluence about 30 miles north of present-day Bismarck, N.D., and settled in with the Mandan Indians, who welcomed them as security against Sioux attacks. They met Toussaint Charbonneau, a 40-year-old trapper wintering there, who, although ignorant of English, spoke a number of Indian languages. Equally important, he had a teenage wife, Sacajawea, a Shoshone who had been captured and traded by the Hidatsa (Minitari). Her tribe were horse-people and lived near the headwaters of the Missouri, two facts that enticed Lewis and Clark to hire Charbonneau and, as part of the deal, arrange for her to accompany them to the area. It would prove burdensome, though, for she delivered a baby boy, Baptiste, who would go with them. Clark took a liking to him and nicknamed him Pompey, even naming and autographing a river cliff prominence (Pompey's Pillar) after him. Later, Clark was to adopt the boy.

A myth of political correctness tells of Sacajawea being the guide for the expedition. Nothing could be further from the truth, as she was six years removed from her people and, when kidnapped, had been taken on a completely different route than that followed by the explorers. She did know Indian herbs, food, and medicine, though, and her presence and that of her child assured others that this was no war party.

Various factors of luck augured the party's success, such as Clark's flaming red hair and York's black skin and "buffalo hair." These would be items of curiosity to up-river Indians. The Corps also had an acrobat who walked on his hands, a one-eyed fiddler, and an air gun that made no explosion when fired. Some Indians previously thought that sound, not the rifle ball, killed, and

could not understand this magic. Lewis' dog always was viewed with larcenous eyes, as Indians used dogs for hauling, camp guards, and eating.

On April 7, 1805, the now seasoned expeditionary force left the village and went northwest for parts unknown. Their vehicles were six small canoes and two large perogues. The extras who accompanied them to the fort returned home with the keelboat. Aboard it were samples of flora and minerals, as well as "barking squirrels" (prairie dogs) and other hides and stuffed animals unknown to the East, such as "beardless goats" (pronghorn antelope). Lewis noted, "I could but esteem this moment of departure as among the most happy of my life."

They entered country that was increasingly wild and where white men had not penetrated. Grizzly bears proved to be a considerable threat, but food was plentiful as buffalo abounded. Frequent entries record that "Musquetoes were troublesum." For a time, they were plagued by the ague, dysentery, and boils. Clark drained a half-pint of fluid from one carbuncle on his ankle. The change of diet from meat to camas bulbs to fish didn't help. They laboriously portaged about 16-miles around Great Falls (now Montana), and reached the three forks of the Missouri River, which they named the Jefferson, Madison, and Gallatin. They were but a short distance northwest of what is now Yellowstone National Park.

Lewis followed the Jefferson fork, as Clark and Sacajawea lingered behind. Seeing some Indians, Lewis tried to entice them with presents to meet him, rolling up his sleeves and pointing to his white skin, calling out, "Tabba-bone." Supposedly, this was Shoshone for "white man," but a mispronunciation could render it as the equivalent of "enemy."

The Shoshone feared this was a trick of their hereditary enemies, the Blackfeet, as they never had seen white men. They scarcely were reassured when Clark, Sacajawea, and the rest of the party caught up with Lewis. However, Sacajawea began to suck furiously on her fingers, indicating she was suckled by these people. She also recognized another woman who had been kidnapped

with her, but had escaped. When a council was called, she recognized her brother, Cameawhait, a Shoshone chief. This helped the Corps in trading for needed horses to cross the Continental Divide.

The explorers were disappointed, for they had hoped that, by now, they would be close to the Pacific. This could not be so, though as these Indians knew no white men, and the salmon (a saltwater fish) they had were from trade, not the Indians' own fishing. Staying with the Shoshone for about a week, during which his 31st birthday occurred, Lewis wrote introspectively that he regretted his "many hours . . . of indolence [and now] would live for mankind, as I have hitherto lived for myself."

They hired a Shoshone guide known as "Old Toby" and his sons to cross the treacherous Bitterroot Mountains, the Continental Divide. After doing yeoman's service, the Indians deserted the party without collecting pay near the Clearwater and Snake rivers. The reason was the intention of the explorers to run ferocious rapids that seemed to swallow up everything in their fury. The Corps were able to run them without serious consequence, though. They proceeded on and came upon the Flathead Indians. One Flathead boy knew Shoshone, and a roundabout process of translation was established. Clark spoke English, and an army man translated it to French for Charbonneau. He, in turn, changed it to Minitari, and Sacajawea converted it to Shoshone, which the Flathead boy rendered in his language.

The group pursued the Clearwater River, which met the Snake River. This flowed into the Columbia, which emptied into the Pacific Ocean. Numerous Indian tribes inhabited the Columbia—Clatsop, Chinook, Salish, to name a few. Most were poverty-stricken and a far cry from the healthy Plains Indians. Many were blinded by age 30, as the sun reflecting off the water while they were fishing took its toll. Clark administered ointments and laudanum. Most didn't improve healthwise, but the Indians felt better for the drug and any placebo effects.

Lewis and Clark were overjoyed to find some Columbia River Indians using white men's curse words and wearing metal trinkets. Both only could be from ships' crews that plied the Pacific shores. The Corps were nearing the western end of their journey and, on Nov. 7, 1805, Lewis declared, "Great joy in camp we are in view of the Ocian." They constructed a rude Fort Clatsop (now rebuilt) by the Columbia River estuary near Astoria, in what today is Oregon, and sent parties in all directions to gather information. There was great excitement when reports of a beached whale reached the fort. Sacajawea, who continued with the expedition, insisted on seeing this leviathan, and she was accommodated. The men busied themselves hunting, making salt, and preparing for the journey home. (The salt cairn is reconstructed and preserved not many miles from the fort.)

THE JOURNEY HOME

The Corps entertained the hope that they might make contact with a coastal ship to return them home, and one ship, the *Lydia,* did arrive, but, through a communication failure or lying by the Indians, the captain believed the Corps already had left over land.

On March 23, 1806, after a rainy and miserable winter, the expedition left Fort Clatsop and, along the way, split into three groups hoping to explore more territory. They felt duty-bound to learn as much as they could and agreed to meet at the confluence of the Yellowstone and Missouri rivers. They traded beads and boats for horses and faced the worst kind of pilfering, even Scannon being nearly dog-napped.

Lewis, whose route took him through the territory of the fierce Blackfeet, invited a small party into his camp. One of them tried to steal soldier Reuben Field's gun and was stabbed for his efforts; another stole a horse and, losing all patience, Lewis "at a distance of thirty steps shot him in the belly." Fearing a large war party might be nearby, they traveled the next 60 miles nearly non-stop.

On the way to meet Clark, Lewis and a one-eyed hunter, Peter Cruzatte—both dressed in elkskin—went into the brush to hunt. Lewis was shot in the buttocks by Cruzatte, who apparently mistook him for an elk. The wound was painful, but no vital parts were damaged, although Lewis privately wondered if the shooting was deliberate.

Downriver, Lewis' party met two Illinois trappers searching for beaver. When they learned about the Blackfeet incident, they backtracked and accompanied Lewis to the rendezvous. There, with the captains' permission, they persuaded John Colter, who later discovered Yellowstone, to leave the party and to show them the beaver areas.

Having rendezvoused with the others, all stopped at the Mandan village in which they had spent the previous winter. Here, Toussaint Charbonneau, Sacajawea, and Baptiste (Pompey) parted company. The trapper was paid about $400–500 for his services.

Upon their return home, all the men received double pay and land grants from a grateful Congress. Several of the men went back to trap the area from which they had come, commencing the era of the mountain men. One became a judge and U.S. Senator, and another a district attorney. Others returned to farming. Clark had some sort of fallout with York, and the latter was reduced to a hired-out slave, a considerable fall from the prestigious body-servant status. Eventually, though, he was freed by Clark.

Lewis was appointed governor of the Louisiana Territory, but ran into personal and political problems. He suffered severe bouts of depression, began to drink heavily, and had to dose himself with drugs more frequently. To clear his name, he set off for Washington, but grew increasingly suicidal. He attempted to kill himself several times and finally succeeded on the Natchez Trace, at Grinder's Stand in Tennessee in 1809. Nevertheless, Meriwether Lewis should be remembered not for the circumstances of his death, but for his life of duty, leadership, and love of country.

Clark was appointed governor and Indian agent of the Missouri Territory. He also was given the rank of brigadier general in the militia—not bad for a bogus captain! He married Julia Hancock, a childhood friend, and named one of their children after Lewis, his comrade-in-arms. After Julia's death, Clark married her cousin, Harriet Kennerly.

Sacajawea died a young woman around 1812 at Ft. Union near the Missouri-Yellowstone confluence. Although she was rumored to die an old lady at Ft. Washakie in Wyoming—indeed, a large gravestone with her name is engraved there on the Shoshone Arapaho Reservation—the evidence for the Ft. Union death is more compelling. Clark adopted young Pompey, who later became a famous linguist and toured Europe in the company of royalty. Eventually, he became a mountain man.

William Clark died in 1838, a good friend of the Indians and, like Meriwether Lewis, a genuine American hero.

Chief Justice Marshall Takes the Law in Hand

Upsetting presidents and setting precedents, he helped forge a nation

By Robert Wernick

IF YOU HAVE BEEN BROUGHT UP pledging allegiance to the flag and the Republic for which it stands, "one nation under God, indivisible, with liberty and justice for all," there is a certain surprise in reading the Constitution and finding that it nowhere contains the word nation (or, for that matter, the word "God").

The Constitution was ratified—though just barely—in 1788, but it took Americans years to decide what this new political experiment was actually going to be. Would it be a cluster of confederated republics? Or a nation in the traditional sense, like France or England?

Today we know what happened and take the result for granted. Yet in 1804, it was the subject of bitter debate, and no less a personage than Thomas Jefferson, the President of the United States, could write, "whether we remain in one confederacy or form into Atlantic and Mississippi confederations, I believe not

very important to the happiness of either part."

The definitive answer binding upon all Americans was written in torrents of blood during the Civil War. Long before that, however, the question began to be answered, and a crucial moment in the gradual shift toward nationhood can be pinpointed to a few months in the year 1803, when two great Americans, who detested each other, took separate and independent actions ensuring that a nation, one and indivisible, would eventually result.

One was Thomas Jefferson, third President. The other was John Marshall, fourth Chief Justice of the United States.

In February of that year Marshall handed down a decision in a case called *Marbury v. Madison.* That was the first time the Supreme Court declared unconstitutional a law that had been duly passed by Congress and signed by the President. A few months after *Marbury*

v. Madison, Jefferson deliberately exceeded what he was pretty certain were the powers of the Presidency, as defined by the Constitution, by buying Louisiana from Napoleon Bonaparte for $15 million.

Jefferson, of course, is one of the most famous figures of American history: his face is on the nickel, his memorial stands in white marble splendor across the water from those of Washington and Lincoln. The graces and crotchets of his character are well known to us. John Marshall, on the other hand, remains an austere and shadowy figure, remembered almost exclusively for having written a handful of brilliant and decisive opinions, their details familiar mainly to historians and constitutional scholars. Just lately, however, perhaps because the role and functions of the Supreme Court are under such hot debate, Marshall has reappeared in the public eye. Two books, *John Marshall,* by Jean

From *Smithsonian,* November 1998, pp. 156-160, 162-173. © 1998 by Robert Wernick. Reprinted by permission.

Edward Smith, and *The Great Chief Justice,* by Charles Hobson, have been published, and they help bring him to life not only as a justice but as a towering, many-talented and very appealing figure.

Marshall came from the same Virginia stock as Jefferson; they were in fact second cousins once removed. But their political opinions were as far apart as their characters. Unlike Jefferson, a slaveholding aristocrat born to wealth, Marshall, the oldest of 15 children, came from a frontier community and was a self-made man. For various reasons, Jefferson did not fight in the American Revolution. As ambassador to France, he was not at the Constitutional Convention of 1787 (SMITHSONIAN, July 1987). Marshall had played a major role in ratifying the Constitution. He was, moreover, tempered by war, having served with George Washington at Valley Forge, and he had to work hard to establish himself as a successful Virginia lawyer. In 1798 President Washington virtually ordered him to run for a seat in Congress.

Marshall remained something of a frontiersman all his life, tall, rangy, plainspoken, self-reliant. Before being appointed to the Supreme Court by President John Adams, he had not only been a frontline soldier, lawyer and legislator but a land speculator, diplomat, pamphleteer and John Adams' Secretary of State. He briefly became a national hero in 1797 when, as one of three American envoys sent to Paris to negotiate a treaty with the government of revolutionary France, he ran up against Citizen, ex-bishop and foreign minister Charles Maurice de Talleyrand. The slippery Talleyrand informed him through three emissaries that America would get the treaty only if it suitably greased Talleyrand's palms. The three emissaries were code-named X, Y and Z. Marshall took the lead in bluntly rebuffing this shakedown as dishonorable and an affront to the United States of America. Marshall's tensely worded message home was later summed up by a memorable sound bite, "Millions for defense, but not one cent for tribute." Americans were so outraged at the

French behavior that war was threatened, all of which further stirred Jefferson's ire at Marshall, perhaps because Jefferson had a weakness for all things French. He was angry enough to claim the whole thing was "a dish cooked up by Marshall." The country knew better. On his return Marshall was lavishly honored by enthusiastic crowds in Philadelphia, then the nation's capital.

Jefferson often dealt with him vindictively. He even used to run down what he called Marshall's "lax lounging manners," partly because Marshall was as perfectly at home in a rowdy tavern as in a law court or an elegant Paris salon, and got on with everybody. On election day Marshall was the candidate who offered the best whiskey to the voters. There were no fancy airs about him. He was famous for his slovenly dress. He often did the shopping for his ailing wife, Polly, a rarity for a man of his standing. They liked to tell the story of how a dandified young man came up to him in the Richmond marketplace once and, not knowing him, said, in effect, "Here, my man. Just take this turkey to my house," and flipped him a coin. The Chief Justice of the United States cheerfully pocketed it and delivered the turkey. It was on his way.

Jefferson, by contrast, lived beyond his means and was always in debt. He envisioned himself as the representative of poor farmers and the slave-owning, agrarian South, telling them that moneyed interests and manufacturers in the Northeastern cities were up to no good. The Louisiana Purchase notwithstanding, Jefferson thought—like some extreme conservatives of today—that the government had no right to do anything not spelled out in the Constitution.

Marshall had learned sacredness of contracts and the value of sound money as a self-made lawyer. During the starvation winter at Valley Forge, Marshall watched local farmers selling food to the British in Philadelphia—who had real money to pay for it—rather than accept the worthless paper issued by the Continental Congress, which did not have the right to tax. He had a lifelong conviction that a country needs a central government with power and responsibility enough to override local interests.

LIBRARY OF CONGRESS

In a romanticized re-creation, Marshall is characterized as the ill-clad orator; no doubt, he is delivering a persuasive speech to his dapper audience.

This was the view of his political party, the Federalists, who believed that the Constitution had authorized the formation of a federal government able to pay the country's debts and provide for its defense. They cited the Preamble to the Constitution as well as Article 1, Section 8, which both asserted that the document's purpose was to "provide for the common Defense and general Welfare." For Federalists, that seemed to cover all sorts of federal initiatives. Jefferson and his party, the Republicans, hated the very idea.

For Jefferson the states were sovereign. It was thus up to any individual state to determine the extent of its powers in settling disputes between the federal and state governments. Though Marshall was not an extreme Federalist, he saw that as a recipe for anarchy. Such decisions, it followed, could best be made by an independent judiciary. Judges, presumably, had nothing to gain from their actions; they alone could be impartial umpires. The heart of the judiciary was the Supreme Court.

In those early years of the Republic, however, the Supreme Court had none of the authority it enjoys today. It heard cases for a few weeks each year; the judges also had to serve as circuit court judges in various legal districts. When gathered in the raw city of Washington they all lived together in a ramshackle boarding-house. Even when the Capitol eventually went up, the Court's quarters were far from supreme; a first-floor committee room served until 1810, and then the justices found themselves in a dark, cramped space beneath the magisterial halls of Congress.

The justices had a tradition in their conferences; they would have wine only when the weather was bad. If it was sunny out, though, Marshall would sometimes say to his colleagues: "Our jurisdiction extends over so large a territory that the doctrine of chances makes it certain that it must be raining somewhere."

Marshall's charm, his taste in wine and whiskey, along with his formidable intellect and legal learning, won the support of colleagues, many of whom, as the years went by, were expressly appointed to disagree with him. In years

on the bench he was obliged to write only one dissenting opinion in a constitutional case.

John Adams appointed him Chief Justice shortly after being defeated by Jefferson in the Presidential election of 1800. Marshall was then Secretary of State, and Adams asked him to stay on till the new Republican administration took over on March 4, 1801. Adams appointed other Federalists at the last minute as well, including one William Marbury, named justice of the peace for the District of Columbia. The nomination was approved by the Senate the day before Jefferson's inauguration. Marbury's commission was duly made out and signed by President Adams at the very end of his term. As Secretary of State, Marshall affixed the great seal of the United States to it. But in the rush of events leading up to the transfer of power, he left it on his desk and didn't send it out.

The Court had a tradition in their conferences; they would have wine only when the weather was bad.

Jefferson was an intensely partisan politician, and he was greatly annoyed by the last-minute appointments of Federalist judges. He regularly accused Federalists of wanting to establish a monarchy and cozy up to Great Britain. He wanted to be rid of all Federalists, Marshall especially.

Jefferson simply ordered that the commissions not be delivered. Marbury was out of the job, and after nine months he turned to the law. He requested that the Court issue a writ of mandamus (in Latin, "we command"), which by law compels a government official to perform a duty. Marbury wanted the new Secretary of State, James Madison, to be forced to deliver to him his duly signed and sealed commission. The result was *Marbury v. Madison,* a case that called forth heated political invective between Federalists and Republicans. It was also a ticklish matter for the

new Chief Justice, who handled it with the intellectual grip, clarity of reasoning and political adroitness that would mark his whole career. His method was always to narrow his focus, brushing aside the extraneous, until he got to the precise point on which a case turned. In Marbury, he managed to find an elegant legal solution that gave something to both sides.

Article 3 of the Constitution had established a Supreme Court but left the organization of other courts to be defined by Congress. An early attempt was the Judiciary Act of 1789, which, in addition to creating some district and circuit courts, in Section 13 took up some of the Supreme Court's jurisdictions, and granted it the power under certain circumstances to issue writs of mandamus "to persons holding office under the authority of the United States."

Marshall found that Marbury clearly had a right to his commission, it having been signed by the President. He had, indeed, been illegally deprived of it by the government. But, Marshall reasoned, in the case at hand the Supreme Court had no power to issue a writ of mandamus, ordering the government to deliver it. Why? Because Section 13 of the Judiciary Act unconstitutionally enlarged the Court's original jurisdiction. The whole of the new nation's laws should depend on the Constitution, so Congress, he reasoned, could not change the jurisdictions and powers of the Court as a matter of political will. Since the power of the Supreme Court to issue a writ of mandamus did not apply, the Court could do nothing for Marbury.

The Republicans at first were delighted. Marshall, after all, had ruled in their favor and Federalist Marbury was out of a job. Moreover, the practical effect of his finding seemed to limit, rather than extend, the Court's power. So the Republicans failed to realize that Marshall's ruling had created a judicial precedent that resounds heavily through our history, especially today. For the first time the Supreme Court had invoked the principle that under the terms of the Constitution it could overturn as unconstitutional a law passed by Congress and signed by a President. It would be 54 years, and long after Marshall's death, before the Supreme Court struck down another law passed by Congress (the Dred Scott Case, argued in 1856–57). The precedent had been set, and in the law precedent counts for almost everything.

Nowadays, though supporters may grouse when the Court refuses to approve some radical reform that they think would render the country far better, everyone takes it for granted that the Supreme Court has the last word. Instead of challenging that right, each side tries to pack the Court with justices who see things their way. The process of matching laws against the Constitution, known as judicial review, is now standard operating procedure. In 1803 it was a defining moment for the Court. The Constitution nowhere expressly states that the Supreme Court has authority to impose its interpretation on the President or Congress.

If Jefferson failed to see what Marshall's decision would mean in the long run, it may have been because the President was involved in a deal with Napoleon that, in May 1803, resulted in the Louisiana Purchase, the acquisition of more than a fourth of what is now the United States.

In effect the agreement guaranteed peace and almost unlimited expansion and prosperity for the American people, at a bargain-basement price. The only trouble was that Jefferson felt sure that the purchase was unconstitutional. After all, a central tenet of his political philosophy was the idea that the federal government could not do a single thing that was not specifically authorized in the Constitution. Jefferson believed the country consisted of sovereign states that retained their sovereignty even after joining the Republic and ratifying the Constitution. He knew that the clause in the Constitution giving the President, with the consent of the Senate, the right to make treaties (Article 2, Section 2) could be stretched to imply that it was legal to annex 828,000 square miles of territory. But if that was so, then other phrases in the Constitution might be made to imply all sorts of things—as they are today. The Constitution would be turned, the President said, into a

blank sheet of paper on which one could write anything one wanted.

If he didn't grab Louisiana, however, his career might be ruined, and his party's future as well, for people were overwhelmingly in favor of it. As many Presidents have done since, he found that principles that had been proclaimed rigid and unchangeable when he was out of power became somewhat more supple when he was actually running the country. He and Congress quietly slipped the constitutional issue under the rug.

The trial of Aaron Burr, a former Vice President, set Jefferson and Marshall further at odds with each other

---

Jefferson hoped that the Louisiana precedent would be soon forgotten, but it was not to be. After the War of 1812, Congress had voted to spend 5 million federal dollars on "internal improvements"—building roads and digging canals. Jefferson's successor, James Madison, vetoed the bill. "The power to regulate commerce among the several states," he wrote, "cannot include a power to construct roads and canals, and to improve the navigation of watercourses in order to facilitate, improve, and secure such a commerce.... To refer the power in question to the clause 'to provide for the common defense and general welfare' would be contrary to the established and consistent rules of interpretation."

Madison's veto was sustained, despite a pointed question put by Senator John C. Calhoun, "On what principle can the purchase of Louisiana be justified?" But—except where slavery was concerned—the tide was beginning to run against "strict construction," and states' rights. People wanted those roads and canals, along with all sorts of other services; and in the long run they were willing to defer to the national government to get them. What was needed, it turned out, was a "broad construction" of the kind that Marshall consistently

placed on the text of the Constitution and that allowed the United States to grow into the great commercial-industrial nation it became—rather than the collection of rural communities of which Jefferson dreamed.

In case after case Marshall kept whittling away at the theory of states' rights. Jefferson could only look on in horror as the black-robed justice, appointed for life, did his work. In vain, as seats on the Supreme Court became vacant, did Jefferson and his successors appoint good Republicans to the Supreme Court. Under the driving logic of the Chief Justice, the newcomers duly studied the Constitution and ended by regularly voting on the nationalist side.

Jefferson was often overwhelmed by Marshall's powers of intellectual persuasion. "So great is his sophistry you must never give him an affirmative answer," he said, "or you will be forced to grant his conclusion. Why, if he were to ask me if it were daylight or not, I'd reply, 'Sir, I don't know, I can't tell.'" Through all the last 20 years of his life, Jefferson saw his party—by then they called themselves Democrats—win all the Presidential elections, till it became for a while the only effective political party. Still, Marshall and his court gained in judicial prestige as they established the judicial branch of the government as the umpire of disputes between the conflicting powers of the state and federal governments.

In 1807, Aaron Burr, who uttered the immortal phrase "Great souls care little for small morals," and who had been Vice President in Jefferson's first term, was picked up on the Mississippi River with nine longboats and 60 adventurers and charged with treason. He claimed he was innocent, but Jefferson was convinced it was part of a plot to threaten the union by creating an independent empire in the Mississippi Valley. When Burr went on trial in Richmond with Justice Marshall presiding as a circuit court judge in Virginia, Burr's defense lawyers asked the court to subpoena certain papers in Jefferson's files.

The President was outraged. Using excuses that are all too familiar today, he refused to hand over the papers, saying they contained state secrets; besides, he argued, a President was not bound to be at the beck and call of a mere judge. Marshall issued the subpoena, a decision that still reverberates in today's newspaper headlines. Though he conceded that as President, Jefferson deserved special treatment because he might have more important things to do, he insisted that under the Constitution the President of the United States is a citizen and not above the law. And thus, like anybody else, obliged to comply with a subpoena. In the end, after threatening to get Marshall thrown off the bench, Jefferson sent the papers—saving what face he could by not formally answering the subpoena.

The jury ultimately handed in a verdict of "Not Guilty." But throughout the proceedings, Jefferson raged against Marshall, writing that the case proved the "error in our Constitution, which makes any branch independent of the nation," and that only the "tricks of the judges" had stood between Burr and the gallows. Marshall, for his part, remained impassive, saying the "court feels no inclination to comment."

Case after case followed, most of them routine, but some inaugurating changes in the very nature of the country. In all of them Marshall followed two fundamental principles. The first was that it was up to the courts to protect the rights of the individual in the face of the massed powers of government, notably the right to keep and enjoy one's own property. The three crucial rights were to life, liberty and property, according to John Locke, who influenced the makers of the Constitution, the other two being guaranteed by the right not to have property taken by the state—except, as the Fifth Amendment allows, under certain limited circumstances and with due recompense. Marshall's second principle involved establishing the extent of federal authority over the states.

In 1810 Marshall received the case of *Fletcher v. Peck,* involving litigation that had been dragging on for 15 years about the Yazoo lands—a plot of some 35 million acres, including most of Alabama and Mississippi. The land had been sold by the legislature of Georgia to a syndicate of speculators for $500,000, a price of 1 ½ cents per acre.

When it was later learned that all but one of the legislators had profited financially from the deal, angry voters threw them all out and elected new ones. The new legislature repealed the act authorizing the sale and ordered the original copy of it burned in a public square. In the meantime, hundreds of more or less innocent private individuals had bought pieces of the land, and wanted their money back. The Supreme Court decided that the motives of the legislators who had voted the original act were irrelevant. The State of Georgia had made a valid contract with the purchasers, and could not declare ownership of property null and void.

Eventually Congress voted $5 million to pay off the Yazoo claimants and bought the land itself, incidentally making a handsome profit for the federal government. Marshall had established once and for all that when a state makes a contract, it is required, like anyone else, to keep it.

In 1819 he took up another epoch-making case, *Dartmouth College v. Woodward.* The college had been privately owned by a self-perpetuating board of trustees under a charter incorporated in 1769 by the British crown. In 1816 a political squabble caused the state legislature to, in effect, take over the college from its trustees. With Daniel Webster as their attorney, the trustees sued and Marshall agreed with them. The original charter, he held, was a contract, and under Article I, Section 10 of the Constitution, no state had the right to pass any "law impairing the Obligation of Contracts."

Gibbons v. Ogden was once described as the "emancipation proclamation of American Commerce."

The state had no more right to break its contract with a corporation than with an individual; a corporation, in fact, must be seen legally as something like an immortal individual. This decision

had the long-range effect of keeping corporations safe from capricious interference by legislators. Corporations were still a relatively new and untested form of social organization. By the end of the 18th century, American states had issued charters for only 310 corporations, and only 8 of them were for commercial purposes (the rest having religious, educational or political aims). After the *Dartmouth College* decision, the number of corporations would rise exponentially till, by the end of the 19th century, they dominated the American economy.

In the same year, Marshall wrote the unanimous decision *McCulloch v. Maryland,* which has been described as the most important case in the history of the Supreme Court because it definitively established the priority of federal law over state law. It involved the Second Bank of the United States, which was chartered by Congress in 1816 and served as the repository for the public funds. But it was basically a private institution that competed with banks chartered by the various states. Banks in the state of Maryland did not appreciate the competition, and so Maryland decided to levy a heavy stamp tax on all banks "not chartered by the legislature," meaning the Second Bank of the United States.

Maryland argued that the federal government was created by the states, and that state law took precedence over federal law in every matter, such as banking, not specifically cited in the Constitution. Marshall, on the other hand, determined that the Constitution was not made by the states but by the people ("We, the people of the United States, . . . do ordain and establish . . ."). Any act of the federal government not directly contrary to the Constitution therefore was the law of the land, whatever a state, or the Supreme Court, might think of its merits. Coining the famous phrase, "The power to tax involves the power to destroy," Marshall declared that the Maryland tax on a bank established by the U.S. Government was void.

In 1824, he struck another devastating blow to states' rights.

It was in the case of *Gibbons v. Ogden,* in a decision once described as the "emancipation proclamation of American commerce," that Marshall's decision nullified a law by which the State of New York granted a monopoly on the use of its waters to the line of steamboats belonging to Robert Fulton and his partner, Robert Livingston. The law had been used to restrain competition by barring a rival line owned by Thomas Gibbons from making the crossing between New Jersey and New York City. This, Marshall held, was in flagrant violation of the constitutional provision giving Congress the power to "regulate Commerce . . . among the several States." All of the now immense regulatory apparatus of the modern American government had its inception in this judgment.

The effect of all such cases was to prevent the states from ever erecting economic walls around their borders. That America moved so rapidly from an overwhelmingly agricultural society to the highly urbanized industrialized and mobile one it would become is in good part owing to the way the Marshall court cleared away efforts to put obstacles in the way of the free flow of trade and people across state boundaries. No wonder Marshall has been described as a definer of the nation.

There were things that Marshall could not do. Judicial conservative though he was, he held views in advance of his time, believing in the equality of women and detesting slavery. But as a judge bound by the laws of the land, there was not much he could do about either, though in 1829 in *Boyce v. Anderson* he ruled that "a slave has volition, and has feelings. . . . He cannot be stowed away as a common package. In the nature of things, and in his character, he resembles a passenger, not a package of goods."

He was also indignant about the fate of the Indian nations being dispossessed of their land to make room for the westward movement. The Cherokees in Georgia had done their best to adjust to the new way of life by abandoning hunting for agriculture and writing a constitution for themselves based on that of the United States. The State of Georgia was nevertheless determined to get rid of them. Marshall was powerless to intervene, but he struck a blow in 1832 in *Worcester v. Georgia* when he declared the Georgia statutes relative to the Indians "repugnant to the Constitution, laws, and treaties of the United States." He ordered the release of Samuel Worcester and Elihu Butler, missionaries who had been arrested and detained for interfering with Georgia's Indian policies.

The State of Georgia ignored the order, and President Andrew Jackson is reported to have said, "Well, John Marshall has made his decision, now let him enforce it." The Cherokees lost all their land and had to embark on their long, tragic march a thousand miles to the west.

Jefferson died on July 4, 1826, on the 50th anniversary of the adoption of the Declaration of Independence he had mostly written. In Philadelphia, the great Liberty Bell tolled to mark his passing. Marshall died in Philadelphia two days after the Fourth of July, nine years later, and to mourn his passing they rang the Liberty Bell yet again.

The two men died unreconciled, each fearful of his country's future. Jefferson saw his beloved union of self-reliant states being pressed "at last into one consolidated mass" by the decisions of the Marshall court. Marshall glumly watched the electoral triumphs of the states' rights candidates while yielding "slowly and reluctantly to the conviction that the Constitution cannot last. The Union," he said, "has been prolonged thus far by miracles. I fear they cannot continue."

In his 74 articles for Smithsonian, *on everything from goats to the Spanish Civil War, the author has exercised a lot of judicial restraint.*

The Florida Quagmire

When the U.S. Army attempted to force the Seminole Indians from their land, it quickly became bogged down in an unwinnable war.

by Floyd B. Largent, Jr.

In the history of the United States, few conflicts have proven as frustrating as the one that erupted in 1835. It lasted for years, was enormously costly in both monetary and human terms, and was fought in a near-jungle setting where the environment itself was hostile. The opponent was a determined native population that used guerrilla tactics to bring a better-equipped American army to a standstill. The locale was the marshes and swamps of Florida. The enemy was the region's Seminole Indians.

The Second Seminole War began in late 1835, when the U.S. Army launched a presidentially mandated campaign to remove the Seminoles to Indian Territory west of the Mississippi River. The army expected little trouble, since other local tribes had already gone with minimal difficulty. It came as something of a shock when the Seminoles rose in a series of preemptive first strikes in late December, smashing military detachments and destroying settlements throughout Florida. The Seminoles then took the war to the Everglades, where they settled in for a drawn-out guerrilla conflict.

President Andrew Jackson, who had sparked the campaign with the Indian Removal Act in 1830, made no secret of his displeasure at the army's inability to contain and remove a few thousand aborigines. Even with 50 women under his command, the president said, he could "whip every Indian that had ever crossed the Suwannee." Those who

failed to show immediate results were swiftly removed. In April 1836, Major General Winfield Scott, the third commander since December, was relieved and eventually appeared before a military court of inquiry. His replacement was Florida territorial governor Richard Call, a civilian and friend of the president. Call fared no better than Scott, and his failure to end the Seminole problem also ended his friendship with Jackson.

Call's replacement was Brevet Major General Thomas Sidney Jesup, who took command on December 9. Born in Virginia and raised in Ohio, Jesup had joined the army as a second lieutenant in 1808, at age 20. Although he had served with distinction in the War of 1812, much of his subsequent career was spent managing supplies and logistics; he'd been the army's quartermaster general since 1818, when he received his brigadier's star. Still, he was an experienced Indian-fighter, having suppressed a Creek uprising in Alabama the previous May.

A physically imposing man with white hair and piercing eyes, Jesup was well-regarded by his troops, who felt he made a sincere effort to take good care of them. Indeed, one of his first acts as commander was to insist that the president supply him with sufficient men and matériel to complete his task, which Jackson agreed to do. Jesup then proceeded to construct a string of fortifications, including Forts Pierce, Lauderdale, Dallas, Jupiter, Meade, and Myers. In addition, he surrounded him-

self with competent subordinates, such as future notables William Harney and Zachary Taylor. Ultimately, Jesup proved the most effective of all the commanders who waged the war against the Seminoles, mainly because of his decision to reject the traditional rules of warfare.

Jesup inherited a royal mess and a stubborn enemy. The Seminoles were a nation of survivors. Their society had been midwifed by war, and fighting was second nature to them. They were a vigorous hybrid of remnant cultures who, decimated by European diseases, constant warfare, and encroaching settlement, had united for survival around 1700.

The Seminoles flourished unmolested for nearly a century. By 1800, they had adopted elements of Euro-American life and were accepted as one of the Five Civilized Tribes, a label they shared with their cousins the Cherokee, Choctaw, Chickasaw, and Creek. Eventually, however, their willingness to harbor runaway slaves—some kept as slaves, others not—led to conflict with the United States. Southern law held that even the descendants of runaway slaves belonged to the original owners, and slave traders' raids on the "Negro Seminole" became common after 1800. The Seminoles retaliated with a series of attacks against white settlements north of the U.S.-Spanish border, and were answered by punitive U.S. Army expeditions in 1816 and 1818, led by future president Andrew Jackson. Hun-

American History, October 1999, pp. 40-46. © 1999 by Cowles Magazines, Inc. Reprinted through the courtesy of Cowles Magazines, publishers of *American History.*

"It seems now to be an established fact that [Indians] can not live in contact with a civilized community and prosper,"
Andrew Jackson told Congress.

dreds of Indians were killed, and many of their darker brethren were sold into slavery during this First Seminole War.

In February 1819, Spain ceded the Florida peninsula to the United States. Over the next decade the U.S. government used military force and legal chicanery to maneuver the Seminoles off their land and onto a marginal reservation in central Florida. In 1830 President Jackson signed the Indian Removal Act, which directed the army and other appropriate agencies to begin transferring the Five Tribes to Indian Territory, using force if necessary. "It seems now to be an established fact that [Indians] can not live in contact with a civilized community and prosper," Jackson told Congress.

The Seminoles were the last to go. The Payne's Landing and Fort Gibson treaties, signed by some chiefs under questionable circumstances in 1832 and 1833, required them to vacate their lands within three years and merge with the Creeks in Indian Territory. The Seminoles refused to abide by the treaty terms. In 1835, when their initial nonviolent protests against the treaty failed to have an effect, 5,000-plus Seminoles began to fade quietly into the dank green refuge of the Everglades.

One of the Indians most opposed to removal was an ex-Creek named Osceola. Indian Agent Wiley Thompson described him as "a bold, manly and determined young chief," an opinion shared by others who encountered him. Born around 1804 in Alabama of a Creek mother and a white father, he was known by whites as Billy Powell. Osceola was noted for his fierce temper, and his attitude towards the United States was not improved when

Thompson, provoked by some unspecified insulting behavior, had him thrown into irons in June 1835. Osceola regained his freedom only after promising to support removal, but, enraged by Thompson's action, he was merely biding his time until he could seek revenge.

Tension mounted throughout the remainder of the year. In October, 1,500 Seminoles gathered and formally elected to resist removal. They further declared that any Seminole accepting the American removal plan would be killed. One of the first to die was Charley Emathla, the most influential of the chiefs supporting removal. Osceola himself carried out the execution on November 26 as Charley Emathla was returning home after selling cattle in preparation for the move. Osceola shot him dead, then scattered the proceeds from the cattle sale on the ground.

The Seminoles struck hard in late December. On the 28th, Osceola's band ambushed and killed agent Thompson and a friend as they strolled outside Fort King. They also killed the fort's sutler and two others. The Indians then dashed 40 miles south to join the force that had obliterated Major Francis Dade's 108-man detachment on the Withlacoochee River near present-day St. Petersburg. Osceola and his men arrived, to their chagrin, after the battle was over and Dade's force had been wiped out almost to the man. On New Year's Eve, Osceola's 250 warriors defeated a force of more than 700 soldiers under the command of General Duncan Clinch on the banks of the Withlacoochee River. Though Clinch's casualties were light, Osceola forced the general into a confused retreat.

Throughout 1836 the army reeled from a series of Seminole onslaughts. The course of the war began to change, however, after Jesup assumed command. During the first few months of 1837, his forces won several skirmishes and persuaded several bands to emigrate with minimal bloodshed. Captured Indians were also sent west, although the darker-skinned among them were enslaved.

Jesup found a worthy enemy in the Seminoles. He admired them; they were remarkably courageous and fierce, and even their women and children fought

when necessary. He was quite aware of the origins of the conflict; as he noted early on, "This ... is a Negro, not an Indian, war." By mid-1837, he had returned approximately 100 Black Seminoles "to their rightful owners." Simultaneously, he respected the black warriors he encountered and insisted that they be treated honorably.

Jesup made no attempt to hide his mixed feelings about the war. It was his opinion that Indians had been unfairly persecuted since colonial times. He believed that the Seminole War was "an unholy cause." But Jesup's first loyalty lay with the army he had so faithfully served for nearly three decades. He prided himself on being, first and foremost, a soldier.

Jesup understood the realities of the campaign. "If I have at any time said aught in disparagement of the operations of others in Florida," he wrote, " ... I consider myself bound, as a man of honor, solemnly to retract it." The public and his superiors, however, demanded quick results. Seeing no way to defeat the Indians fairly, Jesup began to consider other tactics.

General Thomas Sidney Jesup believed that the conflict was "a negro, not an Indian war."

To Jesup's credit, he first attempted to negotiate an honorable end to the conflict. The Seminoles were hungry and weary of being hunted. The war held no real future for them, and they believed their enemy was as eager as they to see it end. By 1837, most were willing to consider emigration. That spring, Jesup invited Seminole tribe members to a council at Fort Mellon, east of Tampa, in anticipation of a forthcoming settlement. The natives proved amenable to a discussion of removal, and Jesup agreed that "their negroes, their bona fide property, shall accompany them West. . . ." In March Jesup was so confident of a settlement that he reported to his superiors, "The war is over."

An unfortunate series of events proved his statement premature. Some Seminoles still lurked in the swamps, and Jesup offended those assembled at Fort Mellon by threatening to import bloodhounds from Cuba to roust out their defiant kin. Then measles broke out in the Seminole camps, further slowing the influx of refugees. Finally, any lasting hope of peace was shattered after Jesup made a secret arrangement with the more willing chiefs to have runaway slaves returned to their owners.

The situation deteriorated even further with the arrival of the slave catchers, who began raiding the Seminole camp in May, capturing any Black Seminoles they could locate and infuriating the Indians. Osceola in particular opposed returning the runaways. Negotiations became increasingly fragile. On the night of June 2, under the influence of Osceola and others, the Seminoles faded back into the forest. The war was on again.

Jesup had lost credibility, and nothing he promised would convince the Seminoles to emigrate willingly. Both Congress and Jackson wasted no time in heaping abuse upon him. Embittered by the criticism, disheartened by the stubbornness and sheer ruthlessness of the enemy, Jesup decided that total war was necessary. "If the war be carried it must necessarily be one of extermination," he declared. "We have, at no former period in our history, had to contend with so formidable an enemy."

Immediately thereafter, Jesup asked to be relieved of his command, as he wanted no part in a war of extermination. The army initially refused his request, although on June 22 Alexander Macomb, the army's commanding general, offered to allow him to withdraw from Florida if he still cared to do so. By then, Jesup had changed his mind. The criticism had so wounded his pride that he was determined to stay on and redeem itself.

What Jesup couldn't achieve by negotiation he elected to accomplish by guile and he began the practice of seizing Seminole leaders under a truce flag, capturing a chief named Wildcat that way in September. He also began threatening captives with death if they didn't lead him to Seminole hideouts. Weary and desperate, the Seminoles continued to negotiate despite Jesup's dishonorable tactics.

Jesup now set his sites on Osceola. In October the chief and a number of his followers arrived under a flag of truce to parley in a camp near Fort Peyton. Jesup sent General Joseph M. Hernandez to talk with them. According to a report he later submitted to President Jackson, Jesup said he told Hernandez. "You have force sufficient to compel obedience, and they must move instantly."

Hernandez ordered Lieutenant James A. Ashby and his men to surround the encampment during the talks. At a prearranged secret signal from Hernandez, Ashby was to send in his troops to make the capture. Perhaps Osceola, who was ill, suspected something. At the start of the conference he said he was too choked up to speak and asked a chief named Coa Hadjo to talk for him. Shortly afterwards Ashby's soldiers moved in and captured the Indians without firing a shot. Osceola was sent to Fort Moultrie in South Carolina, where he died of a throat infection in January 1838. The chief was buried there with full military honors—but minus his head. According to John K. Mahon's *The Second Seminole War,* the doctor who treated Osceola cut off the chief's head, embalmed it, and kept it at home. "If one of his three small sons was disobedient," Mahon wrote, "the doctor would hang the head on the child's bedstead for the night."

The war chief was lionized as a hero by both the press and the public, while Jesup suffered ridicule and derision as the "personification of treachery throughout most of the civilized world." Nevertheless, when a delegation of Cherokee persuaded Seminole chief Micanopy and others to travel to Fort Mellon to parley, Jesup ordered the Seminoles arrested, even though the Cherokee had promised them safe conduct.

By the end of 1837, Jesup had achieved a series of major victories against the Seminoles and had collected and removed some 2,000 individuals. In mid-January he personally led his troops into combat for the first time at the Battle of Lockahatchee. Like most of the fighting, it was a confused skirmish in a region of swamps and marshes. Forced to dismount and move forward on foot, Jesup led volunteers from Tennessee into battle, only to have a Seminole bullet strike him in the face, knocking off his glasses and leaving him with a minor wound. "Waving the Tennesseans on, the general carefully picked up the pieces of his glasses, and then moved to the rear," wrote Mahon.

The last significant American victory occurred at the Battle of Okeechobee on Christmas Day, 1837, when troops under Zachary Taylor overwhelmed a force of 400 warriors led by chiefs Alligator, Arpeika, and Wildcat, who had managed to escape from prison in St. Augustine. By this time Jesup was tired of the whole war, and following a parley with Seminole chief Tuskegee and other warriors, he wrote to Secretary of War Joel Poinsett to propose that the Seminoles be allowed to remain in southern Florida. "We have committed the error of attempting to remove them when the lands were not required for agricultural purposes; when they were not in the way of white immigrants; and when the greater portion of their country was an unexplored wilderness, of the interior of which we were as ignorant as of the interior of China," Jesup reasoned. Poinsett refused. When Jesup received word from Washington, he acted in a characteristic manner by arresting Tuskegee and others under a flag of truce.

Despite the losses of their chiefs, the Seminoles in the swamps of southern Florida continued to skirmish with the army. Finally, to Jesup's palpable relief, he was relieved of command at his own request in April 1838 and replaced by Zachary Taylor. Officially, the Seminole War dragged on for nearly five more years. The last of the Seminoles were never flushed out of their hiding places, and in early 1843 the U.S. Army simply gave up and called off the war. Hostilities continued to flare up occasionally between whites and the remaining Seminoles, most significantly in December 1855. This conflict continued until 1858, when a group of western Seminoles was able to persuade the hostile bands to emigrate. Yet the last of the

Florida Seminoles never stopped resisting white encroachment, and peace wasn't officially negotiated until 1934, nearly one hundred years after the war began.

During the course of the Second Seminole War, the United States removed 3,800 Seminoles to Indian Territory, but at a terrible price. The war lasted for an interminable seven years, 1,500 American soldiers died, and the cost has been estimated at between $20,000,000 and $60,000,000—significantly more than the United States paid for the entire Louisiana Purchase only 52 years earlier. Worst, perhaps, was the national embarrassment caused by the war. The U.S. Army, in its first real showing since the War of 1812, was shocked at the ferocity of the Seminole assault and never recovered from its initial surprise. The result was an immense loss of face, internationally and domestically, which could have been avoided or at last postponed.

While he was certainly no angel, neither was Thomas Jesup the demon he was painted as in his day. An unpretentious and politically unastute soldier, Jesup knew that by following the "civilized rules of war" he would accomplish little and earn the wrath and disdain of his superiors. If he used the natives' tactics against them or invented his own, he would be seen as a monster. Nothing he could do, moral or immoral, was right.

Jesup's failure in the Seminole War haunted him for the rest of his life. In the 22 years after his participation, he received no further promotions. His brevet as major general, awarded in 1828 for long and meritorious service, was never confirmed. After relinquishing the Florida command, Jesup returned to his post as quartermaster general, where he remained until his death in 1860. The Ohioan had served in the army for 52 years, all but 10 of those years in the same post—a record in the U.S. Armed Services. He was instrumental in the subsequent advancement of the western frontier by supervising the construction of a variety of new outposts, including Kansas' Fort Riley, and the refurbishment of existing posts, such as Fort Gibson in Oklahoma. He also oversaw the logistics in the Mexican War of 1845–47, another unpopular war of the era. His high level of competence as quartermaster is unimpeachable, and in 1986 he became one of the first four individuals to be inducted into the U.S. Army's Quartermaster Hall of Fame.

Despite his tactical and moral failings, Thomas Jesup was clearly an intelligent, thoughtful man who well understood his enemy and the venue in which they fought. When he counseled the nation's leaders that theirs was an ill-advised war, they ignored him. When he warned his superiors of what it would take to win a war against the Seminoles, they too ignored him. President Jackson and his successors would have been better served if they had listened to their quartermaster, for, in the end, history has vindicated his viewpoint. Sufficient proof of this can be found in the fact that there are still Seminoles in Florida, and their culture is stronger and more vibrant than ever.

Floyd B. Largent, Jr., is a Texas-based writer, anthropologist, and historian, with a particular interest in Native-American cultures.

"All we want is make us free!"

An 1839 mutiny aboard a Spanish ship in Cuban waters raised basic questions about freedom and slavery in the United States

By Howard Jones

Around 4:00 A.M. on July 2, 1839, Joseph Cinqué led a slave mutiny on board the Spanish schooner *Amistad* some 20 miles off northern Cuba. The revolt set off a remarkable series of events and became the basis of a court case that ultimately reached the U.S. Supreme Court. The civil rights issues involved in the affair made it the most famous case to appear in American courts before the landmark Dred Scott decision of 1857.

The saga began two months earlier when slave trade merchants captured Cinqué, a 26-year-old man from Mende, Sierra Leone, and hundreds of others from different West African tribes. The captives were then taken to the Caribbean, with up to 500 of them chained hand and foot, on board the Portuguese slaver *Teçora*. After a nightmarish voyage in which approximately a third of the captives died, the journey ended with the clandestine, nighttime entry of

THE NEW HAVEN COLONY HISTORICAL SOCIETY

Sengbe Pieh—given the name Joseph Cinqué in Cuba—who is depicted in a painting by Nathaniel Jocelyn.

the ship into Cuba—in violation of the Anglo-Spanish treaties of 1817 and 1835 that made the African slave trade a capital crime. Slavery itself was legal in Cuba, meaning that once smuggled ashore, the captives became "slaves" suitable for auction at the Havana barracoons.

In Havana, two Spaniards, José Ruiz and Pedro Montes, bought 53 of the Africans—including Cinqué and four children, three of them girls—and chartered the *Amistad*. The ship, named after the Spanish word for friendship, was a small black schooner built in Baltimore for the coastal slave trade. It was to transport its human cargo 300 miles to two plantations on another part of Cuba at Puerto Principe.

The spark for the mutiny was provided by Celestino, the *Amistad*'s mulatto cook. In a cruel jest, he drew his hand past his throat and pointed to barrels of beef, indicating to Cinqué that, on reaching Puerto Principe, the 53 black captives aboard would be killed and eaten. Stunned by this revelation, Cinqué found a nail to pick the locks on the captives' chains and made a strike for freedom.

From *American History*, February 1998, pp. 22-28, 71. © 1998 by Cowles Magazines, Inc. Reprinted through the courtesy of Cowles Magazines, publishers of *American History*.

In the small, hot, and humid room beneath the Senate chamber, [John Quincy] Adams challenged the Court to grant liberty on the basis of natural rights doctrines found in the Declaration of Independence.

In this painting by an unknown artist (above, left), the badly weather-beaten schooner Amistad is at anchor in Long Island Sound, while several of the mutineers head for shore in search of provisions. In two of a series of murals painted in 1939 by Hale Woodruff (above, right) for the Amistad centennial, the Africans are depicted during the pre-dawn revolt and on their return home, almost three years later.

On their third night at sea, Cinqué and a fellow captive named Grabeau freed their comrades and searched the dark hold for weapons. They found them in boxes: sugar cane knives with machete-like blades, two feet in length, attached to inch-thick steel handles. Weapons in hand, Cinqué and his cohorts stormed the shadowy, pitching deck and, in a brief and bloody struggle that led to the death of one of their own, killed the cook and captain and severely wounded Ruiz and Montes. Two sailors who were aboard disappeared in the melee and were probably drowned in a desperate attempt to swim the long distance to shore. Grabeau convinced Cinqué to spare the lives of the two Spaniards, since only they possessed the navigational skills necessary to sail the *Amistad* to Africa. Instead of making it home, however, the former

captives eventually ended up off the coast of New York.

Cinqué, the acknowledged leader of the mutineers, recalled that the slave ship that he and the others had traveled on during their passage from Africa to Cuba had sailed away from the rising sun; therefore to return home, he ordered Montes, who had once been a sea captain, to sail the *Amistad* into the sun. The two Spaniards deceived their captors by sailing back and forth in the Caribbean Sea, toward the sun during the day and, by the stars, back toward Havana at night, hoping for rescue by British anti-slave-trade patrol vessels.

When that failed, Ruiz and Montes took the schooner on a long and erratic trek northward up the Atlantic coast.

Some 60 days after the mutiny, under a hot afternoon sun in late August 1839, Lieutenant Commander Thomas Gedney of the USS *Washington* sighted the ves-

sel just off Long Island, where several of the schooner's inhabitants were on shore bartering for food. He immediately dispatched an armed party who captured the men ashore and then boarded the vessel. They found a shocking sight: cargo strewn all over the deck; perhaps 50 men nearly starved and destitute, their skeletal bodies naked or barely clothed in rags; a black corpse lying in decay on the deck, its face frozen as if in terror; another black with a maniacal gaze in his eyes; and two wounded Spaniards in the hold who claimed to be the owners of the Africans who, as slaves, had mutinied and murdered the ship's captain.

Gedney seized the vessel and cargo and reported the shocking episode to authorities in New London, Connecticut. Only 43 of the Africans were still alive, including the four children. In addition to the one killed during the mutiny, nine

Margru was one of the three female captives on board the Amistad. After her return home, she was educated at the American mission school and sent back to the United States to study. She then returned to Africa, where she became principal of the mission's school.

had died of disease and exposure or from consuming medicine on board in an effort to quench their thirst.

The affair might have come to a quiet end at this point had it not been for a group of abolitionists. Evangelical Christians led by Lewis Tappan, a prominent New York businessman, Joshua Leavitt, a lawyer and journalist who edited the *Emancipator* in New York, and Simeon Jocelyn, a Congregational minister in New Haven, Connecticut, learned of the *Amistad's* arrival and decided to publicize the incident to expose the brutalities of slavery and the slave trade. Through evangelical arguments, appeals to higher law and "moral suasion," Tappan and his colleagues hoped to launch a massive assault on slavery.

The *Amistad* incident, Tappan happily proclaimed, was a "providential occurrence." In his view slavery was a deep moral wrong and not subject to compromise. Both those who advocated its practice and those who quietly condoned it by inaction deserved condemnation. Slavery was a sin, he declared, because it obstructed a person's free will inherent by birth, therefore constituting a rebellion against God. Slavery was also, Tappan wrote to his brother, "the

worm at the root of the tree of Liberty. Unless killed the tree will die."

Tappan first organized the "Amistad Committee" to coordinate efforts on behalf of the captives, who had been moved to the New Haven jail. Tappan preached impromptu sermons to the mutineers, who were impressed by his sincerity though unable to understand his language. He wrote detailed newspaper accounts of their daily activities in jail, always careful to emphasize their humanity and civilized backgrounds for a fascinated public, many of whom had never seen a black person. And he secured the services of Josiah Gibbs, a professor of religion and linguistics at Yale College, who searched the docks of New York for native Africans capable of translating Cinqué's Mende language. Gibbs eventually discovered two Africans familiar with Mende—James Covey from Sierra Leone and Charles Pratt from Mende itself. At last the *Amistad* mutineers could tell their side of the story.

Meanwhile, Ruiz and Montes had initiated trial proceedings seeking return of their "property." They had also secured their government's support under Pinckney's Treaty of 1795, which stipulated the return of merchandise lost for reasons beyond human control. To fend off what many observers feared would be a "judicial massacre," the abolitionists hired attorney Roger S. Baldwin of Connecticut, who had a reputation as an eloquent defender of the weak and downtrodden.

Baldwin intended to prove that the captives were "kidnapped Africans," illegally taken from their homeland and imported into Cuba and thus entitled to resist their captors by any means necessary. He argued that the ownership papers carried by Ruiz and Montes were fraudulent and that the blacks were not slaves indigenous to Cuba. He and his defense team first filed a claim for the *Amistad* and cargo as the Africans' property in preparation for charging the Spaniards with piracy. Then they filed suit for the captives' freedom on the grounds of humanity and justice: slavery violated natural law, providing its victims with the inherent right of self-defense.

The case then entered the world of politics. It posed such a serious problem

for President Martin Van Buren that he decided to intervene. A public dispute over slavery would divide his Democratic party, which rested on a tenuous North-South alliance, and could cost him reelection to the presidency in 1840. Working through his secretary of state, slaveholder John Forsyth from Georgia, Van Buren sought to quietly solve the problem by complying with Spanish demands.

Van Buren also faced serious diplomatic issues. Failure to return the Africans to their owners would be a violation of Pinckney's Treaty with Spain. In addition, revealing Spain's infringement of treaties against the African slave trade could provide the British, who were pioneers in the crusade against slavery, with a pretext for intervening in Cuba, which was a long-time American interest.

The White House position was transparently weak. Officials refused to question the validity of the certificates of ownership, which had assigned Spanish names to each of the captives even though none of them spoke that language. Presidential spokesmen blandly asserted that the captives had been slaves in Cuba, despite the fact that the international slave trade had been outlawed some 20 years earlier and the

Grabeau, drawn here from life by William H. Townsend in 1839, had been a blacksmith in his Mende homeland before he was seized by slave dealers and sent to Cuba for sale on the slave market.

children were no more than nine years old and spoke an African dialect.

The court proceedings opened on September 19, 1839, amid a carnival atmosphere in the state capitol building in Hartford, Connecticut. To some observers, Cinqué was a black folk hero; to others he was a barbarian who deserved execution for murder. Poet William Cullen Bryant extolled Cinqué's virtues, numerous Americans sympathized with the "noble savages," and pseudo-scientists concluded that the shape of Cinqués skull suggested leadership, intelligence, and nobility. The New York *Morning Herald*, however, derided the "poor Africans," "who have nothing to do, but eat, drink, and turn somersaults."

To establish the mutineers as human beings rather than property, Baldwin sought a writ of habeas corpus aimed at freeing them unless the prosecution filed charges of murder. Issuance of the writ would recognize the Africans as persons with natural rights and thus undermine the claim by both the Spanish and American governments that the captives were property. If the prosecution brought charges, the Africans would have the right of self-defense against unlawful captivity; if it filed no charges, they would go free. In the meantime, the abolitionists could explore in open court the entire range of human and property rights relating to slavery. As Leavitt later told the General Antislavery Convention in London, the purpose of the writ was "to test their right to personality."

Despite Baldwin's impassioned pleas for justice, the public's openly expressed sympathy for the captives, and the prosecution's ill-advised attempt to use the four black children as witnesses against their own countrymen, Associate Justice Smith Thompson of the U.S. Supreme Court denied the writ. Thompson was a strong-willed judge who opposed slavery, but he even more ardently supported the laws of the land. Under those laws, he declared, slaves were property. He could not simply assert that the Af-

ricans were human beings and grant freedom on the basis of natural rights. Only the law could dispense justice, and the law did not authorize their freedom. It was up to the district court to decide whether the mutineers were slaves and, therefore, property.

Prospects before the district court in Connecticut were equally dismal. The presiding judge was Andrew T. Judson, a well-known white supremacist and staunch opponent of abolition. Baldwin attempted to move the case to the free state of New York on the grounds that Gedney had seized the Africans in that state's waters and not on the high seas. He hoped, if successful, to prove that they were already free upon entering New York and that the Van Buren administration was actually trying to enslave them. But Baldwin's effort failed; the confrontation with Judson was unavoidable.

Judson's verdict in the case only appeared preordained; as a politically ambitious man, he had to find a middle ground. Whereas many Americans wanted the captives freed, the White House pressured him to send them back to Cuba. Cinqué himself drew great sympathy by recounting his capture in Mende and then graphically illustrating the horrors of the journey from Africa by sitting on the floor with hands and feet pulled together to show how the captives had been "packed" into the hot and unsanitary hold of the slave vessel.

The Spanish government further confused matters by declaring that the Africans were both property and persons. In addition to calling for their return as property under Pinckney's Treaty, it demanded their surrender as "slaves who are assassins." The real concern of the Spanish government became clear when its minister to the United States, Pedro Alcántara de Argaiz, proclaimed that "The public vengeance of the African Slave Traders in Cuba had not been satisfied." If the mutineers went unpunished, he feared, slave rebellions would erupt all over Cuba.

Argaiz's demands led the Van Buren administration to adopt measures that constituted an obstruction of justice. To

facilitate the Africans' rapid departure to Cuba after an expected guilty verdict, Argaiz convinced the White House to dispatch an American naval vessel to New Haven to transport them out of the country *before* they could exercise the constitutional right of appeal. By agreeing to this, the president had authorized executive interference in the judicial process that violated the due-process guarantees contained in the Constitution.

Judson finally reached what he thought was a politically safe decision. On January 13, 1840, he ruled that the Africans had been kidnapped, and, offering no sound legal justification, ordered their return to Africa, hoping to appease the president by removing them from the United States. Six long months after the mutiny, it appeared that the captives were going home.

But the ordeal was not over. The White House was stunned by the decision: Judson had ignored the "great [and] important political bearing" of the case, complained the president's son, John Van Buren. The Van Buren administration immediately filed an appeal with the circuit court. The court upheld the decision, however, meaning that the case would now go before the U.S. Supreme Court, where five of the justices, including Chief Justice Roger Taney, were southerners who were or had been slaveowners.

Meanwhile, the Africans had become a public spectacle. Curious townspeople and visitors watched them exercise daily on the New Haven green, while many others paid the jailer for a peek at the foreigners in their cells. Some of the most poignant newspaper stories came from professors and students from Yale College and the Theological Seminary who instructed the captives in English and Christianity. But the most compelling attraction was Cinqué. In his midtwenties, he was taller than most Mende people, married with three children, and, according to the contemporary portrait by New England abolitionist Nathaniel Jocelyn, majestic, lightly bronzed, and strikingly handsome. Then there were the children, including Kale, who learned enough English to become the spokesperson for the group.

The supreme court began hearing arguments on February 22, 1841. Van Buren had already lost the election, partly and somewhat ironically because his *Amistad* policy was so blatantly pro-South that it alienated northern Democrats. The abolitionists wanted someone of national stature to join Baldwin in the defense and finally persuaded former President John Quincy Adams to take the case even though he was 73 years old, nearly deaf, and had been absent from the courtroom for three decades. Now a congressman from Massachusetts, Adams was irascible and hard-nosed, politically independent, and self-righteous to the point of martyrdom. He was fervently antislavery though not an abolitionist, and had been advising Baldwin on the case since its inception. His effort became a personal crusade when the young Kale wrote him a witty and touching letter, which appeared in the *Emancipator* and concluded with the ringing words, "All we want is make us free."

Baldwin opened the defense before the Supreme Court with another lengthy appeal to natural law then gave way to Adams, who delivered an emotional eight-hour argument that stretched over two days. In the small, hot, and humid room beneath the Senate chamber, Adams challenged the Court to grant liberty on the basis of natural rights doctrines found in the Declaration of Independence. Pointing to a copy of the document mounted on a huge pillar, he proclaimed that, "I know of no other law

that reaches the case of my clients, but the law of Nature and of Nature's God on which our fathers placed our own national existence." The Africans, he proclaimed, were victims of a monstrous conspiracy led by the executive branch in Washington that denied their rights as human beings.

Adams and Baldwin were eloquent in their pleas for justice based on higher principles. As Justice Joseph Story wrote to his wife, Adams's argument was "extraordinary . . . for its power, for its bitter sarcasm, and its dealing with topics far beyond the records and points of discussion."

On March 9, Story read a decision that could not have surprised those who knew anything about the man. An eminent scholar and jurist, Story was rigidly conservative and strongly nationalistic, but he was as sensitive to an individual's rights as he was a strict adherent to the law. Although he found slavery repugnant and contrary to Christian morality, he supported the laws protecting its existence and opposed the abolitionists as threats to ordered society. Property rights, he believed, were the basis of civilization.

Even so, Story handed down a decision that freed the mutineers on the grounds argued by the defense. The ownership papers were fraudulent, making the captives "kidnapped Africans" who had the inherent right of self-defense in accordance with the "eternal principles of justice." Furthermore, Story reversed Judson's decision ordering the captives' return to Africa because there was no American legislation

authorizing such an act. The outcome drew Leavitt's caustic remark that Van Buren's executive order attempting to return the Africans to Cuba as slaves should be "engraved on his tomb, to rot only with his memory."

The abolitionists pronounced the decision a milestone in their long and bitter fight against the "peculiar institution." To them, and to the interested public, Story's "eternal principles of justice" were the same as those advocated by Adams. Although Story had focused on self-defense, the victorious abolitionists broadened the meaning of his words to condemn the immorality of slavery. They reprinted thousands of copies of the defense argument in pamphlet form, hoping to awaken a larger segment of the public to the sordid and inhumane character of slavery and the slave trade. In the highest public forum in the land, the abolitionists had brought national attention to a great social injustice. For the first and only time in history, African blacks seized by slave dealers and brought to the New World won their freedom in American courts.

The final chapter in the saga was the captives' return to Africa. The abolitionists first sought damage compensation for them, but even Adams had to agree with Baldwin that, despite months of captivity because bail had been denied, the "regular" judicial process had detained the Africans, and liability for false imprisonment hinged only on whether the officials' acts were *malicious* and without probable *cause*." To achieve equity Adams suggested that the

NEW HAVEN COLONY HISTORICAL SOCIETY

The court proceedings shown above in the Woodruff mural panel, "Trial of the Captive Slaves," proved to be long and tumultuous.

This letter to Lewis Tappan from John Quincy Adams was in response to the gift of a Bible that had been sent to Adams by Cinqué and his comrades after they had been freed by the court and allowed to return home.

Oberlin College, in Ohio, to prepare for mission work among her people. She was educated at the expense of the American Missionary Association (AMA), established in 1846 as an outgrowth of the Amistad Committee and the first of its kind in Africa. Cinqué returned to his home, where tribal wars had scattered or perhaps killed his family. Some scholars insist that he remained in Africa, working for some time as an interpreter at the AMA mission in Kaw-Mende before his death around 1879. No conclusive evidence has surfaced to determine whether Cinqué was reunited with his wife and three children, and for that same reason there is no justification for the oft-made assertion that he himself engaged in the slave trade.

The importance of the *Amistad* case lies in the act that Cinqué and his fellow captives, in collaboration with white abolitionists, had won their freedom and thereby encouraged others to continue the struggle. Positive law had come into conflict with natural law, exposing the great need to change the Constitution and American laws in compliance with the moral principles underlying the Declaration of Independence. In that sense the incident contributed to the fight against slavery by helping to lay the basis for its abolition through the Thirteenth Amendment to the Constitution in 1865.

federal government finance the captives' return to Africa. But President John Tyler, himself a Virginia slaveholder, refused on the grounds that, as Judge Story had ruled, no law authorized such action.

To charter a vessel for the long trip to Sierra Leone, the abolitionists raised money from private donations, public exhibitions of the Africans, and contributions from the Union Missionary' Society, which black Americans had formed in Hartford to found a Christian mission in Africa. On November 25, 1841, the remaining 35 *Amistad* captives, accompanied by James Covey and five missionaries, departed from New York for Africa on a small sailing vessel named the *Gentleman.* The British governor of Sierra Leone welcomed them the following January—almost three years after their initial incarceration by slave traders.

The aftermath of the *Amistad* affair is hazy. One of the girls, Margru, returned to the United States and entered

Howard Jones is University Research Professor and Chair of the Department of History at the University of Alabama. He is the author of numerous books, including Mutiny on the Amistad: The Saga of a Slave Revolt and Its Impact on American Abolition, Law, and Diplomacy, *published by Oxford University Press.*

One hundred and fifty years ago the people attending the first Women's Rights Convention adopted the radical proposition that

"All men & women are created equal"

By Constance Rynder

THE ANNOUNCEMENT OF an upcoming "Woman's Rights Convention" in the *Seneca County Courier* was small, but it attracted Charlotte Woodward's attention. On the morning of July 19, 1848, the 19-year-old glove maker drove in a horse-drawn wagon to the Wesleyan Methodist Chapel in the upstate New York town of Seneca Falls. To her surprise, Woodward found dozens of other women and a group of men waiting to enter the chapel, all of them as eager as she to learn what a discussion of "the social, civil, and religious rights of women" might produce.

The convention was the brainchild of 32-year-old Elizabeth Cady Stanton, daughter of Margaret and Judge Daniel Cady and wife of Henry Stanton, a noted abolitionist politician. Born in Johnstown, New York, Cady Stanton demonstrated both an intellectual bent and a rebellious spirit from an early age. Exposed to her father's law books as well as his conservative views on women, she objected openly to the legal and educational disadvantages under which women of her day labored. In 1840 she provoked her father by marrying Stanton, a handsome, liberal reformer and further defied convention by deliberately omitting the word "obey" from her wedding vows.

Marriage to Henry Stanton brought Elizabeth Cady Stanton—she insisted on retaining her maiden name—into contact with other independent-minded women. The newlyweds spent their honeymoon at the World Anti-Slavery Convention in London where, much to their chagrin, women delegates were denied their seats and deprived of a voice in the proceedings. Banished to a curtained visitors' gallery, the seven women listened in stunned silence as the London credentials committee charged that they were "constitutionally unfit for public and business meetings." It was an insult Cady Stanton never forgot.

Among the delegates was Lucretia Coffin Mott, a liberal Hicksite Quaker preacher and an accomplished public speaker in the American abolitionist movement, who was also disillusioned by the lack of rights granted women. A mother of six, Mott had grown up on Nantucket Island, "so thoroughly imbued with women's rights," she later admitted, "that it was the most important question of my life from a very early age." In Mott, Cady Stanton found both an ally and a role mode. "When I first heard from her lips that I had the same right to think for myself that Luther, Calvin and John Knox had," she recalled, "and the same right to be guided by my own convictions . . . I felt a new born sense of dignity and freedom." The two women became fast friends and talked about the need for a convention to discuss *women's* emancipation. Eight years passed, however, before they fulfilled their mutual goal.

For the first years of her marriage, Cady Stanton settled happily into middle-class domestic life, first in Johnstown and subsequently in Boston, then the hub of reformist activity. She delighted in being part of her husband's stimulating circle of reformers and intellectuals and gloried in motherhood; over a 17-year period she bore seven children. In 1847, however, the Stantons moved to Seneca Falls, a small, remote farming and manufacturing community in New York's Finger Lakes district. After Boston, life in Seneca Falls with its routine household duties seemed dull to Cady Stanton, and she renewed her protest against the conditions that limited women's lives. "My experience at the World Anti-Slavery Convention, all I had read of the legal status of women, and the oppression I saw everywhere, together swept across my soul, intensified now by many personal experiences." A meeting with Lucretia Mott in July of 1848 provided the opportunity to take action.

On July 13, Cady Stanton received an invitation to a tea party at the home of Jane and Richard Hunt, wealthy Quakers living in Waterloo, New York, just three miles west of Seneca Falls. There she again met Lucretia Mott, Mott's younger sister, Martha Coffin Wright, and Mary Ann McClintock, wife of the Waterloo Hicksite Quaker minister. At tea, Cady Stanton poured out to the group "the torrent of my long-accumulating discontent." Then and there they decided to schedule a women's "convention" for the following week. Hoping to attract a large audience, they placed an unsigned notice in the *Courier* advertising Lucretia Mott as the featured speaker.

Near panic gripped the five women as they gathered around the McClintocks' parlor table the following Sunday morning. They had only three days to set an agenda and prepare a document "for the inauguration of a rebellion." Supervised by Cady Stanton, they drafted a "Declaration of Sentiments and Resolutions," paraphrasing the Declaration of Independence. The document declared that "all men and women are created equal" and "are endowed by their Creator with certain unalienable rights. . . ." These natural rights belong equally to women and men, it continued, but man "has usurped the prerogative of Jehovah himself, claiming it as his right to assign for her a sphere of action, when that belongs to her conscience and to her God." The result has been "the establishment of an absolute tyranny over her."

There followed a specific catalog of injustices. Women were denied access to higher education, the professions, and the pulpit, as well as equal pay for equal work. If married they had no property rights; even the wages they earned legally belonged to their husbands. Women were subject to a high moral code, yet legally bound to tolerate moral delinquencies in their husbands. Wives could be punished, and if divorced a mother had no child custody rights. In every way, man "has endeavored to destroy [woman's] confidence in her own powers, to lessen her self-esteem, and to make her willing to lead a dependent and abject life." Above all, every woman had been deprived of "her inalienable right to the elective franchise."

Eleven resolutions demanding redress of these and other grievances accompanied the nearly 1,000-word Declaration. When Cady Stanton insisted upon including a resolution favoring voting rights for women, her otherwise supportive husband threatened to boycott the event. Even Lucretia Mott warned her, "Why Lizzie, thee will

Susan B. Anthony and Elizabeth Cady Stanton remained close friends from the time they met in 1851 until Cady Stanton's death in 1902. Both women became leaders in the fight for women's equality. Lucretia Mott was another of the great women of the nineteenth century.

make us ridiculous!" "Lizzie," however, refused to yield.

Although the gathering was a convention for and of women, it was regarded as "unseemingly" for a lady to conduct a public meeting, so Lucretia's husband, James Mott, agreed to chair the two-day event. Mary Ann McClintock's husband, Thomas, also participated. Henry Stanton left town.

When the organizers arrived at the Wesleyan Chapel on the morning of Wednesday, July 19, they found the door locked. No one had a key, so Cady Stanton's young nephew scrambled in through an open window and unbarred the front door. As the church filled with spectators, another dilemma presented itself. The first day's sessions had been planned for women exclusively, but almost 40 men showed up. After a hasty council at the altar the leadership decided to let the men stay, since they were already seated and seemed genuinely interested.

Tall and dignified in his Quaker garb, James Mott called the first session to order at 11:00 A.M. and appointed the McClintocks' older daughter (also named Mary Ann) secretary. Cady Stanton, in her first public speech, rose to state the purpose of the convention. "We have met here today to discuss our rights and wrongs, civil and political." She then read the Declaration aloud, para-

graph by paragraph, and urged all present to participate freely in the discussions. The Declaration was re-read several times, amended, and adopted unanimously. Both Lucretia Mott and Cady Stanton addressed the afternoon session, as did the McClintock's younger daughter, Elizabeth. To lighten up the proceedings, Mott read a satirical article on "woman's sphere" that her sister Martha had published in local newspapers. Later that evening, Mott spoke to the audience on "The Progress of Reforms."

The second day's sessions were given over to the 11 resolutions. As Mott feared, the most contentious proved to be the ninth—the suffrage resolution. The other 10 passed unanimously. According to Cady Stanton's account, most of those who opposed this resolution did so because they believed it would compromise the others. She, however, remained adamant. "To have drunkards, idiots, horse racing rum-selling rowdies, ignorant foreigners, and silly boys fully recognized, while we ourselves are thrust out from all the rights that belong to citizens, is too grossly insulting to be longer quietly submitted to. The right is ours. We must have it." Even Cady Stanton's eloquence would not have carried the day but for the support she received from ex-slave and abolitionist Frederick Douglass, editor of the antislavery newspaper, *North Star*. "Right is of no sex," he argued; a woman is "justly entitled to all we claim for man." After much heated debate the ninth resolution passed, but by only a small majority.

Thomas McClintock presided over the final session on Thursday evening and read extracts from Sir William Blackstone's *Commentaries on the Laws of England* that described the status of women in English common law. Cady Stanton took questions before short speeches were given by young Mary Ann McClintock and Frederick Douglass. Lucretia Mott closed the meeting with an appeal to action and one additional resolution of her own: "The speedy success of our cause depends upon the zealous and untiring efforts of both men and women, for the overthrow of the monopoly of the pulpit, and for securing to women of equal participation with men in the various trades, professions, and commerce." It, too, passed unanimously.

In all, some 300 people attended the Seneca Falls Convention. The majority were ordinary folk like Charlotte Woodward. Most sat through the 18 hours of speeches, debates, and readings. One hundred of them—68 women (including Woodward) and 32 men—signed the final draft of the Declaration of Sentiments and Resolutions. Women's rights as a separate reform movement had been born.

Press coverage was surprisingly broad and generally venomous, particularly on the subject of female suffrage. Philadelphia's *Public Ledger and Daily Transcript* declared that no lady would want to vote. "A woman is nobody. A wife is everything. The ladies of Philadelphia . . . are resolved to maintain their rights as Wives, Belles, Virgins and Mothers." According to the Albany *Mechanic's Advocate*, equal rights would "demoralize and degrade [women] from their high sphere and noble destiny . . . and prove a monstrous injury to all mankind." The *New York Herald* published the entire text of the Seneca Falls Declaration, calling it "amusing" but conceding that Lucretia Mott would "make a better President than some of those who have lately tenanted the White House." The only major paper to treat the event seriously was the liberal *New York Tribune*, edited by Horace Greeley, who found the demand for equal political rights improper, yet "however unwise and mistaken the demand, it is but the assertion of a natural right and as such must be conceded."

Stung by the public outcry, many original signers begged to have their names removed from the Declaration. "Our friends gave us the cold shoulder, and felt themselves disgraced by the whole proceeding," complained Cady Stanton. Many women sympathized with the convention's goals but feared the stigma attached to attending any future meetings. "I am with you thoroughly," said the wife of Senator William Seward, "but I am a born coward. There is nothing I dread more than Mr. Seward's ridicule." Even the McClintocks and the Hunts refrained

---

As Cady Stanton later put it, "I forged the thunderbolts and she [Susan B. Anthony] fired them."

---

from active involvement in women's rights after the Seneca Falls Convention.

But Cady Stanton saw opportunity in public criticism. "Imagine the publicity given our ideas by thus appearing in a widely circulated sheet like the *Herald*!" she wrote to Mott. "It will start women thinking, and men, too." She drafted lengthy responses to every negative newspaper article and editorial, presenting the reformers' side of the issue to the readers. Mott sensed her younger colleague's future role. "Thou art so wedded to this cause," she told Cady Stanton, "that thou must expect to act as pioneer in the work."

News of the Seneca Falls Convention spread rapidly and inspired a spate of regional women's rights meetings. Beginning with a follow-up meeting two weeks later in Rochester, New York, all subsequent women's rights forums featured female chairs. New England abolitionist Lucy Stone organized the first national convention, held in Worcester, Massachusetts, in 1850. Like Cady Stanton, Stone saw the connection between black emancipation and female emancipation. When criticized for including women's rights in her anti-slavery speeches, Stone countered: "I was a woman before I was an abolitionist—I must speak for the women."

QUAKER REFORMER Susan B. Anthony joined the women's rights movement in 1852. She had heard about the Seneca Falls Convention, of course, and her parents and sister had attended the 1848 Rochester meeting. Initially, however, she deemed its goals of secondary importance to temperance and abolition. All that changed in 1851 when she met Cady Stanton, with whom she formed a

---

life-long political partnership. Bound to the domestic sphere by her growing family, Cady Stanton wrote articles, speeches, and letters; Anthony, who never married, traveled the country lecturing and organizing women's rights associations. As Cady Stanton later put it, "I forged the thunderbolts and she fired them." In time, Susan B. Anthony's name became synonymous with women's rights.

Women's rights conventions were held annually until the Civil War, drawing most of their support from the abolitionist and temperance movements. After the war, feminist leaders split over the exclusion of women from legislation enfranchising black men. Abolitionists argued that it was "the Negro's Hour," and that the inclusion of female suffrage would jeopardize passage of the Fifteenth Amendment to the Constitution, which enfranchised all male citizens regardless of race. Feeling betrayed by their old allies, Cady Stanton and Anthony opposed the Fifteenth Amendment. Their protest alienated the more cautious wing of the movement and produced two competing suffrage organizations.

In 1869, Lucy Stone, Julia Ward Howe—well known author of "Battle Hymn of the Republic"—and others formed the moderate American Woman Suffrage Association, while Cady Stanton, Anthony, Martha Wright, and the radical faction founded the National Woman Suffrage Association (NWSA). Lucretia Mott, now an elderly widow, sought in vain to reconcile the two camps.

Both organizations sought political equality for women, but the more radical NWSA actively promoted issues beyond suffrage. Guided by the original Seneca Falls Resolutions, the NWSA demanded an end to all laws and practices that discriminated against women, and called for divorce law reform, equal pay, access to higher education and the professions, reform of organized religion, and a total rethinking of what constituted a "woman's sphere." Cady Stanton spoke about women's sexuality in public and condemned the Victorian double standard that forced wives to endure drunken, brutal, and licentious husbands. Anthony countenanced—and occasionally practiced—civil disobedience; in 1872 she provoked her own arrest by illegally casting a ballot in the presidential election. By the time the two rival organizations merged in 1890 to form the National American Woman Suffrage Association (NAWSA), much had been accomplished. Many states had enacted laws granting married women property rights, equal guardianship over children, and the legal standing to make contracts and bring suit. Nearly one-third of college students were female, and 19 states allowed women to vote in local school board elections. In two western territories—Wyoming and Utah—women voted on an equal basis with men. But full suffrage nationwide remained stubbornly out of reach. NAWSA commenced a long state-by-state battle for the right to vote.

NAWSA's first two presidents were Cady Stanton and Anthony, by then in their seventies. Old age did not mellow either one of them, especially Cady Stanton. Ever the rebel, she criticized NAWSA's narrow-mindedness and viewed with increasing suspicion its newly acquired pious, prohibitionist allies. NAWSA's membership should include all "types of classes, races and creeds," she stated, and resist the evangelical infiltrators who sought to mute the larger agenda of women's emancipation.

Cady Stanton had long advocated reform of organized religion. "The chief obstacle in the way of woman's elevation today," she wrote, "is the degrading position assigned her in the religion of all countries." Whenever women tried to enlarge their "divinely ordained sphere," the all-male clerical establishment condemned them for violating "God's law." Using the Scriptures to justify women's inferior status positively galled her. In 1895, she published *The Woman's Bible*, a critical commentary on the negative image of women in the Old and New Testaments. Even Anthony thought she had gone too far this time and could do little to prevent conservative suffragists from venting their wrath. During the annual convention of NAWSA, both the book and its author were publicly censured. Henceforth, mainstream suffragists downplayed Cady Stanton's historic role, preferring to crown Susan B. Anthony as the stateswoman of the movement.

Elizabeth Cady Stanton died in 1902 at the age of 86, and Susan B. Anthony died four years later, also at 86. By then a new generation of suffrage leaders had emerged—younger, better educated, and less restricted to the domestic sphere. The now-respectable, middle-class leadership of NAWSA adopted a "social feminist" stance, arguing that women were, in fact *different* from men and therefore needed the vote in order to apply their special qualities to the political problems of the nation.

However, more militant suffragists, among them Quaker agitator Alice Paul and Cady Stanton's daughter, Harriot Stanton Blatch, continued to insist upon women's absolute equality. They demanded a federal suffrage amendment as a necessary first step toward achieving equal rights. Paul's National Woman's Party gained the movement valuable publicity by engaging in confrontational tactics, including picketing the White House, being arrested, and going on hunger strikes while in prison.

Voting rights came in the wake of World War I. Impressed by the suffragists' participation in the war effort, Congress passed what came to be known as the "Susan B. Anthony Amendment" in 1919. Following state ratification a year later, it enfranchised American women nationwide in the form of the Nineteenth Amendment to the Constitution.

It had been 72 years since that daring call for female voting rights was issued at the Seneca Falls Convention. On November 2, 1920, 91-year-old Charlotte Woodward Pierce went to the polls in Philadelphia, the only signer of the Seneca Falls Declaration who had lived long enough to legally cast her ballot in a presidential election.

Constance B. Rynder is a professor of history at the University of Tampa, Florida, and specializes in women's history.

James K. Polk and the Expansionist Spirit

Harlan Hague

James K. Polk, 1795–1849. (Daguerreotype by Mathew B. Brady)

Only days after his inauguration in March 1845, President James K. Polk announced to Secretary of the Navy George Bancroft: "There are four great measures which are to be the measures of my administration: one, a reduction of the tariff; another, the independent treasury; a third, the settlement of the Oregon boundary question; and lastly, the acquisition of California."[1] It was the last two of his "great measures" that elected Polk, for he was swept into the White House by an expansionist fervor that peaked at his election. As President, Polk did not initiate a policy toward the West; he inherited one, based on the tenets of Manifest Destiny.

There was no doubt during the campaign where candidate Polk stood on the expansionist issue. In the spring of 1844, he called publicly for the annexation of both Texas and the Oregon country.[2] At the same time, Martin Van Buren, the assumed presidential candidate of the Democratic Party, announced his opposition to Texas annexation on grounds that it would mean war with Mexico.[3] Andrew Jackson, determined that the United States should have Texas, threw his support behind his fellow Tennessean for the Democratic Party nomination. In the end, Polk was nominated on the ninth ballot, as a compromise after the convention deadlocked on a choice between Van Buren, the lackluster ex-President whose political sun was setting, and Lewis Cass, an expansionist zealot who had won the support of many Westerners and Southerners and the enmity of multitudes. The Whig candidate, Henry Clay, had long opposed annexation of Texas, and the Whig platform ignored the issue. Polk's election assured the admission of Texas, and on 1 March 1845, the Lone Star Republic was invited into the Union by a joint resolution of Congress.

Upon his inauguration, the new President set to work on satisfying his campaign pledge. Polk was particularly concerned that the United States control important West Coast ports. He was not the first American leader to demand that a settlement of the Oregon question must give the United States control of Puget Sound, a region dominated by Britain's Hudson's Bay Company. A port on the Sound would be an Ameri-

can window on the Pacific, a jumping-off point for the Asian trade. Great Britain was just as determined that it would surrender no land north of the Columbia River. Logic seemed to support the British view. British settlement, chiefly the works and farms of the Hudson's Bay Company, was located north of the Columbia in present-day Washington, while American settlement was located south of the river, chiefly in Oregon's Willamette Valley.

Since 1818, the United States and Britain, by agreement, had jointly occupied the Oregon country. During the negotiations that had established joint occupancy, the United States had proposed a division of Oregon at the 49th parallel, but Britain, preferring the Columbia River as a boundary, rejected the offer. The American claim was subsequently pushed northward until it rested at 54°40′, the southern limit of Russian claims which had been established by treaty between Russia and the United States in 1824.

By the early 1840s, interest in a settlement of the Oregon question had increased in both Great Britain and the United States. As presidential candidate in 1844, Polk accepted the demand of the Democratic Party leadership for a boundary at 5440° but only as a political expedient. Indeed in July 1845, after only a few months in office, he offered Richard Pakenham, the British minister in Washington, a boundary settlement at the 49th parallel. Privately, Polk acknowledged that American interests would be protected because the boundary would leave the United States in control of Puget Sound. Pakenham rejected the offer since it did not include free British navigation of the Columbia, a long-standing British condition. When London later showed interest, nevertheless, in the offer, Polk refused to renew it.[4]

The following December, the President explained rather weakly in a message to Congress that he had made the 49th parallel boundary offer only from respect for his predecessors, who had long favored that compromise. Perhaps, though unstated, he had also feared war with Britain. Now, in December, Polk vowed that he would make no other offer. Rather than accommodation, he recommended that notice of termination of joint occupancy be delivered to Britain. At the expiration of the agreement, he said, the United States would pursue its interests aggressively in the Oregon country. London favored accommodation and suggested that the issue be submitted to arbitration. Polk rejected arbitration on grounds that the British had no just claim to Oregon.[5]

The President's rhetoric was mostly bluff and bluster. It was directed as much at the British government and public as American. Polk's objective was more pacific than his words. He simply wanted to stimulate negotiations and to force the British to take the initiative. To Louis McLane, the American minister in London, Polk intimated that he would be receptive to a British restatement of his original proposal, that is, a 49th parallel boundary, though Britain could have all of Vancouver Island, but no free British navigation of the Columbia.[6] Polk expected that his belligerent posture would force the issue.

Many congressmen were alarmed at Polk's notice proposal, fearing that it could lead to war with Britain. Congress debated the proposal for over four months and finally, in April 1846, enacted a measure to give Britain notice to terminate joint occupancy.

In the end, the settlement of the Oregon question may be attributed less to belligerence than to a lack of zeal.[7] By the end of 1845, the British public and the larger part of the government were little interested in Oregon. They were preoccupied with the specter of famine at home because of the potato blight in Ireland and light harvests in Britain.

Great Britain now needed American wheat, and trade relations in general improved in early 1846, leading many, including Polk, to hope for a lowering of tariffs. Furthermore, the fur trade was declining in Oregon, and British leaders were hard pressed to justify defense of a claim to the region below the 49th parallel at the risk of war. Finally, British leaders were convinced that sufficient British access to the sea would be secured if an agreement on a 49th parallel boundary left Britain all of Vancouver Island.

Accordingly, London tendered a proposal to Washington, and a treaty was concluded on these terms in June 1846. Both sides breathed a great sigh of relief. The signing came none too soon, particularly for the United States. Fighting had already begun on the disputed Texas border.

Polk's views on Oregon were contradictory at best. His obligation as leader of a party that was committed to having all of Oregon often conflicted with his own view. His involvement stemmed from political necessity, not personal interest, and he did what he had to do.

A Southerner, Polk was more interested in Texas and California. He was personally and passionately committed to American domination in the Southwest. The Oregon question settled, Polk turned to the Texas question.

Trouble between Mexico and the United States had been brewing since 1836 when Mexico blamed the United States for its loss of Texas. Mexico had never acknowledged the loss and warned the United States not to interfere, a warning that Polk ignored. He had no more sympathy for the arguments of anti-imperialists and anti-slavery leaders who spoke out against Washington's growing interest in Texas.

Polk dispatched agents to the Lone Star Republic in early 1845 to gather information and encourage Texans to call for annexation.[8] Following annexation in March, he sent William S. Parrott to Mexico City with instructions to convince the Mexican leadership to accept the finality of the American annexation of Texas and to resume diplomatic ties with the United States, which the annexation had ruptured. The shaky gov-

ernment of José Joaquín Herrera, mindful of the growing public clamor in Mexico against the American annexation of Texas, was noncommittal. Herrera preferred a British plan that included Mexico's recognition of Texas in return for the Lone Star Republic's rejection of annexation.[9]

Polk applied pressure. His administration accepted the Texas claim to the Rio Grande River boundary, and he moved to reinforce the claim. In mid-June, he ordered Zachary Taylor to move his troops from Louisiana to Texas where they installed themselves on the south bank of the Nueces River, thus inside the disputed territory between that river and the Rio Grande. Polk vowed that no invading force would be allowed to cross the Rio Grande.[10] In spite of the belligerent tone, he considered the Army's deployment a defensive move. Polk was an expansionist, but he was no fool. He did not shrink from the necessity of war, but he sought none, at least not until other measures were exhausted.

Mexico indeed appeared prepared to settle differences amicably. In August from Mexico City, Parrott notified Polk that the government seemed prepared to receive an American emissary. Polk appointed John Slidell his secret agent—during his presidency, Polk would appoint an abundance of secret agents—and instructed him to secure Mexico's acceptance of the Rio Grande boundary and a promise to pay the claims of American citizens against Mexico. And the pièce de résistance: He was to offer Mexico as much as $40 million for California and New Mexico. At the same time, Polk warned Mexico—and Britain and France, as well—against any plan for a European protectorate for California. The Monroe Doctrine would be enforced. Polk's prohibition of European protectorates, a new factor in American hegemony, in time became called the "Polk doctrine."[11]

The Slidell mission was doomed from the start. The Herrera government fell on 2 January to a new revolutionary movement under General Paredes y Arrillaga. Anticipating that the new administration would be no more stable than the former, Polk toyed with the idea of asking Congress for a secret fund of $500,000 to a $1 million which he would transfer to Paredes to strengthen his government during negotiations. He abandoned the scheme when he could not win sufficient support among Democratic leaders.[12]

In early 1846, Polk was intrigued by the possibilities suggested to him by one Alexander J. Atocha. A naturalized American citizen, Atocha was a friend of ex-President Antonio Lòpez de Santa Anna who was overthrown in 1845. Atocha had recently visited General Santa Anna in Havana. He believed that Santa Anna would soon be once again in power and that the general favored a treaty in which Mexico would cede New Mexico and California to the United States. Santa Anna, he said, had told him that $30 million would be a satisfactory sum to conclude the deal, but that the United States must take action to pose such an armed threat that Mexican citizens would be convinced that the cession was the only alternative to destruction.[13] Polk concluded that Atocha was probably not reliable, but the President continued to pursue the diplomacy-by-bribery scheme off and on. Nothing came of it.[14]

Polk's fears for the stability of the new government were well founded. He learned in early April 1846 that Arrillaga, certain that he would be removed from office by an angry citizenry if he agreed to negotiations, had refused to receive Slidell. War now seemed likely. That same day, Polk had told his cabinet that if Mexico rejected his envoy, the American leaders must "take the remedy for the injuries and wrongs we had suffered into our own hands."[15] He now "saw no alternative but strong measures towards Mexico."[16] Slidell counseled Polk that war now was probably the best course.[17]

War was not long in coming. By early May, Polk had decided that war would be necessary to achieve his objectives, which included California and New Mexico and perhaps additional northern Mexican states. He prepared a message for delivery to Congress on 12 May, a delicately worded message, for he was asking Congress for authority to initiate war. Three days before the scheduled delivery date, Polk learned that a Mexican patrol had crossed the

Rio Grande and fired on American troops. In Polk's view, Mexico had invaded American soil. He changed his message, and on 11 and 12 May, Congress, by huge majorities, declared war.

Polk soon clarified his war aims, privately at least. Shortly after the declaration of war, he read a dispatch that Secretary of State James Buchanan planned to send to European governments to notify them of the declaration. Polk was not pleased; he ordered the Secretary to strike from the message a statement that the United States had no intention "to dismember Mexico or make conquests . . . [and] that in going to war we did not do so with a view to acquire either California or New Mexico or any other portion of the Mexican territory." Polk told Buchanan that we would seek indemnities, and Mexico had no other way of indemnifying the United States, save in territory. Buchanan said that unless the assurance that he recommended was included in the message, both England and France would join the war on the side of Mexico. Polk replied testily that before he gave this assurance, he would "meet the war which either England or France or all the Powers of Christendom might wage. . . ." He would stand for no interference.[18] He had long since given his pledge to the American people, at least those of the public who counted, in Polk's estimation. Those who did not support his policy he branded as disloyal and hinted that such behavior was treasonous.

Polk had not forgotten that other prize that must come in a contest with Mexico: California. Polk's initial interest in the Mexican province was the same as his interest in Oregon; that is, its ports. For a while, it seemed that California might fall quietly to the United States. Thomas O. Larkin, American Consul to Mexican California, was making headway in convincing Californians that their destiny lay in an association, initiated by themselves, with the United States.[19] By the mid-1840s, however, there was reason for haste. American immigrants entering California overland were arguing belligerently for a "Texas solution" for California.

In 1845 affairs appeared to take an ominous turn in California. Larkin had written frequently to Washington from Monterey during the past year, telling of the revolutionary ferment among *Californios*. Some *Californio* leaders, said Larkin, favored associating a liberated California with the United States. On the other hand, the Consul warned of apparent British and French intrigues in the province and the interest of some California leaders in seeking protection from a European country.[20] Polk was convinced that Britain wanted California, and he was determined that the United States would not permit Britain or any other foreign power to possess it.[21]

The President was impressed by Larkin's revelations. In October 1845, Polk appointed him his confidential agent with instructions to inform the Californians that though the United States would not interfere in any conflict between California and Mexico, Americans would not permit California's becoming a colony of Britain or France. The United States would not leave its neighbor unprotected. Indeed, Larkin was to assure the Californians that an application for admission into the American union by a free California would be most welcome.[22]

Acting on Larkin's information, members of Polk's cabinet, unquestionably at the President's direction, strengthened American preparedness. Secretary of War George Bancroft ordered Commodore John D. Sloat, commander of the American fleet off the Mexican coast, to be ready to blockade or seize California ports at the first sign of hostilities.[23] Secretary of State Buchanan alerted the American ambassador in London and briefed John Slidell on Larkin's correspondence.[24] Bancroft dispatched Commodore Robert F. Stockton to the West Coast to deliver the letters containing Sloat's new orders and Larkin's appointment. At the same time, Buchanan sent a copy of the appointment letter to Larkin by Marine Lieutenant Archibald H. Gillespie, who was to travel in disguise across Mexico. Gillespie, another of Polk's secret agents, also was ordered to deliver an informational copy of Larkin's letter to

Brevet Captain John D. Frémont, who was exploring in California.

Frémont's role in California affairs was stormy, controversial, and contradictory.[25] Frémont had arrived in California with an expedition of 60 well-armed mountain men early in 1846. He soon offended California authorities and was ordered to leave. Instead, in March he erected barricades atop Hawk's Peak in the Gavilan Mountains near Monterey where he was besieged by a *Californio* force. Frémont soon withdrew, realizing that the affair was essentially personal and that his action could jeopardize Washington's plan to acquire California.[26]

Three months later in the Bear Flag affair, Frémont took a belligerent stance that angered *Californios* more than did the Hawk's Peak incident. He even arrested General Mariano Guadalupe Vallejo, who favored an association of California with the United States. By then, Frémont had seen the copy of Buchanan's letter to Larkin, and he was confident now that he was acting in the best interests of the United States. Questioned by Commodore Sloat in July 1846 about his part in the Bear Flag incident, Frémont replied that he "had acted solely on my own responsibility, and without any expressed authority from the Government to justify hostilities.' "[27]

Perhaps Frémont responded to a higher authority. "How fate pursues a man!" he had observed earlier, upon learning that Gillespie was on his trail.[28] Fate perhaps was on his side, but not his commander in chief. Polk later confided to his diary that Frémont had acted without authority.[29]

During the war in California, Frémont led his own men under the overall command of Commodore Stockton, who had replaced Sloat. When General Stephen Watts Kearny arrived from Santa Fé with an advance unit of his Army of the West, carrying orders that designated him governor of California, Frémont refused to recognize his authority.[30] A court-martial board in Washington the following January found Frémont guilty of mutiny and ordered him discharged from the service.

After a review of the court record and consultation with his cabinet, Polk con-cluded that the facts of the case did not prove mutiny. He dismissed that conviction, but let stand conviction on two lesser charges: disobedience of orders and conduct prejudicial to good order and military discipline. The President, influenced by the cabinet, also thought the sentence of dismissal from the Army too severe. Accordingly, he set aside the sentence and ordered Frémont to report for duty. The decision, he groaned, was "a painful and a responsible duty."[31] Frémont rejected Polk's clemency, for to accept would be to acknowledge guilt. He resigned from the Army and returned to California.

In the heated controversies between Kearny and Stockton and between Kearny and Frémont, Polk sided with Kearny. After a full examination of the correspondence in May 1847, Polk con-cluded that he was "fully satisfied that General Kearny was right, and that Commodore Stockton's course was wrong. Indeed, both he [Stockton] and Lieut.-Col. Frémont, in refusing to rec-ognize the authority of General Kearny, acted insubordinately and in a manner that is censurable."[32]

At war's end, there was some con-cern in California that Washington would not insist in the peace treaty on retention of the province. Those that knew something of the origins of the New York Volunteer Regiment, which arrived in California in spring 1847, were less fearful. Polk had directed Colonel Jonathan D. Stevenson to re-cruit mechanics who would agree that they would, at war's end, accept their discharges and settle in California or the closest United States territory. The East-ern press, from the regiment's inception, guessed that its principal purpose was colonization rather than war.[33] Shortly before the end of the war, Polk confided in a letter to his brother that California indeed would be retained, and New Mexico as well, as war indemnifications. Further-more, the longer Mexico continued hos-tilities by its "stubbornness," said Polk, the greater the indemnities.[34]

Publicly, Polk said little about Cali-fornia's destiny, for he did not wish to enter the debate on whether the United States intended to retain Mexican terri-tory. He was no longer stating publicly, as he had before, that the United States had no intention to retain Mexican prop-erties after the signing of a peace treaty.[35] His reluctance to make his po-sition known baffled and angered the public. The public should have remem-bered that Polk at the outset of the war had similarly refused to clarify his war objectives.

At war's end, when it appeared that Polk might be forced to bow to powerful elements in the Democratic Party who were arguing for annexation of all of Mexico, Nicholas Trist signed the Treaty of Guadalupe Hidalgo for the United States, which established a boundary just south of San Diego Bay, virtually the same boundary that Polk had sought in the Slidell mission. The President's well-known quarrel with Trist would be overlooked, and the administration, ac-cording to the New Orleans *Picayune,* would be content to "swallow its disap-pointment, and California and New Mexico at the same time."[36]

Polk left to his successors the ques-tion of slavery which would be-come central to the issue of Westward Expansion for the next 15 years. During his presidency, Polk adopted a position that could have prevented sectional cri-sis if his successors had been so wise. He understood better than his contem-poraries, and successors as well, the true nature of the issue of slavery in the Western territories. He assailed fellow Southerner John C. Calhoun for his ex-tremist stance on the expansion of slav-ery. At the same time, he rejected the Wilmot Proviso which would have pre-vented slavery in any territory acquired from Mexico at the end of the war. In-deed, he favored the extension of the 1820 Missouri Compromise line of 36°30′ to the Pacific.

Polk saw no contradiction in his po-sition. He was simply convinced that slavery would never exist in the territory south of the 36°30′ line.[37] A Southern man who wished to be president to all the people, he would permit slavery in the federal territories since he believed that it would never take hold there. If this view had prevailed, there might have been no Civil War.

Polk decided that he was going to enjoy retirement more than the presidency, and he left the office without regret. He was dismayed, however, to be succeeded by a Whig, especially by Zachary Taylor, whom he held in low regard. His opinion of Taylor undoubtedly reached rock-bottom during a coach ride to the Capitol on inauguration day. Polk was shocked when the President-elect, in the course of polite conversation, said that Oregon and California should establish an independent government, since they were so far removed from the United States. Polk, for some time, had been anxious that Congress form a government for California, fearing that otherwise the territory could be lost to the Union by the formation of a separate government, precisely the course the new President seemed to advocate. Polk concluded that Taylor was a "well-meaning old man," though uneducated and politically ignorant.[38]

If Polk's election in 1844 can be traced at least partly to the American people's expansionist spirit, then it can be argued that the voters' rejection of the Democrats in 1848 can be interpreted as a repudiation of the siren song of Manifest Destiny.[39] Yet, Polk's contributions, the fruit of the expansionist spirit, were embraced and defended. His "Polk Doctrine," which warned Europe not to interfere in the affairs of the North American continent, was subsequently embraced by the American people. During the four-year tenure, over one-half million square miles of territory were added to the United States, a number second only to Jefferson's Louisiana Purchase.[40] Even ill-gotten gains, like horse thieves and harlots in the family tree, can be accepted with resignation or amusement, even some pride, when separated by a sufficient lapse of time.

Notes

1. James K. Polk, *Polk: The Diary of a President, 1845–1849*, Allan Nevins, ed. (New York, 1952), xvii.
2. See, for example, Polk to Chase *et al*, 23 Apr. 1844, in James K. Polk, *The Correspondence of James K. Polk*, Wayne Cutler and James P. Cooper, Jr., eds. (Nashville, TN, 1989), 105–106.
3. Polk, *Diary*, xxiii.
4. Frederick Merk, *The Oregon Question: Essays in Anglo-American Diplomacy and Politics* (Cambridge, MA, 1967), 410; Jesse S. Reeves, *American Diplomacy under Tyler and Polk* (Gloucester, MA, 1967, a reprint of the 1907 publication of The Johns Hopkins Press), 252–253.
5. Merk, *The Oregon Question*, 219–220.
6. *Ibid.*, 343.
7. For an elaboration of the view following, see Merk, *The Oregon Question*, 415–416, and Norman A. Graebner, *Empire on the Pacific: A Study in American Continental Expansion* (Santa Barbara, CA, reprint, 1983), 137–140.
8. Commodore Robert F. Stockton, the most energetic among the agents, appeared bent on provoking a war with Mexico. See, generally, Glenn W. Price, *Origins of the War with Mexico: The Polk-Stockton Intrigue* (Austin, TX, 1967). Texas President Anson Jones, who later wrote an account of the intrigues of Stockton and his Texan and American cohorts, charged that Polk secretly sought to provoke war at the point, 112.
9. Charles Sellers, *James K. Polk: Continentalist, 1843–1846* (Princeton, NJ, 1966), 259.
10. Neal Harlow, *California Conquered: War and Peace on the Pacific, 1846–1850* (Berkeley, 1982), 55; Paul H. Bergeron, *The Presidency of James K. Polk* (Lawrence, KS, 1987), 62.
11. Polk, *Diary*, 10; Bernard DeVoto, *Year of Decision: 1846* (Boston, 1942), 16–17. Slidell's mission was to be kept secret to prevent foreign powers, particularly Britain or France, from interfering with it. Polk, *Diary*, 10.
12. Graebner, *Empire on the Pacific*, 121.
13. Polk, *Diary*, 50–53; Sellers, *Polk: Continentalist*, 401.
14. Polk, *Diary*, 53; Bergeron, *Polk*, 70–71, 83, 103; Sellers, *Polk: Continentalist*, 427–428, 430–431.
15. Polk, *Diary* (4-7-1846), 69–70. Polk believed that the British ambassador had influenced the Mexican government to reject Slidell *Ibid.* (4-18-1846), 71–72], perhaps assuming that the Mexican issue would be sufficiently irritating to the United States to encourage the settlement of the Oregon question.
16. Polk, *Diary* (4-18-1846), 71.
17. Graebner, *Empire on the Pacific*, 152.
18. Polk, *Diary* (5-13-1846), 90–92.
19. For Larkin's role in trying to persuade Californians, see Harlan Hague and David J. Langum, *Thomas O. Larkin: A Life of Patriotism and Profit in Old California* (Norman, OK, 1990), especially chapter 7.
20. Larkin's role in the approach to war with Mexico is told in *Ibid.*, chapter 7.
21. Polk, *Diary* (10-14-1845), 19. Spence and Jackson indeed conclude that Polk's concern about British designs on California became "one of the cornerstones of his foreign policy." John Charles Frémont, *The Expeditions of John Charles Frémont: The Bear Flag Revolt and the Court-Martial*, Mary Lee Spence and Donald Jackson, eds., vol. 2 (Urbana, 1973), xxi. If that is true, then Larkin's influence on American foreign policy during Polk's presidency looms large. Polk's fear of European interference would extend to the end of the war. As late as December 1847, he argued that a premature withdrawal of the American Army from Mexico might open the way to European intervention. Robert W. Johannsen, *To the Halls of the Montezumas: The Mexican War in the American Imagination* (New York, 1985), 304.
22. Buchanan to Larkin, 17 Oct. 1845, in George P. Hammond, ed., *The Larkin Papers: Personal, Business, and Official Correspondence of Thomas Oliver Larkin, Merchant and United States Consul in California*, 10 vols. (Berkeley, 1951–1968), 4: 44–46.
23. Bancroft to Sloat, 17 Oct. 1845, in Robert E. Cowan, ed., "Documentary," *California Historical Society Quarterly*, 2 (July 1923): 167–170.
24. Buchanan to McLane, 14 Oct. 1845, cited in Robert Glass Cleland, "The Early Sentiment for the Annexation of California: An Account of the Growth of American Interest in California, 1835–1846," *The Southwestern Historical Quarterly* (Jan. 1915), 243; Buchanan to Slidell, 10 Nov. 1845, cited in Howard William Gross, "The Influence of Thomas O. Larkin Toward the Acquisition of California," M.A. thesis, University of California, Berkeley, 1937, 112.
25. For an overview, see: Harlow, *California Conquered*, principally chapters 6–8; Hague and Langum, *Thomas O. Larkin*, 120–130, 136–139.
26. John Charles Frémont, *Memoirs of My Life* (Chicago: Belford, Clarke & Company, 1887), 460.
27. Frémont, *Memoirs*, 534. In later life, Frémont, probably influenced by Jessie, his wife, claimed that the letter from Buchanan that was shown him in spring 1846 was actually meant for *himself* not Larkin, that *he*, not Larkin, had been appointed Polk's confidential agent. The record does not support his claim. See Hague and Langum, *Thomas O. Larkin*, 128–130.
28. Frémont, *Memoirs*, 486.
29. Frémont, *Expeditions*, 2: xxix.
30. This tangled story is best told in Harlow, *California Conquered*, chapters 14, 15.
31. Polk, *Diary* (2-16-1848), 303. See also Frémont, *Expeditions*, 468n, 469n.
32. Polk, *Diary* (5-4-1847), 226.
33. Graebner, *Empire on the Pacific*, 156.
34. *Ibid.*, 158–159.
35. *Ibid.*, 161–162.
36. Quoted in *Ibid.*, 213–214.
37. Polk, *Diary*, xvi, 189–190, 376.
38. *Ibid.*, 389.
39. This argument is suggested in Graebner, *Empire on the Pacific*, 227.
40. Polk, *Diary*, xvii.

Harlan Hague is the author, with David J. Langum, of Thomas O. Larkin: A Life of Patriotism and Profit in Old California *(1990), winner of the Caroline Bancroft Prize. He is currently editing a collection of unpublished Larkin letters and working on a biography of Stephen Watts Kearny for the University of Oklahoma Western Biographies series. Recipient of a number of grants, including NEH, the Huntington Library, and the Sourisseau Academy, Hague is particularly interested in Mexican California, exploration and travel, and environmental history.*

The Lives of Slave Women

Deborah Gray White

Deborah Gray White is associate professor of history and Africana studies at Rutgers University, New Brunswick, New Jersey. This chapter is adapted from her book, Ar'nt I a Woman? Female Slaves in the Plantation South, *published in 1984 by W. W. Norton.*

Slave women have often been characterized as self-reliant and self-sufficient, yet not every black woman was a Sojourner Truth or a Harriet Tubman. Strength had to be cultivated. It came no more naturally to them than to anyone else, slave or free, male or female, black or white. If slave women seemed exceptionally strong it was partly because they often functioned in groups and derived strength from their numbers.

Much of the work slaves did and the regimen they followed served to stratify slave society along sex lines. Consequently slave women had ample opportunity to develop a consciousness grounded in their identity as females. While close contact sometimes gave rise to strife, adult female cooperation and dependence of women on each other was a fact of female slave life. The self-reliance and self-sufficiency of slave women, therefore, must be viewed in the context not only of what the individual slave woman did for herself, but what slave women as a group were able to do for each other.

It is easy to overlook the separate world of female slaves because from colonial times through the Civil War black women often worked with black men at tasks considered by Europeans to be either too difficult or inappropriate for females. All women worked hard, but when white women consistently performed field labor it was considered temporary, irregular, or extraordinary, putting them on a par with slaves. Actress Fredericka Bremer, visiting the ante-bellum South, noted that usually only men and black women did field work; commenting on what another woman traveler sarcastically claimed to be a noble admission of female equality, Bremer observed that "black (women) are not considered to belong to the weaker sex."[1]

Bremer's comment reflects what former slaves and fugitive male slaves regarded as the defeminization of black women. Bonded women cut down trees to clear lands for cultivation. They hauled logs in leather straps attached to their shoulders. They plowed using mule and ox teams, and hoed, sometimes with the heaviest implements available. They dug ditches, spread manure fertilizer, and piled coarse fodder with their bare hands. They built and cleaned Southern roads, helped construct Southern railroads, and, of course, they picked cotton. In short, what fugitive slave Williamson Pease said regretfully of slave women was borne out in fact: "Women who do outdoor work are used as bad as men."[2] Almost a century later Green Wilbanks spoke less remorsefully than Pease in his remembrances of his Grandma Rose, where he implied that the work had a kind of neutering effect. Grandma Rose, he said, was a woman who could do any kind of job a man could do, a woman who "was some worker, a regular man-woman."[3]

It is hardly likely, though, that slave women, especially those on large plantations with sizable female populations, lost their female identity. Harvesting season on staple crop plantations may have found men and women gathering the crop in sex-integrated gangs, but at other times women often worked in exclusively or predominantly female gangs.[4] Thus women stayed in each other's company for most of the day. This meant that those they ate meals with, sang work songs with, and commiserated with during the work day were people who by virtue of their sex had the same kind of responsibilities and problems. As a result, slave women appeared to have developed their own female culture, a way of doing things and a way of assigning value that flowed from their perspective as slave women on Southern plantations. Rather than being squelched, their sense of womanhood was probably enhanced and their bonds to each other strengthened.

Since slaveowners and makers seemingly took little note of the slave woman's lesser physical strength, one wonders why they separated men and women at all. One answer appears to be that gender provided a natural and easy way to divide the labor force. Also probable is that despite their limited sensitivity regarding female slave labor, and the double standard they used when evaluating the uses of white and black

From *Southern Exposure,* November/December 1984, pp. 32-39. Adapted from *Ar'n't I a Woman? Female Slaves in the Plantation South* by Deborah Gray White. © 1984 by Deborah Gray White. Reprinted with permission of W. W. Norton & Company, Inc.

female labor, slave-owners did, using standards only they could explain, reluctantly acquiesce to female physiology. For instance, depending on their stage of pregnancy, pregnant women were considered half or quarter hands. Healthy nonpregnant women were considered three-quarter hands. Three-quarter hands were not necessarily exempt from some of the herculean tasks performed by men who were full hands, but usually, when labor was being parceled out and barring a shortage of male hands to do the very heavy work or a rush to get that work completed, men did the more physically demanding work. A case in point was the most common differentiation where men plowed and women hoed.[5]

A great deal of both field labor and nonfield labor was structured to promote cooperation among slave women.

Like much of the field labor, nonfield labor was structured to promote cooperation among women. In the Sea Islands, slave women sorted cotton lint according to color and fineness and removed cotton seeds crushed by the gin into the cotton and lint. Fence building often found men splitting rails in one area and women doing the actual construction in another. Men usually shelled corn, threshed peas, cut potatoes for planting, and platted shucks. Grinding corn into meal or hominy was women's work. So too were spinning, weaving, sewing, and washing.[6] On Captain Kinsler's South Carolina plantation, as on countless others, "old women and women bearin' chillun not yet born, did cardin' wid handcards." Some would spin, others would weave, but all would eventually learn from some skilled woman "how to make clothes for the family . . . knit coarse socks and stockins."[7]

"When the work in the fields was finished women were required to come home and spin one cut a night," reported a Georgian. "Those who were not successful in completing this work were punished the next morning."[8] Women had to work in the evenings partly because slaveowners bought them few ready-made clothes. On one South Carolina plantation each male slave received annually two cotton shirts, three pairs of pants, and one jacket. Slave women, on the other hand, received six yards of woolen cloth, six yards of cotton drilling, and six yards of cotton shirting a year, along with two needles and a dozen buttons.[9]

Perhaps a saving grace to this "double duty" was that women got a chance to interact with each other. On a Sedalia County, Missouri, plantation, women looked forward to Saturday afternoon washing because, as Mary Frances Webb explained, they "would get to talk and spend the day together."[10] Quiltings, referred to by former slaves as female "frolics" and "parties," were especially convivial. Anna Peek recalled that when slaves were allowed to relax, they gathered around a pine wood fire in Aunt Anna's cabin to tell stories. At that time "the old women with pipes in their mouths would sit and gossip for hours."[11] Missourian Alice Sewell noted that sometimes women would slip away and hold their own prayer meetings. They cemented their bonds to each other at the end of every meeting when they walked around shaking hands and singing, "fare you well my sisters, I am going home."[12]

The organization of female slave work and social activities tended not only to separate women and men, but also to generate female cooperation and interdependence. Slave women and their children could depend on midwives and "doctor women" to treat a variety of ailments. Menstrual cramps, for example, were sometimes treated with a tea made from the bark of the gum tree. Midwives and "doctor women" administered various other herb teas to ease the pains of many ailing slaves. Any number of broths—made from the leaves and barks of trees, from the branches and twigs of bushes, from turpentine, catnip, or tobacco—were used to treat whooping cough, diarrhea, toothaches, colds, fevers, headaches, and backaches.[13] According to a Georgia ex-slave, "One had to be mighty sick to have the services of a doctor." On his master's plantation "old women were . . . responsible for the care of the sick."[14] This was also the case on Rebecca Hooks's former Florida residence. "The doctor," she noted, "was not nearly as popular as the 'granny' or midwife, who brewed medicines for every ailment."[15]

Female cooperation in the realm of medical care helped foster bonding that led to collaboration in the area of resistance to abuses by slaveholders. Frances Kemble could attest to the concerted efforts of the black women on her husband's Sea Island plantations. More than once she was visited by groups of women imploring her to persuade her husband to extend the lying-in period for childbearing women. On one occasion the women had apparently prepared beforehand the approach they would take with the foreign-born and sympathetic Kemble, for their chosen spokeswoman took care to play on Kemble's own maternal sentiments, and pointedly argued that slave women deserved at least some of the care and tenderness that Kemble's own pregnancy had elicited.[16]

Usually, however, slave women could not be so outspoken about their needs, and covert cooperative resistance prevailed. Slaveowners suspected that midwives conspired with their female patients to bring about abortions and infanticides, and on Charles Colcock Jones's Georgia plantation, for example, this seems in fact to have been the case. A woman named Lucy gave birth in secret and then denied that she had ever been pregnant. Although the midwife attended her, she too claimed not to have delivered a child, as did Lucy's mother. Jones had a physician examine Lucy, and the doctor confirmed what Jones had suspected, that Lucy had indeed given birth. Twelve days later the decomposing body of a full-term infant was found, and Lucy, her mother, and the midwife were all hauled off to court. Another woman, a nurse, managed to avoid prosecution but not suspicion. Whether Lucy was guilty of murder, and whether the others were accessories, will never be known because the court could not shatter their collective defense that the child had been stillborn.[17]

The inability to penetrate the private world of female slaves is probably what kept many abortions and infanticides from becoming known to slaveowners. The secrets kept by a midwife named Mollie became too much for her to bear. When she accepted Christianity these were the first things for which she asked forgiveness. She recalled, "I was carried to the gates of hell and the devil pulled out a book showing me the things which I had committed and that they were all true. My life as a midwife was shown to me and I have certainly felt sorry for all the things I did, after I was converted."[18]

Health care is not the only example of how the organization of slave work and slave responsibilities led to female cooperation and bonding; slave women also depended on each other for childcare. Sometimes, especially on small farms or new plantations where there was no extra woman to superintend children, bondswomen took their offspring to the field with them and attended to them during prescheduled breaks. Usually, however, infants and older children were left in the charge of an elderly female or females. Josephine Bristow, for example, spent more time with Mary Novlin, the nursery keeper on Ferdinand Gibson's South Carolina plantation, than she spent with her mother and father, who came in from the fields after she was asleep: "De old lady, she looked after every blessed thing for us all day long en cooked for us right along wid de mindin'."[19] In their complementary role as nurses, they ministered to the hurts and illnesses of infants and children.[20] It was not at all uncommon for the children's weekly rations to be given to the "grannies" as opposed to the children's parents.[21] Neither the slaveowner nor slave society expected the biological mother of a child to fulfill all of her child's needs. Given the circumstances, the responsibilities of motherhood had to be shared, and this required close female cooperation.

Cooperation in this sphere helped slave women overcome one of the most difficult of predicaments—who would provide maternal care for a child whose mother had died or been sold away? Fathers sometimes served as both mother and father, but when slaves, as opposed to the master, determined maternal care, it was usually a woman who became a child's surrogate mother. Usually that woman was an aunt or a sister, but in the absence of female relatives, a non-kin woman assumed the responsibility.[22] In the case of Georgian Mollie Malone, for example, the nursery superintendent became the child's substitute mother.[23] When Julia Malone's mother was killed by another Texas slave, little Julia was raised by the woman with whom her mother had shared a cabin.[24] On Southern plantations the female community made sure that no child was truly motherless.

Because black women on a plantation spent so much time together, they inevitably developed some appreciation of each other's skills and talents. This intimacy enabled them to establish the criteria by which to rank and order themselves. The existence of certain "female jobs" that carried prestige created a yardstick by which bondswomen could measure each other's achievements. Some of these jobs allowed for growth and self-satisfaction, fringe benefits that were usually out of reach for the field laborer. A seamstress, for example, had unusual opportunities for self-expression and creativity. On very large plantations the seamstress usually did no field work, and a particularly good seamstress, or "mantua-maker," might be hired out to others and even allowed to keep a portion of the money she earned.[25] For obvious reasons cooks, midwives, and female folk doctors also commanded the respect of their peers. Midwives in particular often were able to travel to other plantations to practice their art. This gave them an enviable mobility and also enabled them to carry messages from one plantation to the next.

Apart from the seamstresses, cooks, and midwives, a few women were distinguished as work gang-leaders. On most farms and plantations where there were overseers, managers, foremen, and drivers, these positions were held by men, either black or white. Occasionally, however, a woman was given a measure of authority over slave work, or a particular aspect of it. For instance

Louis Hughes noted that each plantation he saw had a "forewoman who . . . had charge of the female slaves and also the boys and girls from twelve to sixteen years of age, and all the old people that were feeble."[26] Similarly, a Mississippi slave remembered that on his master's Osceola plantation there was a "colored woman as foreman."[27]

Clearly, a pecking order existed among bondswomen—one which they themselves helped to create. Because of age, occupation, association with the master class, or personal achievements, certain women were recognized by other women—and also by men—as important people, even as leaders. Laura Towne met an aged woman who commanded such a degree of respect that other slaves bowed to her and lowered their voices in her presence. The old woman, Maum Katie, was according to Towne a "spiritual mother" and a woman of "tremendous influence over her spiritual children."[28]

A slaveowner lamented that Big Lucy, one of his oldest slaves, had more control over his female workers than he did.

Sometimes two or three factors combined to distinguish a particular woman. Aunt Charlotte was the aged cook in John M. Booth's Georgia household. When Aunt Charlotte spoke, said Booth, "other colored people hastened to obey her."[29] Frederick Douglass's grandmother wielded influence because of her age and the skills she possessed. She made the best fishnets in Tuckahoe, Maryland, and she knew better than anyone else how to preserve sweet potato seedlings and how to plant them successfully. She enjoyed what Douglass called "high reputation," and accordingly "she was remembered by others."[30] In another example, when Elizabeth Botume went to the Sea Islands after the Civil War, she employed as a house servant a young woman named Amy who performed her tasks slowly and sullenly, until an older woman named Aunt Mary arrived from Beaufort. During slavery Amy and Aunt Mary had both worked in the house but Amy had learned to listen and obey Aunt Mary. After Aunt Mary arrived the once obstreperous Amy became "quiet, orderly, helpful and painstaking."[31]

The leadership of some women had a disruptive effect on plantation operations. Bennet H. Barrow repeatedly lamented the fact that Big Lucy, one of his oldest slaves, had more control over his female workers than he did: "Anica, Center, Cook Jane, the better you treat them the worse they are. Big Lucy the Leader corrupts every young negro in her power."[32] A self-proclaimed prophetess named Sinda was responsible for a cessation of all slave work for a considerable period on Butler Island in Georgia. According to a notation made by Frances Kemble in 1839, Sinda's prediction that the world would come to an end on a certain day caused the slaves to lay down their hoes and plows in the belief that their final emancipation was imminent. So sure were Sinda's fellow slaves of her prediction that even the lash failed to get them into the fields. When the appointed day of judgment passed uneventfully Sinda was whipped mercilessly. Yet, for a time, she had commanded more authority than either master or overseer.[33]

Bonded women did not have to go to such lengths in order to make a difference in each other's lives. The supportive atmosphere of the female community was considerable buffer against the depersonalizing regimen of plantation work and the general dehumanizing nature of slavery. When we consider that women were much more strictly confined to the plantation than men, that many women had husbands who visited only once or twice a week, and that slave women outlived slave men by an average of two years, we realize just how important the female community was to its members.

If we define a stable relationship as one of long duration, then it was probably easier for slave women to sustain stable emotional relationships with other bondswomen than with bondsmen. This is not to say that male-female relationships were unfulfilling or of no consequence. But they were generally fraught with more uncertainty about the future than female-to-female relationships, especially those existing between female blood kin. In her study of ex-slave interviews, Martha Goodson found that of all the relationships slaveowners disrupted, through either sale or dispersal, they were least likely to separate mothers and daughters.[34] Cody found that when South Carolina cotton planter Peter Gaillard divided his estate among his eight children, slave women in their twenties and thirties were twice as likely to have a sister with them, and women over 40 were four times more likely to have sisters with them than brothers. Similarly, daughters were less likely than sons to be separated from their mother. Over 60 percent of women aged 20 to 24 remained with their mothers when the estate was divided, as did 90 percent of those aged 25 to 29.[35] A slave song reflected the bonds between female siblings by indicating who took responsibility for the motherless female slave child. Interestingly enough, the one designated was neither the father nor the brother:

A motherless chile see a hard time.
Oh Lord, help her on de road.
Er sister will do de bes' she kin,
Dis is a hard world, Lord, fer a motherless chile.[36]

If female blood ties did indeed promote the most enduring relationships among slaves, then we should probably assume that like occupation, age, and personal achievement these relationships helped structure the female slave community. This assumption should not, however, obscure the fact that in friendships and dependency relationships women often treated non-relatives as if a consanguineous tie existed. This is why older women were called Aunt and Granny, and why unrelated women sometimes called each other Sister.[37]

While the focus here has been on those aspects of the bondswoman's life that fostered female bonding, female-to-female conflict was not uncommon. It was impossible for harmony always to prevail among women who saw so much of each other and who knew so much about one another. Lifelong friendships were founded in the hoe gangs and sewing groups, but the constant jockeying for occupational and social status created an atmosphere in which jealousies and antipathies smoldered. From Jesse Belflowers, the overseer of the Allston rice plantation in South Carolina, Adele Petigru Allston heard that "mostly amongst the Women" there was a "goodeal of quarling and disputing and telling lies."[38] The terms of a widely circulated overseer's contract advised rigorous punishment for "fighting, particularly amongst the women."[39] Some overseers followed this advice. According to Georgian Isaac Green, "Sometimes de women uster git whuppin's for fightin'."[40]

Occasionally, violence between women could and did get very ugly. Molly, the cook in James Chesnut's household, once took a red hot poker and attacked the woman to whom her husband had given one of her calico dresses.[41] Similarly, when she was a young woman in Arkansas, Lucretia Alexander came to blows with another woman over a pair of stockings that the master had given Lucretia.[42] In another incident on a Louisiana cotton plantation, the day's cotton chopping was interrupted when a feisty field worker named Betty lost her temper in the midst of a dispute with a fellow slave named Molly and struck her in the face with a hoe.[43]

The presence of conflict within interpersonal relationships between female slaves should not detract from the more important cooperation and dependence that prevailed among them. Conflict occurred *because* women were in close daily contact with each other and because the penalties for venting anger on other women were not as severe as those for striking out at men, either black or white. It is not difficult to understand how dependency relationships could become parasitical, how sewing and washing sessions could become "hanging courts," how one party could use knowledge gained in an intimate conversation against another.

Just how sisterhood could co-exist with discord is illustrated by the experience of some black women of the

South Carolina and Georgia Sea Islands between 1862 and 1865. On November 7, 1861, Commodore S. F. DuPont sailed into Port Royal Sound, quickly defeated the Confederates, and put Union troops ashore to occupy the islands. Almost before DuPont's guns ceased firing, the entire white population left the islands for the mainland. A few house servants were taken with the fleeing whites but most of the slaves remained on the islands. The following year they and the occupying army were joined by a host of government agents and Northern missionaries. Several interest groups were gathered in the islands and each had priorities. As Treasury agents concerned themselves with the cotton, and army officers recruited and drafted black soldiers, and missionaries went about "preparing" slaves for freedom, the black Sea Islanders' world was turned upside down. This was true for young and middle-aged men who served in the Union army, but also for the women who had to manage their families and do most of the planting and harvesting in the absence of the men.[44]

During the three years of upheaval, black female life conformed in many ways to that outlined here. Missionaries' comments indicate that certain women were perceived as leaders by their peers. Harriet Ware, for instance, identified a woman from Fripp Point on St. Helena Island named Old Peggy as "the leader." This woman was important because she, along with another woman named Binah, oversaw church membership. Ware's housekeeper Flora told her, "Old Peggy and Binah were the two whom all that came into the Church had to come through, and the Church supports them."[45]

On the Coffin's Point Plantation on St. Helena Island, a woman named Grace served her fellow women at least twice by acting as spokeswoman in disputes over wages paid for cotton production. On one occasion the women of the plantation complained to Mr. Philbrick, one of the plantation superintendents, that their wages were not high enough to permit them to purchase cloth at the local store. They were also upset because the molasses they bought from one of the other plantation superintendents was watered down. As Grace spoke

in their behalf, the women shouted words of approval. At least part of the reason for Grace's ascendancy stemmed from the fact that she was among the older women of the island. She was also a strong and diligent worker who was able despite her advanced age to plant, hoe, and harvest cotton along with the younger women.[46]

Ample evidence exists of dependency relationships and cooperation among Sea Island women throughout the war years. In slavery sick and "lying-in" women relied on their peers to help them, and the missionaries found this to be the case on the islands during the Union occupation as well. For instance, Philbrick observed that it was quite common for the blacks to hire each other to hoe their tasks when sickness or other inconveniences kept an individual from it. In 1862 some of the Coffin's Point men were recruited by government agents to pick cotton elsewhere in the Sea Islands. This left many of the women at Coffin's Point completely responsible for hoeing the land allotted to each. Women who were sick or pregnant stood to lose their family's allotment since neglected land was reassigned to others. However, the women saw to it, according to Philbrick, that "the tasks of the lying-in women [were] taken care of by sisters or other friends in the absence of their husbands." No doubt these "other friends" were women, since in the same letter Philbrick noted that the only men left on the plantation were those too old to work in the cotton.[47]

Another missionary, Elizabeth Hyde Botume, related similar episodes of female cooperation. Regardless of the circumstances surrounding a pregnancy, it was common for the women of Port Royal to care for, and keep company with, expectant and convalescing mothers. Several times Botume was approached by a spokeswoman seeking provisions for these mothers. Sometimes she gave them reluctantly because many of the women were not married. Usually, however, she was so impressed by the support that the pregnant women received from their peers that she suspended judgment and sent clothes and groceries for the mothers and infants. On one occasion she was approached by

several women who sought aid for a woman named Cumber. The women were so willing to assist one of their own that Botume remarked abashedly: " . . . their readiness to help the poor erring girl made me ashamed."[48] These were not the only instances of cooperation among the black women. Some moved in with each other and shared domestic duties; others looked after the sick together.[49] With so many of the men away, women found ways of surviving together and cooperating. Predictably, however, along with the "togetherness" went conflict.

Many situations held possibilities for discord. Charles P. Ware, a missionary from Boston, wrote that the work in the crops would go more smoothly if only he could get the women to stop fighting. At least some of the fights were caused by disputes over the distribution of the former mistress's wardrobe. According to Ware, when a woman said, "I free, I as much right to ole missus' things as you," a fight was sure to erupt.[50] Harriet Ware witnessed a fight in which the women "fired shells and tore each other's clothes in a most disgraceful way." The cause of the fight was unknown to her but she was sure it was the "tongues of the women." Jealousy, she noted, ran rampant among the women, and to her mind there was "much foundation for it."[51]

The experiences of the Sea Islands women in the early 1860s comprised a special episode in American history, but their behavior conformed to patterns that had been set previously by bonded women on large plantations. Historians have shown that the community of the quarters, the slave family, and slave religion shielded the slave from absolute dependence on the master and that parents, siblings, friends, and relatives served in different capacities as buffers against the internalization of degrading and dependent roles. The female slave network served as a similar buffer for black women, but it also had a larger significance. Treated by Southern whites as if they were anything but self-respecting women, many bonded females helped one another to forge their own independent definitions of womanhood, their own notions about what women should be and how they should act.

Notes

1. Fredericka Bremer, *Homes of the New World*, 2 vols. (New York, 1853), 2: 519; Frances Anne Kemble, *Journal of a Residence on a Georgian Plantation*, ed. John A. Scott (New York, 1961 [1863]), p. 66. See also: Harriet Martineau, *Society in America*, 3 vols. (London, 1837), 2: 243, 311–12.

2. Benjamin Drew, *The Refugees: A North Side View of Slavery*, in *Four Fugitive Slave Narratives* (Boston, 1969), p. 92.

3. George Rawick, ed., *The American Slave, A Complete Autobiography*, 19 vols. (Westport, CT, 1972), Ga., vol. 13, pt. 4: 139.

4. Frederick Olmsted, *A Journey in the Seaboard Slave States* (New York, 1856), pp. 430–32; Olmsted, *The Cotton Kingdom*, ed. David Freeman Hawke (New York, 1971), p. 176; William Howard Russell, *My Diary North and South (Canada, Its Defenses, Condition and Resources)*, 3 vols. (London, 1865), 1: 379–80; Solomon Northrup, *Twelve Years a Slave, Narrative of Solomon Northup* in Gilbert Osofsky, ed., *Puttin' on Ole Massa* (New York, 1969), pp. 308–309; Rawick, *American Slave*, Ark., vol 10, pt. 5: 54; Ala., vol. 6: 46, 336; Newstead Plantation Diary 1856–58, entry Wednesday, May 6, 1857, Southern Historical Collection (SHC), University of North Carolina at Chapel Hill; Adwon Adams Davis, *Plantation Life in the Florida Parishes of Louisiana 1836–1846 as Reflected in the Diary of Bennet H. Barrow* (New York, 1943), p. 127; Frederick Olmsted, *A Journey in the Back Country* (New York, 1907), p. 152; *Plantation Manual*, SHC, p. 4; Eugene Genovese, *The Political Economy of Slavery: Studies in the Economy and Society of the Slave South* (New York, 1961), p. 133; Stuart Bruchey, ed., *Cotton and the Growth of the American Economy: 1790–1860* (New York, 1967), pp. 176–80.

5. See note 4.

6. J. A. Turner, ed., *The Cotton Planters Manual* (New York, 1865), pp. 97–98; Guion B. Johnson, *A Social History of the Sea Islands* (Chapel Hill, NC, 1930), pp. 28–30; Jenkins Mikell, *Rumbling of the Chariot Wheels* (Columbia, SC, 1923), pp. 19–20; Bruchey, *Cotton and the Growth of the American Economy*, pp. 176–80.

7. Rawick, *American Slave*, S.C., vol. 2, pt. 2: 114.

8. Ibid., Ga., vol. 13, p. 3: 186.

9. *Plantation Manual*, SHC, p. 1.

10. Rawick, *American Slave*, Ok., vol. 7: 315.

11. George P. Rawick, Jan Hillegas, and Ken Lawrence, ed., *The American Slave: A Composite Autobiography, Supplement, Series 1*, 12 vols. (Westport, CT, 1978), Ga., Supp. 1, vol. 4: 479.

12. Rawick, *American Slave*, Mo., vol 11: 307.

13. For examples of cures see: Ibid., Ark., vol. 10, pt. 5: 21, 125; Ala., vol. 6: 256, 318; Ga., vol. 13, pt. 3: 106.

14. Ibid., Ga., vol. 12, pt. 1: 303.

15. Ibid., Fla, vol. 17: 175; see also: Rawick *et al.*, *American Slave, Supplement*, Miss. Supp. 1, vol. 6: 317; Ga. Supp. 1., vol. 4: 444; John Spencer Bassett, *The Southern Plantation Overseer, as Revealed in His Letters* (Northampton, MA, 1923), pp. 28, 31.

16. Kemble, *Journal of a Residence on a Georgian Plantation*, p. 222.

17. Robert Manson Myers, ed., *The Children of Pride: A True Story of Georgia and the Civil War* (New Haven, CT, 1972), pp. 528, 532, 542, 544, 546.

18. Charles S. Johnson, ed., *God Struck Me Dead: Religious Conversion Experiences and Autobiographies of Negro Ex-Slaves* in Rawick, *American Slave*, vol. 19: 74.

19. Rawick, *American Slave*, S.C., vol. 2, pt. 1: 99.

20. Ibid., Ga., vol. 12, pt. 2: 112; S.C., vol 2, pt. 2: 55; Fla., vol. 17: 174; see also Olmsted, *Back Country*, p. 76.

21. See, for instance, *Plantation Manual*, SHC, p. 1.

22. Rawick, *American Slave*, Ala., vol. 6: 73.

23. Rawick *et al.*, *American Slave, Supplement*, Ga. Supp. 1, vol. 4, pt. 3: 103.

24. Rawick, *American Slave*, Tex., vol. 5, pt. 3: 103.

25. Hughes, *Thirty Years a Slave*, p. 39; Rawick, *American Slave*, Fla., vol. 17: 158; S. C., vol. 2, pt. 1: 114; White Hill Plantation Books, SHC, p. 13.

26. Hughes, *Thirty Years a Slave*, p. 22.

27. Ophelia Settle Egypt, J. Masuoha, and Charles S. Johnson, eds., *Unwritten History of Slavery: Autobiographical Accounts of Negro Ex-Slaves* (Washington, 1968 [1945]), p. 41.

28. Laura M. Towne, *Letters and Diary of Laura M. Towne Written from the Sea Islands of South Carolina 1862–1884*, ed. Rupert Sargent Holland (New York, 1969 [1912]), pp. 144–45.

29. See also: Kemble, *Journal of a Residence on a Georgian Plantation*, p. 55.

30. Rawick, *American Slave*, Ga. vol. 13, pt. 3: 190.

31. Frederick Douglass, *My Bondage and My Freedom* (New York, 1968 [1855]), p. 36.

32. Elizabeth Hyde Botume, *First Days Amongst the Contrabands* (Boston, 1893), p. 132.

33. Davis, *Plantation Life in the Florida Parishes*, p. 191. See also pp. 168, 173.

34. Kemble, *Journal of a Residence on a Georgian Plantation*, pp. 118–19.

35. Martha Graham Goodson, "An Introductory Essay and Subject Index to Selected Interviews from the Slave Narrative Collection" (Ph.D. diss., Union Graduate School, 1977), p. 33.

36. Cheryll Ann Cody, "Naming, Kinship, and Estate Dispersal: Notes on Slave Family Life on a South Carolina Plantation, 1786 to 1833," *William and Mary Quarterly* 39 (1982): 207–09.

37. Rawick, *American Slave*, Ala., vol. 7: 73.

38. Herbert G. Gutman, *The Black Family in Slavery and Freedom, 1750–1925* (New York, 1976), pp. 216–22.

39. J. H. Easterby, ed., *The South Carolina Rice Plantations as Revealed in the Papers of Robert W. Allston* (Chicago, 1945), p. 291.

40. Bassett, *The Southern Plantation Overseer*, pp. 19–20, 32.

41. Rawick, *American Slave*, Ga., vol. 12, pt. 2: 57.

42. C. Vann Woodward, Ed., *Mary Chestnut's Civil War* (New Haven, CT, 1981), pp. 33–34.

43. Norman Yetman, *Voices from Slavery* (New York, 1970), p. 13.

44. J. Mason Brewer, *American Negro Folklore* (New York, 1968), p. 233.

45. Willie Lee Rose, *Rehearsal for Reconstruction: The Port Royal Experiment* (New York, 1964), p. 11.

46. Elizabeth Ware Pearson, ed., *Letters from Port Royal: Written at the Time of the Civil War* (New York, 1969 [1906]), p. 44.

47. Ibid., pp. 250, 303–04.

48. Ibid., p. 56.

49. Botume, *First Days Amongst the Contrabands*, p. 125.

50. See for instance: Ibid., pp. 55–56, 58, 80, 212.

51. Pearson, *Letters from Port Royal*, p. 1133.

52. Botume, *First Days Amongst the Contrabands*, pp. 210–11.

Eden Ravished

The Land, Pioneer Attitudes, and Conservation

Harlan Hague

Harlan Hague teaches history of the American West and American environmental history at San Joaquin Delta College, Stockton, California. He is the author of Road to California: The Search For a Southern Overland Route *and articles on western exploration and trails.*

In O. E. Rölvagg's *Giants in the Earth,* a small caravan of Norwegian immigrants stopped on the prairie, and the riders got down from their wagons. They scanned the landscape in all directions and liked what they saw. It was beautiful, all good plowland and clean of any sign of human habitation all the way to the horizon. After so much hoping and planning, they had finally found their place in the new land. One of the men, Per Hansa, still had difficulty comprehending what was happening:

"This vast stretch of beautiful land was to be his—yes, his. . . . His heart began to expand with a mighty exultation. An emotion he had never felt before filled him and made him walk erect. . . . 'Good God!' he panted. 'This kingdom is going to be mine!' "

Countless others who went to the West reacted like Rölvaag's Per Hansa. They entered the Promised Land with high expectations, possessed the land and were possessed by it. They changed the land and in time were changed by it.

The influence of the West on the American mind has interested historians ever since Frederick Jackson Turner read his momentous essay in 1893 to a meeting of the American Historical Association. In the essay, Turner concluded: "The existence of an area of free land, its continuous recession, and the advance of American settlement westward, explain American development." Turner went on to describe in some detail the various ways the western environment changed the frontiersman, molding him into the American. The processes and result of this evolution were in the end, by implication, favorable.

Writing in the early 1890s, Turner did not detect one of the most important themes, if not the most important, of the westward movement, a theme which would have immense impact on the shaping of the American character. This was the belief that the resources of the West were inexhaustible. Henry Nash Smith, in his influential *Virgin Land,* caught the point that Turner missed:

"The character of the American empire was defined not by streams of influence out of the past, not by a cultural tradition, nor by its place in a world community, but by a relation between man and nature—or rather, even more narrowly, between American man and the American West. This relation was thought of as unvaryingly fortunate."

This cornucopian view of the West was the basis of the frontiersman's attitude toward and his use of the land.

The typical trans-Mississippi emigrant in the last half of the nineteenth century accepted the assumption of inexhaustible resources. Yet the view of the West as an everlasting horn of plenty had been proven false long before the post–Civil War exodus. For example, commercial hunting of the sea otter along the California coast, which had begun in 1784, reached its peak around 1815; by the mid-1840s, the numbers of the animals had declined alarmingly, and the otter was soon hunted almost to extinction. The beaver's fate was similar. Soon after Lewis and Clark told about the teeming beaver populations in western streams, trappers moved westward to harvest the furs. They worked streams so relentlessly that the beaver began to disappear in areas where it had always been plentiful. By 1840, the beaver had been trapped virtually to oblivion. No mountain man in the 1820s would have dreamed there could ever be an end to the hardy little animal. Yet unbridled exploitation had nearly condemned the beaver to extinction. The lesson was lost on Westerners.

Pioneers were not noticeably swayed by the arguments of the naturalists, who publicized the wonders of nature or went further and pled for its preservation. William Bartram, a contemporary of Jefferson, wrote eloquently about the beauty of American nature in his *Travels.* Originally published in 1791, his book was more popular in Europe than in the United States, which had yet to discover its aesthetic environment. John James Audubon had more influence in this country upon publication of his *Birds of America* series (1827–1844) and his subsequent call for protection of wildlife. Francis Parkman, while not famed as a naturalist, wrote firsthand accounts about the scenic West and the Indian inhabitants who lived in harmony with nature. It is no wonder that Parkman, who was enthralled with the outdoors, admired Indians and mountain men more than the settlers he encountered during his western travels.

There was indeed a whole body of romantic literature and art during the first half of the nineteenth century that might have persuaded Americans that environmental values could be measured in terms other than economic. William Cullen Bryant wrote with such depth of feeling about the simple pleasures of the outdoors that he is still known as one of our foremost nature poets. The founding spirit of transcendentalism, Ralph Waldo Emerson, wrote in his first book, *Nature:*

"In the presence of nature, a wild delight runs through the man.... In the woods, is perpetual youth.... In the woods, we return to reason and faith.... The currents of the Universal Being circulate through me; I am part or particle of God.... In the wilderness, I find something more dear and connate than in streets or villages."

Emerson's contemporary, Henry David Thoreau, was even less restrained in his adoration of untamed nature when he wrote: "In Wildness is the preservation of the World." At the same time, Thomas Cole and the Hudson River school of landscape painters captured on canvas the essence of nature that the romantic writers had recorded in prose and poetry. And farther west, beyond the Mississippi River, George Catlin, Karl Bodmer, and Alfred Jacob Miller were painting the exotic wilderness that increasingly drew the attention of Americans.

Unmoved by praise of the aesthetic quality of the environment, frontiersmen were even less impressed by warnings that its resources were not without end. Every American generation since the colonial period had been told of the virtue of using natural resources wisely. An ordinance of Plymouth Colony had regulated the cutting of timber. William Penn had decreed that one acre of trees be left undisturbed for every five acres cleared. In 1864, only a moment before the beginning of the migration that would cover the West within one generation, George Perkins Marsh published his book *Man and Nature,* the most eloquent statement up to that time of the disastrous result that must follow careless stewardship of the land. "Man has too long forgotten," he wrote, "that the earth was given to him for usufruct alone, not for consumption, still less for profligate waste." That is, man could and should both cherish and use the land, but he should not use it up. The significance in Marsh's warning was the recognition that the land could be used up.

While American ambassador to Italy, Marsh had theorized that ancient Rome's fall could be traced to the depletion of the empire's forests. He predicted a like fate for the United States if its resources were similarly squandered. Marsh's book appears to have been widely read by American intellectuals and probably favorably influenced the movements for national parks and forestry management. In it, indeed, were the seeds of the conservation movement of the early twentieth century. Yet it is unlikely that many frontiersmen read or were aware of—or at least they did not heed—Marsh's advice.

Pioneers heard a different drummer. They read descriptions about the West written by people who had been there. Lansford W. Hastings's glowing picture of California and Oregon thrilled thousands:

"In view of their increasing population, accumulating wealth, and growing prosperity, I can not but believe, that the time is not distant, when those wild forests, trackless plains, untrodden valleys, and the unbounded ocean, will present one grand scene, of continuous improvements, universal enterprise, and unparalleled commerce: when those vast forests, shall have disappeared, before the hardy pioneer; those extensive plains, shall abound with innumerable herds, of domestic animals; those fertile valleys, shall groan under the immense weight of their abundant products: when those numerous rivers shall team [*sic*] with countless steam-boats, steam-ships, ships, barques and brigs; when the entire country, will be everywhere intersected, with turnpike roads, rail-roads and canals; and when, all the vastly numerous, and rich resources, of that now, almost unknown region, will be fully and advantageously developed."

Once developed, hopeful emigrants learned, the area would become the garden of the world. In the widely-distributed *Our Western Empire: or the New West Beyond the Mississippi,* Linus P. Brockett wrote that "in no part of the vast domain of the United States, and certainly in no other country under the sun, is there a body of land of equal extent, in which there are so few acres unfit for cultivation, or so many which, with irrigation or without it, will yield such bountiful crops."

Other books described the routes to the Promised Land. The way west was almost without exception easy and well-watered, with plenty of wood, game, and grass.

There was not just opportunity on the frontier. Walt Whitman also saw romance in the westward migration:

> *Come my tan-faced children,*
> *Follow well in order, get your weapons ready,*
> *Have you your pistols? have you your sharp-edged axes?*
> *Pioneers! O pioneers!*
> *For we cannot tarry here,*
> *We must march my darlings, we must bear the brunt of danger,*
> *We the youthful sinewy races, all the rest on us depend,*
> *Pioneers! O pioneers! . . .*
> *We primeval forests felling,*
> *We the rivers stemming, vexing we and piercing deep the mines within,*
> *We the surface broad surveying, we the virgin soil upheaving*
> *Pioneers! O pioneers!.*
> *Swift! to the head of the army!-swift! spring to your places,*
> *Pioneers! O Pioneers!*

The ingredients were all there: danger, youth, virgin soil. Well might frontiersmen agree with Mark Twain who wrote that the first question asked by the American, upon reaching heaven, was: "Which way West?" Thoreau also thought a westward course the natural one:

"When I go out of the house for a walk ... my needle always settles between west and south-southwest. The future lies that way to me, and the earth seems more unexhausted and richer on that side.... westward I go free. I must walk toward Oregon."

Emigrants felt this same pull but for different reasons. Thoreau's West was a wild region to be enjoyed for itself and preserved untouched, while the West to the emigrants was a place for a new start.

The pioneers would conquer the wilderness and gather its immeasurable bounty. This did not imply that Westerners were oblivious to the beauty of the land. Many were aware of the West's scenic attractions but felt, with the influential artist Thomas Cole, that the wilderness, however beautiful, inevitably must give way to progress. In his "Essay on American Scenery," Cole described the sweet joys of nature—the mountains, lakes, rivers, waterfalls, and sky. The essay, dated 1835, is nostalgic. Cole closed his paean with an expression of "sorrow that the beauty of such landscapes are quickly passing away . . . desecrated by what is called improvement." But, after all, he added, "such is the road society has to travel!" Clearly, Cole, like most of his nineteenth-century readers, did not question the propriety of "improvement" or the definition of "progress."

The belief in the inexhaustability of western resources was superimposed on an attitude toward the land that Americans had inherited from generations past. In the Judeo-Christian view, God created the world for man. Man was the master of nature rather than a part of it. The resources of the earth—soil, water, plants, animals, insects, rocks, fish, birds, air—were there for his use, and his proper role was to dominate. It was natural then for God's children to harvest the rich garden provided for them by their Creator. They went into the West to do God's bidding, to use the land as he willed, to fulfill a destiny.

This attitude of man-over-nature was not universal. Like most primitive cultures throughout history, it was not held by the American Indian. The Indian saw himself as a part of nature, not its master. He felt a close kinship with the earth and all living things. Black Elk, a holy man of the Oglala Sioux, for example, believed that all living things were the children of the sky, their father, and the earth, their mother. He had special reverence for "the earth, from whence we came and at whose breast we suck as babies all our lives, along with all the animals and birds and trees and grasses." Creation legends of many tribes illustrate the Indian's familial attachment to the earth and his symbiotic relationship with other forms of life.

The land to Indians was more than merely a means of livelihood for the current generation. It belonged not only to them, the living, but to all generations of their people, those who came before and those who would come after. They could not separate themselves from the land. Of course, there were exceptions. Some Indians fell under the spell of the white trader who offered them goods that would make their lives easier, not to say better. As they became dependent on white man's goods, the land and its fruits began to assume for them an economic value that might be bartered for the conveniences produced by the white man's technology. This is not to say that the Indian attitude toward the land changed. Rather it illustrates that some Indians adopted the white man's view.

To European-Americans, the western Indians' use of the land was just another proof of their savagery. The pioneers had listened to the preachers of Manifest Destiny, and they knew that the nomadic tribes must stand aside for God's Chosen People who would use the land as God intended.

And so they returned to Eden. While some went to California and some to Oregon, the most coherent migration before the rush for California gold began in 1849 was the Mormon exodus to Salt Lake Valley. The latter was not typical of the westward movement. The persecuted saints entered the West not so much for its lure as because of its inaccessibility. In 1830, the same year that the Mormon Church was founded, Joseph Smith announced a revelation which would lead eventually to—or at least foresaw—the great migration:

> "And ye are called to bring to pass the gathering of mine elect . . . unto one place upon the face of this land [which] . . . shall be on the borders by the Lamanites [Indians]. . . . The glory of the Lord shall be there, and it shall be called Zion. . . . The righteous shall be gathered out from among all nations, and shall come to Zion, singing with songs of everlasting joy!"

Mormons who trekked to the Utah settlements in the late 1840s and 1850s knew they were doing God's bidding.

Other emigrants were just as sure that the Lord had prepared a place for them.

"Truly the God in Heaven" wrote an Oregon-bound traveler in 1853, "has spread in rich profusion around us everything which could happily man and reveal the Wisdom and Benevolence of God to man." Oregon Trail travelers often noted in their journals that they were going to the "Promised Land." In A. B. Guthrie's *The Way West,* Fairman, who would be leaving Independence shortly for Oregon, proposed a toast "to a place where there's no fever." McBee, another emigrant, impatient to get started, responded:

"'Y God, yes, . . . and to soil rich as anything. Plant a nail and it'll come up a spike. I heerd you don't never have to put up hay, the grass is that good, winter and all. And lambs come twice a year. Just set by and let the grass grow and the critters berth and get fat. That's my idee of farmin'.'"

It seems that most emigrants, in spite of the humor, did not expect their animals or themselves to wax fat in the new land without working. God would provide, but they must harvest.

Following close on the heels of the Oregon Trail farmers, and sometimes traveling in the same wagon trains, were the miners. This rough band of transients hardly thought of themselves as God's children, but they did nevertheless accept the horn-of-plenty image of the West. Granville Stuart wrote from the California mines that "no such enormous amounts of gold had been found anywhere before, and . . . they all believed that the supply was inexhaustible." Theirs was not an everflowing cornucopia, however, and each miner hoped to be in the right spot with an open sack when the horn tipped to release its wealth.

The typical miner wanted to get as rich as possible as quickly as possible so he could return home to family, friends, and a nabob's retirement. This condition is delightfully pictured in the frontispiece illustration in Mark Twain's *Roughing It.* A dozing miner is seated on a barrel in his cabin, his tools on the floor beside him. He is dreaming about the future: a country estate, yachting, carriage rides and walks in the park with a lady, an ocean voyage and a tour of Europe, viewing the pyramids. The dreams of other miners, while not so grand, still evoked pleasant images of home and an impatience to return there. This yearning is obvious in the lines of a miner's song of the 1850s:

Home's dearest joys Time soon destroys,
Their loss we all deplore;
While they may last, we labor fast
To dig the golden ore.

When the land has yielded its riches:

Then home again, home again,
From a foreign shore,
We'll sing how sweet our heart's delight,
With our dear friends once more.

Miners' diaries often reflected these same sentiments, perhaps with less honeyed phrases but with no less passion.

A practical-minded argonaut, writing in 1852 from California to his sister in Alabama, explained his reason for going to the mines: "I think in one year here I can make enough to clear me of debt and give me a pretty good start in the world. Then I will be a happy man." What then? He instructed his sister to tell all his friends that he would soon be "back whare (*sic*) I can enjoy there [*sic*] company." Other miners thought it would take a little longer, but the motives were the same. A California miner later reminisced:

"Five years was the longest period any one expected to stay. Five years at most was to be given to rifling California of her treasures, and then that country was to be thrown aside like a used-up newspaper and the rich adventurers would spend the remainder of their days in wealth, peace, and prosperity at their eastern homes. No one talked then of going out 'to build up the glorious State of California.' "

The fact that many belatedly found that California was more than worked-out diggings and stayed—pronouncing the state glorious and themselves founding fathers—does not change their motives for going there.

There was a substantial body of miners, perpetually on the move, rowdies usually, the frontier fraternity boys, whose home was the mining camp and whose friends were largely miners like themselves. They rushed around the West to every discovery of gold or silver

in a vain attempt to get rich without working. Though they had no visions of returning east to family and fireside, they did believe that the West was plentifully supplied with riches. It was just their bad luck that they had not found their shares. Their original reason for going to the mining camps and, though they might enjoy the camaraderie of their fellows, their reason for staying was the same as that of the more genteel sort of miner who had come to the western wilderness, fully expecting to return to the East. More than any other emigrant to the West, the miner's motive was unabashed exploitation. For the most part, he did not conserve, preserve, or enrich the land. His intention, far from honorable, was rape.

The cattleman was a transition figure between the miner who stripped the land and the farmer who, while stripping the land, also cherished it. The West to the cattleman meant grass and water, free or cheap. The earliest ranchers on the plains raised beef for the eastern markets and for the government, which had decreed that the cow replace the buffalo in the Plains Indians' life-style. The Indians, except for a few "renegades," complied, though they were never quite able to work the steer into their religion.

It was not long before word filtered back to the East that fortunes could be made in western stock raising. James Brisbin's *Beef Bonanza; or, How to Get Rich on the Plains,* first published in 1881, was widely read. Readers were dazzled by the author's minutely documented "proof" that an industrious man could more than double his investment in less than five years. Furthermore, there was almost no risk involved:

"In a climate so mild that horses, cattle, and sheep and goats can live in the open air through all the winter months, and fatten on the dry and apparently withered grasses of the soil, there would appear to be scarcely a limit to the number that could be raised."

Experienced and inexperienced alike responded. Getting rich, they thought, was only a matter of time, not expertise.

Entrepreneurs and capital, American and foreign, poured into the West. Most

of the rangeland was not in private ownership. Except for small tracts, generally homesteaded along water courses or as sites for home ranches, it was public property. Though a cattleman might claim rights to a certain range, and though an association of cattlemen might try to enforce the claims of its members, legally the land was open, free, and available.

By the mid-1880s, the range was grossly overstocked. The injury to the land was everywhere apparent. While some began to counsel restraint, most ranchers continued to ravish the country until the winter of 1886–1887 forced them to respect it. Following that most disastrous of winters, which in some areas killed as much as 85 percent of range stock, one chastened cattle king wrote that the cattle business "that had been fascinating to me before, suddenly became distasteful. . . . I never wanted to own again an animal that I could not feed and shelter." The industry gradually recovered, but it would never be the same. More land was fenced, wells dug, and windmills installed. Shelters for cattle were built, and hay was grown for winter feeding. Cattle raising became less an adventure and more a business.

In some cattlemen there grew an attachment, if not affection, for the land. Some, especially after the winter of 1886–1887, began to put down roots. Others who could afford it built luxurious homes in the towns to escape the deficiencies of the countryside, much as twentieth-century townsmen would build cabins in the country to escape the deficiencies of the cities. Probably most cattlemen after the winter of 1886–1887 still believed in the bounty of the West, but a bounty which they now recognized would be released to them only through husbandry.

Among all those who went into the West to seek their fortunes, the frontier farmers carried with them the highest hopes and greatest faith. Their forebears had been told for generations that they were the most valuable citizens, chosen of God, and that their destiny lay westward. John Filson, writing in 1784 about frontier Kentucky, described the mystique of the West that would be understood by post–Civil War emigrants:

"This fertile region, abounding with all the luxuries of nature, stored with all the principal materials for art and industry, inhabited by virtuous and ingenious citizens, must universally attract the attention of mankind." There, continued Filson, "like the land of promise, flowing with milk and honey, a land of brooks of water, . . . a land of wheat and barley, and all kinds of fruits, you shall eat bread without scarceness, and not lack any thing in it."

By 1865 the Civil War had settled the controversy between North and South that had hindered the westward movement, the Homestead Act had been passed, and the Myth of the Garden had replaced the Myth of the Desert. By the grace of God and with the blessing of Washington, the frontier farmer left the old land to claim his own in the new:

Born of a free, world-wandering race,
Little we yearned o'er an oft-turned sod.
What did we care for the father's place,
Having ours fresh from the hand of God?

Farmers were attracted to the plains by the glowing accounts distributed by railroads and western states. Newspapers in the frontier states added their accolades. The editor of the Kansas Farmer declared in 1867 that there were in his state "vast areas of unimproved land, rich as that on the banks of the far famed Nile, . . . acres, miles, leagues, townships, counties, oceans of land, all ready for the plough, good as the best in America, and yet lying without occupants." Would-be emigrants who believed this sort of propaganda could sing with conviction:

Oh! give me a home where the buffalo roam,
Where the deer and the antelope play;
Where never is heard a discouraging word,
And the sky is not clouded all day.

There was a reason for the sky's clarity, the emigrants learned when they arrived on the plains. It was not long before many had changed their song:

We've reached the land of desert sweet,
Where nothing grows for man to eat;
I look across the plains
And wonder why it never rains.

And, finally, sung to the cadence of a "slow sad march":

We do not live, we only stay;
We are too poor to get away.

It is difficult to generalize about the experience of pioneer farmers. Those who continued their journeys to the Pacific Coast regions were usually satisfied with what they found. It was those who settled on the plains who were most likely to be disillusioned. Their experience was particularly shattering since they had gone to the West not just to reap in it but also to live in it. Most found not the land of milk and honey they expected, but, it seems, a life of drudgery and isolation.

The most persistent theme in the literature of the period is disenchantment. This mood is caught best by Hamlin Garland. In *Main-Travelled Roads,* Garland acknowledged two views of the plains experience when he wrote that the main-travelled road in the West, hot and dusty in summer, muddy and dreary in fall and spring, and snowy in winter, "does sometimes cross a rich meadow where the songs of the larks and bobolinks and blackbirds are tangled." But Garland's literary road is less cluttered: "Mainly it is long and wearyful, and has a dull little town at one end and a home of toil at the other. Like the main-travelled road of life it is traversed by many classes of people, but the poor and the weary predominate."

The opposite responses to the plains are more pronounced in O. E. Rölvaag's *Giants in the Earth,* one of the most enduring novels of the agricultural West. Per Hansa meets the challenge of the new land, overcomes obstacles and rejoices in each success, however small. He accepts the prairie for what it is and loves it. Meanwhile, his wife, Beret, is gradually driven insane by that same prairie. Where Per Hansa saw hope and excitement in the land, Beret saw only despair and loneliness. "Oh, how quickly it grows dark out here!" she cries, to which Per Hansa replies, "The sooner the day's over, the sooner the next day comes!" In spite of her husband's optimistic outlook, Beret's growing insanity dominates the story as it moves with gloomy intensity to its tragic end. It is significant that Per Hansa dies, a victim of the nature that he did not fear but could not subdue.

Willa Cather, the best-known novelist of nineteenth-century prairie farm life, treated relationships between people and their environment more sensitively than most. While her earlier short stories often dwell on themes of man against the harsh land, her works thereafter, without glossing over the severity of farm life, reveal a certain harmony between the land and those who live on it and love it. Her characters work hard, and suffer; but they are not immune to the loveliness of the land.

The histories of plains farming dwell more on processes than suffering, but accounts that treat the responses of the settlers to their environment generally verify the novelists' interpretations. According to the histories, the picture of desperation painted by Garland and Rölvaag applies principally to the earliest years of any particular frontier region. By the time sod houses acquired board floors and women were able to visit with other women regularly, Cather's images are more accurate.

The fact that pioneer farmers were not completely satisfied with what they found in the Promised Land does not alter their reasons for going there. They had gone into the West for essentially the same reason as the trappers, miners, and cattlemen: economic exploitation. Unlike their predecessors, they also had been looking for homes. Yet, like them, they had believed fervently in the Myth of Superabundance.

The irrational belief that the West's resources were so great that they could never be used up was questioned by some at the very time that others considered it an article of faith. George Perkins Marsh in 1864 warned of the consequences of a too rapid consumption of the land's resources. In 1878, John Wesley Powell attacked the Myth of the Garden when he pointed out that a substantial portion of western land, previously thought to be cultivable by eastern methods, could be farmed successfully only by irrigation. Overgrazing of grasslands resulted in the intrusion of weeds and the erosion of soil, prompting many ranchers, especially after the devastating winter of 1886–1887, to contract their operations and practice range management. Plowing land where rainfall was inadequate for traditional farming methods resulted in wind and water erosion of the soil. Before the introduction of irrigation or dry farming techniques, many plains farmers gave up and returned eastward. The buffalo, which might have numbered fifty million or more at mid-century, were hunted almost to extinction by 1883. Passenger pigeons were estimated to number in the billions in the first half of the nineteenth century: around 1810, Alexander Wilson, an ornithologist, guessed that a single flock, a mile wide and 240 miles long, contained more than two billion birds. Yet before the end of the century, market hunting and the clearing of forest habitats had doomed the passenger pigeon to extinction. Examples of this sort led many people to the inescapable conclusion that the West's resources were not inexhaustible.

At the same time a growing number of people saw values other than economic in the West. Some plains farmers struggling with intermittent drought and mortgage could still see the beauty of the land. Alexandra in Cather's *O Pioneers!* could see it: "When the road began to climb the first long swells of the Divide, Alexandra hummed an old Swedish hymn. . . . Her face was so radiant" as she looked at the land "with love and yearning. It seemed beautiful to her, rich and strong and glorious. Her eyes drank in the breadth of it, until her tears blinded her."

Theodore Roosevelt wrote often of the "delicious" rides he took at his Badlands ranch during autumn and spring. He described the rolling, green grasslands; the prairie roses; the blacktail and white-tail deer; the songs of the skylark; the white-shouldered lark-bunting; and the sweet voice of the meadowlark, his favorite. Of a moonlight ride, he wrote that the "river gleams like running quick-silver, and the moonbeams play over the grassy stretches of the plateaus and glance off the wind-rippled blades as they would from water." Lincoln Lang, a neighbor of Roosevelt's, had the same feeling for the land. He called the Badlands "a landscape masterpiece of the wild, . . . verdant valleys, teeming with wild life, with wild fruits and flowers, . . . with the God-given atmosphere of truth itself, over which unshackled Nature, alone, reigned queen."

Even miners were not immune to the loveliness of the countryside. Granville Stuart, working in the California mines, was struck by the majestic forests of sugar pine, yellow pine, fir, oak, and dogwood. He described the songs and coloration of the birds and the woodpeckers' habit of storing acorns in holes that they meticulously pecked in tree limbs. He delighted in watching a covey of quail near his cabin each day. "Never was I guilty of killing one," he added. Bret Harte lived among the California miners, and his stories often turn to descriptions of the picturesque foothills of the Sierra Nevada. After the birth of "The Luck" in Roaring Camp, the proud, self-appointed godfathers decorated the baby's "bower with flowers and sweetsmelling shrubs, . . . wild honey-suckles, azaleas, or the painted blossoms of Las Mariposas. The men had suddenly awakened to the fact that there were beauty and significance in these trifles, which they had so long trodden carelessly beneath their feet."

Success of some sort often broadened the frontiersman's viewpoint. The miner, cattleman, or farmer who had succeeded in some way in his struggle with the land had more time and inclination to think about his relationship with it. Viewing his environment less as an adversary, the Westerner began to see what was happening to it.

At times, concern for the environment led to action. The mounting protests of Californians whose homes and farms had been damaged by the silt-laden runoff from hydraulic mining finally led to the outlawing of this mindless destruction of the land. Frederick Law Olmsted, who had designed New York's Central Park, initiated an era in 1864 when he and some friends persuaded Congress to grant to the state of California a piece of land in California's Sierra Nevada for the creation of a park, merely because the land, which included Yosemite Valley and the Mariposa Big Trees, was beautiful and the public would enjoy it. The idea took hold, and other parks soon followed, Yellowstone in 1872 being the first public "pleasuring ground" under federal management. The new art of landscape photography showed Easterners the wonders of the West, without the hardships of getting there, and revealed to many Westerners a land they inhabited but had never seen. With the improvement in transportation, principally railroads, more and more people ventured into the West to see these wonders firsthand.

A growing awareness that unrestrained exploitation was fast destroying the natural beauty of the West and that its resources, by the end of the nineteenth century widely acknowledged to be finite, were being consumed at an alarming pace led to considerable soul-searching. Frederick Jackson Turner, who had most eloquently described the influence that the great expanses of western land had on the shaping of American character, also hinted that the disappearance of available land was likely to cause some serious disruptions in American society. "The frontier has gone," he wrote, "and with its going has closed the first period of American history."

If the first phase of American history, in which a dominant theme was the advance of the frontier, ran from 1607 to 1890, the second phase began with the emergence of the conservation movement which would lead to the alteration of fundamental attitudes toward the land nurtured during the first phase. While based generally on concern for the environment, the movement split in the early twentieth century into two factions. One faction argued for wise management of the country's resources to prevent their being wasted. This "utilitarian conservation," was not a break with the frontier view of exploitation. It was a refinement. While the frontier view was one of rapid exploitation of inexhaustible resources, the utilitarian conservationists rejected the myth of inexhaustibility and advocated the careful use of finite resources, without rejecting the basic assumption that the resources were there to be exploited. This view of conservation led to the setting aside and management of forest reserves, soil and water conservation projects, and irrigation and hydroelectric programs.

The other faction, whose ideology has been called "aesthetic conservation," clearly broke with the frontier past when its members argued for the preservation of areas of natural beauty for public enjoyment. This group's efforts bore fruit in the establishment of national and state parks, monuments and wilderness areas. There are indications that the two factions are drawing closer together in the umbrella ecology movement of the 1970s, perhaps eventually to merge.

It is senseless to compare nineteenth-century frontier attitudes toward the land with today's more enlightened views. Faced seemingly with such plenty—billions of passenger pigeons, millions of buffalo, innumerable beaver, endless seas of grass, vast forests of giant trees, mines to shame King Solomon's—excess was understandable and probably inevitable. Excess in this case meant waste. Here the Turner thesis is most meaningful, for the belief in the inexhaustibility of resources in the West generated the unique American acceptance of waste as the fundamental tenet of a life-style. For this, the frontiersman is not entirely blameless. But certainly, he is less blameworthy than the neo-pioneer who continues, against reason and history, to cling hopefully to the myth of inexhaustibility. Yet there were examples, however few, and voices, however dim, that the frontiersman might have heeded. It remains to be seen whether Americans today have learned the lesson their ancestors, four generations removed, failed to comprehend.

BIBLIOGRAPHIC NOTE

There are few comprehensive surveys of the evolution of American attitudes toward the environment. Three useful sources are Stewart L. Udall, *The Quiet Crisis* (New York: Holt, Rinehart, 1963); Hans Huth, *Nature and the American: Three Centuries of Changing Attitudes* (Berkeley: University of California, 1957); and Roderick Nash, *Wilderness and the American Mind,* rev. ed. (New Haven: Yale University, 1973), the last particularly concerned with the American response to wilderness. Frederick Jackson Turner's frontier thesis, which inevitably must be considered in any study of the relationship between Americans and their environment, is in his *The Frontier in American History* (New York: Henry Holt, 1921). Invaluable to an understanding of what Americans thought the West was is Henry Nash Smith, *Virgin Land: The American West as Symbol and Myth* (New York: Vintage Books, 1950). The most influential book of the twentieth century in the development of a land ethic is Aldo Leopold, *A Sand County Almanac* (New York: Oxford University, 1949).

Selections from historical materials and literature were blended in this study to illustrate western emigrants' expectations for and responses to the new country. In addition to titles listed in the text, literary impressions of nature are in Wilson O. Clough, *The Necessary Earth: Nature and Solitude in American Literature* (Austin: University of Texas, 1964) and John Conron, The *American Landscape: A Critical Anthology of Prose and Poetry* (New York: Oxford University, 1974). Useful bibliographies of the literature of the westward movement are Lucy Lockwood Hazard, The *Frontier in American Literature* (New York: Thomas Y. Crowell, 1927) and Richard W. Etulain, *Western American Literature* (Vermillion, S.D.: University of South Dakota, 1972). Bibliographies of historical materials are in Ray Allen Billington, *Westward Expansion, 4th* ed. (New York: Macmillan, 1974), and Nelson Klose, *A Concise Study Guide to the American Frontier* (Lincoln: University of Nebraska, 1964).

Assault in the Senate

A violent confrontation in 1856 between Representative Preston Brooks and Senator Charles Sumner became a benchmark on the nation's road to civil war.

By David E. Johnson

On May 19, 1856, Senator Charles Sumner of Massachusetts took to the Senate floor to deliver a much-anticipated address entitled "The Crime Against Kansas." At issue was the 1854 Kansas-Nebraska Act, which left the determination of slave status for the new territories to their settlers—the doctrine of popular sovereignty. The act had repealed the 1820 Missouri Compromise, which prohibited slavery north of latitude 36° 30′, and sparked heated debate in Congress and violence in Kansas. It was time, Sumner declared, to "redress a great transgression."

> *Senator Charles Sumner once declared, "Nothing against slavery can be unconstitutional."*

Elected to the Senate in 1851, Sumner was a powerful and classical speaker who had come to represent the voice of abolitionists. In his speech, the senator intended to lash the Democratic administration of President Franklin Pierce for allowing popular sovereignty to become "popular slavery." A full Senate and packed galleries listened with rapt atten-

tion as Sumner began one of the most memorable speeches of the era.

He opened with a discourse on the Missouri Compromise, the Kansas-Nebraska Act, and the doctrine of popular sovereignty. Sumner blamed the worsening situation in Kansas on fraudulent elections, a lack of presidential will, and the devotion of some to "the one idea, that Kansas, at all hazards, must be made a slave state." Sumner took a dim view of the various remedies proposed to end the conflict. The only just and peaceful solution, he argued, was the admission to the Union of Kansas as a free state.

Sumner then changed the subject to offer his thoughts on three senators who supported the administration's position. Those "who have raised themselves to eminence on this floor in championship of human wrongs," he declared, included Virginia's James Mason, Stephen A. Douglas of Illinois, and Andrew Pickens Butler of South Carolina. Butler, a respected, 59-year-old Senate veteran, represented the interests of many slave holders and had clashed with Sumner before. He happened to be away during Sumner's speech, in which the Massachusetts senator stated that Butler had chosen "the harlot, Slavery" for his mistress.

Continuing the following day, Sumner expanded his harsh characterization of Butler, stating that the South Carolinian "touches nothing which he does not disfigure with error, sometimes of principle, sometimes of fact." Sumner

decried the "shameful imbecility from slavery" of Butler's native state. If South Carolina's entire history was wiped out, he concluded, civilization would lose "less than it has already gained by the example of Kansas." Stephen Douglas, pacing the floor in the rear of the Senate chamber, shook his head at Sumner's words and muttered, "that damn fool will get himself killed by some other damn fool."

Sumner took his seat at the conclusion of his address, as Senators Mason and Douglas responded in outrage at the personal nature of his attacks. Michigan Senator Lewis Cass called the speech "the most un-American and unpatriotic that ever grated on the ears." Sumner was not finished, however, and answered Douglas' retorts by referring to the Illinois politician as a "noisome, squat, and a nameless animal" who was "not the proper model for an American Senator." When Douglas took exception to the insult, Sumner mocked him for filling the Senate with the "offensive odor" of his tongue.

In the wake of Sumner's scalding attack on slavery, the *New York Tribune* declared that "Mr. Sumner has added a cubit to his stature," while private letters praised the "lofty moral tone" of his delivery. The personal attacks on Butler and Douglas, however, shocked and disappointed many of Sumner's fellow Republicans. Congressional observers could not recall a prepared speech containing such intemperate language. New York

From *American History*, June 1999, pp. 52-59. © 1999 by Cowles Magazines, Inc. Reprinted through the courtesy of Cowles Magazines, publishers of *American History*.

Senator William Seward disapproved of the speech's bitter tone, while renowned statesman and orator Edward Everett noted that "from a man of character of any party I have never seen anything so offensive." While Sumner's inspired defense of a free Kansas had initially filled the chamber with electricity his words now hung uneasily in the May air.

THE MOST UNSETTLED MAN in Washington, D.C., that evening was Representative Preston S. Brooks of South Carolina. Brooks was not only a close neighbor and political supporter of Andrew Butler, but also the senator's nephew. Then in his second term, the 36-year-old moderate Democrat was a well-liked veteran of the Mexican War. Brooks was present in the Senate chamber on May 19 during Sumner's opening remarks and had heard of Sumner's conclusions of May 20. After carefully reading the printed text of the speech, he found it as offensive as he had anticipated.

Brooks felt that Sumner had dishonored both Butler and South Carolina and decided that a proper response was in order. According to traditional Southern rules of conduct, such an insult was not avenged in a court of law, but handled with pistols in the presence of witnesses. Dueling, however, could only be staged between men of the same social class, and Brooks concluded that by disparaging the absent Butler, Sumner had shown himself to be no gentleman. A good thrashing with a cane or whip, therefore, was the only fitting penalty. Brooks realized that the elderly Butler could not possibly flog the younger and more powerfully built Sumner, so he decided to do it himself.

On the morning of May 21, Brooks armed himself with a solid, gold-headed, gutta-percha walking stick and made his way to the Capitol grounds. As he paced back and forth between the Senate and the steps of the Capitol, Virginia Representative Henry A. Edmundson greeted him with a cheerful "you are going the wrong way for the discharge of your duties." Brooks somberly replied that unless Sumner apologized for his offensive remarks, he was going to punish him. Though somewhat taken aback, Edmundson inquired as to how he might be of assistance. Brooks stated that he wanted Edmundson to take no part in the affair, but only to be present. As the two maintained their vigil for Sumner, Brooks commented that "it was time for southern men to stop this coarse abuse used by the abolitionists. . . ." The congressmen waited until 12:30 P.M. before entering the Capitol, convinced that Sumner had eluded them.

By 11:00 A.M. the following day, Brooks was waiting in the porter's lodge at the Pennsylvania Avenue entrance to the Capitol. Edmundson again approached him. "I cannot overlook the insult," Brooks said when he saw his colleague. He had planned for each possible contingency. If Sumner walked to the Capitol, he would tend to him at the gate; if he came by carriage, Brooks would run across the yard and confront the senator before he entered the building. Edmundson pointed out, however, that if Brooks had to run across the grounds and up so many flights of steps he would be too tired to contend with the 6'4" Sumner. Finding this logic persuasive, Brooks abandoned the plan and entered the Capitol.

The Senate had adjourned early that day due to the death of a Missouri congressman. Sumner had remained at his desk, where he was busy writing letters and signing copies of his Kansas speech. Brooks entered the chamber and took a seat in the rear. Edmundson soon joined him and attempted small talk while Brooks impatiently waited for a number of women in the gallery to leave. Agitated by this latest delay, Brooks decided to send a note to Sumner asking the senator to meet him outside. Edmundson noted, however, that Sumner would probably just ask Brooks to come to his desk. Finally, the women departed and Sumner was alone.

"My attention at this time was so entirely withdrawn from all other objects, that . . . I saw nobody," Sumner later testified. He heard his name spoken and he looked up from his writing to see the unfamiliar figure of Brooks standing over his desk.

"Mr. Sumner," Brooks began, "I have read your speech carefully, and with as much calmness as I could be expected to read such a speech. You have libeled my state, and slandered my relation, who is aged and absent, and I feel it to be my duty to punish you for it." As he finished his introduction, Brooks brought his cane down upon Sumner's head. The light chastisement he had intended to administer quickly turned into a severe beating.

Sumner attempted to stand, but his legs were trapped under the desk, which was bolted to the floor. Reeling under the blows with his arms extended in weak defense, he finally wrenched the desk from the floor with his thighs. He staggered down the aisle as Brooks snapped his cane in two over the senator's head. Brooks continued the attack with the shattered remnant of his cane. By this time Sumner was insensible, and witnesses rushed to the scene to restrain Brooks and assist Sumner. "I did not wish to hurt him much, but only whip him," Brooks said as he left the chamber.

Dazed and covered with blood, Sumner was moved from the Senate floor to a small anteroom where Dr. Cornelius Boyle arrived to treat him. He found the victim "bleeding very copiously" with "marks of three wounds on the scalp." Two of the cuts required two stitches each to close. Boyle judged the gashes "simply as flesh wounds" and advised

South Carolina Senator Andrew Pickens Butler became friendly with Sumner when the Massachusetts senator took office in 1851. Their opposing views on slavery, however, soon cooled their friendship and led to Sumner's harsh remarks.

A HOT TIME IN THE OLD TOWN

Washington, D.C., in the mid-1850s was a lively place. The hotels and bars along Pennsylvania Avenue teemed with patrons discussing the widening rift between the North and South. Capitol Hill became one of the city's main social attractions as people flocked to the Senate and House galleries to watch their senators and representatives spar over the nation's future.

The debate over slavery heated up following the passage of the 1854 Kansas-Nebraska Act, increasing tension in Washington. Iowa Senator James W. Grimes wrote in 1859 that the "Capitol resounds with the cry of dissolution and the cry is echoed through the city." Congressional debates between pro-slavery Democrats and free-state Republicans degenerated into heated arguments and shoving matches. Political opponents scowled at each other on the city's streets. With no firearms laws on the books, many men carried guns.

Politicians went to work ready to defend themselves, turning Congress into a veritable armory. South Carolina Senator James H. Hammond described the scene of the contentious debates over the election of a new speaker of the House in December 1859: "Every man on the floor of both Houses is armed with a revolver—some with two revolvers and a Bowie Knife." Senator Grimes noted that "members of both sides are mostly armed with deadly weapons, and the friends of both are armed in the galleries." Preston Brooks, in fact, had once half-seriously suggested that congressman be required to check their guns before entering the House.

The most spectacular confrontation between the opposing political factions took place in the House of Representatives in the early hours of February 6, 1858. After several hours of angry debate over the fate of slavery in Kansas Territory, representatives lay scattered throughout the House, sleeping at their desks or stretched out on sofas. As Republican Galusha Grow of Pennsylvania walked through the Democratic side of the House at about 2:00 A.M., Democrat Lawrence Keitt called him a "Black Republican puppy" and told him to return to his side. Grow replied that he would speak wherever he pleased. Keitt muttered "We'll see about that," and reached for Grow's throat.

Representatives leapt to their feet and the fight quickly became a full-scale brawl. Keitt was knocked to the floor, and Grow slugged Reuben Davis of Mississippi. Democrats and Republicans grappled and punches flew. A spittoon sailed through the air and Wisconsin's John Potter charged into the pack, "striking right and left with tremendous vigor." The melee continued as congressmen shouted for the sergeant-at-arms to do something. Suddenly, William Barksdale's wig fell onto the floor and someone stepped on it. The Tennessee representative retrieved his hairpiece but put it on backwards. The resulting eruption of laughter was enough to cool tempers and end the brawl. When fighting on a much larger scale divided the country three years later, however, restoring peace would not prove so easy.

—Eric Ethier

his patient to go home and rest. Brooks was soon arrested on a charge of assault, then released on bail.

The reaction to Brooks' attack on Sumner reflected the nation's increasing sectionalism. "We consider the act good in conception, better in execution, and best of all in consequence," trumpeted the *Richmond Enquirer*. "A Good Deed," echoed the *Richmond Whig*. These newspapers were joined in their sentiments by the *Petersburg Intelligencer, Washington Republic*, and nearly every newspaper in South Carolina.

While a few Southerners expressed reservations about the time, place, or method of attack, few challenged the act itself. "Every southern man sustains me," Brooks noted, "the fragments of the stick are begged for as sacred relics." Admirers sent Brooks a number of ceremonial canes as gifts, including one inscribed, "Hit him again."

Not everyone in the North agreed with the language of Sumner's speech. Daniel Webster's son Fletcher noted that the senator should have taken "the precaution of wearing an iron pot on his head" before making such insulting remarks. Generally, however, Northern reaction to the assault was one of indignation. Editorials assailed "Bully Brooks" as a "villainous assassin" and the "apotheosis of brutality." He had attacked, it was said, not only Sumner but the principle of free speech. Meanwhile, Sumner's printed address began to sell in the thousands.

The young Republican Party recognized the political significance of Sumner's caning and rallied around the incident. Francis Blair, a Southern Unionist editor who opposed the extension of slavery, wrote Sumner that he had "done more to gain the victory than any other." To many Northerners, Sumner's empty Senate seat became a symbol of the anti-slavery movement, freedom of speech, civilized discourse, and the depravity of slave holding Southerners.

This fact was not lost on Southern leaders. Though toasted at banquets and heralded by his colleagues, Preston Brooks began to worry about the negative political repercussions of his act. Seeking to contain the damage, he described his confrontation with Sumner as "a personal affair" and said he had not intended to "offend [the] dignity of the senate." Brooks' efforts notwithstanding, the *Macon Telegraph* judged the fallout from the attack to be a "stronger impetus to the Black Republicans than anything else which could be imagined of a hundred times its importance."

IN THE INCIDENT'S AFTERMATH, Congress investigated the matter. A Senate committee concluded that it had no jurisdiction over a member of the House and therefore could not discipline a representative. Meanwhile, a more volatile House committee of three Republicans and two Democrats began questioning 27 witnesses, including Sumner, on May 26.

The Republicans sought to prove the attack on Sumner was "at the hazard of the life assailed." It was not only an example of Southern vigilante justice, they claimed, but an assault with intent to kill an innocent man. The Democratic representatives saw Brooks' attack as a simple defense of honor brought about by continual abolitionist slander.

Significantly, Dr. Boyle testified that Sumner's injuries were not serious and that he "might have taken a carriage and driven as far as Baltimore on the next day without any injury." The Republican majority committee, however, voted 3–2 along party lines to recommend the expulsion of Brooks from the House. After a bitter House debate the resolution fell short of the required two-thirds majority by the vote of 121–95. Only one Southerner voted against Brooks.

On July 14, Preston Brooks addressed the House. "If I cannot preserve my self-respect and constitutional rights together with a seat in this body," he declared, "I must renounce the last rather than the former." Brooks answered the charge that he had intended to kill Sumner, explaining that it "was expressly to avoid taking life that I used an ordinary cane." Had he used a horsewhip, he added, the stronger Sumner might have wrested it from him and forced him into more violent action. "And now, Mr. Speaker," Brooks concluded, "I announce to you and this House that I am no longer a member of the Thirty-fourth Congress." Preston Brooks walked out of the House chamber and returned home to South Carolina, where he was triumphantly reelected to his seat. He was fined $300 for the attack and was back at his desk within a few weeks.

The assault had more lasting effects on Charles Sumner. Despite the apparent superficial nature of his injuries, Sumner remained out of the Senate for more than three years. Within days of the attack Sumner became feverish, and the glands in his head and neck swelled, probably as a result of septicemia. Dr. Boyle found fluid building under his pa-

tient's scalp. Sumner's brother George dismissed the doctor, whose care he judged inadequate. Sumner began to lose weight and complained of pressure on his brain. His symptoms fit those associated with anemia.

Months passed and Sumner fared little better. The stress of politics and the memory of his ordeal plagued him, and the resulting nervousness aggravated his mysterious condition. He worried about losing his mental faculties and moved from one health spa to another, gaining only temporary relief. In September, Dr. Marshall S. Perry examined Sumner in Philadelphia and found him "not in a position to expose himself to mental or bodily excitement without the risk of losing his *life*."

Sumner's condition was the object of much discussion throughout the country. Abolitionists considered him a martyr to the cause. Northern supporters talked of him as a senator for life, and Sumner received 35 votes for the 1856 Republican vice-presidential nomination. Short of making public appearances, Sumner did what he could to support the party. He was reelected to the Senate in January 1857, but remained something of an invalid. In the South he was accused of faking his illness and derided for cowardice. Washington's *Union*, for example, attributed Sumner's absence to "his wounded pride."

Sumner continued to seek relief from his ailments and spent considerable time in Europe. He regained some of his vigor, but suffered a relapse in England when he was advised that his brain "would give way under the pressure of public life in America." He returned briefly to the Senate in December 1857, but still found the pressures of the capital too much.

Sumner swore that when he returned to his post his next speech would "be to my last speech in the Senate of the United States as first proof brandy to molasses and water." The senator's nervousness and insecurities gradually dissipated, and he finally found his health returning in 1859. In December, Sumner returned full-time to his seat in the Senate.

Sumner found Washington an even more tensely divided place than it had been in 1856. Although Preston Brooks had died suddenly in early 1857 and Andrew Pickens Butler had passed away a few months later, Sumner found his enemies as numerous as ever, which only increased his antipathy toward the practice of slavery. On June 4, 1860, he read a four-hour speech to the Senate entitled "The Barbarism of Slavery," the long-delayed follow-up to the 1856 effort that had caused him such trouble. The speech brought the outspoken senator additional threats of reprisal, but no one ever repeated Brooks' tactics.

On the night he was assaulted, Charles Sumner had confessed that he "could not believe that a thing like this was possible." By 1860, however, violence over the slavery issue had become almost commonplace. Kansas Territory had been overrun by skirmishing bands of pro-slavery and anti-slavery guerrilla forces, and in October 1859 John Brown had raided the federal armory at Harper's Ferry, Virginia, in an attempt to ignite a slave rebellion. Civil war now seemed inevitable.

David E. Johnson specializes in the history and politics of the South.

Unit Selections

Key Points to Consider

❖ How and why did the Civil War change from a limited conflict to almost total war? What kept Abraham Lincoln from issuing the Emancipation Proclamation earlier, and why did he finally take the step?

❖ Discuss the experiences of black Americans during the war, both those who served in the military and those who remained within Southern lines.

❖ William Sherman's march through Georgia enraged Southerners who saw it as a barbaric campaign of senseless destruction. Does the essay on this subject (see "Sherman's War") make a convincing case that it actually was both brilliant and humane? Explain.

❖ Was Radical Reconstruction doomed to fail? What would it have taken on the part of the North to prevail over the opposition of white Southerners?

DUSHKINONLINE **Links**   **www.dushkin.com/online/**

27. **The American Civil War**
    http://www.janke.washcoll.edu/civilwar/civilwar.htm
28. **Anacostia Museum/Smithsonian Institution**
    http://www.si.edu/organiza/museums/anacost/
29. **Abraham Lincoln Online**
    http://www.netins.net/showcase/creative/lincoln.html
30. **Gilder Lehrman Institute of American History**
    http://vi.uh.edu/pages/mintz/gilder.htm
31. **Secession Era Editorials Project**
    http://history.furman.edu/benson/docs/

These sites are annotated on pages 4 and 5.

Sectional disputes had been commonplace even before the Constitution was drawn up, and were reflected in some of its provisions. The reason why a two-thirds majority in the senate was made necessary to pass treaties, for instance, was to prevent two sections from pushing through an agreement that was disadvantageous to the third. Commercial and manufacturing interests were powerful in the North. These interests favored such policies as high tariffs to protect industries, and federal support for the construction of turnpikes, canals, and railroads to enlarge markets. The agricultural South wanted low tariffs to reduce the prices of the imports that they bought and opposed the taxes necessary for transportation improvements. These issues were manageable, however, and did not stir up a great deal of public emotion.

Slavery was another matter. Part of the controversy over slavery involved economics, to be sure. Northerners were afraid that the spread of slavery into newly acquired territories would inhibit the growth of "free" farming. Southerners were equally adamant that their institution of labor be permitted to exist wherever it proved viable. Compromises over this matter were hammered out in 1820 and 1850, but these amounted only to truces that proved unsatisfactory to both sides. The difference between compromises over tariffs and over slavery was that the latter issue contained a moral ingredient. More and more Northerners came to regard slavery as an evil system, as time went on, and demanded that it be abolished. Southerners stoutly defended the institution, arguing that it was beneficial to both blacks and whites. Incidents such as the Brooks-Sumner affair discussed in unit three, fueled public emotions that had been absent in debates over whether to construct some canal or turnpike.

Moderates in both national parties, realizing that the issue had the potential to split the nation, tried to keep it offstage. The Democratic Party managed to stay together until almost the very end, although there were defections. The Whig Party collapsed under the strain. The subsequent emergence of the Republican Party brought things to a head. This party drew almost its entire strength from the North, and Southerners began to regard it as the party of abolitionism. The Republican presidential candidate in 1860, Abraham Lincoln, stated that although he opposed the expansion of slavery he had no intention of trying to move against it where it already existed. Southerners believed that prohibiting the spread of slavery would be merely the first step towards abolishing the institution—their way of life—altogether. Lincoln's victory in 1860 caused Southern states to begin seceding from the union, and his refusal to let them go in peace led to the Civil War.

Four selections deal with military aspects of the war. " 'The Doom of Slavery': Ulysses S. Grant, War Aims, and Emancipation, 1861–1863" describes how the struggle changed from a limited conflict to a concept of total war against Southern resources and morale. Author Brooks Simpson argues that General Ulysses S. Grant realized that slavery was at the bottom of the conflict. In "Lee's Greatest Victory," Robert Krick recounts General Robert E. Lee's masterly conduct of the battle of Chancellorsville. The victory was a costly one, however, as one of Lee's best generals, "Stonewall" Jackson, was accidently killed by his own men. Next, "Sherman's War" argues against the common view that Sherman's march through Georgia was a ruthless campaign of terror and destruction. Author Victor Davis Hanson writes to the contrary, seeing the campaign as "brilliant, effective, and, above all, humane."

There are two essays that treat the conduct of blacks during the war. In "Pride and Prejudice in the American Civil War," Susan-Mary Grant examines the experiences and legacy of black soldiers who contributed more to the conflict, and who suffered more losses, than is commonly realized. "The Struggle for Black Freedom before Emancipation" shows how blacks themselves sought freedom before the Emancipation Proclamation. Some simply fled the farms and plantations and made their way to free areas, others stayed home but were able to redefine their conditions in the direction of greater rights and privileges.

Thomas Dyer, in "A Yankee Scarlett O'Hara in Atlanta," tells the fascinating story of an ardent Unionist who lived in Atlanta during the war. Cyrena Bailey Stone's recently-discovered diary provides an eyewitness account of daily life in Atlanta during the latter months of the conflict. The essay "Bats, Balls, and Bullets: Baseball and the Civil War" denies the popular myth that the game of baseball was invented in 1839 by Abner Doubleday, who went on to become a general in the Civil War. Author George Kirsch shows that the sport actually had evolved from several bat-and-ball games over decades. A fairly modern version was being widely played during the Civil War, especially by Northerners. After the war, a number of Northern and Southern journalists predicted that exhibition tours of leading teams would help dissipate sectional hatreds.

A struggle took place after the war ended over how the South should be reintegrated into the union. The most important issue was what status blacks would have in the society. Moderates such as Lincoln wished to make reconstruction as painless as possible, even though this meant white domination of the Southern states. "Radical" or "advanced" Republicans wished to guarantee freedpeople the full rights of citizenship, using force if necessary to achieve this goal. Southern whites resisted "Radical Reconstruction" any way they could and, when Northern will eroded, ultimately prevailed. Eric Foner's "The New View of Reconstruction" argues that even though Radical Reconstruction failed in the short run, it provided an "animating vision" for the future.

The Civil War and Reconstruction

"The Doom of Slavery": Ulysses S. Grant, War Aims, and Emancipation, 1861–1863

Brooks D. Simpson

Like many northerners, Ulysses S. Grant went to war in 1861 to save the Union—and nothing more—in what he predicted would be a short conflict. By 1863, after two years of bloody struggle against a stubborn enemy, Grant came to understand that a war to preserve the Union must of necessity transform that Union. Central to that revolutionary transformation was the acceptance of emancipation as a war aim and the enrollment of ex-slaves in the bluecoat ranks. The intensity of Confederate resistance compelled Union commanders to accept this notion, while the influx of black refugees into Yankee camps helped to force a decision. In 1861 Grant believed that the Union should keep hands off slavery if a quick peace and rapid reconciliation was desired. By 1863 circumstances had changed. Notions of a limited conflict gave way to the concept of a total war waged against Southern resources and morale as well as manpower. New means were needed to attain victory. To save the Union one must destroy slavery. Grant's experiences as a field commander are illustrative of this process, suggesting the interaction between the progress of the war effort, the escalation of Southern resistance, and the transformation of war aims to encompass emancipation.

From war's beginning Grant realized that at the core of the dispute was the institution of slavery. His position on the peculiar institution was ambiguous, and he left no detailed explanation of his feelings for historians to examine. Marriage to the daughter of a slaveholder entangled him in slavery: he worked alongside slaves, his wife owned four house servants, and he was a slaveholder for a short period. Yet family slaves heard him speak out against the institution, he did not succumb to the blatant prejudices of his age, and he freed the slave he owned at a time when the money a sale might have brought could have been a great boon. He showed no interest in protecting slavery, let alone perpetuating it.[1]

Moreover, Grant understood that the advent of war in the spring of 1861 would affect slavery, no matter the outcome. Southerners were risking the foundation of their society even as they defended it. "In all this I can but see the doom of Slavery," he told his father-in-law. "The North do not want, nor will they want, to interfere with the institution. But they will refuse for all time to give it protection unless the South shall return soon to their allegiance." The disruption of the Southern economy by war would render it vulnerable to international competition, reducing the worth of slaves "so much that they will never be worth fighting over again." Slavery would be destroyed as a consequence of prolonged conflict, a casualty of events rather than the target of Union policy.[2]

Nevertheless, a quick Northern victory, achieved before hatred could become deep-seated, might minimize the impact of the conflict upon slavery. And Grant believed that such a rapid triumph was possible. Startled by the vigorous reaction of Northerners in Sumter's aftermath, he ventured that if Southerners ever discovered what they had wrought, "they would lay down their arms at once in humble submission." Confidently he predicted a Northern triumph in a conflict "of short duration." With "a few decisive victories" by the North the "howling" Confederates would flee the field. "All the states will then be loyal for a generation to come, negroes will depreciate so rapidly in value that no body will want to own them and their masters will be the loudest in their declamations against the institutions in a political and economic view." If slavery was to suffer, it would be as a byproduct of the conflict, not because of deliberate policy decisions to eradicate it. Indeed, to take such steps might only prolong the conflict by engendering resistance born of bitterness.[3]

In June, Grant was commissioned colonel of the 21st Illinois. Soon his regiment was dispatched to Missouri to hunt down scattered rebel detachments. Grant kept a close eye on his men, mak-

The author wishes to acknowledge the assistance provided by a research grant from Wofford College. He thanks Richard H. Sewell and Allan G. Bogue for their advice and counsel and John Y. Simon and David L. Wilson for their encouragement.

From *Civil War History*, Vol. 36, No. 1, March 1990, pp. 36-56. © 1990 by Kent State University Press. Reprinted by permission.

ing sure that they did not disturb citizens along the line of march. He reasoned that a well-behaved army would contradict rumors of a marauding bunch of Yankees bent upon plunder, eroding fears and enhancing the chances of a quick and easy peace. Such considerations were especially crucial in Missouri, where the population was nearly evenly divided between loyalists and secessionists. With the state still teetering on the edge of secession, it was of utmost importance that Grant maintain discipline among his new recruits. He did so, with good results. While there existed "a terrible state of fear among the people" when his troops arrived, he added that within a few weeks they discovered that the bluecoats "are not the desperate characters they took them for." He was convinced that "if orderly troops could be marched through this country . . . it would create a very different state of feeling from what exists now."[4]

Efforts to foster good feeling, however, met a serious obstacle in the stubborness of the local citizens. "You can't convince them but that the ultimate object is to extinguish, by force, slavery," he complained to his father. To his wife Julia he revealed concern that the war was getting out of hand. Not only were the citizens "great fools," but they "will never rest until they bring upon themselves all the horrors of war in its worst form. The people are inclined to carry on a guerilla Warfare that must eventuate in retaliation and when it does commence it will be hard to control."[5] Should the war transcend conventional limits, it would embitter both victor and vanquished, making it all the more difficult to achieve a lasting peace. Moreover, to abandon notions of a limited war fought between armies, in favor of a people's struggle, carried with it revolutionary implications. While both sides may have gone to war to preserve something—the North to save the Union, the South to protect a way of life—the resulting conflict, should it spill over its initial boundaries, promised to transform American society whatever the result.

Signs of Confederate determination caused Grant to reconsider his earlier notions about a short war. "I have changed my mind so much that I don't

know what to think," he told his sister. While he still believed that the rebels could be crushed by spring, "they are so dogged that there is no telling when they may be subdued." As resistance stiffened, Grant adopted a tougher policy toward secessionist sympathizers, arresting several to prevent them from relaying information, seizing a prosouthern paper, and warning businessmen not to trade with Confederates. If Southerners wanted to broaden the scope of the war, Grant was willing to respond in kind.[6]

Inevitably such a struggle affected the institution of slavery. While Grant did not go to war to free the slaves, he had maintained that Northerners would not prop up slavery while the South continued to fight. Eventually Union field commanders found themselves confronted with the problem of what to do about slavery in the war zone. Despite Grant's avowed disinclination to become involved in political questions, his actions toward civilians, property, and fugitive slaves inescapably carried with them political overtones. In August, General John C. Frémont ordered Grant to take command of troops concentrating in southeast Missouri. Arriving at Cape Girardeau on August 30, Grant observed "Contrabands, in the shape of negroes," working on the fortifications. "I will make enquiries how they come here and if the fact has not been previously reported ask instructions," he informed Frémont's headquarters at St. Louis. Grant was trying to avoid initiating policies which interfered with slavery.[7]

Unknown to Grant, Frémont, tired of harassment by Confederate sympathizers, struck at slavery the same day. His abolitionism, bolstered by a visit from Owen Lovejoy, and his ambition combined to convince him to issue a proclamation which imposed martial law on Missouri, confiscated the property of active Confederate supporters, and declared their slaves free. Local commanders wired Grant for instructions. "Protect all loyal Citizens in all their right[s]," Grant replied, "but carry out the proclamation of Genl Fremont upon all subjects known to come under it." Frémont's order was soon countermanded by Lincoln, but it had alerted

Grant to the possibility that the war could assume a wider scope and thus involve him in the very political questions he wished to avoid.[8] Lincoln's removal of Frémont several weeks later also reminded the new brigadier of the cost of violating established policy.

Grant's decision to invade Kentucky in September 1861 provided him with an opportunity to issue a proclamation outlining war aims, and the contrast with Frémont's missive was marked. Through August, Kentucky had managed to preserve a precarious neutrality in the sectional conflict. Neither side had set foot in the state, although it was obvious that sooner or later Union troops would have to violate its neutrality if they intended to launch an offensive to recapture Tennessee. Grant had been sent to southeast Missouri to plan for just such an invasion, but Confederate forces conveniently relieved him of the onus of disrupting the status quo first by invading Kentucky on September 3. The Rebel commander, General Leonidias Polk, had made a serious error, one on which Grant seized in moving his troops across the Ohio River into Paducah, Kentucky, on September 6.

Once installed at Paducah, Grant issued his own proclamation. He had invaded Kentucky, "not to injure or annoy, . . . but to respect the rights, and to defend and enforce the rights of all loyal citizens." It was a purely defensive move. "I have nothing to do with opinions. I shall deal only with armed rebellion and its aiders and abetors." Nothing was said about slavery. Grant issued special instructions "to take special care and precaution that no harm is done to inoffensive citizens."[9]

Grant's proclamation was as much a political statement as that issued by Frémont. Both were issued in states still technically loyal to the Union, and both reflected the lack of a declaration of overall war aims from Washington. Frémont, anxious to make a name for himself, had sought to place the war effort on advanced ground; Grant's announcement reflected his own belief that the war was one for reunion, not revolution. In contrast to Frémont, who saw his handiwork annulled by Lincoln, Grant's statement stood. It still remained for the Lincoln administration to make known its policy in order to guide military commanders in their actions.

Although Lincoln's action in countermanding Frémont's proclamation helped people understand what his policy was not, Grant was unsure of what government policy was, especially as it applied to black refugees. Within two weeks of the occupation of Paducah, blacks began entering Union lines, intent on making good their escape from slavery. Like Grant, Kentucky blacks knew that the presence of Union troops meant the disruption of slavery, regardless of the unwillingness of Union commanders to play abolitionist. And, if the Yankee army would not come to the blacks, they would go to it. The slaveholders followed, demanding the return of their property. They were willing to overlook the irony that they were asking the assistance of a government that many of them were rebelling against to protect their right to own slaves, when many of them had justified secession precisely because they had no faith that the same government would protect that right. Grant wired Washington for instructions. None came.[10]

Left on his own, and aware that fugitive slave legislation was still in force, Grant ordered the return of at least one slave. Some two months later he finally received definite guidelines on what to do. Major General Henry W. Halleck succeeded Frémont in November with orders to convince civilians in his command that the sole purpose of the war was to uphold "the integrity of the Union." The day after he assumed command Halleck issued General Orders No. 3, which closed Union lines to black fugitives.[11]

Grant received the order with mixed feelings. To be sure, he still held fast to his belief that the sole object of the war was to restore the Union. "My inclination is to whip the rebellion into submission, preserving all constitutional rights," he told his father. But Grant was willing to admit the possibility that this might not be possible. "If it cannot be whipped in any other way than through a war against slavery," he continued, "let it come to that legitimately. If it is necessary that slavery should fall that the

Republic may continue its existence, let slavery go." The general was willing to consider the possibility that slavery's demise might be a goal of Union war policy, instead of being merely the consequence of the disruptive impact of military operations. But he was not yet ready to take that step. Aware that many Northern newspapers had seized upon Halleck's order to renew their criticism of the narrow scope of Union war aims, Grant charged that such papers "are as great enemies to their country as if they were open and avowed secessionists." Adopting such broad goals would mean that the prospects for reunion and reconciliation would give way to a bitter struggle requiring the North to conquer the entire South.[12]

Despite his reaction to press criticism of Halleck's order, Grant was ambivalent about it. "I do not want the Army used as negro catchers," he explained in approving the return of a fugitive to a loyal master, "but still less do I want to see it used as a cloak to cover their escape. No matter what our private views may be on this subject there are in this Department positive orders on the subject, and these orders must be obeyed." While he still agreed that the army's mission did not include emancipation, he was not willing to endorse active support of slavery in all instances, especially in the face of growing resistance. Noting that it was not the military's policy "to ignore, or in any manner interfere with the Constitutional rights of loyal citizens," he denied the same protection to secessionist slaveholders when he refused to honor a Confederate master's demand for the return of a fugitive who had sought refuge in Grant's camp. "The slave, who is used to support the Master, who supported the rebellion, is not to be *restored* to the Master by Military Authority." The slaveholder might appeal to the civil authorities, but Grant did not "feel it his duty to feed the foe, or in any manner contribute to their comfort." This position, violating the letter of Halleck's order, went further in the direction of emancipation than existing congressional legislation outlining confiscation policy, which concerned only those slaves actively employed in support of the rebellion.[13]

Grant let slip his growing antislavery convictions on other occasions. During the fall of 1861 his forces sparred with Polk's units, and the two armies met once in a pitched battle at Belmont, Missouri. Inevitably, prisoners were taken at these clashes, and Grant met with Polk several times on a truce boat to arrange exchanges and discuss other issues. At the conclusion of one meeting, drinks were served, and Polk offered a toast: "George Washington!" No sooner had Grant tipped the glass to his lips, however, when Polk added, "the first rebel." Chagrined, Grant protested that such sharp practice was "scarcely fair" and vowed to get even. The opportunity came several weeks later, at another truce boat conference. This time Grant proposed a toast: "Equal rights to all." Heartily assenting, Polk began to down the contents of his glass, when Grant quickly added, "white and black." A sputtering Polk admitted that Grant had achieved his object.[14]

Nor was Grant willing to tolerate actions which exceeded the bounds of conventional warfare. In January 1862, upon receiving reports that several of his pickets had been shot by civilians, he ordered that the surrounding area "should be cleaned out, for six miles around, and word given that all citizens making their appearance in within those areas are liable to be shot," thus establishing the Civil War version of a free-fire zone. These orders restored stability. A week later, he instructed the local commander to release all civilians captured under these orders and to allow all slaves to return to their masters.[15]

During early 1862 Grant remained uncertain about the correct policy to pursue toward fugitives, and his capture of Fort Donelson on February 16 added to the problem. Halleck wanted to consolidate Grant's gains by erecting fortifications to hold Donelson and its twin, Fort Henry, and instructed Grant to use slaves owned by secessionists to do the work. Grant sent division commander John A. McClernand out to capture slaves to increase the available work force. At least one expedition interpreted its orders liberally, seizing "mostly old men, women and children." The commander had violated Halleck's order, and the fugitives had to be returned. Grant finally halted McClernand, explaining, "It leads to constant mistakes and embarassment to have our men running through the country interpreting confiscation acts and only strengthens the enthusiasm against us whilst it has a demoralizing influence upon our own troops."[16]

The incident caused Grant a great deal of embarrassment. He reminded his troops that Halleck's order about returning fugitive slaves was still in force and must be observed. Union lines were flooded with slaveholders seeking to recover their slaves, proving that General Orders No. 3 continued to be a necessity. Halleck had issued a new order, reminding officers that civil courts, not military authorities, were empowered to rule on the status of slaves. Keeping fugitives out of camp would keep Grant out of trouble, or so he thought. But the image of Union soldiers returning "old men, women and children" to their masters was too much for many Northerners, and newspapers attacked Grant's action. "I have studiously tried to prevent the running off of negroes from all outside places," an exasperated Grant explained, "as I have tried to prevent all other marauding and plundering." It was not a matter of personal preference. "So long as I hold a commission in the Army I have no views of my own to carry out. Whatever may be the orders of my superiors, and law, I will execute." If Congress passed legislation "too odious for me to execute," he promised to resign. He enforced a strict observance of Halleck's order to avoid more trouble, including the arrest of any soldiers violating the order.[17]

Even when orders from Washington finally arrived, they did not ease Grant's mind. In March he received notification of new War Department guidelines which instructed soldiers not to return fugitives. One suspects that incidents in Grant's own command had contributed to the new directive. In response Grant pointed out the ramifications of such a policy. He had heard from former U.S. Representative J. M. Quarles that Confederate enlistments had risen around Clarksville, Tennessee, in reaction to the use of fugitives by a Union post com-

mander. The post commander told Grant that "the return of those two negroes would do more good, & go further to cultivate a union sentiment in & about Clarksville than any other act." Grant forwarded the case, uncertain how to respond in light of the new directives, but expressed his opinion that the blacks should be returned.[18]

As Grant realized, federal policy toward fugitive slaves was intertwined with efforts at reconciliation. After Fort Donelson, he believed that one more Union victory would end the conflict, an impression made plausible by circumstances in his command. Many Tennesseans were declaring their loyalty to the Union; others were enlisting in Grant's regiments. Confederate deserters reported great discontent in rebel ranks. "With one more great success I do not see how the rebellion is to be sustained," Grant told his wife. He thought that the question of fugitive slaves would simply disrupt the reconciliation process at a time when the end seemed so near. But the bloodbath at Shiloh in April disabused Grant of these hopes. He later claimed that the battle changed his thinking about the conduct of the war. After Shiloh, "I gave up all idea of saving the Union except by complete conquest." Previous policies to "protect the property of the citizens whose territory was invaded, without regard to their sentiments," went out the door, and Grant began to make war not only on Confederate armies but the resources which sustained the war effort.[19]

But Grant's change in attitude was a little slower in coming than he liked to recall later. "This war could be ended at once," he told his wife in June, two months after Shiloh, "if the whole Southern people could express their unbiased feeling untrammeled by leaders. The feeling is kept up however by crying out Abolitionest against us and this is unfortunately sustained by the acts of a very few among us." He detailed instances where Tennesseans "inclined to Union sentiments" watched as soldiers encouraged their slaves to escape. This did little to assist reconciliation. Still, as Grant took command of the District of West Tennessee in June, he expressed his confidence that as soon as his district

was "reduced to working order" its residents would "become loyal, or at least law-abiding." Others were not so sure. Dr. Edward Kittoe, a friend of Grant's patron Congressman Elihu B. Washburne, complained, "We curry favour of these secessionists, and real Union men do not fare as well as they: we are obsequious to them, we feed them, we guard their property, we humble ourselves to gain their favor, and in return we receive insult and injury." Unionists were "disgusted," and both officers and men "feel outraged . . . and very naturally ask is this the way to crush this rebellion." To Kittoe the answer was obvious: "The iron gauntlet must be used more than the silken glove to crush this serpent."[20]

Grant's early hopes for reconciliation were dashed when he observed the temper of the people. Far from anxiously awaiting reunion, most west Tennesseans remained defiantly loyal to the Confederate cause, chafing under occupied rule. They cheered on the small bands of guerrillas who sought to disrupt and disturb Grant's operations. As Grant struggled to secure his lines from raiders, he began to reassess his beliefs about limited war in the face of escalating Confederate resistance. The intensity of the Southern attack at Shiloh, while alarming, remained within the bounds of conventional warfare: but when resisting citizens and marauding guerrillas expanded the scope of conflict beyond these limits, Grant had to meet the challenge. It was combatting a restive populace in occupied territory, stalking guerrillas, and absorbing black refugees, not merely Shiloh, that persuaded Grant to abandon limited war for total war. He did so with surprising speed. On July 1, he ordered the *Memphis Avalanche* to shut down after the paper had complained about the behavior of Union troops. Within days a Unionist paper, the *Bulletin,* replaced it. Two days later he took steps to halt guerrilla activities by ordering that property losses sustained by his army would be made up by assessments on the property of Confederate sympathizers. All captured guerrillas would not be treated as prisoners of war, leaving open the possibility of execution. The order provoked one Mississippian to protest Grant's "infamous and fiendish proclamation . . . characteristic of your infernal policy. . . . Henceforth our motto shall be, Blood for blood, and blood for property."[21]

Grant also tired of dealing with Confederate sympathizers in Memphis. On July 10 he issued a special order directing families of Confederate officers and officeholders to move south. Although the order was later modified to allow such families to remain in Memphis upon taking a pledge not to aid enemy operations, it outraged Confederate General Jeff Thompson, who promised revenge. In contrast, a local Unionist applauded the order: "I would suggest that all persons who *uphold,* and *preach* Secession in our midst be required to 'skedaddle' to the land of *'secession'*."[22]

As Federal units probed southward across the Tennessee-Mississippi border, blacks continued to flood into Union lines. Their sheer numbers negated any further attempts at exclusion. If whites were "sullen" at the sight of the bluecoats, Kittoe told Washburne, "the darkies seemed joyous at our presence." Grant's soldiers realized that their mere presence destroyed slavery, "Where the army of the Union goes, *there slavery ceases forever,*" wrote a Wisconsin captain. "It is astonishing how soon the blacks have learned this, and they are flocking in considerable numbers already in our lines." Another officer noted, "All that came within our lines were received and put to work and supplied with clothing and subsistence. This policy was viewed by the soldiers with very general approbation."[23]

Grant moved slowly at first in responding to these new circumstances. "It is hard to say what would be the most wise policy to pursue towards these people," he wrote Washburne. He put blacks to work fortifying Memphis from Confederate attack, much as he had used blacks at Donelson. But he remained unsure of his responsibilities in other cases, and, rather than invite more criticism by acting on his own, he asked for instructions. After arresting Confederate sympathizer Francis Whitfield on July 17, 1862, Grant had to decide what to do with Whitfield's slaves, who, since they were women and children, could

not be used on fortifications. Whitfield, understandably, wanted the slaves sent south to relatives. Grant, preoccupied with enemy movements, asked Halleck what to do. The general-in-chief responded that if Grant had no use for or reason to detain the slaves, "let them go when they please."[24]

Halleck could have been more helpful to the befuddled Grant. On the day of Whitfield's arrest, Congress passed a second confiscation act which declared that slaves owned by rebels who came in contact with Union forces were free. Certainly Halleck should have been aware of this legislation, but he failed to pass policy directives down to his subordinates. Promulgation of a policy did not necessarily guarantee its immediate implementation and enforcement. Grant was not officially informed of the passage of the act for several weeks. Halleck finally instructed him to "clean out West Tennessee and North Mississippi of all organized enemies," eject civilian sympathizers, and confiscate rebel property. "It is time that they should begin to feel the presence of war on one side."[25]

Grant planned to make the war even more oppressive for Southern whites. He cracked down on the activities of Confederate sympathizers and guerrillas, following Halleck's advice to "handle that class without gloves." As William T. Sherman put it to Secretary of the Treasury Salmon P. Chase, "The Government of the United States may now safely proceed on the proper rule that all in the South are enemies of all in the North, and not only are they unfriendly, but all who can procure arms now bear them as organized regiments or as guerrillas." Grant also took steps to close down trade with the enemy, especially cotton speculators. To Chase he declared that such trade profited only "greedy" speculators and the enemy, failed to "abate [the] rancorous hostility" of Rebels, and hurt the war effort. Doubtless Grant's new toughness was due to his realization that the war had taken on a new character, but he was also frustrated with his present situation, holding territory while hunting down pesky guerrilla bands. If he could not attack the South in battle, he would find another way to strike back.[26]

Washburne apprised Grant of the new attitudes in Washington. "This matter of guarding rebel property, of protecting secessionists and of enforcing 'order No. 3' is 'played out' in public estimation. Your order in regard to the Secessionists of Memphis taking the oath or leaving, has been accepted as an earnest of vigorous and decided action on your part. . . . The administration has come up to what the people have long demanded—a vigorous prosecution of the war by all the means known to civilized warfare." Such measures included striking at slavery. "The negroes must now be made our auxiliaries in every possible way they can be, whether by working or fighting." The general "who takes the most decided step in this respect," Washburne hinted, "will be held in the highest estimation by the loyal and true men in the country."[27]

Grant followed Washburne's advice, freed of the responsibilities of playing slave catcher. "I have no hobby of my own with regard to the negro, either to effect his freedom or to continue his bondage," he told his father. "If Congress pass any law and the President approves, I am willing to execute it." His headquarters established guidelines for the enforcement of the new confiscation legislation. Blacks would no longer be turned away: instead, they would be put to work. Manpower needs would be met by impressing the slaves belonging to Confederate masters. Uncertain as to the scope of the legislation, Grant excluded unemployed blacks from the lines, and prohibited soldiers "from enticing Slaves to leave their masters." The order had an immediate impact. "If the niggers come into camp for a week as fast as they have been coming for two days past," a Wisconsin private noted some two days after Grant issued his order, "we will soon have a waiter for every man in the Regt."[28]

The result pleased Grant. "The war is evidently growing oppressive to the Southern people," he told his sister. "Their *institution* are beginning to have ideas of their own and every time an expedition goes out more or less of them follow in the wake of the army and come to camp." The general employed them as teamsters, cooks, and hospital attendants, but there was not enough work for all. "I don't know what is to become of these poor people in the end but it [is] weakening the enemy to take them from them."[29]

With the approach of fall the black refugee problem assumed serious dimensions. Grant's troops, busy repelling Confederate offensives near Corinth, found the flood of fugitives obstructing movements and causing health problems. They described the blacks coming by the hundreds each night, "bearing their bundles on their heads and their pickaninnies under their arms." Chaplain John Eaton of the 27th Ohio recalled that the influx of refugees resembled "the oncoming of cities": once in camp, the bedraggled blacks produced "a veritable moral chaos." Sherman wrote his senator brother that "if we are to take along and feed the negroes who flee to us for refuge" on top of clothing and transportation shortages, military movements would bog down. "A perfect stampede of contrabands" confronted William S. Rosecrans, who was preparing to advance against enemy positions. Rosecrans sent them behind his lines to shield them from guerillas, complaining, "But what a burden what shall be done with them then."[30]

At first Grant tried to make use of the refugees, putting them to work in the Corinth fortifications. He sent the women and children to campsites east of Corinth and asked Secretary of War Edwin M. Stanton what he should do next. Some people in Chicago thought they would make excellent servants, a practice Stanton permitted for nearly a month until an adverse reaction in the Midwest, encouraged by electioneering Democrats, forced him to rescind the order.[31] Grant then decided to establish camps for the blacks and to let them bring in the cotton and corn crops under his supervision. They would live off the land, receive wages for their work, and strive toward providing for themselves. The Union authorities would exercise a form of guardianship over the refugees, for Grant did not believe that blacks fresh from slavery were prepared to take on the responsibilities of freedom immediately. He sought to provide them with

some means of making the transition. His plan would allow him to provide for all blacks entering Union lines, not only the males able to work for the army.

Grant explained his reasoning to Chaplain Eaton, whom he had placed in charge of the project. Racial prejudice, Grant believed, was fundamentally a product of mistaken beliefs about behavior. One of those beliefs held by many whites was that blacks would not work of their own free will. Grant's plan would allow blacks to refute that stereotype. Once blacks assisting the military and working on the plantations had proved that they were responsible, whites would begin to accept the idea of handing a musket to a black man, and blacks could enlist in the Union army. And once blacks had fought for their freedom and demonstrated again that they were responsible and hard-working, whites could begin to entertain the idea of granting citizenship, even the ballot, to blacks. "Never before in those early and bewildering days had I heard the problem of the future of the Negro attacked so vigorously and with such humanity combined with practical good sense," Eaton recalled.[32]

Grant, who had once believed that the military should not interfere with slavery, now was pushing a plan of de facto emancipation, using military supervision to oversee the transition from slavery to freedom. It also reflected his belief that racial prejudice was best countered and conquered by actual demonstrations of its falsehoods. If his plan was paternalistic, at least it held out the prospect of progressive change. Of course, it also provided a solution to the problems of conducting military operations while disposing of a potential disaster by promising relief from the disease-ridden conditions currently confronting the freedmen. Grant took an active interest in Eaton's progress, ordering supplies and assistance whenever needed, and making sure that his subordinates followed suit.[33]

Perhaps the most notable aspects of Grant's solution to the refugee problem was that, for once, he acted without asking his superiors for advice. Not until four days after he had ordered Eaton's appointment did Grant tell Halleck what

he was doing and ask for instructions. Halleck, too busy to be bothered by these problems, approved of Grant's policy, although he had only a vague idea of what his subordinate was doing. In fact, the Lincoln administration seemed more interested in taking steps which would halt Grant's plans in their tracks. On September 22, 1862, Lincoln had made public a preliminary version of the Emancipation Proclamation, promising that he would put it into force on January 1, 1863. He sought to take advantage of those hundred days to encourage Tennesseans to reenter the Union on their own, holding out the prospect that if the Volunteer State returned it could do so with slavery intact, since the proclamation applied only to areas under Confederate control. On October 21, 1862, Lincoln informed both Grant and military governor Andrew Johnson of his plan. He wanted them to hold elections for congressmen wherever they could do so. The President hoped that Tennesseans would rejoin the Union "to avoid the unsatisfactory prospect before them."[34]

Grant, who once had held high hopes for the prospect of a speedy reunion, was skeptical of Lincoln's plan. Months before he had heard reports of Unionist speakers such as Emerson Etheridge being mobbed by Rebels; certainly the actions of Memphis's residents struck a telling blow against stories of latent Unionism. Now guerrilla bands were firing on Union steamers with civilians on board. Sherman suggested various ways to punish the guerrillas; Grant approved the expulsion of secessionist families as adequate retaliation. Other policies suggested an intensification of the war effort. With fall came reports of families suffering from a lack of food and shelter. Grant, convinced that those "not actively engaged in rebellion should not be allowed to suffer" amidst plenty, decided that "the burden of furnishing the necessary relief . . . should fall on those, who, by act, encouragement or sympathy have caused the want now experienced." Some of the troops agreed. They were tired of guarding secessionist property: one private wrote that it made his regiment "squirm like a Sarpent." He concluded that there were "few if any

Union men" in the area. Another veteran later remarked that the troops believed by now that "they did not go South to protect Confederate property."[35]

Nevertheless, Grant was not one to question presidential policy. On December 9, 1862, he issued a proclamation to the people of west Tennessee calling for elections in the 8th, 9th, and 10th Congressional districts. All "legal voters" as of 1860 were permitted to participate in the balloting, which would take place on Christmas Eve. Grant was more impressed with the sentiments displayed by the Mississippians, who "show more signs of being subdued than any we have heretofore come across." A reporter noted that many Mississippians wanted to reenter the Union "at whatever cost" before Lincoln's proclamation came into play.[36]

Confederate forces under Nathan Bedford Forrest and Earl Van Dorn had no intention of allowing the election to proceed. They launched an offensive that not only disrupted an attempt by Grant to take Vicksburg but also made it impossible to hold elections. Grant was too busy conducting military operations to take much notice. Attempts at reestablishing loyal governments were futile until military operations rendered territory secure from guerrillas. As the new year started, Grant instructed Brigadier General Stephen A. Hurlbut, commanding at Memphis, to transfer ten secessionist families to Confederate lines for every guerrilla raid launched by the enemy. The general's patience was wearing thin, and protecting his supply lines against cavalry thrusts and armed bands sapped too much energy, time, and men from offensive operations.[37]

But guerrillas proved to be only one of the problems disrupting Grant's control of his own lines. Despite Eaton's project, the flood of refugees threatened to overwhelm Union camps. As Grant reestablished his position around Corinth and Memphis, he sought help from Halleck. "Contraband question becoming serious one," he telegraphed the general-in-chief. "What will I do with surplus negroes?" He glimpsed one possible solution as he shifted his forces to the west bank of the Mississippi opposite Vicksburg in the aftermath of his

failed December offensive. It had long been a favorite belief of Union commanders that if the course of the river was diverted through the construction of a canal, Vicksburg, stripped of its western water barrier, would be rendered vulnerable. Grant, although somewhat skeptical, was willing to try the idea himself, using blacks to do the work. The project illustrated Grant's priorities. The problem presented by black refugees was first and foremost a military problem. Their presence obstructed military movements, disrupted camps, and promised to increase disease and disorder. Grant spared his soldiers of these risks as well as lessened the burden of digging trenches in the dirty swamps by employing black laborers. Military needs having been met, other concerns took over, as Grant worried about the conditions under which the blacks worked.[38]

But this solution was at best a stopgap measure. Nothing seemed to stop the influx of refugees. On February 12, 1863, Grant decided to issue an order excluding blacks from his lines. Soldiers were instructed to stop "enticing" blacks to enter Union camps; freedmen should remain on their plantations and work out a labor arrangement with the planters. "Humanity dictates this policy," he explained to Halleck. "Planters have mostly deserted their plantations taking with them all their able bodied negroes and leaving the old and very young. Here they could not have shelter nor assurances of transportation when we leave." The army was simply not equipped materially or mentally to take on any more freed men. As Grant told one subordinate, "the question is a troublesome one. I am not permitted to send them out of the department, and such numbers as we have it is hard to keep them in."[39]

Unfortunately for Grant, he was caught once more by a shift in administration policy. Halleck told Grant that reports had reached the War Department "that many of the officers of your command not only discourage the negroes from coming under our protection, but, by ill-treatment, force them to return to their masters." Obviously Grant's exclusion order had not gone over well with

the top brass. "This is not only bad policy in itself," Halleck continued, "but is directly opposed to the policy adopted by the government." In the wake of the Emancipation Proclamation, Washington decided to make war in earnest. Halleck—whose General Orders No. 3 in 1861 had epitomized the conservative attitude toward blacks—justified the new approach. "The character of the war has very much changed within the last year. There is now no possible hope of a reconciliation with the rebels. The union party in the south is virtually destroyed. There can be no peace but that which is enforced by the sword. We must conquer the rebels, or be conquered by them."[40]

With this acceptance of a total war approach against the Confederacy came new attitudes toward the treatment of black slaves by the Union army. It is the policy of the government to withdraw from the enemy as much productive labor as possible," Halleck explained, preaching with the passion of the recently converted. "Every slave withdrawn from the enemy, is equivalent to a white man put *hors de combat.*" Freedmen were to be used "so far as practicable as a military force for the defence of forts, depots, &c. . . . And it is the opinion of many who have examined the question without passion or prejudice, that they can also be used as a military force." Grant was instructed to assist this process by using his "official and personal influence to remove prejudices on this subject," and to assist General Lorenzo Thomas in efforts to organize black regiments."[41]

War had become revolution, taking the very path which Grant had outlined to Eaton the previous November. To arm ex-slaves was to make real the greatest fear of many a white Southerner by equipping blacks with the means to achieve revenge. Grant, who had grown weary of previous attempts at reconciliation, welcomed the change. "Rebellion has assumed that shape now that it can only terminate by the complete subjugation of the South or the overthrow of the Government," he informed Major General Frederick Steele, instructing him to provide for all the black refugees already in his lines and to "encourage all negroes, particularly middle aged males to come within our lines," obviously with an eye toward recruiting them. Then Grant welcomed Thomas to headquarters and did all he could to facilitate his mission. "At least three of my Army Corps Commanders take hold of the new policy of arming the negroes and using them against the rebels with a will," he told Halleck, adding: "You may rely on my carrying out any policy ordered by proper authority to the best of my ability." When several officers tendered their resignations over the new policy, Grant recommended that they be dismissed from the service instead.[42]

While Thomas proceeded with his mission, Grant embarked on yet another campaign against Vicksburg. Crossing the Mississippi below the city, Grant's army won five battles within three weeks, destroyed several factories at Jackson, and laid seige to Vicksburg itself in one of the most brilliant campaigns of the war. His troops took the war to the Southern people. Grant instructed commanders to make sure that their troops would "live as far as possible off the country through which they pass and destroy corn, wheat crops and everything that can be made use of by the enemy in prolonging the war. Mules and horses can be taken to supply all our wants and where it does not cause too much delay agricultural implements may be destroyed. In other words cripple the rebellion in every way."[43]

During the seige he received news that Thomas's recruits had engaged in their first battle at Milliken's Bend, some twenty miles upriver from Vicksburg. At first giving way, the blacks launched a vicious counterattack, spurred on in part by reports that Confederates were murdering blacks taken prisoner in the initial assault. Milliken's Bend proved blacks could fight, and many whites who were skeptical of black enlistment were won over when they heard accounts of the clash. Grant himself was pleased, endorsing the report of the Union commander at the battle with the comment that while the soldiers "had but little experience in the use of fire arms" they had been "most gallant and I doubt not but with good officers they will make good troops."[44]

But in the aftermath of the battle stories began to surface that the Confederates had executed captured black soldiers. Initially Grant was unsure whether such acts had official Confederate sanction, or if they had been perpetrated by "irresponsible persons"; but additional reports suggested that Confederate General Richard Taylor had approved the measures. Grant told Taylor that if the Confederates were initiating a policy, "I will accept the issue. It may be you propose a different line of policy towards Black troops and Officers commanding them to that practiced towards White troops? If so," Grant added, "I can assure you that these colored troops are regularly mustered into the service of the United States," and all Union authorities "are bound to give the same protection to these troops that they do to any other troops." Such a statement had revolutionary implications, for now Grant was demanding that prisoners in blue uniforms be treated equally, whether their skin was black or white. While Taylor denied the stories, he pointed out that all black prisoners would be turned over to state authorities in accordance with Confederate policy. Grant, accepting Taylor's denial of responsibility, was not so gracious about Confederate policy toward black POWs, commenting that "I cannot see the justice of permitting one treatment for them, and another for the white soldiers." But the exchange proved Grant's willingness to accept the notion that equal treatment followed naturally from emancipation, an idea which promised to transform American society.[45]

By the summer of 1863 Ulysses S. Grant's thoughts on the relationship between slavery, war, and reunion had undergone a drastic change from the ones he voiced during his early weeks of field command. He had always assumed that slavery would be a casualty of the war, but his initial passivity toward "the peculiar institution," fueled by a desire to achieve a quick and painless peace based on reconciliation, had given way in the face of fierce Confederate resistance. Once it had become obvious that the war would be long, Grant grasped that Union military operations would help turn it into a social and economic revolution by disturbing the very foundation of Southern society. Moreover, he now welcomed that challenge. To Lincoln he explained that he was giving "the subject of arming black troops my hearty support." The enlistment of blacks, "with the emancipation of the negro, is the heavyest blow yet given the Confederacy. . . . By arming the negro we have added a powerful ally. They will make good soldiers and taking them from the enemy weaken him in the same proportion they strengthen us."[46]

Such measures signalled the death of slavery. "The people of the North need not quarrel over the institution of Slavery," Grant reassured Washburne. "What Vice President Stevens [Alexander H. Stephens] acknowledges the corner stone of the Confederacy is already knocked out. Slavery is already dead and cannot be resurrected. It would take a Standing army to maintain slavery in the South" now. Then Grant injected a personal note. "I never was an Abolitionest, [not even what could be called anti slavery," he admitted, "but . . . it became patent to my mind early in the rebellion that the North & South could never live at peace with each other except as one nation, and that without Slavery." To save the Union, one must first destroy slavery. Any other settlement would be flawed. With that in mind, he argued that no peace should be concluded "until this question is forever settled." War had become revolution, and Ulysses S. Grant had been both witness and participant in the process. As he told a committee of Memphis unionists, he, like they, had come to "acknowledge human liberty as the only true foundation of human government."[47]

Notes

1. On Grant and slavery see Brooks D. Simpson, "Butcher? Racist? An Examination of William S. McFeely's *Grant: A Biography*," *Civil War History* 33 (March 1987), 63–83.
2. Ulysses S. Grant to Frederick Dent, April 19, 1861, in John Y. Simon, ed., *The Papers of Ulysses S. Grant*, 16 vols. to date (Carbondale, Ill.: Southern Illinois University Press, 1967–88), 2:3–4.
3. Ulysses S. Grant to Mary Grant, April 29, 1861, ibid., 2:13–14; Grant to Jesse Root Grant, May 6, 1861, ibid., 2:21–22. In fact,

Grant expressed some concern lest slaves rise up in insurrection against their masters.

4. Ulysses S. Grant to Julia Dent Grant, July 19, 1861, ibid., 2:72–73.

5. Ulysses S. Grant to Julia Dent Grant, August 3, 1861, ibid., 2:82–83; Grant to Jesse Root Grant, August 3, 1861, ibid., 2:80–81.

6. Ulysses S. Grant to Mary Grant, August 12, 1861, ibid., 2:105; Grant to John C. Kelton, August 14, 1861, ibid., 2:111; Grant to William H. Worthington, August 26, 1861, ibid., 2:139–40.

7. Ulysses S. Grant to John C. Kelton, August 30, 1861, ibid., 2:154–55.

8. Dudley Taylor Cornish, *The Sable Arm: Negro Troops in the Union Army, 1861–1865* (New York: Norton, 1966), 12–15; John Cook to Ulysses S. Grant, September 11, 1861, Simon, ed., *Grant Papers*, 2:220, and Grant to Cook, September 12, 1861, ibid., 2:243–44. Frémont issued a new proclamation on September 11 in line with Lincoln's policy.

9. Ulysses S. Grant, "Proclamation," September 6, 1861, and Grant to E. A. Paine, September 6, 1861. ibid., 194–95.

10. Ulysses S. Grant to Lorenzo Thomas, September 21, 1861, ibid., 2:291 and annotation.

11. Kenneth Williams, *Lincoln Finds A General*, 5 vols. (New York: Macmillan, 1949–59), 3:106–12.

12. Ulysses S. Grant to Jesse Root Grant, November 27, 1861, Simon, ed., *Grant Papers*, 3:227.

13. Ulysses S. Grant to John L. Cook, December 25, 1861, ibid., 3:342–43; William S. Hillyer (Grant staff officer) to L. F. Ross, January 5, 1862, ibid., 3:373–74; Charles F. Smith to Grant, January 4, 1862, ibid., 3:431.

14. James Grant Wilson, *Life and Public Services of Ulysses Simpson Grant* (New York: De Witt, 1885), 24.

15. Ulysses S. Grant to E. A. Paine, January 11, 19, 1862, Simon, ed., *Grant Papers*, 4:32, 68–69.

16. Henry W. Halleck to Ulysses S. Grant, February 8, 1862, and Grant to Halleck, February 11, 1862, ibid., 4:193–94; General orders No. 46, Department of the Missouri, February 22, 1862, ibid., 4:291; Grant to McClernand, February 18, 1862, ibid., 4:243; Grant to J. C. Kelton, February 22, 1862, ibid., 4:267–68; Grant to McClernand, February 22, 1862, ibid., 4:470.

17. General Orders No. 14, District of West Tennessee, February 26, 1862, ibid., 4:290–91; Grant to Elihu B. Washburne, March 22, 1862, ibid., 4:408; Grant to Philip B. Fouke, March 16, 1862, ibid., 4:377; Grant to Marcellus M. Crocker, March 17, 1862, ibid., 4:384; Grant to William T. Sherman, March 17, 1862, ibid., 4:382–83.

18. Ulysses S. Grant to Nathaniel H. McLean, March 31, 1862, ibid., 4:454; Philip B. Fouke to Grant, March 30, 1862, ibid., 4:454.

19. Ulysses S. Grant to George W. Cullum, February 23, 25, 1862, ibid., 4:276, 286; Grant to William T. Sherman, February 25, 1862, ibid., 4:289; Grant to Philip B. Fouke, March 16, 1862, ibid., 4:377; Grant to Nathaniel H. McLean, March 15, 30, 1862, ibid., 4:368, 447–48; Grant to Julia Dent Grant, March 18, 1862, ibid., 4:389; Ulysses S. Grant, *Personal Memoirs of U.S. Grant*, 2 vols. (New York: Charles L. Webster and Co., 1885–86), 1:368–69.

20. Ulysses S. Grant to Julia Dent Grant, June 12, 1862, Simon, ed., *Grant Papers*, 5:142–43; Kittoe to Washburne, June 24, 1862, Lloyd Lewis–Bruce Catton Research Notes, Ulysses S. Grant Association, Southern Illinois University.

21. Grant to Elihu B. Washburne, June 19, 1862, Simon, ed., *Grant Papers*, 5:146; Grant to William S. Hillyer, July 1, 1862, ibid., 5:181–82 and annotation; General Orders No. 60, District of West Tennessee, July 3, 1862, ibid., 5:190–91 and annotation.

22. "Union" to Grant, July 12, 1862, William S. Hillyer Papers, University of Virginia; see Simon, ed., *Grant Papers*, 5:192–94.

23. Seymour D. Thompson, *Recollections with the Third Iowa Regiment* (Cincinnati, 1864), 275; William P. Lyon, *Reminiscences of the Civil War* (San Jose, Calif.: Muirson and Wright, 1907), 53; Kittoe to Washburne, June 24, 1862, Lewis-Catton Research Notes, Ulysses S. Grant Association.

24. Ulysses S. Grant to Elihu B. Washburne, June 19, 1862, Simon, ed., *Grant Papers*, 5:146; Grant to Halleck, July 19, 1862, and Halleck to Grant, July 19, 1862, ibid., 5:218–19. See also Grant to Halleck, July 8[7], 1862, ibid., 5:199.

25. Herman Belz, *Emancipation and Equal Rights: Politics and Constitutionalism in the Civil War Era* (New York: Norton, 1978), 36–40; General Orders No. 72, District of West Tennessee, August 11, 1862, Simon, ed., *Grant Papers*, 5:273–74; Halleck to Grant, August 2, 1862, ibid., 5:243–44.

26. Grant to Halleck, July 28, 1862, and Halleck to Grant, August 2, 1862, ibid., 5:243–44; Grant to William W. Rosecrans, August 10, 1862, ibid., 5:282; Grant to Isaac F. Quinby, July 26, 1862, ibid., 5:238–41; Grant to Salmon P. Chase, July 31, 1862, ibid., 5:255–56; Grant to Rosecrans, August 7, 1862, ibid., 5:271; Sherman to Chase, August 11, 1862, quoted in John B. Walters, *Merchant of Terror: General Sherman and Total War* (Indianapolis: Bobbs-Merrill, 1973), 57–58.

27. Washburne to Grant, July 25, 1862, Simon, ed., *Grant Papers*, 5:226.

28. Grant to Jesse Root Grant, August 3, 1862, ibid., 5:264; General Orders No. 72, District of West Tennessee, August 11, 1862, ibid., 5:273–74; Stephen Ambrose, ed., *A Wisconsin Boy in Dixie: The Selected Letters of John K. Newton* (Madison. Wis.: The University of Wisconsin Press, 1961), 27–28.

29. Grant to Mary Grant, August 19, 1862, Simon, ed., *Grant Papers* 5:311.

30. Samuel H. M. Byers, *With Fire and Sword* (New York: Neale, 1911), 45; John Eaton, *Grant, Lincoln, and the Freedmen* (New York: Longmans, Green and Co., 1907), 2; William T. Sherman to John Sherman, September 3, 1862, William T. Sherman Papers, LC; Rosecrans to Grant, September 10, 1862, Simon, ed., *Grant Papers*, 6:32.

31. Grant to Thomas J. McKean, September 16, 1862, ibid., 6:54; James M. Tuttle to Edwin M. Stanton, September 18, 1862, ibid., 6:317; V. Jacque Voegeli, *Free But Not Equal: The Midwest and the Negro During the Civil War* (Chicago: University of Chicago Press, 1967), 60–61.

32. Eaton, *Grant, Lincoln and the Freedmen*, 9–15.

33. Ibid., 18–32. For additional discussion about Grant, Eaton, and the development of this policy at Corinth and at Davis Bend, Mississippi, which Grant hoped would become "a negro paradise," see Cam Walker: "Corinth: The Story of a Contraband Camp," *Civil War History* 20 (March 1974), 5–22; Steven J. Ross, "Freed Soil, Freed Labor, Freed Men: John Eaton and the Davis Bend Experiment," *Journal of Southern History* 44 (May 1978), 213–32; Louis S. Gerteis, *From Contraband to Freedman: Federal Policy Toward Southern Blacks, 1861–1865* (Westport, Conn.: Greenwood Press, 1973); and Janet Sharp Hermann, *The Pursuit of a Dream* (New York: Oxford University Press, 1981), 37–60.

34. Grant to Halleck, November 15, 1862, and Halleck to Grant, November 16, 1862, Simon, ed., *Grant Papers*, 6:315; Lincoln to Johnson and Grant, October 21, 1862, ibid., 7:3.

35. General Orders No. 4, Department of the Tennessee, November 3, 1862, ibid., 6:252–53; William W. Lowe to John A. Rawlins, August 18, 1862, ibid., 5:314; John W. Brinsfield, "The Military Ethics of General William T. Sherman: A Reassessment," *Parameters*, Vol. 12, No. 2 (1980), 42; Fred A. Shannon, ed., *The Civil War Letters of Sergeant Onley Andrus* (Urbana: University of Illinois Press, 1947), 25–26; Bruce Catton, *Grant Moves South* (Boston: Little, Brown, 1960), 336.

36. Ulysses S. Grant, "Proclamation," December 9, 1862, Simon, ed., *Grant Papers* 7:3–4; Grant to Halleck, December 14, 1862, ibid., 7:31–32; Thomas W. Knox, *Camp-Fire and Cotton-Field* (New York: Blelock and Co., 1865), 233.

37. Grant to Steven A. Hurlbut, January 3, 1863, Simon, ed., *Grant Papers*, 7:167–68.

38. Grant to Halleck, January 6, 1863, ibid., 7:186; Grant to George W. Deitzler, February 2. 1863, ibid., 7:278; Eaton, *Grant, Lincoln and the Freedmen*, 44.

39. Special Field Orders No. 2, Department of the Tennessee, February 12, 1863, ibid., 7:339; Grant to Halleck, February 18, 1863, ibid., 7:338, Catton, *Grant Moves South*, 401–2.

40. Halleck to Grant, March 30, 1863, Simon, ed., *Grant Papers*, 8:93n.

41. Halleck to Grant, March 30, 1863, ibid., 8:93n.

42. Grant to Frederick Steele, April 11, 1863, ibid., 8:49; Grant to Halleck, April 19, 1863, ibid., 91–92.

43. Grant to Stephen A. Hurlbut, May 5, 1863, ibid., 8:159–60.

44. Cornish, *The Sable Arm*, 144–45; Grant to Lorenzo Thomas, June 16, 1863, Simon, ed., *Grant Papers* 8:328.

45. Grant to Richard Taylor, June 22, 1863, ibid., 400–401 and annotation; Grant to Taylor, July 4, 1863, ibid., 468–69 and annotation. [Grant was unaware of Federal policy on the treatment of black prisoners of war, expressed in General Orders No. 100, issued April 24. Lincoln, perhaps because of this incident, issued an executive order on July 30, promising to retaliate in kind if Confederate officials mistreated black prisoners.] Cornish, *The Sable Arm*, 165–68.

46. Grant to Lincoln, August 23, 1863, Simon, ed., *Grant Papers*, 9:196.

47. Grant to Washburne, August 30, 1863, ibid., 9:217–18; Grant to Rue Hough and others, August 26, 1863, ibid., 9:203.

The image of the American Civil War as a 'white man's fight' became the national norm almost as soon as the last shot was fired. **Susan-Mary Grant** looks at the experience and legacy of the conflict for black Americans.

PRIDE AND PREJUDICE IN THE AMERICAN CIVIL WAR

. . . You can say of the colored man, we too have borne our share of the burden. We too have suffered and died in defence of that starry banner which floats only over free men. . . . I feel assured that the name of the colored soldier will stand out in bold relief among the heroes of this war. . . .

(Henry S. Harmon, 3rd United States Colored Infantry, October 1863)

Far better the slow blaze of Learning's light,
The cool and quiet of her dearer fane,
Than this hot terror of a hopeless fight,
This cold endurance of the final pain,
Since thou and those who with thee died for right
Have died, the Present teaches, but in vain!

(Paul Laurence Dunbar, 'Robert Gould Shaw.')

In 1897, over thirty years after the end of the American Civil War, a very special monument to that war was erected opposite the Statehouse in Boston. Designed by the Irish-born sculptor Augustus Saint-Gaudens, it depicted in profile the figure of Robert Gould Shaw, the twenty-five-year-old white officer of the North's showcase black regiment, the Massachusetts 54th, leading his men through Boston on their way to South Carolina in 1863. An unusual piece of sculpture, Saint-Gaudens had worked hard to avoid representing the black troops in any kind of stereotypical manner, portraying them instead as noble patriot soldiers of the American nation. Both in its novelty and in its sentiment the monument remains impressive according to the art critic Robert Hughes, 'the most intensely felt image of military commemoration made by an American.'

However, the Saint-Gaudens monument in no way reflected the general mood of the American people towards those black troops who had fought in the conflict, as the poet Paul Laurence Dunbar's response to Shaw's sacrifice reveals. Between 1863, when Henry Harmon expressed his optimism about history's treatment of the black soldier, and 1897, the American nation had all but forgotten that black troops had ever played a role in the Civil War. Both Saint-Gaudens and Dunbar were working at a time when segregation was beginning to bite in the South with the 'Jim Crow' Laws, but the exclusion of black troops from the national memory of the Civil War began long before the 1890s. In the Grand Review of the Armed Forces which followed the cessation of hostilities very few blacks were represented. Relegated to the end of the procession in 'pitch and shovel' brigades or intended only as a form of comic relief, neither the free black soldier nor the former slave was accorded his deserved role in this poignant national pageant. Rather than a war fought for liberty, in which the role of the African-American soldier was pivotal, the image of the American Civil War as a 'white man's fight' became the norm almost as soon as the last shot was fired.

The relationship between the black soldier and the 'land of the free' has always been ambiguous. The involvement of black troops in America's wars from colonial times onwards followed a depressing pattern. Encouraged to enlist in times of crisis, the African-American soldier's services were clearly unwelcome in time of peace. Despite this, the link between fighting and freedom for African-Americans was forged in the earliest days of the American nation, and once forged proved resilient. During the colonial era, South Carolina enacted legislation that offered freedom to slaves in return for their military services. By the conclusion of the American Revolution military service was regarded as a valid and successful method of achieving freedom for the slave, as well as an important expression of patriotism and loyalty to the nation.

It was unsurprising, therefore, that when hostilities commenced between North and South in 1861 blacks throughout the North, and some in the South too, sought to enlist. However, free blacks who responded to Abraham Lincoln's call for 75,000 volunteers found that their services were not required by a North in which slavery had been abolished but racist assumptions still prevailed. Instead they were told that the war was a 'white man's fight,' and offered no role for them. The notable black leader, Frederick Douglass, himself an escaped slave, summed the matter up:

> Colored men were good enough to fight under Washington. They are not good enough to fight under McClellan. They were good enough to fight under Andrew Jackson. They are not good enough to fight under Gen. Halleck. They were good enough to help win American independence but they are not good enough to help preserve that independence against treason and rebellion.

Douglass further recognised that unless the issues of arming free blacks and of freeing the slaves were addressed, the Union stood slim chance of success. The Union, however, showed little sign of heeding his warnings. In the early months of the conflict the *National Intelligencer* reinforced the view that the war 'has no direct relation to slavery. It is a war for the restoration of the Union under the existing constitution.' Yet under the pressures of conflict it became increasingly difficult to maintain such a limited policy. This was particularly true for those generals in the field who found themselves having to deal with both the free black population and a growing number of slaves who, dislocated by the war, were making their way to Union lines. Whilst the Federal Government prevaricated on the question of arming blacks for a variety of mainly political reasons, the Union generals found themselves faced with a problem that required immediate resolution. Consequently, the first moves towards both arming blacks and freeing slaves during the American Civil War came not from Washington but from the front line.

Initial steps in this direction proved clumsy, though an important precedent as far as the slaves were concerned was set early on in the conflict. In 1861 Benjamin A. Butler, in charge of Fortress Monroe in Virginia, declared that all slaves who escaped to Union lines were 'contraband of war' and refused to uphold the terms of the Fugitive Slave Law, which bound him to return to their owners. Butler's policy did not have much of an impact on attitudes in Washington, but it did reinforce the views of those who felt that slavery was of great military use to the Confederacy and ought to be attacked on those grounds alone. In Missouri in 1861, John C. Fremont, commander of the Department of the West, declared all slaves owned by Confederate sympathisers to be free. Lincoln insisted that Fremont modify his announcement to bring it into line with the 1861 Confiscation Act, which removed slaves only from those actively engaged in hostilities against the Union.

In late March 1862, Major General David Hunter, commander of the Department of the South, emancipated all slaves held in Georgia, South Carolina and Florida, and forced as many escaped male slaves as he could find into military service. Not only was Hunter's announcement rejected by Lincoln, but the aggressive manner in which he went about recruiting blacks for the Union army served only to alienate the very people he was attempting to help. Thomas Wentworth Higginson, the white officer in charge of what became the First South Carolina Volunteers, was in no doubt that the suspicion his troops expressed towards the Federal Government was the natural legacy of bitter distrust bequeathed by the abortive regiment of General Hunter.' More successful were the efforts of Jim Lane in Kansas. A former US Senator and a brigadier general in the Union army, Lane chose simply to ignore the War Department and raised a black regiment, the First Kansas Colored Volunteers, in 1862. This regiment was finally recognised the following year, by which time it had already seen active service against the Confederacy.

Although the War Department sanctioned the recruitment of black troops in August 1862, black regiments were not properly raised until after Lincoln's Emancipation Proclamation of January 1st, 1863. The decision came at a time when the war was not going well for the Union, and coincided with the first draft in the North. In some ways this helped. Racist objections to the arming of blacks could easily, if cynically, be countered on the grounds that it was better that a black soldier die than a white one. As John M. Broomall, Congressman from Pennsylvania noted:

> I have never found the most *shaky* constituent of mine, who, when he was drafted, refused to let the blackest negro in the district go as a substitute for him.

Abraham Lincoln acknowledged such sentiments in his famous letter to James Conkling, written in August, 1863, in which he defended his emancipation decision. 'You say you will not fight to free negroes. Some of them seem willing to fight for you,' Lincoln noted, 'but no matter. . . . I thought that whatever Negroes could be got to do as soldiers leaves just so much less for white soldiers to do, in saving the Union'. He concluded:

> . . . there will be some black men who can remember that, with silent tongue and clenched teeth, and steady eye, and well-poised bayonet, they have helped mankind on to this great consummation; while, I fear, there will be some white ones unable to forget that, with malignant heart, and deceitful speech, they have strove to hinder it.

For many blacks, Lincoln's latter point was the important one. They were initially confident that their acceptance, however reluctantly granted, by the Union army offered them the opportunity both of short-term military glory and longer-term acceptance into the nation as a whole. As Frederick Douglass put it:

> Once let the black man get upon his person the brass letters US, let him get an eagle on his button, and a musket on his shoulder and bullets in his pocket, and there is no power on earth which can deny that he has earned the right to citizenship in the United States.

Corporal James Henry Gooding, a former seaman and volunteer in the Massachusetts 54th, anticipated that 'if the colored man proves to be as good a soldier as it is confidently expected he will, there is a permanent field of employment opened to him, with all the chances of promotion in his favor.' The First Arkansas Colored Regiment had an equally optimistic view of the future. They gleefully marched into battle singing, to the tune of 'John Brown's Body':

> We have done with hoeing cotton, we have done with hoeing corn,
> We are colored Yankee soldiers, now, as sure as you are born;
> When the masters hear us yelling, they'll think it's Gabriel's horn,
> As it went sounding on.

They will have to pay us wages, the
wages of their sin,
They will have to bow their foreheads
to their colored kith and kin,
They will have to give us house-room,
or the roof shall tumble in!
As we go marching on.

Not everyone shared such optimism. One black New Yorker argued that it would be foolish for blacks to heed the Union's call to arms since the race had no reason 'to fight under the flag which gives us no protection.' Initially, this pessimistic view appeared to be the more realistic. The white response to the raising of black regiments was far from positive, and inspired a backlash against the whole idea of emancipation. Notwithstanding racist arguments in favour of blacks rather than whites being killed, most whites did not believe that blacks would make effective soldiers, seeing them as cannon fodder at best. Attitudes began to change only with the battlefield successes of several of the black regiments. Even before its official recognition by the War Department, Jim Lane's black regiment had performed well in Missouri, prompting one journalist to write that it was 'useless to talk any more about negro courage. The men fought like tigers, each and every one of them.' Skirmishes between Thomas Wentworth Higginson's First South Carolina and the rebels, and between Benjamin Butler's Second Louisiana Native Guards and Confederate cavalry and infantry regiments were equally decisive in terms of proving that the black troops could and would fight, but did little to alter the northern public's perception of the black regiments. The first major engagement for those came in the spring of 1863, with an assault on Port Hudson on the Mississippi in Louisiana. The assault itself was misconceived, and the Union army suffered a defeat, but for the black troops who had fought there Port Hudson proved a turning point of sorts. One lieutenant reported that his company had fought bravely, adding 'they are mostly contrabands, and I must say I entertained some fears as to their pluck. But I have none now'. The New York *Times* was similarly impressed:

Those black soldiers had never before been in any severe engagement. They were comparatively raw troops, and were yet subjected to the most awful ordeal that even veterans ever have to

experience—the charging upon fortifications through the crash of belching batteries. The men, white or black, who will not flinch from that will flinch from nothing. It is no longer possible to doubt the bravery and steadiness of the colored race, when rightly led.

If further proof were required that the black soldier had potential, one of the Civil War's most bloody engagements, the battle of Milliken's Bend, fought shortly after the Port Hudson defeat, provided it. Here, too, raw black recruits found themselves facing substantial Confederate forces. In the black units engaged, casualties ran to 35 per cent and for the Ninth Louisiana Infantry alone casualties reached 45 per cent. The cost was high but, as at Port Hudson, white commanders declared themselves impressed with the behaviour under fire of the black troops. Charles A. Dana, the Assistant Secretary of War, concluded that:

The sentiment in regard to the employment of negro troops has been revolutionized by the bravery of the blacks in the recent Battle of Miliken's Bend. Prominent officers, who used in private to sneer at the idea, are now heartily in favor of it.

At the same time as black soldiers were proving their valour on the Mississippi at Port Hudson and Milliken's Bend, the North's most famous black regiment, the Massachusetts 54th, was preparing to set off for its first major campaign and a place in the history books. Fort Wagner, on the northern tip of Morris Island in South Carolina, was the main defence both for Charleston and for Battery Gregg which overlooked the entrance to Charleston Harbour. The taking of the fort would have been a significant prize for the Union forces, enabling them to attack Fort Sumter and hopefully Charleston itself. Originally, the plan had been to use the 54th in a minor supporting role, but its commander, Robert Gould Shaw, recognised the importance of being seen to take an active part in the forthcoming engagement and campaigned vigorously for his regiment to be given a more prominent place in the attack. He was successful, and the 54th received orders to head the attack on the fort on July 18th, 1863.

As with Port Hudson, the attack on Fort Wagner, one of the most heavily defended of the Confederate forts, was doomed to failure, and the Union forces sustained heavy casualties. The Massachusetts 54th lost over half its men, including Shaw who was shot through the heart as he took the parapet of the fort. His troops held the ground he had reached for barely an hour. Yet in the more general battle against racism Fort Wagner, like Port Hudson, was a significant success. The New York *Tribune* reminded its readers that:

If this Massachusetts Fifty-fourth had faltered when its trial came, two hundred thousand colored troops for whom it was a pioneer would never have been put into the field. . . . But it did not falter. It made Fort Wagner such a name to the colored race as Bunker Hill has been for ninety years to the white Yankees. . . . To this Massachusetts 54th was set the stupendous task to convince the white race that colored troops would fight,—and not only that they would fight, but that they could be made, in every sense of the word, soldiers.

Thanks in part to the bravery of the Massachusetts 54th, therefore, by the end of 1863 the Union army had recruited some 50,000 African-Americans—both free blacks and former slaves—to its ranks. By the end of the war this number had risen to around 186,000, of which 134,111 were recruited in the slave states. African-American troops comprised 10 per cent of the total Union fighting force, and some 3,000 of them died on the battlefield plus many more in the prisoner of war camps, if they made it that far. Overall, one third of all African-Americans who fought were casualties of the Civil War.

The propaganda success of the assaults on Port Hudson, Milliken's Bend and Fort Wagner were, however, only part of the story as far as the African-American troops were concerned. The fact that blacks had shown that they could fight in no way diminished the prejudice they experienced in the Union army. Nor did it resolve the crux of the issue which was that the war, for many of the black troops, was in essence a very different conflict from that experienced by the whites. In purely practical terms, the conditions experienced by African-American troops were far inferior to those experienced by some white ones. It is important not to overstate this, however. By the time the black regiments were raised and sent into the field the Civil War had been going on for almost two years. Fresh recruits, therefore, of whatever colour, found themselves facing a rebel army with much more combat experience. At Milliken's Bend, for example, the most experienced officers had been in uniform for less than a month. Even worse, some of the black troops had received only two days of target practice prior to the battle, and in a war where fast reloading was crucial for survival they simply lacked the necessary skill.

The African-American regiments also received a greater proportion of fatigue duty than many of the white regiments, thereby denying them essential fighting experience. The quality of weapons distributed to them was also not always on a par with those the white regiments received, although again it is important to bear in mind that adequate weaponry was a problem for many regiments, both black and white. Medical care for the black regiments was equally inadequate, and a particular problem given the high rate of combat casualties in these regiments. Many of the black troops, being relatively new to the field, had little immunity to the diseases that infected the camps, and the problem was compounded by a white assumption that blacks were not as susceptible to disease as whites. Finding surgeons to work with black troops was also difficult. Again, racism alone does not account for this. By 1863 there was a general shortage of physicians in the Union army, and those that could put up with the rigours of camp life had long ago been snapped up by regiments formed earlier in the war.

Unfortunately, deliberately prejudicial policies compounded the more general problems that the African-American regiments faced after 1863. Most obviously, blacks were never promoted on a par with whites. Benjamin Butler, in mustering in the Louisiana regiments, had created a mixed officer class. Jim Lane in Kansas did likewise, and since he was acting against orders anyway he never troubled himself to defend his actions. However, when Governor Andrew sought to appoint black officers to the Massachusetts 54th and 55th, he was told that white officers only would be accepted. Similarly, when Jim Lane's

Kansas regiments were officially recognised, its black officers were not. In the South, Nathaniel Prentiss Banks, on taking over from Butler, promptly set about removing all the black officers, usually by forcing them to resign. In many cases the argument used to defend such blatant racism was that blacks lacked the necessary literacy skills and knowledge to cope with high command. In many cases, particularly as far as the contraband regiments were concerned, there was an element of truth to the charge. The white officers were no more capable in this regard than the blacks: the only difference was that the white officers were not being put under the microscope to the same extent. By the conclusion of the war only one in 2,000 black troops had achieved officer rank, and these mostly by the indirect route of becoming either chaplains or physicians.

Of all the discriminatory policies to impact on the African-American regiments, however, the most damning related to pay. At the outset there was no indication that the War Department intended to pay black troops less than whites. When Governor Andrew was granted permission to raise the Massachusetts 54th, he was instructed to offer $13 per month, plus rations and clothing, along with a bounty of $50 for signing up and $100 on mustering out. However in June 1863, the War Department decided that black troops were entitled to only $10 per month, of which $3 should be deducted for clothing. The reasoning was that the raising of black regiments came under the Militia Act of 1862, which specified the lower rate of pay on the grounds that it was intended for noncombatants.

The matter prompted an angry backlash from black troops and many of the officers. Governor Andrew, embarrassed at the turn of events, offered to make up the difference out of his own pocket, but the 54th would not let him. There was a principle at stake. As one black volunteer put it:

Now it seems strange to me that we do not receive the same pay and rations as the white soldiers. Do we not fill the same ranks? Do we not cover the same space of ground? Do we not take up the same length of ground in a graveyard that others do? The ball does not miss the black man and strike the white, nor the white and strike the black.

Corporal John B. Payne, of the Massachusetts 55th, declared his unwillingness 'to fight for anything less than the white man fights for'. The issue of pay went beyond prejudice alone. It represented the crux of the problem for those black regiments who fought in the Civil War, and threw into sharp focus many of the inconsistencies and contradictions that lay at the heart of Union war aims. The Union had, from the outset, been faced with two distinct yet linked problems: the role of the free black and the future of the slave. Equality and emancipation were not synonymous, yet one could not be addressed without affecting the other. The question over the citizenship right of free northern blacks went hand in hand with the larger and more troubling question of slavery—for many the root cause of the conflict. Northern blacks were well aware of this and, unlike northern whites, could not and would not avoid the wider implication of the conflict. Many blacks saw the Civil War as a battle for emancipation long before it became apparent that Lincoln shared this view and far ahead of a northern public who regarded it as a war for the restoration of the Union as it had been, with slavery intact. Frederick Douglass, for one, was of the opinion that the future of the American Republican experiment itself rested on the triumph of the black soldier and the freed slave. For Douglass, the evil of slavery had corrupted the white man as much as it had degraded the slave, and the Civil War was an opportunity not just to end the institution but to rededicate the nation to the principles set out in the Declaration of Independence. Freedom for both white and black depended not just on a Union victory but on complete reassessment of the national ideal. As he summed it up to a Boston audience in 1862:

My friends, the destiny of the colored American, however this mighty war shall terminate, is the destiny of America. We shall never leave you. The allotments of Providence seem to make the black man of America the open book out of which the American people are to learn lessons of wisdom, power, and goodness—more sublime and glorious than any yet attained by the nations of the old or the new world. Over the bleeding back of the American bondsman we shall learn mercy. In the very extreme difference of color and feature of the negro and the Anglo-Saxon, shall be learned the highest ideas of sacredness of man and the fullness and protection of human brotherhood.

Ultimately, the problem facing both African-American soldiers and their spokesmen in the North was that their vision of the meaning of the Civil War clashed with that of the majority of whites. For blacks, the Civil War offered an opportunity not just to end slavery, but to redefine American national ideals. Their determination to fight in the face of hostility and prejudice left their dedication to these ideals in no doubt whatsoever. In this regard, their experience of the Civil War gave them a far more expansive, optimistic and demanding vision of the nation's future than it did many whites. As George Stephens of the Massachusetts 54th noted 'this land must be consecrated to freedom, and we are today the only class of people in the country who are earnestly on the side of freedom'. This was not a message that whites wished to hear.

Ultimately, the nation as a whole chose to ignore both the sacrifice of the black regiments and the implications of their involvement in America's greatest national crisis. As North and South came together over an increasingly selective interpretation of what the Civil War had been about, the opportunity to reconstruct the nation on a new basis of equality was thrown away. On Memorial Day 1871, speaking at the Tomb of the Unknown Soldier at Arlington, Frederick Douglass lamented the call 'in the name of patriotism to forget the merits of this fearful struggle, and to remember with equal admiration those who struck at the nation's life, and those who struck to save it.' In the end, the need to find some common ground between North and South encouraged the growth of a patriotism that rejected the pride of those black troops who had fought and died for the nation.

On May 31st, 1997, a hundred years after the Saint-Gaudens monument was first unveiled, a re-dedication ceremony was held at the site. The day included an historical reenactment of Shaw's troops leaving for the South and a speech by General Colin Powell in which he drew parallels between the Union's decision to raise black regiments during the Civil War and the contemporary army's leading role in the fight for racial equality in America today. Despite Powell's words, the many thousands of books written on the American Civil War to date and the cinematic success of the Hollywood film about the Massachusetts 54th, *Glory,* the war continues to be regarded by many as a white man's war. The overt racism of 1897 has dissipated, yet the significance of the black soldier in America's bloodiest conflict continues to be downplayed.

FOR FURTHER READING:

Ira Berlin, et al., *Slaves No More: Three Essays on Emancipation and the Civil War* (Cambridge University Press, 1992); Joseph T. Glatthaar, *Forged in Battle: The Civil War Alliance of Black Soldiers and White Officers* (Penguin/Meridian Books, 1991); Hondon B. Hargrove, *Black Union Soldiers in the Civil War* (McFarland, 1988); James G. Hollandsworth, Jr., *The Louisiana Native Guards: The Black Military Experience During the Civil War* (Louisiana State University Press, 1995); Ervin L. Jordan, Jr., *Black Confederates and Afro-Yankees in Civil War Virginia* (University Press of Virginia, 1995); Edwin S. Redkey (ed.), *A Grand Army of Black Men: Letters from African-American Soldiers in the Union Army, 1861–1865* (Cambridge University Press, 1992).

***Susan-Mary Grant** is a lecturer in history at the University of Newcastle upon Tyne. She is the author of* The American Civil War *(UCL Press, 1999).*

The Struggle for Black Freedom before Emancipation

Wayne K. Durrill

Wayne K. Durrill teaches American history at the University of Cincinnati.

The Civil War has recently become a hot ticket. The movie, *Glory,* the PBS series "The Civil War" by Ken Burns, and James McPherson's recent Pulitzer Prize-winning account of the conflict have all dramatized the continuing relevance of the war as a defining experience for a people and a nation. These stories, however, have often neglected an important part of that defining experience: the role of black people in securing their own emancipation. Most accounts of war date emancipation from Lincoln's famous proclamation and the military campaigns that followed. Even *Glory,* which traces the heroic deeds of black soldiers from Massachusetts, portrays slaves in the lowcountry of South Carolina as incompetent and ineffectual, persons who simply waited for Northern free black liberators to march South and rescue them from bondage.

However, even this relatively enlightened view of the role of black people in their own emancipation is historically inaccurate. As Ira Berlin and his colleagues have shown in their monumental multi-volume series, *Freedom: A Documentary History of Emancipation,* slaves throughout the South squeezed freedom in dribs and drabs from their own local situation as opportunities arose in wartime. In Kentucky, where blacks re-mained in bondage until after the Civil War, slaves fled to Tennessee where they could join the Union army as laborers and later as soldiers, and thereby free themselves and sometimes their families. Others stayed home, testing the limits of servitude in a volatile and dangerous situation, always with an eye toward establishing claims to property and place, as well as to their own humanity. These black struggles for freedom within slavery are sometimes difficult to visualize. Indeed, they seem to be a contradiction in terms. Yet they did occur, and with an intensity and regularity that historians have only just begun to uncover. As an example of such struggle, let us examine the story of how one group of North Carolina slaves redefined the rules of slavery in the crisis of war so as to create for themselves a larger space in which to carry on a life separate from their white masters.

In September of 1861, after the fall of federal forces off Hatteras Island on North Carolina's Outer Banks, Major General John Wool, Union commander of the island, reported that "negro slaves" were "almost daily arriving at this post from the interior." They came in small groups, many traveling over one hundred miles from the counties bordering the Albemarle Sound. At Columbia, on the eastern edge of the Sound and about five miles from William Pettigrew's plantation, a certain planter had brought his slaves to town for "safe-keeping." The militia had already mustered there and the town had a jail if he needed it. But shortly after their arrival, thirteen of the man's slaves quietly stole a boat and sailed for Hatteras, setting in motion a chain of events that quickly spread through counties all around the Sound. One planter complained that news of the escape had spread among slaves in the area, and he reasoned, "We may look for others to leave soon." In response, slave owners throughout the Sound region began to move to the up-country, taking with them as many of their slaves as they could support on the land available to them.

William Pettigrew, one of the richest planters in Washington County, North Carolina, grasped the crisis early on and resolved to remove his slaves before planting began the following spring. On 4 March 1862, the planter arranged for twenty-five Confederate cavalrymen to descend upon Magnolia plantation. The move took the slaves by surprise, and all were captured. That day, men, women, and children were loaded onto wagons guarded by armed troopers, and began a long journey upcountry. After a nine-day forced march, Pettigrew and the slaves came to Haywood, a small crossroads community about fifty miles west of Raleigh where the planter had located a small farm for sale. He purchased the farm as his base camp in the

From *OAH Magazine of History* Vol. 8, No. 1, Fall 1993, pp. 7-10. Adapted from *War of Another Kind: A Southern Community in the Great Rebellion* by Wayne K. Durrill. © 1990 Oxford University Press, Inc. Reprinted by permission.

upcountry, but it was too small to support any but a handful of his slaves. The others he drove on foot fifty miles further west where he leased out eighty-seven of them in nineteen groups to fifteen different planters.

The exchange of slaves for promissory notes, however, signified more than simply a purchase of labor. It included a broader transfer of power from one planter to another. For this reason, William Pettigrew insisted that persons who hired his slaves provide them with certain goods in the coming year, mostly food, clothing, and shoes. The planter might have provided the goods himself and factored the cost into his asking price. But he did not. Instead, he included in the contract detailed directions specifying what each slave should receive. In doing so, Pettigrew ensured that his slaves' new master would become the sole source of some crucial goods for them, thus giving the new master enormous leverage over the hired-out slaves. By his actions, Pettigrew produced not merely new employers for his slaves, but new masters.

Such contracts, however, did not settle all questions of a planter's dominance and a slave's submission in the upcountry. Planters and slaves, in fact, had always created their own mutual expectations, in part by contesting the rules by which they lived. Before the war, this had not been a conflict among equals, to be sure. Instead, the struggle between planter and slave presumed an unequal resolution; the master would rule and the slave submit. But in 1862, the relations between planters and slaves had changed dramatically, even in the upcountry. Many of the Pettigrew slaves worked for new masters who might or might not be skilled in managing human property. Would these men have the wherewithal to nail the meat-house door shut, call in the slave patrol, or face down a personal challenge? No one knew. But William Pettigrew's slaves were determined to find out.

Mary Jane, for example, decided early on to see just what kind of master she had been assigned. William Pettigrew had hired her out as a cook to a planter named George Foushee, along with a slave named Dick Lake, his wife

Jenny, and their five children. Mary Jane complained "mostly of colick" during her first three weeks at Foushee's place. In that period, she rendered "very little service" in the planter's view. According to Foushee, "She don't seem to be very bad off, just sick enough to keep her from work." The planter further wondered if "a good deal of it is deception." To find out, Foushee asked Dick Lake about her, and the slave's answer confirmed the planter's suspicions. According to Lake, Mary Jane had "never done much the year she was in a family way." Mary Jane had a history of probing the limits of her master's power.

Similarly, Jenny took advantage of the change of masters to renew work rules she had known at Magnolia plantation. She had just borne a child and informed Foushee that she had "never been required to do any work until her child was eight weeks old." She also objected to Foushee's plan to put her to work in the fields. At Magnolia she always had labored as a cook and now complained that she "could not work out."

When members of the slave family initiated the same contest that took place on the Foushee plantation, Caveness could not comprehend their actions for what they were.

Mary Jane, Jenny, and their fellow slaves did not wish simply to avoid work by refusing to labor for their masters. Most, in fact, worked steadily and with a will. In late March, a friend of William Pettigrew's who saw some of the planter's slaves "most every Sunday" in church, reported them at work and "well satisfied" with their new circumstances. Therefore, the action taken by Mary Jane and Jenny must be inter-

preted as having some more specific purpose. Mary Jane had succeeded in making pregnancy a privileged status at their old plantation. Here, she renewed the rule by making a public event of her refusal to work while pregnant. Similarly, she served notice upon George Foushee that Pettigrew slaves could not be required to work when ill, no matter how slight the planter thought evidence of any malady appeared. Jenny, for her part, sought to reinforce two rules. The first would give women a special status when pregnant. The second would renew a longstanding division between housework and fieldwork that served as the basis for some very important and very sharp distinctions among the Pettigrew slaves themselves.

George Foushee understood all of this on a practical level. Doubtless, he could never admit publicly, or perhaps even to himself, that Mary Jane and Jenny's actions constituted a challenge to the local rules that governed relations between masters and slaves. But Foushee did have the presence of mind to remain calm. He reported by letter to William Pettigrew the two slaves' failure to work diligently. But Foushee did not propose that either he or Pettigrew take any action. The planter concluded his account of Mary Jane's behavior by saying simply, "I hope she will be better hereafter."

Mary Jane did become better. After she had made her point, she returned to work as usual. Other planters, however, did not fully appreciate the give-and-take that an exercise of a master's power required, particularly when the power of masters had been so undermined by Union military activity on the North Carolina coast. Or perhaps some planters sensed in small challenges larger issues that George Foushee had overlooked.

A. E. Caveness is a case in point. Caveness had hired one slave family from William Pettigrew—Jack, his pregnant wife, Venus, and their six young children. The children must have been young because the entire family hired out for twenty-five dollars, less than the cost of hiring a single prime male field hand. Caveness got a good deal more than he bargained for, however, when he paid his pittance to William Pettigrew. When members of the slave family initiated the same contest that took place on the Foushee plantation, Caveness could not comprehend their actions for what they were. In his view, the slaves attempted to "over-run" him. Finally, in a fit of ill-temper, the planter whipped the oldest child, a gal named Sarah, for what he considered her "laziness and disobedience."

The girl's parents objected violently to this. They "made a great ado about it," according to one account, so much so that Caveness felt compelled to "take Venus in hand." At that point, Venus "started off" down the plantation road and, as she walked, turned to the planter and told him off. What exactly she uttered that day remained a matter of dispute. Caveness claimed that she shouted, I am "going to the Yankees." Doubtless, she had no such intention—if she even spoke these words. Venus and her family had just made the nine-day trek from the coast on foot. She well knew that she needed food and extra clothing for such a journey, that Confederate troops blanketed eastern North Carolina and would demand a pass from her, and that William Pettigrew would hire a slave catcher to find her long before she reached federal lines. Later, Venus's husband claimed that she had said no such thing. By the slave's account, Venus told Caveness that she intended to walk to the plantation of William Campbell, Pettigrew's friend, presumably to lodge a complaint against her new master for his actions. Whatever the exact words, Venus had made her point in producing this small drama—pubicly and loudly. She feared no man, planter or otherwise, and if she chose to oppose that man, she would make her claim a matter of public debate.

Caveness "ordered her to come back," but Venus refused and continued walking down the road. The planter then got his whip and followed her. Some distance from the house, he finally caught up with her. Again, Caveness commanded Venus to return to the plantation. Once more, the slave refused and voiced her intention to leave. At that point, the planter lost all patience and good sense. Caveness began to whip Venus, at which time Jack, who evidently had followed the two, "got in between them." The planter then "fell to

work on Jack, and drove both slaves back to the house."

But Venus had succeeded in her purpose even as she and her husband bore the lashes of the planter's whip. Caveness complained that "the fuss might have been heard all over the neighborhood." If he hoped to exercise any power over Pettigrew's slaves, Caveness now would have to submit to the scrutiny of his neighbors, both black and white. Each side in this conflict would mobilize its supporters. The battle between master and slave over who would rule the family, and particularly the children of Venus and Jack, became a public controversy.

In one sense, the customary rights of slaves acting within the rules of paternalism had been renewed. Yet, there was more to the story than a restoration of peaceable relations between masters and slaves.

The next day, Caveness traveled to William Campbell's plantation, where he hoped to make his case to the county's planters. To Campbell, he gave an account of the basic facts in the matter. But Caveness made no attempt to justify his actions. Instead he simply announced a solution. He demanded that Campbell, who had been charged with managing William Pettigrew's interest in Chatham and Moore counties, write to the slaves' owner seeking "permission to conquer them." If Pettigrew refused to grant him such authority, Caveness demanded that their master "take them away." By this ultimatum, Caveness cast the conflict in terms of fundamental is-

sues—in this case, the interest of planters in dominating their slaves. Essentially, Caveness argued that all planters must stand with him, no matter what the specifics of this case, in order to preserve their power over slaves as a whole.

Meanwhile, Venus and Jack also made their opinions known throughout the neighborhood. The couple communicated their interpretation of the conflict to slaves belonging to William Campbell who, in turn, approached their master after Caveness returned home. They told Campbell that Caveness had "not been good "to Pettigrew's slaves. They argued that Caveness was "a man of bad temper," and he acted "very ill" to Jack and his family. In particular Campbell's slaves charged that Caveness had refused to give Jack and his family "enough to eat," even though he had "plenty of meat and bread" to sell to other persons in the neighborhood.

During the next two weeks, Jack and Venus appealed directly to William Campbell. When Campbell visited the family, Jack accused Caveness of abusing them "without any just cause." To support the charge, the slave pointed out that recently Caveness had "knocked Edith [his youngest child] down with a handspike." The blow cut the little girl "severely on the head." And "since the first difficulty with Venus," Caveness had "knocked [her also] down with a chair." That piece of viciousness caused Venus to miscarry. On 10 June, she was reported "very bad off." Moreover, after he struck Venus, Caveness "threatened to kill her if she did not get up and go to work," according to Jack's account.

Jack therefore requested that Campbell write to William Pettigrew in order to give the planter the slaves' version of events. In the letter, Jack argued that he and his family had "worked harder" that spring than they had "ever worked in their lives," but Caveness could not be satisfied. Therefore, he implored William Pettigrew to remove them from Caveness's plantation. Jack declared his family "willing to live anywhere," even "on half feed," as long as they would "not be abused." We "did not want to put you to any trouble," Jack told his master, "but we can not stand it."

In the end, Jack and his wife prevailed. Their story had a ring of truth that even Caveness himself made no attempt to deny. Moreover, Caveness's poor reputation in the area precluded his attempt to mobilize planter opinion in his cause. Campbell considered Caveness "very hard to please" and "a very passionate man." Finally, Caveness did not help his own case when he admitted to Campbell that if he had carried his gun along, he would have "killed some of them."

But all of this might have come to nothing if Venus had not made the dispute a public event. By mobilizing local opinion, both black and white, Jack and Venus forged a means by which the Pettigrew slaves could shape their own destiny, at least in some small part. William Campbell considered his slave's version of events "only negro news" and therefore, "only to be used as such." Yet, he recommended to William Pettigrew that Jack and his family be removed from Caveness' plantation to a place where they would be "well cared for." "If Caveness is not willing to keep them and treat them humanely as other negroes are treated in this part of the country," wrote Campbell, "I should take them away."

In one sense, the customary rights of slaves acting within the rules of paternalism had been renewed. Yet, there was more to the story than a restoration of peaceable relations between masters and slaves. The abuse by Caveness of Venus and her children provided an unprecedented opportunity to challenge a slaveholder. Caveness had made certain guarantees to Pettigrew—physical safety and an adequate subsistence for the slaves—that he failed to fulfill. And ironically, by insisting on Pettigrew's rights in his property, Venus advanced her own claim as a human being. Indeed, she used those double-edged claims to turn Caveness's own class against him; she forced Pettigrew and others to recognize not only her right to safety and subsistence but also her right to be heard and recognized as a person. In doing so, Venus and Jack and all the other Pettigrew slaves participated in a much larger defining moment, the self-emancipation of America's slaves in the crucible of the Civil War.

Lee's Greatest Victory

During three days in May 1863, the Confederate leader took astonishing risks to win one of the most skillfully conducted battles in history. But the cost turned out to be too steep.

by Robert K. Krick

The ability of Robert E. Lee and Thomas J. ("Stonewall") Jackson never showed itself more vividly than during three days of battle in May 1863 around a rustic crossroads called Chancellorsville. At the battle's denouement, which might be considered the highest tide of the Confederacy, the two Virginians capped a reversal of fortunes as dramatic as any recorded in more than three centuries of American military affairs.

Joseph Hooker had stolen a march on Lee as completely as anyone did during the entire war.

During the last day of April the Federal commander Joseph Hooker had stolen a march on Lee as completely as anyone did during the entire war. In an amazing strategic initiative Hooker took his army far around Lee's left, across two rivers, and into an admirable position around Chancellorsville. His fellow general George G. Meade, a saturnine man and no admirer of Joseph Hooker when in the sunniest of moods, exclaimed jubilantly on April 30: "Hurrah for old Joe! We're on Lee's flank and he doesn't know it."

The army with which Joe Hooker stole his march on Lee was a tough, veteran aggregation that had suffered from ill use at the hands of a series of inadequate leaders. Most recently Ambrose E. Burnside had butchered more than twelve thousand of his brave men in a hopeless attack near Fredericksburg the preceding December. Earlier the Army of the Potomac had endured mishandling from a boastful bully named John Pope, whose tenure in command was numbered in days, not in months, and the brilliant but timid George B. McClellan had led the same regiments to the brink of victory—but never quite over the threshold—on famous fields in Virginia and Maryland.

General Hooker's rise to high rank during the war grew from a blend of training at West Point and experience in Mexico, with more than a tincture of political maneuvering. Bravery under fire in the 1862 campaigns won the general a name for valor and the nickname Fight-ing Joe. (According to some accounts the catchy name was coined by accident when two newspaper headlines—THE FIGHTING and JOE HOOKER—overlapped in some fashion.) Hooker had shamelessly schemed against Burnside, motivated in part by a wholesome distaste for Burnside's ineptitude but also by a powerful degree of personal ambition.

Abraham Lincoln concluded in January 1863 that Burnside must go and reluctantly identified Hooker as the officer to inherit the mantle. In a patient and appropriately famous letter the President bluntly informed Hooker that he was appointing him despite the "great wrong to the country" inherent in his behavior toward Burnside. "I have heard, in such way as to believe it," Lincoln continued, "of your recently saying that both the Army and the Government needed a Dictator. Of course it was not for this, but in spite of it, that I have given you the command. Only those generals who gain success, can set up dictators. What I now ask of you is military success, and I will risk the dictatorship."

During the three months between Hooker's appointment and the onset of the campaigning season, Lincoln must have been very much gratified by the accomplishments of his

From *American Heritage*, March 1990, pp. 66-79. © 1990 by Forbes, Inc. Reprinted by permission of *American Heritage* magazine, a division of Forbes, Inc.

new commander. A contemporary wrote that Hooker when young was a "very expert" baseball player, who could "take a ball from almost in front of the bat, so eager, active and dexterous were his movements." When applied to military administration, that same controlled zeal made the Army of the Potomac a much improved military implement. Joe Hooker ironed ineptitude and indolence out of the medical services, flogged quartermaster and commissary functions into a fine pitch of efficiency, revitalized the cavalry arm, and inaugurated an intelligence-gathering system far ahead of its time in that staff-poor era. The soldiers noticed the changes and took heart from them.

The men also relished their new commander's reputation as a profane, hard-drinking sort of fellow. "Our leader is Joe Hooker, he takes his whiskey strong," they sang in admiration of one of the general's two most widely mooted social traits. The other rumored trait resulted in a persistent tradition that remains in circulation to this day. General Hooker's campaign to tighten up the Army of the Potomac extended to controlling the prostitution that flourished on its fringes. Supposedly the general's name somehow became an appellation for the quarry of the overworked provost detachments enforcing his order. Joe Hooker's own reputation as a womanizer fed the story conveniently. Firm evidence that the etymology of the word hooker antedates 1863 by more than a decade has done little to check the legend.

Hooker's ranking subordinates by and large did not share the enthusiasm of the men in the ranks. The officer corps of the Old Army was a generally conservative body, both politically and morally. One immediate subordinate, the intensely pious O. O. Howard, doubtless felt particularly uneasy about Hooker, and Hooker reciprocated. Soon after the war he told an interviewer that Howard was "a good deal more" qualified to "command a prayer meeting" than an army corps. "He was always a woman among troops," said Hooker. "If he was not born in petticoats, he ought to have been, and ought to wear them. He was always taken up with Sunday Schools and the temperance cause."

Other corps commanders of note included George G. Meade and Daniel E. Sickles. General Meade, the snappish patrician who was destined to replace Hooker, seems in retrospect the most capable man who wore Union general's stars in the war's Eastern theater. Dan Sickles, by contrast, was a bawdy, rambunctious adventurer. Three years before Chancellorsville he escaped conviction for the public murder of his wife's lover on the then novel ground of temporary insanity. After the war he served as intermittent paramour to the queen of Spain.

Federal operations at Chancellorsville suffered dramatically from two absences. Much of Hooker's cavalry spent the crucial days on a largely irrelevant raid, leaving the main army bereft of its essential screening-and-reconnaissance function. Worse, the army's enormously capable chief of artillery, Henry J. Hunt, was off in a rear area, where Hooker had consigned him after the two had quarreled.

The men of the Army of Northern Virginia benefited from any number of subjective advantages over their familiar foemen of the Army of the Potomac, but no Southerner could help worrying over the apparent disparity of force. Although no one knew enemy strengths with precision—and, in fact, often neither side could firmly establish its own strength—Federals north of the Rappahannock clearly had a vast preponderance in numbers. The actual figures approximated 130,000 against 60,000.

The Northern army brought seven corps to the field of Chancellorsville. The Confederates countered with two, and one of the two was at less than one-half of its strength. The missing divisions had gone southeastward to the vicinity of Suffolk, Virginia, in quest of the foodstuffs that already dwindled at an alarming rate. The question now was whether the agrarian South could feed its armies on its own soil.

The two supporting arms that came up short for Hooker at Chancellorsville never looked better on Lee's side of the line than they did in that spring of 1863. The colorful Southern cavalry general James E. B. Stuart, universally called Jeb after his initials, stood at the height of his personal and professional powers,

tirelessly alert and active and energetic. As for the Southern artillery, it continued to labor under tremendous disadvantages in weaponry and ammunition but during the past winter had revolutionized its tactics by converting to a battalion system. Since the first whiff of gunpowder, cannon had suffered from the tendency of infantry officers to misuse the big guns simply as larger infantry weapons. In 1861 batteries assigned to brigades fought under infantry direction, often from positions at either end of the line. High ground, low ground, heavy enemy pressure, or no enemy pressure, it was all the same: Put the guns with the infantry. But now Confederate artillery would move and fight in clusters, usually of at least four four-gun batteries, and the higher-ranking artillerymen commanding these larger clusters would enjoy some degree of autonomy. Some of the South's brightest and best young men rode at the head of the reorganized guns.

Federal horsemen attempted to open the campaign that led to the Battle of Chancellorsville at the end of the second week in April. Gen. George Stoneman, commanding Hooker's cavalry, was to take the greater part of the available mounted force and cross the Rappahannock far upstream northwest of Fredericksburg, Virginia. The horse soldiers, Hooker hoped, would ricochet with deadly effect through Confederate rear areas, freeing Federal prisoners, tearing up railroads, breaking an aqueduct on the James River, and forcing a frightened Lee to fall back from Fredericksburg. In the event, heavy rains sluiced the bottoms out of Virginia's clay roads, and the raiding force did not cross the Rappahannock until April 29, after a substantial portion of Hooker's infantry had done so. Still, it is hard to avoid blaming the delay as much on Stoneman as on uncooperative weather.

Once launched, the cavalry raid caromed almost aimlessly about central Virginia, causing some localized discomfort but achieving not a thing of real military worth. Stuart detached just enough regiments to contain the raid within certain wide limits, harassing its rear and flanks and gathering in stragglers. One of the interesting reflections modern students draw from the Chancellorsville campaign is that the Federal cavalry raid, prudently checked by just the right number of Confederates, presaged in mirror image the cavalry situation a few weeks later at Gettysburg. There Stuart wasted his substance in a meaningless raid while his army fought blindly, and the Federals reacted prudently. It was as though the Federals had gone to school at Chancellorsville on the apt use of the mounted arm, with Stuart as teacher.

In the last two days of April, Hooker brought to a successful conclusion the huge turning maneuver that placed the center of his flanking element at the country crossroads of Chancellorsville. That polysyllabic name, whose ending suggests a busy settlement, actually belonged to a single building. The Chancellor kin who built the heart of the structure late in the eighteenth century expanded it into a wayside inn opened in 1815. By 1860 two additions had swelled the building into a really sizable structure, but dwindling traffic on the roads that met in the yard had reduced its function to that of a one-family residence. The Chancellors called their home Chancellorsville in the same fashion that other Southern homes were called Mount Vernon or Belle Hill. No one else lived within a half-mile of the crossroads, and only a few within several miles.

An environmental feature that contributed to Chancellorsville's meager dimensions also levied a heavy impact on military operations nearby. The land lay largely desolate under the dense, scrubby growth of a region known as the Wilderness of Spotsylvania. About seventy square miles of the Wilderness sprawled along the south bank of the Rapidan and Rappahannock rivers, stretching about three miles farther south than Chancellorsville and about two miles farther east. A numerically superior army ensnarled in those thickets, and confined to easy maneuver only on the few poor roads, would lose much of its advantage.

Joe Hooker pushed the head of his mighty army eastward to the edge of the Wilderness early on Friday, May 1, 1863. About three miles from the Chancellorsville crossroads the Federals came face-to-face with a commanding wrinkle of the earth's surface, atop which stood a little wooden Baptist church bearing the name of Zoan. The Zoan Church ridge represented about as succulent a military prize as Joe Hooker could have found just then in his zone of operations. It was high ground (none higher to the east, short of Europe); it straddled a key road; and most important, it rose on open ground just east of the entangling tendrils of the Wilderness.

Confederates on top of the prize ridge had been feverishly digging earthworks overnight on the orders of the division commander Richard H. Anderson. Despite the trenches, Hooker could have dislodged Anderson's relative handful of men and occupied Zoan Church without much exertion. Perhaps he would have, had not Stonewall Jackson ridden into the uncertain tableau and dominated the unfolding action with his force of personality. Stonewall ordered Anderson's men to pack their entrenching equipment and attack. Anderson left no account of his reaction, but he must have wondered how he and Jackson and a few assorted regiments could accomplish much.

As Jackson began pressing against the Northerners lapping around the western base of the ridge, he used two critically important parallel roads. The old Orange Turnpike came out of Fredericksburg past Zoan, through Spotsylvania County, and then on to Orange County and Orange Courthouse. About a decade before the Civil War local entrepreneurs had undertaken to supplant that century-old thoroughfare with a toll road paved on one of its lanes with planks. Elsewhere in the vicinity men of vision were putting their money into railroads; but trains and their trappings required vast capital outlay, and the plank-road people reasoned that everyone owned wheeled wagons already.

The brand-new Orange Plank Road proved to be a wretched idea economically, but in May 1863 it drew troops of both sides like a magnet because it formed a second usable corridor through the Wilderness. Hooker had moved east

on both the Turnpike and the Plank Road, which near Zoan Church ran generally parallel to and a mile or so south of the older right-of-way. As the morning wore on, Confederates pushed west against both heads of Hooker's army on the two roads.

Hooker had collapsed within himself, and now he began inexorably pulling his mighty army down with him.

Jackson, soon joined by Lee in person, superintended an almost chaotic blend of Confederate regiments and brigades in the advance. Southern units arriving from various points funneled off into the Turnpike or the Plank Road at Jackson's whim and in response to unfolding exigencies, without much regard for command and control at levels below the corps commander in person. Their élan and their leader's determination were steadily reclaiming the ground of the earlier Federal advance when yet another transportation corridor swung the action entirely into the Confederate column.

Just before the war more prescient investors had founded and funded a railroad to run from Fredericksburg out to Orange and into fertile Piedmont Virginia. By the time the conflict halted work, the route had been surveyed and the line graded. The level stretch of cuts and fills and grades lay uncluttered by even the first stringers or rails, but it constituted a convenient third passage through the Wilderness. The unfinished railroad ran westward, parallel to the two wagon roads and about a mile south of the Plank Road. Gen. A. R. ("Rans") Wright's brigade, three regiments and a battalion of infantry from Georgia, sliced ahead along that convenient conduit and forced a reorientation of the

Federal line by ninety degrees. Contending lines that had stretched for miles from north to south readjusted to Wright's lunge. Hooker's right swung up away from Wright and left the Federals at the end of the first day of battle (and the first day of May) arrayed in a huge, irregular, shallow V. The apex of the broad V lay at or near Chancellorsville while one arm ran northeast toward the river and the other sprawled west toward Wilderness Church. (See map.)

Hooker hoped halting his advance would "embolden the enemy to attack him." His wish came true.

Before Jackson and Wright buffeted his right, Hooker himself had squandered a wonderful opportunity on his left. The V Corps of the Army of the Potomac, ably led by Meade, began May 1 by moving steadily eastward along the River Road. This fourth east-west route curled far north of the Turnpike and the Plank Road and led eventually past Banks Ford on the river into Fredericksburg. Meade moved vigorously ahead until his skirmishes reached the vicinity of Mott's Run, within hailing distance of Banks Ford. Federals holding the southern mouth of that ford would serve a number of highly desirable ends. By that hour, however, Joe Hooker had recoiled from the presence of the legendary Stonewall Jackson with such abruptness that he sought no opportunities, only shelter. Hooker had collapsed within himself, and now he began inexorably pulling his mighty and well-tempered army down with him.

General Hooker dished out bravado loudly and often during the Chancellorsville campaign, but his boasts seem in retrospect to have been feeble attempts to brace up his own wavering spirits. On

the evening before his advance of May 1, Hooker drummed out a staccato general order assuring his men "that the operations of the last three days have determined that our enemy must either ingloriously fly or come out from behind his defenses and give us battle on our own ground, where certain destruction awaits him." There can be little doubt that Hooker really meant that. Lee surely would react to Hooker's clever and successful movement to Chancellorsville, and to the Federal cavalry roaming in his rear, by sidling south away from the unhappy combination facing him. Good ground on the North Anna River would allow the Confederates a chance to regroup and start over. Even after a century and a quarter it is difficult to come to grips with Lee's daring choice. At the time Hooker clearly was flabbergasted.

With a difficult May 1 behind him, Hooker blustered anew. "It's all right . . . I've got Lee just where I want him," the Federal commander insisted to an incredulous subordinate. At headquarters Hooker declared, "The rebel army is now the legitimate property of the Army of the Potomac." To another audience he said, "The enemy is in my power, and God Almighty cannot deprive me of them." And he finally summarized his professed contentment in a written circular to his corps commanders. "The major general commanding trusts," he wrote incautiously, "that a suspension in the attack to-day will embolden the enemy to attack him." The first three boasts proved to be empty, but Hooker's written wish came true with a vengeance.

Across the lines that evening of May 1 the Confederate commanders weighed the situation somewhat more judiciously. Just about a mile from Hooker's headquarters at Chancellorsville, Lee and Jackson crouched together over a small fire on seats improvised from abandoned U.S. cracker boxes. R. E. Lee, who had ridden up toward the river on his right in a personal reconnaissance during the afternoon, told Jackson that poor roads, steeply cut stream beds, and Federals dense on the ground combined to deny the Confederates any opportunity there.

The two men sent their respective engineer officers on a moonlit scout directly toward the enemy center at Chancellorsville. T. M. R. Talcott of Lee's staff later wrote vividly of that tense experience. His companion, J. Keith Boswell of Jackson's staff, had no chance to record his impressions; Boswell fell dead from a volley that struck him as he rode at Stonewall's side a few hours later. The two capable young men came back convinced that the Federal center offered no opening whatsoever for an assault.

Jackson had a last quiet word with his chief, then rode away. The two men never saw each other again.

Other young men scouting through the darkness of the Wilderness sent back reports through the night that gradually suggested a way to get at Hooker. It would be horribly risky under the circumstances, but perhaps Lee and Jackson might be able to snake a column westward all the way across the enemy's front, around his right, and clear up behind him. Stonewall's favorite preacher, Beverly Tucker Lacy, knew some of the ground in the western reaches of the Wilderness because his brother lived there. Charles Beverly Wellford, a veteran of the army and now running the family iron furnace just down the road, knew more of the ground. Catharine Furnace (named for the matriarch of the Wellford clan) burned charcoal in enormous volume and owned thousands of acres nearby from which to harvest charcoal wood. Jackson's mapmaker Jedediah Hotchkiss, a converted New York Yankee now as zealously Southern as any native, wandered the woods roads with Wellford and Lacy and came back

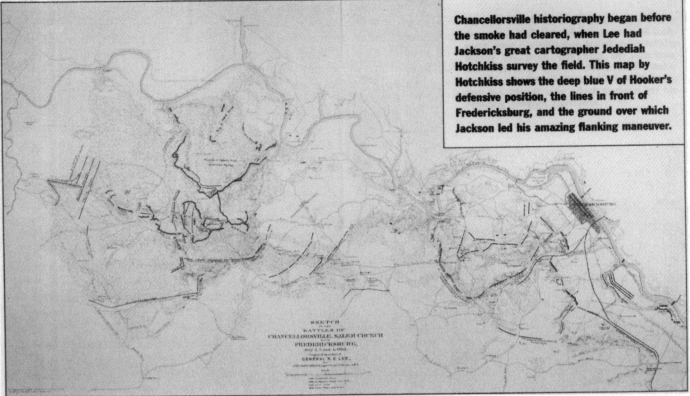

Chancellorsville historiography began before the smoke had cleared, when Lee had Jackson's great cartographer Jedediah Hotchkiss survey the field. This map by Hotchkiss shows the deep blue V of Hooker's defensive position, the lines in front of Fredericksburg, and the ground over which Jackson led his amazing flanking maneuver.

MAP DIVISION, NEW YORK PUBLIC LIBRARY

with some sketches. Jeb Stuart sent cavalry in the same direction under General Lee's boisterous twenty-seven-year-old nephew Fitzhugh Lee.

Very early on May 2 Lee reached his decision. Jackson would take two-thirds of the already heavily outnumbered Army of Northern Virginia and disappear on a daylong march over the horizon. With startling nonchalance the two commanders agreed that Lee would stand firm and act belligerent with no more than seventeen thousand men at his back while Jackson ventured far out on a limb with twice that many troops. An attack by Hooker of even moderate earnestness would simply destroy the Confederate army.

A rough pencil sketch of the roads showed that the desperate gamble might have a chance. Lee and Jackson and others pored over the map. At one point the army commander carefully arranged a handful of broomstraws on the edge of a box and then, by way of example to Jackson, swept them helter-skelter onto the ground. Jackson had a last quiet word with his chief, then rode away. R.

E. Lee and Stonewall Jackson never met again.

Lee at once set out upon the delicate mission of beguiling his opposite number. The tactical dogma of the day held that one or at most two companies of the ten that made up a regiment should go forward on skirmish or outpost duty. Those advance guards could give early warning of approaching enemy, fire a quick volley, and then scurry back to the

LIBRARY OF CONGRESS

Gen. Joseph Hooker, Lee's luckless adversary.

main line. Driving in hostile skirmishers was familiar business; so was finding their comrades behind them in a ratio of about nine to one. On May 2 Lee sent swarms of skirmishers toward the enemy, sometimes using all his men out in front, leaving no main line but creating the impression of great strength. Confederate units launched vigorous feints that Federals repulsed stoutly and with some smugness. Meanwhile, Jackson pushed on through the woods toward Hooker's rear, carrying a quiver full of thunderbolts.

Jackson's fabled flank march actually unfolded with far less stealth than any Confederate wanted. Barely one mile beyond the intersection where Lee and Jackson parted, the flanking column ran into its first taste of trouble. On high ground just before the road dropped into a bottom around Catharine Furnace, a gap in the woods allowed Federals a mile and a quarter away to see the Southerners moving steadily past the open space. Of course Northern artillery opened fire at the closely packed target; of course the Confederates double-timed past the hot spot. General Lee knew of this early difficulty, but then there began a long, tense silence that dragged on for endless hours.

The long-range shells spiraling across more than a mile annoyed their intended victims and no doubt hurt a few of them, but they constituted no real military impediment. A more serious threat gradually developed at the second milepost when Dan Sickles pushed his troops southward to the vicinity of Catharine Furnace to find out what all those moving Southerners were up to. Men of the 23d Georgia spread in an arc above the furnace as a flank guard fought against an increasing tide of Federals. The Georgians finally fell back to the cut of the same unfinished railroad that had played a role the day before in shaping the battle lines. By this time Jackson's entire infantry column had marched past. The Georgia regiment fell apart finally, and all but a handful of men became prisoners. Emory Fiske Best, the regiment's twenty-three-year-old colonel, was among those who escaped. A court-martial cashiered him just before Christmas, but his 23d Georgia had done well for a long time.

The bluecoats of Sickles's corps who captured the Georgians were pleased by their success, but in fact their prime quarry had eluded danger. The last two infantry brigades in Jackson's column turned back and easily repulsed any further advance by Sickles beyond the railroad. High open ground around the Wellford house, bisected by the narrow woods road climbing out of dense thickets, provided the Southern rear guard with a ready-made stronghold. The extensive trains of ambulances and ordnance wagons scheduled to follow Jackson's infantry avoided the furnace pressure point by detouring around it to the south and west on another set of primitive traces. Jackson was free to pursue his great adventure.

The narrowness of the wagon tracks Jackson followed toward his goal proved to be both a blessing and a curse. The Southern column needed secrecy, and the Wilderness that closed in all around provided it. But the column also needed to move fast, and that the primitive roads did not encourage. Even so,

Jackson's two-week-old circular about marching habits kept the march moving: two miles in fifty minutes, then ten minutes' rest, then do it again, and again, and again.

A little more than four miles from his starting point Stonewall Jackson reached the Brock Road. This was the main north-south route in the vicinity, and it led north around the enemy right. Jackson turned south. Someone attributed to Stonewall the military aphorism "Always mystify, mislead, and surprise the enemy." Moving the wrong way with almost thirty thousand men might accomplish that end, if anyone was watching. The wrong-way march lasted only long enough to cross two gentle ridgelines. Then Jackson turned off into the trees again on another set of woods tracks and angled northward parallel to the Brock Road.

Union men of the XI Corps whiled away their last moments of grace playing cards and writing letters.

Soldiers marching at the head of Jackson's corps rejoiced when, about two miles beyond the detour, they came to a small stream flowing across the road. Standing water dotted gullies throughout the Wilderness, but the stream supplied them with their first source of drinkable water along the route. It gurgled across the road at just about precisely the halfway point along the march. When Jackson's van reached the stream, the tail of his attenuated corps had not left the starting blocks six miles to the rear.

Officers prodded dusty and tired men through the enticing water and on their way. When Jackson reached the Brock Road again, he poured his troops onto it, and they surged northward. At the in-

tersection of the Plank Road he planned to turn right and cover the two miles to Wilderness Church, there to demolish Hooker's dangling flank. Gen. Fitzhugh Lee met Jackson at the intersection and led him east on the Plank Road to show him why that idea no longer made good sense. From a high plateau in the yard of a farmer named Burton, young Lee pointed out to Jackson the Federal line running west beyond Wilderness Church. To attack down the Plank Road would be to hit the enemy in front, canceling most of the advantages won by so much sweat and at such great risk.

Stonewall Jackson was about the most famous man on earth that spring; Fitz Lee knew he had served him well and prepared to bask in the glow of a deserved kudos. Instead, the dour Stonewall gazed intently across the intervening ground at his quarry without a glance at his disappointed benefactor. Turning without a word, Jackson hurried back to the head of his column on the Brock Road and pointed it up the road still farther north. Two extra miles of marching would complete the wider circuit now necessary. Good generals adapt to tactical verities, and Jackson was very good indeed at what he did. He paused long enough to scribble a four-sentence dispatch to Lee, then headed eagerly on with his men.

The Federals on whom Jackson planned to unleash his tidal wave belonged to the XI Corps under O. O. Howard. General Howard was new to his post, but the men in the ranks knew Jackson all too well. Stonewall had brought them to grief more than once in the past year while they served under Gen. Nathaniel Banks and Gen. Franz Sigel. That unhappy past, combined with the German origins of many of the men, left them the unpopular and misunderstood outcasts of the Army of the Potomac. After the battle many of them came to believe, or at least to claim, that they had known full well that Confederates by the tens of thousands lurked in the woods. But in the late afternoon of May 2, without access to hindsight, the infantrymen of the XI Corps whiled away their last moments of grace playing cards and writing letters and cooking food that they would never eat.

Several miles away Joe Hooker sat on the veranda of the pleasant Chancellorsville Inn and composed brash communiqués.

General Jackson could not wait for his entire column to snake through the narrow woods and uncoil across Howard's exposed flank. Despite all the risks he had successfully run and the superb opportunity that lay before him, Jackson knew that the inexorable slide of the sun toward the horizon had now become his greatest foe. The stern, devout Jackson was about as close to an Old Testament warrior as the Civil War produced, but he could not make the sun stand still. After pushing two-thirds of his men into three long, parallel lines, Jackson could wait no longer.

The two main Confederate lines, separated by only about one hundred yards, stretched for nearly a mile on either side of the Turnpike. They stood squarely at right angles to the unwitting Federal line strung out along the road and facing south. When the Southern avalanche struck, the bravest Northerner turning to confront this surprise attack from the rear would be outflanked by a mile to his right and a mile to his left. In naval parlance, Jackson had "crossed the T" on his quarry by forming the cap of the T and looking down its shank.

Sometime after 5:00 P.M. Stonewall Jackson reached under his coat and pulled his watch out of an inside pocket. Conflicting accounts place the moment at 5:15 or as late as 6:00. Jackson looked up from the watch at the handsome, capable Robert E. Rodes, a Virginian commanding the division waiting in the front line. "Are you ready, General Rodes?"

"Yes, sir."

"You can go forward then."

That quiet colloquy launched the II Corps and moved thousands of men through the brightest moment of the fabled Army of Northern Virginia. A nod from Rodes to a young officer named Blackford, who had grown up in nearby Fredericksburg but commanded Alabamians on this day, triggered the attack. Bugles told skirmishers to advance. About twenty thousand infantrymen followed close behind through dense brush that tugged at their tattered uniforms. As the Rebels gained momentum, they broke into a hoarse, savage roar that escalated into the spine-chilling high-pitched shriek of the Rebel yell.

The dense two-mile line of Southern soldiers drove forest animals in front of its advance like beaters flushing game on an African safari, and many Northern troops got their first intimation that something was afoot in the woods behind them when animals scurried and fluttered past, hurrying eastward. Some Federals laughed and cheered the bizarre natural phenomenon. Then the paralyzing tremolo of the Rebel yell came floating after the wildlife.

An officer yelled, "You are firing into your own men!" The 18th N. Carolina's major cried, "It's a lie!"

Howard's unfortunate division and brigade commanders generally did their best in an impossible situation. No soldiers could have stood in the circumstances thrust upon the XI Corps—even had the Confederates been unarmed, and the Federals equipped with twentieth-century weapons not yet dreamed of. Troops simply do not stand when surprised from behind by hordes of screaming enemies. Leaders with those foreign names that made the rest of the army look askance encouraged brief rallies that inevitably spilled back in rout. Schurz, Krzyzanowski, Schimmelfennig, von Gilsa, von Einsiedel, and dozens more scrambled in vain to stem the wide and deep tide sweeping against and over them.

Capt. Hubert Dilger won a great name for himself by firing a piece of artillery with steadfast courage in the face of Jackson's legions. This freshly immigrated German, known as Leatherbreeches because of some doeskin pants he wore, retired so stubbornly that Army legend held that he fell back only by reason of the recoil of his gun at each discharge.

Federals fleeing from the intolerable spot whence Jackson had erupted found little support as they ran eastward. Dan Sickles had taken most of his III Corps down toward the furnace to cope with Jackson's rear guard. The panicky fugitives ran back not onto a stalwart line of friends but into a comfortless vacuum.

Only the failure of one inept Confederate officer saved the Federal army from unmitigated disaster. Alfred H. Colquitt was a Georgia politician of starkly limited military attainments. Chance put this weak reed on the right end of Jackson's four-brigade frontline cutting edge. The spare fifth brigade of the front division fell in just behind Colquitt, ready to deploy into the first good seam popped open by the attack. Colquitt and his peers operated under strict orders to move straight and steadily ahead, ignoring matters on either side; they would exploit Jackson's strenuously won advantage while other troops tidied up around the edges and behind them.

Despite his unmistakable instructions, Colquitt came to a dead stop shortly after the attack began. One of the general's staff excitedly reported enemy off to the right. The highly capable young Stephen Dodson Ramseur of North Carolina, commanding the brigade just to the rear and stymied by Colquitt's halt, found to his immense disgust that "not a solitary Yankee was to be seen" in that direction. Colquitt had single-handedly obliterated the usefulness of two-fifths of Jackson's front line. Almost immediately after the battle Lee sent Colquitt into exile far away from the Army of Northern Virginia; by contrast, Georgians thought enough of Colquitt to elect him governor twice and then send him to the U.S. Senate.

Even without the 40 percent of his front line lost through incompetence, Jackson had enough men in place to sweep the field. His troops devoured more than two miles of the Federal line in about two hours. But near the end of

Mississippians on the Sunken Road: one of the starkest views of battle dead recorded during the war.

their triumphant plunge toward Chancellorsville the Southerners were themselves taken by surprise as the result of a bizarre accident. The 8th Pennsylvania Cavalry had spent that afternoon at the commanding artillery position known as Hazel Grove, about one mile south of the Turnpike at a point two miles east of where Jackson struck. An acoustical shadow kept those troopers and others around them from hearing, or at least clearly comprehending, the disaster that had befallen their friends far away to their right and rear. When the Pennsylvanians responded to a routine but outdated order to head north to the main road, then east to Hooker's headquarters at Chancellorsville, they stumbled into the midst of Jackson's columns. Surprised Southerners quickly dispersed the equally surprised Pennsylvania boys, who fought bravely but vainly in a sea

of gray. Gen. Alfred Pleasonton, who had command of the Federal cavalry, later wove the charge of the 8th into a vast panorama of self-serving lies that he concocted as his official report of the battle. Eventually Pleasonton won his well-earned reputation as the Civil War's Munchausen, but at the time the survivors could only fume impotently.

As darkness fell, the men of the Federal XI Corps completed a frantic run for shelter that in many instances took them all the way back to the river and across the pontoon bridges. One officer called these German fugitives the Flying Dutchmen; another, hoarse from his vain efforts to shout up a rally, said that "the damned Dutchmen ran away with my voice." To finish with these poor XI Corps fellows, it must be reported that they ran afoul of similarly grotesque bad luck a few weeks later at Gettysburg and

suffered an almost identical thrashing. Before year's end, though, many of the same men participated in the dramatic spontaneous charge that captured Missionary Ridge in Tennessee.

Dan Sickles's boys of the Federal III Corps blundered through their own personal nightmare after darkness fell. Thousands of them crashed about in the baffling Wilderness, far south of the position they had left when ordered to explore the area around Catharine Furnace and southwest of friendly lines still intact. When the III Corps troops groped back toward Chancellorsville in the darkness, they bumped into blazing muskets and thundering cannon, all fired by the Federal XII Corps. The number of men killed by friends in this hellish, confused pitch-black tangle cannot be ascertained with any certainty. Some Northern witnesses marveled that anyone survived, and Gen. Henry Warner Slocum, commanding the XII Corps, wrote that "the damage suffered by our troops from our own fire . . . must have been severe."

When this combat between bluecoats erupted, Confederates in the vicinity ducked for cover and expected the worst, only gradually coming to the soothing understanding that the storm excluded them. Meanwhile, a handful of Confederates as confused as were Slocum and Sickles inflicted a mortal wound on their own hero—and perhaps on the national prospects of their young country.

Stonewall Jackson's considerable military virtues did not include an intuitive grasp of terrain. Perhaps because of that, the general customarily worked hard and long in seeking understanding of ground where he would fight. In the smoke-smeared moonlight that evening of May 2, Jackson rode out before the amorphous tangle of troops that constituted his front line. The general and an entourage of staffers and couriers poked about in the Wilderness, looking for a route that would provide access to some point behind Chancellorsville, blocking the Federal retreat. When the little cavalcade headed back toward Confederate lines, it came athwart two North Carolina brigades. The noise of the horses prompted one of the brigades to fire a wild volley obliquely across the road from its southern edge. An officer with the general shouted a desperate plea to cease firing. "You are firing into your own men!" he yelled.

The major of the 18th North Carolina, just north of the road, bellowed: "It's a lie! Pour it into them, boys!"

This volley struck dead Jackson's faithful engineer officer, J. Keith Boswell, and inflicted mortal hurts on at least three others in the party. Three of its bullets hit Stonewall Jackson. Two shattered his left arm; the third pierced his right hand. Horrified subordinates gathered around the stricken leader, bound his wounds, and laboriously carried him from the field. At one point three young staff members lay around Jackson's litter in a hurricane of artillery fire, shielding him with their bodies as canister struck sparks from the road all around them. Twice men carrying a cor-

ner of the litter went down. The second time Jackson fell squarely on his mangled shoulder, renewing the arterial bleeding that already had cost him much of his vitality. Eventually the worried and sorrowful party delivered their general to a field hospital near Wilderness Tavern. There his medical director amputated Jackson's savaged arm just below the shoulder early on May 3. The bullet extracted from the general's right palm was round, one of the projectiles fired by the obsolete smoothbore muskets still carried by a surprising number of ordnance-poor Confederate units.

The steady rhythm of artillery at Hazel Grove built to a crescendo that won the battle for Lee.

By the time Jackson awakened from his anesthetic, artillery fire from the nearby battlefield was shaking the earth beneath him. During the night after Jackson's wounding, command of his corps passed to Jeb Stuart, who was dragooned into this unaccustomed temporary role because the only available infantry general of adequate rank had been wounded soon after Jackson went down. Col. Edward Porter Alexander, a fine young artillerist from Georgia, reported to Stuart that a high, open knoll called Hazel Grove offered a wonderful artillery vantage point and persuaded the general to capture it. At about 1:00 A.M. Stuart sent J. J. Archer's brigade of Tennessee and Alabama regiments to the vicinity, and at the first hint of dawn the Southern troops stormed out of the woods into the clearing. They reached the hilltop just in time to capture four guns and one hundred men of a Federal rear guard; Joe Hooker had decided during the night to abandon Hazel Grove, the key to the battlefield.

The newly installed battalion system of artillery, which ensured ready availability of ample guns in large, mobile masses, allowed Alexander to rush about fifty pieces of the right size and type to Hazel Grove. There they took under fire the Federal artillery some twelve hundred yards away at Fairview (still another Chancellor family farmhouse) and at the Chancellorsville crossroads itself. Although the gunners of the Army of Northern Virginia had achieved well-earned fame, they were accustomed to suffering under the fire of better-made and more modern Federal weapons that hurled far more reliable ammunition. The advantage of ground offered by Hazel Grove, however, combined with successful implementation of the battalion concept, resulted in a situation in which, said the army's leading historian, Douglas Southall Freeman, "the finest artillerists of the Army of Northern Virginia were having their greatest day."

One particularly noteworthy round fired from Hazel Grove spiraled over Fairview and headed unerringly for the Chancellorsville Inn. As the shell descended toward its target, General Hooker was leaning against one of the large white porch columns, looking out from the second-story veranda. The shell did not explode (an all-too-typical result from the Southern perspective; one officer on this day insisted that he kept track and only about every fifteenth round went off). The hurtling iron hit Hooker's pillar, though, and the impact knocked it and pieces of the porch in every direction. Lt. Col. Logan Henry Nathan Salyer of the 50th Virginia lay across the top of a piano in the inn's first-floor parlor, where Federal captors had taken him after he went down with a saber wound in the head. Salyer roused himself enough to ask scurrying staff officers what had happened, and they responded with an early and inaccurate report that Hooker had been killed. Salyer rejoiced quietly, but in fact Hooker was only stunned and paralyzed. He ostensibly conveyed to Gen. Darius N. Couch the command of the army, but as the day continued, it became apparent that he retained so many strings on Couch that the latter really wielded no substantial authority.

General Couch and his colleagues recognized that their army still enjoyed clear advantages in numbers and position. Could they commit the large body of unused men to action, they might still grind Lee's weak force to bits, Jackson's dazzling success of the previous day notwithstanding. But Hooker held his army passive and allowed Lee the luxury of choosing the time and place at which decisive actions developed.

Nevertheless, R. E. Lee experienced considerable difficulty on the morning of May 3. Almost all of the Federal infantry lines that Lee had to break that morning stood in the dense Wilderness. Southern brigades plunged into the brush and fought blindly against equally bemused Northern units, generally accomplishing little and ballooning the already dreadful casualty lists. Other brigades wandered through the storm without either doing much good or suffering much loss. "It would be useless to follow in detail the desperate fighting which now ensued. . . ." That admission by Edward Porter Alexander, a ranking Confederate officer who revisited the field after the war before writing a classic history, suggests the nature of the woods fighting on May 3.

Among the casualties of this hourslong brawl was Gen. Hiram G. Berry of Maine, shot down with a mortal wound as he crossed the road near Chancellorsville. But perhaps the most important Federal casualty, viewed from the long perspective of posterity, was Col. Nelson Appleton Miles of the 61st New York. Miles went down with a bullet in the abdomen, recovered, and went on to become commander in chief of the U.S. Army near the turn of the century. At about the time Miles gained his highest command, private citizens both North and South purchased huge chunks of the battlefield of Chancellorsville in hopes that the War Department would accept them as a donation to form a national military park on the order of those newly designated at Gettysburg and elsewhere. The Army chose not to accept the largess of those public-spirited preservationists. Gettysburg was one thing, but the scenes in which the U.S. Army had been humiliated in 1863 (and

where a rebellious Southerner punctured General Miles) certainly did not deserve protection. The portion of the battlefield preserved today, contains only a small fragment of what our forebears sought to protect almost a century ago.

Lee took the bad news with the same calm he always displayed, but his heart must have sunk.

Early during the woods fighting two Confederate generals became casualties of different sorts. Gen. John R. Jones of Virginia was one of Stonewall Jackson's special projects that turned out poorly. Jones had been accused of cowardice so blatant that it resulted in a formal court-martial, a shocking event in the general officer corps of an army fabled for its bravery. The court cautiously exonerated Jones two weeks before Chancellorsville. On May 3, however, the demands of combat among the bullets snapping through the trees proved to be too much for Jones. He left the field and resigned.

Another of Jackson's projects, E. F. Paxton, went into the morning's fight with the unshakable premonition that he would be killed at once. Paxton had known Jackson as a fellow communicant at Stonewall's beloved Presbyterian church before the war. When Paxton lost an election to be major of the 27th Virginia, Jackson calmly found means to promote him several ranks to brigadier general, out of reach of the whims of the electorate. Much of the army disdained this proceeding as another instance of Jackson's much mooted wretched judgment in selecting subordinates. Paxton had had little opportunity to confirm or disprove this conventional wisdom when he led his famous Stonewall Brigade into action on May 3. He knew he would not

survive the battle and prepared for death by studying his wife's photograph and reading his Bible by the scant predawn light. Moments after the action opened Paxton fell dead, surviving only long enough to reach for the pocket where he kept his treasured pictures.

Over all of the infantry chaos that morning there throbbed the steady rhythm of Confederate artillery at Hazel Grove, building to a crescendo that won the battle for Lee. The two divisions that had remained with Lee for the past day and a half pressed toward Chancellorsville from the south and east. Jackson's men under Stuart closed in from the west. Before the morning was far gone, the two Confederate wings reunited at last, ending that aspect of Lee's incredible gamble and providing the general with the chance to reassert direct control over his whole army. Gradually the consolidated Southern force swept Hooker's brave but poorly led legions back to the Chancellorsville intersection. A brief, confused stand there bought Hooker a few minutes. Then Confederates swarmed over the crossroads and around the burning inn in a frenzied victory celebration.

Into this animated scene rode R. E. Lee on his familiar gray horse. "His presence," wrote an officer who was there, "was the signal for one of those outbursts of enthusiasm which none can appreciate who have not witnessed them. The fierce soldiers with their faces blackened with the smoke of battle, the wounded crawling with feeble limbs from the fury of the devouring flames, all seemed possessed with a common impulse. One long, unbroken cheer, in which the feeble cry of those who lay helpless on the earth blended with the strong voices of those who still fought, rose high above the roar of battle, and hailed the presence of the victorious chief. He sat in the full realization of all that soldiers dream of—triumph; and as I looked upon him in the complete fruition of the success which his genius, courage, and confidence in his army had won, I thought that it must have been from such a scene that men in ancient days rose to the dignity of gods."

The impromptu celebration fizzled out when dreadful news arrived from Fredericksburg. Lee's eleven-thousand-

Federal wounded rest at Marye's Heights, where not long before Sedgwick's men had met Alabama regiments under Wilcox.

man rear guard there, under Gen. Jubal A. Early, had been facing twice as many Federals under Gen. John Sedgwick. When a Mississippi colonel named Thomas M. Griffin incautiously (and against regulations) accepted a flag of truce during the morning of May 3, Northern officers saw just how thin was the line opposing them. Adjusting their formations and tactics accordingly, the Federals pounded across the plain below Marye's Heights and burst over the stone wall and Sunken Road that had caused their army so much grief the previous December. This penetration of the rear guard opened a path to Lee's rear for Sedgwick's force. A government photographer accompanying the advancing Federals took some shots of the captured ground, among them one of freshly dead Mississippians in the Sunken Road that gave stark testimony

of the price of their colonel's impolitic behavior. The film captured one of the most graphic views of battle dead taken during the entire war.

Sedgwick's apparently wide-open opportunity to slice westward and do Lee some harm came to an abrupt obstacle about four miles west of Marye's Heights, at Salem Church. Gen. Cadmus Marcellus Wilcox and his brigade of five tough, veteran Alabama regiments began May 3 guarding Banks Ford on the Rappahannock River, two miles due north of Salem Church. Wilcox moved alertly toward Fredericksburg and the action developing there during the morning. When Early's line at Marye's Heights fell apart, Wilcox hurried across country and threw skirmishers in Sedgwick's path. The Alabama men retarded their enemy's advance from positions on each gentle crest and at fence rows perpen-

dicular to the road. Finally at Salem Church they made a stout stand.

Lee received the bad news from eastward with the same calm poise he always displayed, but his heart must have sunk within him. He turned Gen. Lafayette McLaws onto the Turnpike back toward Salem Church and later followed in person. Wilcox and his men stood at bay near the little brick building when McLaws arrived with reinforcements. The simple Southern Baptist sanctuary, built in 1844 by the farming brethren who worshiped in it, now served as a make-do fortification. Bluecoated infantry charged up to and around the building while Alabamians fired out the windows. Hundreds of men fell in the yard, in the church itself, and in the small log church school sixty yards to the east.

But McLaws and his men made the Salem Church ridge too strong to breach, and fighting flickered out late on May 3. The next day Confederates from the church and from Early's bypassed rear guard bottled Sedgwick up with his back to the Rappahannock. Soon after midnight of May 4–5, this Union detachment retreated back over the river under desultory shell fire and light infantry pressure.

Salem Church survives today, covered both inside and out with battle scars. All but a tiny fragment of the Salem Church ridge, however, disappeared during the past few years as gas stations and shopping centers destroyed the battlefield. Huge earth-moving machines chewed up and carried away the ground of the ridge itself, leaving the building a forlorn remnant of the historic past isolated on its little vestigial crest.

After Sedgwick headed for cover at the end of May 4, Lee could return his attention to Hooker's main army. The Federals had built a strong and deep line of earthworks shaped like an enormous capital V. The flanks were anchored on the river, and the apex stretched south to a point only one mile north of Chancellorsville. Within that sturdy fastness Joe Hooker continued to cooperate with Lee's objectives by holding his force quietly under the eyes of Southern detachments that he outnumbered by about four to one. When Lee was able to return to the Chancellorsville front on May 5, the men he brought back with him from around Salem Church improved the odds to some degree but not nearly enough to approach parity. Federal losses totaled about eighteen thousand during the campaign, but Lee had incurred some twelve thousand casualties as well and was still greatly overmatched. Even so, the Confederate commander was looking for some means to launch a renewed offensive against Hooker when, on the morning of May 6, his scouts reported that all the Federals had retreated north of the river during the night.

That same day, Joe Hooker announced in an order to the entire army: "The events of the last week may swell with pride the heart of every officer and soldier of this army. We have added new luster to its former renown . . . and filled [the enemy's] country with fear and con-

sternation." By contrast, Lee's congratulatory order to his troops, dated May 7, gave thanks to God "for the signal deliverance He has wrought" and encouraged divine services in the army to acknowledge that debt.

Historians continue to discuss many aspects of the campaign without any hint of unanimity. Was Joe Hooker drunk most of the weekend? After the war the general conclusion was that he had stopped drinking on accession to army command, leaving him unsettled after a lifetime of consistent bibulousness; new evidence suggests that he did indeed indulge his habit during the Chancellorsville weekend. Did R. E. Lee conclude from the evidence of his

Jackson's wife told him he was dying. "My wish is fulfilled," he said. "I have always desired to die on Sunday."

incredible victory that there was virtually nothing his battle-tested infantry could not do, leading to overconfidence at Gettysburg? The army had performed at an astoundingly high level during the first three days of May, and Lee soon did ask nearly impossible feats from it; on the other hand, the leaders of a tenuous revolutionary experiment could hardly afford to play conservatively against staggering negative odds.

Chancellorsville gave Lee the leverage to move the war out of torn and bleeding Virginia. His raid into Pennsylvania held the potential for great success, but it came to grief at Gettysburg, two months to the day after Chancellorsville.

The combination of bold strategy and even bolder tactics employed by the Confederate leaders at Chancellorsville turned an apparently impossible situation into a remarkable triumph. But the most important scenes in that tragic drama ultimately unfolded not around the old inn or at Hazel Grove but in an

outbuilding of a country house twenty-five miles to the southeast at Guinea Station. Stonewall Jackson seemed to be recovering favorably from the loss of his arm when an ambulance carried him to the Chandler place at Guinea on the hot fourth of May. His progress continued good for two more days at this new resting place farther from the dangers and distractions of the front. Then, early on the morning of May 7, Jackson awakened with a sharp pain in his side that his medical staff readily and worriedly diagnosed as pneumonia. The disease made rapid inroads on the general's weakened system, and doctors began to hint that he might not recover.

The grim news spread through the ranks. The loss of mighty Stonewall would transform the glorious name of Chancellorsville into the blackest of blots. Mrs. Jackson reached her husband's bedside on May 7, and three days later it was she who had to rouse Thomas Jackson from his delirium to warn him that he was dying. "I will be an infinite gainer to be translated," the fading man responded, and later: "My wish is fulfilled. I have always desired to die on Sunday."

In the early afternoon of a lovely spring Sunday, May 10, Stonewall Jackson called out for Gen. A. P. Hill and for Maj. Welles J. Hawks of his staff as his mind wandered to battles won and streams crossed at the head of his troops. At three o'clock a spell of calm intervened, broken only by the sobs of family and friends in the room and by the general's desperate gasping for breath. As the clock neared the quarter hour, Jackson spoke quietly from the bed: "Let us cross over the river, and rest under the shade of the trees." Then, as he so often had done during the year just past, Stonewall Jackson led the way.

Robert K. Krick is chief historian of Fredericksburg and Spotsylvania National Military Park, which preserves portions of Chancellorsville battlefield. He is the author of eight books; his Stonewall Jackson at Cedar Mountain *was published by the University of North Carolina Press.*

A Yankee Scarlett O'Hara in Atlanta

Thomas G. Dyer discovers the secret diary of a Unionist in the heart of the Confederacy who saw the American Civil War at uncomfortably close quarters.

SCARLETT O'HARA dominates the world's image of the American Civil War. But recent research has uncovered a real-life woman, Cyrena Bailey Stone, whose experiences offer a completely new perspective on wartime Atlanta.

Scarlett was a Confederate. Cyrena was a Unionist. Tempestuous, headstrong Scarlett had a conditional attachment to the Confederacy. Steady, courageous Cyrena possessed a principled allegiance to the Union. Scarlett fled Atlanta during the harrowing days of battle and siege. Cyrena stayed. 'This is my home', she wrote on the eve of the great battle for the city in July 1864, '& I wish to protect it if possible.'

We know about Cyrena Stone because of the recent appearance of a diary, anonymously kept during the seven months leading up to the Battle of Atlanta. The document reflects the experience of Cyrena, who recorded the tumult that marked the beginning of the Confederacy's death agony. Aware of the danger of keeping such a journal, she carefully protected her identity, and artfully obscured the identities of fellow members of a secret 'Union Circle' living in the rebel city.

An intensive research effort eventually identified Cyrena Stone, a native Vermonter who had lived in Atlanta for ten years, as the author of the diary. She and her husband, Amherst Stone, an am-

bitious lawyer, were at the heart of the Unionist community in Atlanta. By early 1864, however, Amherst had fled Atlanta on a blockade-running errand, and had been imprisoned in the North. Cyrena remained in the couple's home on the outskirts of the city. Under conditions of constant stress and danger, she kept her diary and in doing so made a record of a hitherto unknown part of the Civil War.

Throughout the war, Cyrena led a life governed by a passionate commitment to the Union. Although she coped with the challenges of everyday life in the Confederate city, she had difficulty in dealing with the suffocating political atmosphere of a region she believed had

Cyrena Stone

CYRENA ANN BAILEY STONE was born in 1830 in East Berkshire, Vermont, the daughter of a Congregationalist minister and Yankee tinkerer, Phinehas Bailey. Although the details of her childhood are sketchy, she apparently attended common schools in East Berkshire and in a series of villages in Vermont and eastern New York where she and the rest of the extensive Bailey brood lived as her father moved from pastorate to pastorate. The Bailey family was quite poor, but Cyrena's childhood was more or less typical, although marked by death of her mother and several siblings.

In 1850, she married Amherst Willoughby Stone, the son of a prosperous Vermont farmer. Young Stone became a lawyer. He was exceedingly ambitious and sought his fortune in the American South. After their marriage, the two settled in Georgia and eventually in Atlanta where Stone became a prominent businessman-lawyer. With prominence came prosperity, and the two settled into a comfortable existence in a large house on the outskirts of Atlanta, a mile from the centre of the city with its population in 1860 of about 10,000 persons.

As the secession crisis neared, Cyrena and Amherst felt the tugs of patriotism that pulled at transplanted northerners living in the South. Although tested by the defection of Amherst's brother to the southern cause and by her husband's ambivalent loyalties, Cyrena retained a remarkably consistent and courageous loyalty to the Union. During the war, she was reviled, threatened, and arrested, but she managed to escape imprisonment and continued to work with other Unionists in Atlanta to subvert the Confederate cause. When Amherst left for the North on a blockade-running mission in 1863, she remained in their home, persisting in her loyalist activities and awaiting the arrival of William T. Sherman and the Union army.

After the war, she and Amherst returned to Georgia where he became a federal official. She died in 1868 in her native Vermont at the age of 38.

steeped itself in treason. For Cyrena Stone, the Confederacy was a confining, stifling sarcophagus. She and the other Atlanta Unionists longed for the coming of the Union army to 'roll away the stone from the tomb into which Secession has consigned us—without any embalming'.

Relationships with other Unionists did much to sustain Cyrena throughout the war but took on a slightly different character in 1864. Many of the men had escaped through the lines, and her Unionist contacts were almost always with the women who remained. The symbols of national loyalty took on greater importance as the Union army approached. Throughout the conflict, Cyrena kept a small American flag, secreting it in a variety of hiding places, at one time in a jar of preserved fruit, at another in her sugar canister. Atlantans with Union sympathies would regularly visit the Stone household to see the flag, which it was illegal to possess in the Confederacy. One woman came furtively as she did not want her husband to know of her interest 'in the advance of the Federals'. When Cyrena retrieved the hidden banner the tearful woman kissed it 'reverently'.

Cyrena had altered her behaviour in order to cope with the constant probings and tauntings by Confederates who hoped to entrap her in a seditious act that could be interpreted as treason. She learned to control herself in these settings just as she hid her emotions from those who lived in her household. In social situations—and contact did continue with loyal Confederates—war news would invariably be interpreted in the best possible light for the rebel cause. Confederate loyalists would, of course, show enthusiasm. Downcast Unionists, sometimes shocked by Confederate claims, would try to react in ways that would minimise suspicion. At times, Cyrena would fight against normal reactions to wartime news, biting her lips to keep the colour in them, fighting back a blush: 'The face must keep its colour—white or red—though the heart stops beating or flames up in scorching pain' she wrote. When Unionists met unexpectedly on the street, they greeted each other correctly, without seeming overly friendly, in order not to arouse suspicion. After receiving some good news about the progress of the war, Cyrena encountered a Unionist man ('staunch & true') walking with a Confederate officer. 'Very slightly and sedately,' the Unionist bowed toward her, but after he had passed, 'something, which often impels us to look back, made me turn my head; at that instant, his head turned too, & his face was covered with smiles'. Intuition, Cyrena concluded, 'schooled as it has been these years—tells us where to laugh & when not to'.

Rumours of the movements of both Confederate and Union armies dominated many of Cyrena's conversations and preyed constantly on her mind. Sorting out fact from fiction proved difficult, and Cyrena and the other Unionists had their spirits lifted by reports of Yankee advances. Just as often, however, those spirits would be dashed by Confederate propaganda that glossed over setbacks and inflated advantages. Cyrena learned to read between the lines of reports and to weigh them carefully.

'Sherman defeated, & Johnston pursuing!' read one propaganda-filled report in early May. 'I like such defeats & such pursuits as these prove to be,' Cyrena wrote, for she had learned that the day before the Union general George Thomas had taken Tunnel Hill, and that Dalton had been evacuated by the Confederates, that place which was so impregnable'. Confederate General Joseph E. Johnston fell back toward Atlanta for strategic advantage, the reports ran, 'so that when he does make a stand—dead Yankees will be piled higher than Stone Mountain'. Cyrena saw through the hyperbole. 'The battles are usually reported in this style,' she observed. 'The vandals were mowed down without number. No loss on our side. One man killed, and three slightly wounded.' Retreats became orderly repositionings with no straggling and no loss of armaments. 'History will probably show the truthfulness of these so-called—"official reports" ' Cyrena concluded cynically.

Early in the war, Atlantans had become accustomed to battles fought several hundred miles away. As Margaret

Inside the captured city. A view down Marietta Street in the heart of Atlanta just after the Union forces occupied the Confederate stronghold.

Mitchell later speculated, perhaps they had developed a wishful habit of believing that a great distance would always separate Atlanta from the real war. By the late spring of 1864, however, the Union army was only eighty-five miles to the north, having marched and fought through the rugged, mountainous north Georgia terrain. The city stood in imminent peril, and every day the threat increased. The Unionists dreamed of having Yankees in the streets of Atlanta. They talked incessantly about it among themselves, but it would have been foolhardy to suggest the probability, much less the desirability, of it in any other quarter. If the Confederates had developed their capacity for self-delusion over nearly four years of war, Cyrena had carefully kept her grip on reality, and though she had dreamed of the coming of the Yankees, she tried not to be too emotional; a tall order for a Unionist caught behind the Confederate lines for more than three years.

The closer the Yankee army drew to Atlanta, the more changes Cyrena and the other Unionists began to see in the behaviour and attitudes of Confederate Atlantans. Fear cooled Confederate loyalty, and cold reality warmed attachment to the Union. One Unionist commented to Cyrena that 'it was getting to be a fine thing to be a Union man. Hats are lifted when I meet some who would not speak to me a year ago. It is now "Why, how do you do Mr. Roberts?—very glad to see you" '. Cyrena also reported a conversation between two Atlanta Confederate 'ladies' and another Union friend. 'I know you can protect me when the Yankees come', one woman said. 'You have friends among them & I am coming right to your house to stay, & I shall be all right.' On May 24th, Cyrena recorded the transformation of the city. 'This has been a wild day of excitement,' she wrote.

> 'From early morning until now —engines have screamed—trains thundered along; wagons laden with government stores, refugees, Negroes and household stuff have rattled out of town. Every possible conveyance is bought, borrowed, begged or stolen'.

She exulted at the sudden transformation of the most ardent Confederate

For Cyrena, the cannon thunder was grand and wonderful music . . . 'our redemption anthem.'

citizens into refugees from the city, noting with unrestrained pleasure the 'packing up & leaving' of those who had boasted about the impregnability of Atlanta. It was, she said, 'perfectly marvellous to behold'.

A 'delirium of fear and excitement' seized the city. There was a 'wild upheaving' as military camps and fortifications multiplied. At night, she could see campfires in the nearby woods. During the day she could hear the sound of bugles and see large groups of soldiers moving about the city and in the open country near her house. For a few days, the Stones' slaves had claimed to hear the sound of cannon at night and in the early morning (like many Unionists, the Stones owned slaves). Cyrena was dubious; they had imagined the sounds, she told them. But on the morning of May 27th, they coaxed her outside to hear for herself what had been more audible since early morning. Once in the yard, Cyrena caught 'the faintest echo of booming guns'. The sound 'awakened the wildest joy I have ever known,' she wrote. For Cyrena, the muffled cannon thunder was grand and wonderful music, 'the first notes of our redemption anthem'. The cannon could not yet be heard in the city, and when Cyrena told a friend who lived inside Atlanta that the guns could be heard from her house, the woman hurried out to hear for herself. 'Mrs. M_____ a Southern lady . . . clapped her hands for joy and beckoned "Come boys!—come on!— we're waiting for you!" '

On June 2nd, militia companies arrived and crowded into the area around the Stone residence. Those who had mounts helped themselves to the ripened oats in the field on Cyrena's property. 'It makes no difference,' she wrote, 'the fences are fast disappearing—let it all go.' Four days later, on June 6th, the mi-

litia vacated the woods and departed for the front. Many of the men were 'in tears,' protesting that they had no interest in fighting the Yankees, and affirming that they would 'much rather fight the people who brought this war upon our country, and forced us to leave our homes to murder and be murdered'.

In addition to calling up the militia to defend Atlanta, the Confederates impressed large numbers of slaves to shore up the city's defences. Some resisted. Four such resisters escaped and made their way to the Stone house, where they pleaded with Cyrena to hide them. Cyrena took them in, hiding them in the cotton house between the stored bales. There they were fed and hidden for several days until, presumably, they made their escape.

On July 5th, the sounds of distant guns suddenly diminished, and an eerie calm settled on Atlanta. Cyrena feared that the latest rumours of a great defeat of the Yankees could be true, although she knew the Confederates would continue to paint a false picture of military successes in order to boost what little remained of civilian and military morale. The position of the main Union armies was unknown while General Johnston, it was said, had retreated to the Chattahoochee during the night. The uncertainty stretched nerves to snapping point.

Waiting for liberation became excruciatingly difficult. Every tidbit of news, every sound of battle, yielded multiple, often conflicting interpretations. The roar of the cannon resumed and sounded much closer, but the accuracy and significance of that, too, could be debated. On the night of July 18th, the noise of the guns seemed so close that it made Cyrena believe that surely the Union Army would march into Atlanta by morning.

In the sixteen months since her husband had left, Cyrena had grown lonely. The slaves remained and so did her white servants, Tom and Mary Lewis, but Cyrena felt isolated. The exodus of refugees since mid-May had gradually emptied the neighbourhood. 'All of my neighbours have gone—am alone on the hill,' Cyrena wrote on the morning of July 19th, 1864. A friend pleaded that she come into the city and stay with her, but Cyrena decided to remain in the house that she and Amherst had built.

By the morning of July 19th, Joseph F. Johnston had been removed from the Confederate command and replaced by General John Bell Hood. The evening before, Union forces had advanced to within two miles of Peachtree Creek, approximately three miles northwest of the Stones' house. On the morning of July 20th, fighting at Peachtree Creek began, and after a day of bitter, bloody battle, the Confederates were defeated. The next day, July 21st, was stupefyingly hot, as Union and Confederate forces prepared for another engagement that night that might decide the contest for Atlanta. Federal troops sought control of Bald (or Leggett's) Hill, which stood less than two miles from Cyrena's house. A bitter struggle for the hill continued throughout the day.

Cyrena remained at home in the midst of frantic Confederate activity. Her house was just inside the fortified ring of the Confederate city defences, with the troops of General Benjamin Cheatham's corps encircling it. Early in the morning, her yard 'swarmed' with hungry soldiers, who climbed onto the porch with dozens of requests for biscuits, milk, and utensils. 'Yes—yes yes—to every one,' was Cyrena's reply,

'thinking their wants would come to an end sometime, but they only increased'.

An injured Confederate colonel came to the house and asked if he could have a room. She said that he might. But would he protect them? 'Certainly madam, as long as we remain here,' he replied. A kindly man, he spoke tearfully of his own family. Then suddenly, 'a horrid whizzing screaming thing,' came flying through the air and burst with a loud explosion above the house. Cyrena was shaken. Although she had become accustomed to the 'roaring of cannon & rattle of musketry,' this was her first exposure to artillery fire. She ran to the colonel. He told her the Yankees were 'trying the range of their guns.' Another shell fell but without exploding. Cyrena had been reassured by the colonel's presence, but orders soon came for his unit to move out. She understood the reasons for the departure. 'I can see there is no feeling of security in the positions held by these forces', she wrote. 'They are on the move continually'.

Within the previous few days, other visitors had become temporary members of Cyrena's household. Robert Webster, a black barber who had aided Union prisoners, and his wife, Bess, had taken refuge there. A few nights before, Confederate soldiers had suddenly burst into

their home, 'pretending to search for runaway Negroes', and while holding guns against the couple's throats had stolen all of their valuables: 'silk dresses —jewellry watches & spoons were carried off'. The couple were now hiding in Cyrena's barn, protected by a 'kind officer', who was also staying there.

Throughout the day, the sounds of battle increased, 'becoming fiercer each hour.' By the end of the afternoon, a 'horrible pall of battlesmoke' hung over the entire area, darkening the sky. In the dusk, Tom Lewis breathlessly ran into the house. 'I tell you,' he said, 'We've got to git away from here now, for the men are falling back to the breastworks, & they're going to fight right away.' No sooner had Tom spoken

> when an army of cannon came pouring onto the grove & yard. An officer came up quickly & said —"They are falling back & will soon fight at the breastworks. It will not be safe for you to remain here madam" . . . A dark night fell suddenly upon the earth, and how dark the night that shut down upon my heart! Not a star illumined it; hope, courage all gone—no husband or brother near, and an army of men around our home; cannons belching forth a murderous fire not far away, & these silent ones in the yard, look so black & vengeful, as if impatient of a moment's quiet.

Nearly distraught, Cyrena went quickly from room to room —'not knowing what to do, or where to go; what to save—if anything could be saved, or what to leave.' The soldiers who accompanied the officer took charge, rolled up the carpets, and quickly packed many of the Stones' household items. The troops belonged to the Washington artillery from New Orleans. A young lieutenant told Cyrena that they were gentlemen. 'My heart thanked them for their sympathy', Cyrena wrote that night in her diary, 'but I thought they little knew upon what "traitor" they were bestowing it.'

A soldier, 'Mr Y', suddenly appeared. He had come to see if Cyrena was safe. Mr. Y and the Louisiana lieutenant then went to Hood's headquarters, where they learned that there would be no significant fighting that night. The soldiers anticipated early orders to fall

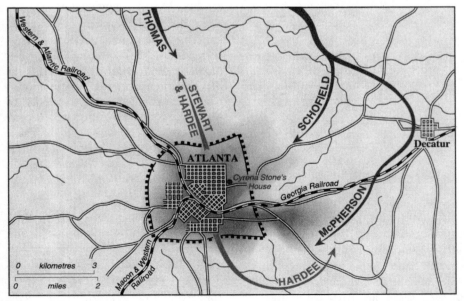

Map of the battle for Atlanta: the fall of the strategic Southern stronghold cut the Confederacy in two and helped seal its fate, to the delight of the secret Unionist sympathisers in the besieged city.

Cyrena Stone's house lay inside strong defences like these, which held up the northern advance for months. Unionists within longed for their liberation.

Cyrena survived the battle and siege and remained in Atlanta for some weeks after the Federal occupation. She was among the sizable number of the citizens who chose to go to the North during the forced evacuation of the city. Prior to leaving, she had a reunion with a Vermont cousin, a Union officer who sought her out in the wrecked city. Cyrena was, he said, 'the noblest woman he ever saw' and 'had remained true to the flag all this time'. She had been, he reported, 'shunned and excluded from society' but had 'endured all for righteousness sake'. Cyrena and her husband were reunited in the North in late 1864 and returned to their native Vermont. Eventually, she went back to Georgia, but never to Atlanta where she had composed her dramatic record of Unionist life in the South—an account completely at odds with the stereotype and fiction that surround the Civil War contest for Atlanta.

back on Atlanta, and thought that the city would probably be abandoned by the Confederate army. Cyrena's first trip as a refugee was put off until morning.

At midnight, seated in the parlour of her 'dismantled home', with the rolled carpets standing in the corners, she had the presence of mind to write up the day's events and remembered pleasant times past spent in the parlour on 'sabbath twilights', singing old hymns with friends and family. Outside, she saw 'lurid light from the fires dotting the yard & grove.' They shone 'fitfully in the darkness, revealing groups of soldiers here & there—some asleep on the earth, & some leaning against trees in a listless way as if life had no longer any gladness for them'. Now she felt completely alone and nearly despondent 'as the red waves of War rush madly by—sweeping away our pleasant Home'.

Early in the morning, Cyrena said good-bye to the members of the Washington Artillery, who had been ordered to move on. She thanked them, promising always to 'remember their kindness and sympathy'. Before leaving, she packed away most of her books in a large closet, abandoned the piano because there was 'no earthly way of removing it', and left gallons of preserved

pickles and 'nice blackberry wine'. She also had to leave behind most of her menagerie—chickens, pigs, and cats. Later that day, almost unbelievably, the kindly Mr Y went back to the house and with the aid of 'some army negroes who were not afraid of shells' brought the piano and a favourite cat to Cyrena.

By nine o'clock on the morning of July 22nd, 1864, Cyrena had left the home she loved:

> A strong feeling came over me as I passed down the shaded walk, where I had so often sauntered the peaceful summer evenings; but I looked not back, for I felt as if leaving those pleasant scenes forever. If such upheavings—such sunderings & losses, were to be the entrance gate into the larger life of liberty for which I had sighed—if this dark narrow way full of thorns & briers that so pierce & lacerate, led out into the broad shining land of my Country– I would go fearless, casting back no look of regret & longing for what I left behind.

Cyrena walked the mile to her friend's house, in the company of Mr Y who brought several small wagonloads of her possessions. After the migration, in the midst of the fury of the battle for Atlanta, her diary abruptly ceases in mid-sentence.

FOR FURTHER READING

Albert Castel, *Decision in the West: The Atlanta Campaign of 1864* (Lawrence: University Press of Kansas, 1992) Daniel W. Crafts, *Reluctant Confederates: Upper South Unionists in the Secession Crisis* (Chapel Hill: University of North Carolina Press, 1989) Carl N. Degler, *The Other South: Southern Dissenters in the Nineteenth Century* (New York: Harper and Row, 1974) Drew Gilpin Faust, *Mothers of Invention: Women of the Slaveholding South in the American Civil War* (Chapel Hill: University of North Carolina Press, 1996) Frank Klingberg, *The Southern Claims Commission* (Berkeley: University of California Press, 1955) James Michael Russell, *Atlanta, 1847–1890: City Building in the Old South and the New* (Baton Rouge: Louisiana State University Press, 1988)

Thomas G. Dyer is University Professor of Higher Education and History at the University of Georgia. He is the author of Secret Yankees: The Union Circle in Confederate Atlanta *(Johns Hopkins University Press, 1999).*

Sherman's War

The General's march through Georgia is usually remembered as a ruthless campaign of indiscriminate terror, waged against helpless civilians rather than Southern soldiers. But Victor David Hanson argues that it was brilliant, effective, and, above all, humane.

BY THE FALL OF 1864 NO ARMY IN either Europe or America was as mobile, self-supporting, and lethal as William Tecumseh Sherman's, which was composed of soldiers in prime physical condition expert in the handling of modern firearms. Their general was in some sense not merely the most powerful man in America but also the most dangerous person in the world. The Macon *Telegraph* warned its readers: "It would seem as if in him all the attributes of man were merged in the enormities of the demon, as if Heaven intended in him to manifest depths of depravity yet untouched by a fallen race. . . . Unsated still in his demoniac vengeance he sweeps over the country like a simoom of destruction."

The advent of Sherman's army must have been a terrifying experience for an agrarian society. The southern Central Valley of California where I live is similarly about three hundred miles from north to south; its eastern corridor between the Sierra Nevada and state freeway 99 is a belt about forty to sixty miles wide that comprises the richest farmland in the world. To comprehend anything comparable to Sherman's coming into Georgia is to imagine a huge column of mobile burners, starting out in the state capital to the north at Sacramento and descending to torch all the farmland of this valley southward to Bakersfield. Everything between San

Francisco and Los Angeles would be as desolate as the sixty-mile-wide corridor between Atlanta and Savannah.

I can imagine in my homeland, situated in the exact center, continuous columns of marchers coming down through Fresno and sweeping east to the Sierra Nevada, burning and destroying as they moved through small towns, tearing up the main railroad from San Francisco to Los Angeles, section by section, each day. I can envision that Americans from a different region of the country, with different accents and customs—perhaps Easterners, whom we often automatically distrust and do not fully fathom still—would come onto this farm, lecture and berate us, and strip our residence of everything I now gaze upon: furniture, silver, paintings, rugs, ancestral clocks, the sum of the collective acquisition of five generations of family members who have lived in this same house.

DOUR, TOUGH MEN, MORE DANGEROUS than any trespassers I have run off on evening walks from this small 120-acre farm, would ride in, camp, sleep, and feast as they saw fit, destroying our pump and water well and killing our five dogs and assorted pets. To understand Sherman's onslaught would be to see torched the barn outside my window, constructed by my great-grandfather well over a hundred years ago, trees

stripped of fresh fruit, and bins of stored raisins, nuts, and dried fruits—the past year's work and the only chance of cash for the future—consumed or simply dumped. Fences and outbuildings, liter-

> *For a century critics would assert that what Sherman did in Georgia was either amoral or irrelevant to the Union cause.*

ally everything wooden, would be collected and burned. Some of the flotsam and jetsam would be the result of gratuitous thievery: my grandmother's silver platter used for target practice, some two thousand books in my study thrown on the dirt and trampled in the alleyway. To imagine Sherman's arrival would be to see flames on every large farm in this immediate vicinity, made worse with the realization that heroic defense meant instant death and, worse still, that the ravagers were not always the ignorant and illiterate but occasionally the learned, who would hector me about how the destruction of my farm was inevitable—the moral wages of my support for the evil of slavery and the treachery of sedition. In short, our 120-year-old farm, where now five separate family households reside, would resemble the Canning plantation after Sherman's army moved through it on November 28, 1864: "We could hardly believe it was our home. One week before it was one of the most beautiful places in the state. Now it was a vast wreck. Gin-house, packing screws, granary—all lay in ashes. Not a fence was to be seen for miles... he army had turned their stock into the fields and destroyed what they had not carried off. Burning cotton and grain filled the air with smoke, and even the sun seemed to hide its face."

In my impotence I would hate the arrogant Eastern Americans who had ruined a century of my family's work and destroyed my community, and I would despise more the architect of that desolation, heartless and crazy Bill Sherman. But I would also never again think that either my neighbors or I had the right—or power—to hold slaves, much less either the prerogative or the ability to declare California and the property of the federal government within it as our region's own. We would have no doubts that we were defeated.

And I would hope that my sixteen-year-old son, Billy Hanson, who, like his deceased grandfather and namesake, has lived his entire life amid these vineyards and orchards, would not be rotting in some field nearby after he had armed himself with the assorted obsolete weaponry of this farm to charge bravely into the murderous line of the army of the United States in order to save our property—and along with it the idea of States' Rights and thus ultimately human bondage itself. Finally, again, I would hope that the commander of such an army was not a man like William T. Sherman, who would say of our ruin and our gallant anger: "Those people made war on us, defied and dared us to come south to their country, where they boasted they would kill us and do all manner of horrible things. We accepted their challenge, and now for them to whine and complain of the natural and necessary results is beneath contempt."

For the next century critics would argue over the rectitude, effectiveness, and difficulty of the March to the Sea, as-serting that what Sherman did in Georgia was either amoral or irrelevant to the Union cause. Others added that Sherman had not been assiduous in collecting freed slaves—purportedly more than fifty thousand directly in his path were ready to flee—and that he had wrecked the entire tradition of the practice of just war that once had expressly spared civilians. Before addressing these criticisms systematically, I must note the irony in each.

H OW IN A MORAL SENSE COULD THE March to the Sea be too barbaric in destroying Southern property yet at the same time not effective enough in killing Confederate soldiers? How could Sherman's men be too lax in freeing slaves? How could his march be considered too easy when Grant and Lincoln—men known for neither timidity nor hysteria—feared for the very destruction of Sherman's army when he requested permission to attempt it? And how else could Sherman move his colossal army to the east and be in position to march northward other than by living off the land and destroying property? Was he to pay for the food of slaveowners in prized Federal dollars with promises that such capital would not be forwarded to purchase more bullets for Lee and Johnston? Were his men to eat hardtack while secessionists fared better? Keep clear of railroads, as locomotives sped by with food, ammunition, and guns to kill Northerners in Virginia? Bypass slaveowning plantationists in a war to end slavery?

As for the charge that Sherman's brand of war was amoral, if we forget for a moment what constitutes "morality" in war and examine acts of violence per se against Southern civilians, we learn that there were few, if any, gratuitous murders on the march. There seem also to have been less than half a dozen rapes, a fact acknowledged by both sides. Any killing outside of battle was strictly military execution in response to the shooting of Northern prisoners. The real anomaly seems to be that Sherman brought more than sixty thousand young men through one of the richest areas of the enemy South without unchecked killing or mayhem. After the war a Con-federate officer remarked of the march through Georgia: "The Federal army generally behaved very well in this State. I don't think there was ever an army in the world that would have behaved better, on a similar expedition, in an enemy country. Our army certainly wouldn't."

If civilians were not killed, tortured, or raped, was the march of the army nonetheless amoral? The historian John Bennett Walters has argued that it was, because soldiers traumatized and robbed noncombatants and wrecked their homes: "An invading army, without any claim on military necessity, had thrown away every inclination toward mercy for weakness and helplessness. The Federal troops had resorted to the sheer brutality of overpowering strength to despoil a people of their material resources and to injure irreparably their finer sensibilities."

The true moral question, though, is not whether civilians are fair game in war but whether the property and tranquillity of civilians who support chattel slavery and rebellion are fair game in a war precipitated over refusal to end that institution—whether, in other words, the supporters of apartheid have abandoned prior claim on the "finer sensibilities." If one believes that slavery is a great evil and that secession constitutes treason, then Sherman was surely right that the best mechanism to end both, short of killing civilians, was to destroy the property of both the state and the wealthy, thereby robbing those fighting on behalf of slaveholding and rebellion of both the material and psychological support of their own citizenry. That seems to me very much a "military necessity."

We must here make a vital distinction between "total" war and a war of "terror." Sherman surely waged the latter, seeking to shock the enemy through the destruction of its landscape and the wreckage of its hopes to such a degree that it would desist from supporting the killing of Union troops. But that terror was not total, and he never resorted to any of the barbarities of the modern age—ethnic cleansing, concentration camps, mass killing, indiscriminate bombing, and torture—to achieve his ends. His march has nothing in common with the dirty wars of the twentieth century, wherein revolutions, coups, and ethnic hatreds have usually had no moral agenda and have never been part of an effort to stop enslavement. When Sherman reached Savannah, Southern generals asked him for the protection of their own families, surely proof that they at least did not think they were entrusting their women and children to a terrorist.

T HE LATE TWENTIETH CENTURY has increasingly come to declare *all* war evil. Since peace is considered the natural state of relations, we live in an era of "conflict resolution" and "peace studies," in which some degree of moral guilt is freely assessed equally both to those who kill to advance evil and those who kill to end it, to those who are aggressive and to those who resist aggrandizement. Regardless of cause or circumstances, we all in the end must become "victims" of those who have the greater power, which transcends national boundaries: politicians, corporations, the military. Indeed, "evil" itself is to be seen as a relative idea.

Yet there is always a timeless, absolute difference between slavery and freedom, and those who battle for abolition and those who kill to defend slavery are qualitatively different and can be recognized as such. There would have been a real difference between a Confederate America and a Union America. Sherman's war against property belongs to a particular context, inseparable from the question of slavery. So I am confused when present-day historians write that they are disturbed, for example, to learn that Sherman's men killed bloodhounds in Georgia, as if the gratuitous killing of pets, some of which were accomplished trackers of slaves and Union prisoners, mattered very much when half a million blacks in Georgia had been slaves until Bill Sherman's dog-killers set thousands of them free.

Once the free Southern leadership and its citizenry chose to fight and kill on behalf of human bondage, the destruction of their private property, unlike attacks against Northern farms, took on the logic of retribution and atonement. Was this a fair rationale for Union soldiers when their own Founding Fathers

had owned slaves and had seen no reason to bar the practice in either the Constitution or the Bill of Rights? Lincoln grasped perfectly this American dilemma and thus sought to eradicate the evil of slavery, at least in the beginning of his efforts, peaceably, with compensation, and over time, as all American society might slowly evolve to a consensus about the immorality of bondage.

Southerners, in contrast, wanted no part of that national dialogue, because they knew precisely where it would end up: abolition and a federal government now strong enough to enforce its moral culture on particular states. Southern leaders precipitated the war because they correctly saw Federal policy as leading immutably to the end of their way of life—a way of life whose material riches for a few were to be perpetually supported by the bondage of African blacks.

W AS SHERMAN'S MARCH EFFECTIVE? There seem to be two approaches involved in this answer, and both result in the affirmative. If for a moment we forget the actual material damage done the Confederacy and consider where Sherman's army started and where it finished, the march in itself was the definitive act of retribution against the South. Sherman's capture of Atlanta probably saved Lincoln the election. The very fact that he could march unharmed through the South eroded all support in the North for Democrats and Copperheads who advocated negotiated peace or surrender under the guise of settlement. Overseas there would be no further talk of recognizing the Confederacy.

Moreover, in purely strategic terms, Sherman was now three hundred miles closer to the last major source of Confederate resistance, Lee's army in Virginia. Until Sherman reached Savannah, Grant was holding Lee firmly in his grasp and waging, whether intended or not, a brutal and steady war of annihilation. When Sherman reached the Atlantic—as he had foreseen all along—the complexion of that death lock changed radically: Lee was faced with the prospect of a lethal force marching steadily northward at his rear,

devouring the source of supply for his army, and ruining the homes of his soldiers in the trenches. Whereas before, Lee had kept Grant out of Richmond and had the option either to threaten Washington or to just stay still, now he had to move either northward over Grant or southward through Sherman.

Had Sherman not torched a single Southern estate, his march would never-

---

Had Sherman not torched a single Southern estate, his march would nevertheless have been strategically brilliant.

---

theless have been strategically brilliant for its role in the coordination of the Union armies—and psychologically devastating to the Confederate cause. As the artillery officer Thomas Osborn wrote when Sherman and his men reached Savannah: "Thus the immediate object of the campaign is completed. This army has been transferred from the middle of the country to the sea coast, this city captured and the lines for supplies for General Lee's army south of here are destroyed. The Confederacy proper is now southern Virginia and North and South Carolina. It has no other territory now at its disposal for military operations and this campaign has shown there is not much more left to it, except General Lee's army and the small force in our front."

Damage, of course, Sherman did. Even by 1870 the assessed valuation of farms in Georgia was little more than a third what it had been ten years earlier. Unfortunately for the poor of the South, the ripples of Sherman's plunge into the Georgian countryside continued for decades; the result of his depredations against the plantations and state was to create years of general economic stagnation that would affect both the free black and white poor. Sherman's apologists—and in the years after the armi-

What Sherman's men left of a train carrying ordnance to Confederate soldiers under Gen. John Bell Hood.

stice they continued to shrink as the horror of frontal infantry assault was forgotten—would defend his actions on three grounds: First, better that Southerners be poor and alive in Georgia than rotting in the mud of northern Virginia—and the South's only apparent strategy of salvation was the doomed quest to crush Grant's Army of the Potomac; second, the poverty of a few hundred thousand citizens for decades was to be reckoned against the bondage of millions of slaves for centuries; and third, war cannot be "refined." Revolutionaries suffer inordinately when they precipitate war, lack the high moral ground, and turn out to be impotent. Sherman would come to be hated in a way Grant never would be because he humiliated and impoverished the South with ease and impunity, rather than kill Southern youth with difficulty and at great cost.

THE MARCH THROUGH GEORGIA made all subsequent campaigns by the Army of the West easier. Hundreds

of thousands of Confederate civilians, once so critical in encouraging their men at the front, now would have precisely the opposite effect. When Sherman turned north into the Carolinas, Confederate soldiers wrote their governor: "It is not in the power of the Yankee Armies to cause us to wish ourselves at home. We can face them, and can hear their shot and shell without being moved; but, Sir, we cannot hear the cries of our little ones and stand." This natural reaction had been foreseen by Sherman: "I attach more importance to these deep incisions into the enemy's country, because this war differs from European wars in this particular: we are not only fighting hostile armies, but a hostile people, and must make old and young, rich and poor, feel the hard hand of war, as well as their organized armies. I know that this recent movement of mine through Georgia has had a wonderful effect in this respect. Thousands who have been deceived by their lying newspapers to believe that we were being whipped all the time now realize the truth, and have

no appetite for a repetition of the same experience."

Whereas much has been written of the destruction of Southern morale, too little has been devoted to the radically changed spirit in the North brought on by Sherman's march. Lincoln put it best as he summed up the Union effort in his annual message to Congress on December 6, 1864: "[We] have *more* men *now* than we had when the war *began....* We are *gaining* strength, and may, if need be, maintain the contest indefinitely." Grant's army was a force vital to the preservation of the Union and the destruction of the best Confederate soldiers in the field, but neither Grant nor the Army of the Potomac—given the frightful casualties of summer 1864 and the absence of movement forward—could embolden the American populace to continue the war.

Americans might now sing "Marching Through Georgia" or read poems about "The March to the Sea"; they would never write hymns to celebrate Cold Harbor or read verses about "The

Wilderness." Sherman—in light of his army's speed, his preservation of Union lives, his transection of the Confederacy, the sheer hatred he incurred from the South, and his gift for the language of doom—captured the mind of America. In a little more than thirty days he had redefined the entire Civil War as a death struggle between yeomen farmers and the privilege of aristocratic plantationists, and the verdict of that ideological contest was plain for all to see in the burning estates of central Georgia. Had Sherman not taken Atlanta, Lincoln might not have been re-elected President; had he lost his army in Georgia, a negotiated peace would have been a real possibility; and had he rested on his laurels in Savannah, Grant would have fought Lee for another six months to a year. It is true that Sherman redefined the American way of war, but his legacy was not Vietnam but rather the great liberating invasions of Europe during World War II, in which Americans marched right through the homelands of the Axis powers. Sherman, in short, invented the entire notion of American strategic doctrine, one that would appear so frequently in the century to follow: the ideal of a vast moral crusade on foreign soil to restructure a society through sheer force of arms.

W E SHOULD KEEP IN MIND THAT the timing the war's close in April 1865 was not fortuitous. The Confederacy collapsed at that particular moment not because of Thomas's smashing victory in Tennessee nearly six months earlier, or because Grant had finally obliterated Lee, but rather because Sherman's gigantic army of Union veterans was now rapidly approaching Lee's rear. The South itself acknowledged this. The obituary for Sherman in the Americus, Georgia, *Daily Times* conceded that he "was the victorious general who really subdued the Confederacy. By his devastations in Georgia the morale of Lee's army was so reduced and his ranks so thinned that Grant's success was possible, so that at last Sherman and not Grant was entitled to the credit of Appomattox."

Moreover, Sherman's marches precipitated the war's end at a great savings in lives on both sides. More Southerners

deserted, gave up, or simply ceased fighting because of Sherman's march than were killed in Grant's attacks. "Of course I must fight when the time comes," Sherman wrote his daughter, "but wherever a result can be accomplished without Battle I prefer it."

Was he sometimes lax in recruiting slaves into his army on his march? Yes. Did it ultimately matter? No. It is true that Sherman did not welcome very young, female, or aged freed slaves to join his march. He was interested primarily in taking on fit young male ex-slaves to serve in his engineering and pioneering corps—the thousands of impressive black troopers who would later carve a path through the Carolinas and march so proudly in review in Washington at war's end.

As events turned out, Sherman still had thousands of blacks in his army when it was all over; he had freed thousands more during his march—best estimates put them at more than twenty-five thousand, or almost a third of the size of his own force—and his efforts at destroying the plantation culture of the South had accelerated the general emancipation in the mere six months left after he cut through Georgia. Later he would put it succinctly: "My aim then was, to whip the rebels, to humble their pride, to follow them to their inmost recesses, and make them fear and dread us. 'Fear of the Lord is the beginning of wisdom.' I did not want them to cast in our teeth what General Hood had once done in Atlanta, that we had to call on their slaves to help us to subdue them. But, as regards kindness to the race, encouraging them to patience and forbearance, procuring them food and clothing, and providing them with land whereon to labor, I assert that no army ever did more for that race than the one I commanded in Savannah."

Finally, and most important, did Sherman bring on the evils of total conflict so well known to the modern age? He did not. The best of the Union generals—Thomas and Grant in particular—were bulldogs, not greyhounds, and it was they, not Sherman, who turned war into an anonymous process of an industrial state, where cannon, rifle, and manpower were thrown promiscuously

into the inferno, with little regard to past custom or protocol and even less chance that individual achievement or skill in arms in themselves might win the day.

H OWEVER INEXACT THE COMPARISON, the difference between World War I and World War II sheds some light on the respective manner in which Grant and Sherman each fought the South, and the contrast is not, as might be expected, entirely to Sherman's detriment. From 1914 to 1918 the Allies, Grant-like, waged a horrific war of annihilation in the trenches against the armies of autocracy that ultimately ruined their entire military but left the populations of the Central Powers largely unscathed—and eager to find scapegoats. Another world war followed a mere two decades later. After World War II and the savage and systematic demolition of the German and Japanese landscapes—far in excess of what even Sherman might have imagined or condoned—neither society warred again, and there has been peace in Europe and Japan thus far not for twenty years but for half a century. No German or Japanese civilians after 1945 could ever underestimate the power of the British and American military, or think that their culture had been betrayed rather than conquered, or believe that their support for murderous regimes did not have personal consequences. Germans had far more respect for—and fear of—Patton in 1945 than they had had for Pershing in 1918.

For Sherman, then, the attack on property and infrastructure was permissible, if the war was an ideological one against anarchy, treason, and slavery and if it would lead to a permanent peace based on just principles. Terror, as a weapon to be employed in war by a democratic army, must be proportional, ideological, and rational: proportional—Southerners, who fought to preserve men as mere property, would have their property destroyed; ideological—those who would destroy property would do so as part of a larger effort of abolition that was not merely strategic but ethical as well; and rational—burning and looting would not be random, nor killing gratuitous, but rather ruin was to have a certain logic, as railways, public buildings, big plantations, all the visible and often official infrastructure of a slave society, would be torched, while the meager houses of the poor and the persons themselves of the Confederacy would be left relatively untouched.

The issues of age and property are also often forgotten in Sherman's march, but again they are decisive. Sherman constantly stressed his affection for "his boys" and the need to save his army; he showed a shocking lack of concern for those of adult age in the Confederacy who had carried through secession. Yet it seems to me a far more moral act to make the middle-aged and elderly, male and female alike, who fight wars for property pay for their folly with their possessions, than to exterminate those youngsters, without possessions, and with little real knowledge of the politics that put them in harm's way.

THE HISTORIAN B. H. LIDDELL HART best summed up Sherman's view of what constituted real savagery: "It was logical, and due to reasoning that was purely logical, that he should first oppose war; then, conduct it with iron severity; and, finally, seize the first real opportunity to make a peace of complete absolution. He cared little that his name should be execrated by the people of the South if he could only cure them of a taste for war. And to cure them he deliberately aimed at the noncombatant foundation of the hostile war spirit instead of its combatant roof. He cared as little that this aim might violate a conventional code of war, for so long as war was regarded as a chivalrous pastime, and its baseness obscured by a punctilious code, so long would it be invested with a halo of romance. Such a code and such a halo had helped the duel to survive long after less polite forms of murder had grown offensive to civilized taste and gone out of fashion."

It is true that Sherman redefined warfare, but his legacy is not Vietnam—it is the liberating invasions of Europe during World War II.

I am also surprised not at the contrasts drawn between Sherman and Grant—their differences in strategic thinking, their close friendship, and their shared responsibility for winning the war invite obvious and spirited comparisons that have merit on both sides—but rather at the absence of contrasts drawn between Sherman and Lee. Lee, who wrecked his army by sending thousands on frontal charges against an entrenched enemy and who himself owned slaves, enjoys the reputation of a reluctant, humane knight who battled for a cause—States' Rights and the sanctity of Southern soil—other than slavery. Sherman, who was careful to save his soldiers from annihilation and who freed thousands of slaves in Georgia, is too often seen as a murderous warrior who fought for a cause—federalism and the punishment of treason—other than freedom.

Lee, as Sherman noted, crafted the wrong offensive for an outmanned and outproduced South, which led to horrendous casualties; Sherman's marches drew naturally on the material and human surpluses of the North and so cracked the core of the Confederacy, with few killed on either side. Lee wrongly thought the Union soldier would not fight as well as the Confed-

erate; Sherman rightly guessed that the destruction of Southern property would topple the entire Confederacy. The one ordered thousands to their deaths when the cause was clearly lost; the other destroyed millions of dollars of property to hasten the end of bloodshed. Yet Sherman, who fought on the winning side, who promised in the abstract death and terror, who was unkempt, garrulous, and blunt, is usually criticized; Lee, who embodies the Lost Cause, who wrote of honor and sacrifice, and who was dapper, genteel, and mannered, is canonized. Historians would do better to assess each on what he did, not on what he professed.

Sherman's most impressive statue, a forty-three-foot-high equestrian rendition of the general on the march, still towers in Washington, D.C., in a beautiful, small park at Fifteenth Street and Pennsylvania Avenue, between the Treasury Department and the Ellipse. Few Washingtonians know where the statue is, and fewer still of those who lunch in the park seem ever to approach the monument itself. If they did, they would discover, on the north side of the granite base, beneath the mounted general, Sherman's own declaration that the proper purpose of battle was to make society right: "War's Legitimate Object Is More Perfect Peace."

Victor Davis Hanson, a classics professor at California State University, is the author of six books, including Fields Without Dreams *and* Who Killed Homer? *This article is adapted from his most recent one,* The Soul of Battle: From Ancient Times to the Present Day, How Three Great Liberators Vanquished Tyranny, *just published by the Free Press.*

Bats, Balls, and Bullets

Baseball and the Civil War

George B. Kirsch

A TERRIBLE TENSION CLOUDED THE EARLY MONTHS OF 1861. All over a partially divided America, people went about their lives with one eye fixed on the horizon of national life, looking for signs of what was to be: the breakup of the Union? peace? war? But life went on, and soon one of the newest but most dependable signs of spring appeared. In dozens of American cities and towns, baseball players set to work preparing their minds, bodies, and—in those days before stadiums, artificial turf, and professional groundskeepers—their grass and dirt playing fields for another season of play.

Then, in mid-April, just as the ball teams were getting warmed up, news of the firing on Fort Sumter in South Carolina sent shock waves through North and South alike. It was war, time to take up swords and muskets and lay aside bats and balls—or so it seemed at first. Instead, baseball went to war with the men in blue and gray, changed as they changed, and emerged stronger than ever to help reunite them in their own national game.

Legend assigns a Civil War connection of sorts to the very origins of baseball itself. Abner Doubleday, the Civil War general who some say aimed the first cannon in defense of Fort Sumter

and who distinguished himself in the Battle of Gettysburg in 1863, is the central character in the myth of baseball's creation promulgated by the present-day professional baseball league, Major League Baseball, and the National Baseball Hall of Fame in Cooperstown, New York. According to a historical commission headed in 1907 by Abraham Mills, president of professional baseball's National League, Doubleday invented the modern rules of the game in 1839 at Cooperstown. The tale rests entirely on the testimony of one Abner Graves, who recalled playing ball with Doubleday as a boy in that bucolic town in upstate New York. Albert G. Spalding, the noted baseball luminary and sporting goods magnate, fully endorsed Graves's story at the time, but later admitted: "It certainly appeals to an American's pride to have had the great national game of Base Ball created and named by a Major General in the United States Army."

Though the Doubleday-Cooperstown myth remains powerful in the American imagination, scholars have long since proven it false. Research has revealed that Doubleday enrolled as a cadet at West Point in the fall of 1838 and possibly never even visited Cooperstown. Although he may have played ball with Graves during his boyhood, in his pub-

lished writings he never mentioned anything about a role in the creation of baseball. The Mills Commission's conclusion rested entirely on an elderly man's recollection of an event that had occurred 68 year earlier. And Graves's mental capacity at the time of his testimony is suspect; a few years later, he shot his wife and was committed to an institution. Furthermore, Mills had known Doubleday ever since the men served together in the Civil War, but his friend apparently had never said anything about his supposed brainstorm in Cooperstown.

If Abner Doubleday did not invent baseball, then who did? The answer is that no one person created the sport; rather, it evolved in stages from earlier bat-and-ball games, especially rounders, an English game often called "townball" in the United States. New England varieties of townball were called "round ball" or "base." The version of the sport that became widely known as the "Massachusetts game" matched sides of 8 to 15 men on a square field with bases or tall stakes (up to five feet high) at each corner. The batter stood midway between first and fourth (home) base and tried to hit a ball made of yarn tightly wound around a lump of cork or rubber and covered with smooth calfskin. The

From *Civil War Times*, May 1998, pp. 30-39. © 1998 by Cowles Magazines, Inc. Reprinted through the courtesy of Cowles Magazines, publishers of *American History*.

cylindrical bat varied in length from three to three and a half feet and was often a portion of a rake or pitchfork handle. It normally was held in one hand. The pitcher threw the ball swiftly overhand, and the batter could strike the ball in any direction, there being no foul territory. After hitting the ball, the striker ran around the bases until he was put out or remained safely on a base. He could be retired if the catcher caught three balls he missed, if a fielder caught a ball he hit before it hit the ground, or if a fielder struck him with a thrown ball while he ran the bases (called "soaking" or "burning" the runner). Usually one out ended the inning, and the first team to score a previously agreed upon number of runs won the game.

Though the Massachusetts version of baseball thrived during the late 1850s, it faced a formidable rival in New York City's version of the game, which boomed in popularity after 1857. Modern baseball derives most immediately from the latter, specifically, from the game created by the New York Knickerbocker Base Ball Club during the mid-1840s. Some baseball historians believe that a man named Alexander J. Cartwright first suggested that the Knickerbockers try aligning the bases along a diamond instead of a square and placing the batter at home plate. At the very least, Cartwright was the chief organizer of the club and the man responsible for codifying its first rules—namely, that the ball had to be pitched underhand, not overhand; that a ball knocked outside the area bounded by first and third bases was foul; and that a player was out if a ball he hit was caught on the fly or on the first bounce, or if a fielder touched him with the ball as he ran between bases. "Soaking" the runner was prohibited, three outs retired a side from the field, and 21 runs (called "aces") decided the game, provided each side had had an opportunity to make an equal number of outs. The Knickerbockers played their first intraclub games in the Murray Hill section of Manhattan, then moved to the Elysian Fields of Hoboken, New Jersey, in 1846. Their pastime spread very slowly until the late 1850s, when baseball mania swept across the greater New York City region.

At the time hostilities between North and South broke out in 1861, no one knew which form of the game would come to enjoy the greatest popularity, but it was already clear that there were striking parallels between team sports and war. During the late 1850s and early 1860s, the sporting press frequently pointed out the similarities. In wrapping up its review of the 1857 season, a journal called the *New York Clipper* remarked that the players "will be compelled to lay by their weapons of war, enter into winter quarters, there to discuss and lay plans for the proper conducting of next season's campaign." Yet sportswriters were acutely aware of the crucial differences between play and mortal struggle. "God forbid that any balls but those of the Cricket and Baseball field may be caught either on the fly or bound," read a March 1861 *Clipper* article, "and we trust that no arms but those of the flesh may be used to impel them, or stumps, but those of the wickets, injured by them."

After the struggle began, a Rochester reporter noted that "many of our first class players are now engaged in the 'grand match' against the rebellious 'side,' and have already made a 'score' which, in after years, they will be proud to look upon." Another remarked, "Cricket and Baseball clubs . . . are now enlisted in a different sort of exercise, the rifle or gun taking the place of the bat, while the play ball gives place to the leaden messenger of death. . . . Men who have heretofore made their mark in friendly strife for superiority in various games, are now beating off the rebels who would dismember the glorious 'Union of States.' " In April, a Union soldier encamped with his regiment at Culpeper Court House, Virginia, reported, "If General Grant does not send them to have a match with Gen. Lee, they are willing to have another friendly match, but if he does, the blue coats think that the leaden balls will be much harder to stop than if thrown by friendly hands on the club grounds."

Soldier-athletes also believed that baseball was useful in preparing them for the more deadly contests of the battlefield. The Rochester *Express* noted that with "the serious matter of war . . .

upon our hands . . . , physical education and the development of muscle should be engendered by indulgence in baseball."

Thousands of Northern baseball club members enlisted in the Union army, and a few volunteered for the Confederate cause. The sportsmen who marched off to war took with them their love of play—and sometimes their bats and balls. Military authorities permitted recreation for soldiers at appropriate times and places because it provided useful diversion. The U.S. Sanitary Commission recommended that to preserve the health of soldiers, "when practicable, amusements, sports, and gymnastic exercises should be favored amongst the men." Baseball was listed among the approved pastimes. Officers encouraged sport to relieve the boredom of camp life. Organized games also helped to motivate men during training, to foster group cohesion and loyalty, and to improve recruits' physical fitness.

The *Clipper* praised the practice of athletic games in camp, noting the "beneficial effect they have on the spirits and health, and how they tend to alleviate the monotony of camp life." The journal also remarked that sports had helped create "a wholesome rivalry between companies and regiments, and augment the *esprit de corps* of the same, to an extent that to those who have not witnessed it would appear marvelous." Baseball was even allowed in certain prison camps. A prominent Southern nine, for example, originated at Johnson's Island, Ohio, where inmates learned the New York game while being held by Union forces.

Baseball-playing soldiers improvised makeshift grounds for their games, constructed rudimentary equipment, and arranged contests both in camp and ever perilously close to enemy positions. One enthusiast sent the *Clipper* the score of a match played on the parade ground of the "Mozart Regiment, now in Secessia" in October 1861. He wanted to report the sports news to civilians on the homefront, "lest you imagine that the 'sacred soil' yields only to the tramp of the soldier; that its hills echo only the booming gun, and the dying shriek." The game, he wrote, totally

Voices from the Stands . . .

In our February issue, we asked readers to send us their thoughts on baseball and its connection to the Civil War. Here is a sampling of what we received.

All men have a hidden desire to compete and win. Baseball is a sport played for the fun of it, and the final score is soon forgotten. War is fought on an extremely serious level, and the outcome is etched in our souls forever.

Victor M. Wein
Pittsburgh, Pennsylvania

You pick up a bat and your back yard becomes the site of the final game of the World Series. It's the bottom of the ninth, the game is tied, and you are the batter, the pitcher, and the announcer all at once. You throw the ball in the air, swing, and drive it past the spot of dirt that is second base. You round that spot with your arms held high and celebrate the possibility of knowing such joy.

Now, you're at Gettysburg. You stand on Seminary Ridge and look out across those fields and wonder, Would I have climbed the fence along the Emmitsburg Road and kept going? Those who did were average people, and perhaps you, too, could have risen to such heroic heights. You walk toward the copse of trees and quietly celebrate the possibility of that kind of commitment.

Austin E. Gisriel
Williamsport, Maryland

I see the hitter at the plate, all alone, facing nine opponents. Yet he remains part of a team. In the Civil War, the Rebs and the Yanks stood in lines, firing away at the other side. Each was a part of a team—a company, regiment, or brigade—but they faced the enemy as individuals, each with his own doubts and fears.

C.J. Calenti
Poughkeepsie, New York

In baseball and in war, two distinct teams compete on a field with a set of rules that are fairly static, but open to interpretation. Strategies are employed to win that often evolve during the course of the conflict. The two teams could be from opposite ends of town, the country, or even the world. But, cultural, ethnic, and racial differences aside, they react the same way: from both we learn about ourselves.

James Dossey
Baker, Louisiana

Soldiers on both sides, at least those who survived the war, stood in later years and cheered baseball's early legends and told their sons about the game. Baseball was played near battlefields grown still by the passage of time, and baseball, like those veterans, will always be remembered.

Bo Bourisseau
Mountville, Ohio

"erased from their minds the all absorbing topic of the day."

Soldiers played both the Massachusetts and New York versions of the game, arranging pickup games within their own regiments or challenging rival units. According to an often-repeated story, on Christmas 1862 more than 40,000 Union soldiers witnessed an encounter between the 165th New York Infantry and an all-star squad that included future National League president A.G. Mills. While it is possible that the game actually occurred, the size of the crowd has undoubtedly been exaggerated.

Generally, the men sported within the relative security of their encampments, though sometimes they violated army regulations and competed outside their fortifications and beyond their picket lines. George H. Putnam remembered a contest among Union troops in Texas that was aborted by a surprise enemy assault. "Suddenly there came a scattering fire of which the three fielders caught the brunt," he wrote; "the center field was hit and was captured, the left and right field managed to get into our lines." The Northern soldiers repulsed the Confederate attack, "but we had lost not only our center field but . . . the only baseball in Alexandria."

While baseball enthusiasts enjoyed their favorite sport in army camps, the game suffered some understandable setbacks on the home front. With so many sportsmen off at war, and with civilian anxieties focused on battlefield news, interest in playful contests naturally waned. Yet the sport persisted, and even progressed, under the trying conditions. In a review of the 1861 season in the New York City area, the *Clipper* reported, "The game has too strong a foothold in popularity to be frowned out of favor by the lowering brow of 'grim-visaged war.'"

The New York form of the game gained momentum in New England when a tour by the Brooklyn Excelsiors excited Boston's sporting fraternity. In Philadelphia, baseball overtook cricket in popularity during the early 1860s. Near the end of the war, the Federal capital experienced a baseball revival thanks in part to resident New Yorkers who worked in the U.S. Treasury Department and played for the National and Union clubs on the grounds behind the White House. In the South, the Union conquest of New Orleans took baseball back deep into Dixie, where the war had virtually snuffed out the sport before it could become firmly established. And in the West, a contingent of "Rocky Mountain Boys" played the New York game in Denver in 1862.

As it was before the war, the Middle Atlantic region was at the core of baseball fever. New York, New Jersey, and Pennsylvania inaugurated the sport's first championship system as well as several intercity all-star contests and club tours. The early 1860s also ushered in an era of commercialism and professionalism, as William H. Cammeyer of Brooklyn and other entrepreneurs enclosed fields and charged admission fees. Before and during the Civil War, amateur clubs offered various forms of compensation—direct payments, jobs or gifts—to premier players such as James Creighton and Al Reach. The National Association of Base Ball Players, founded in 1857, continued to supervise interclub play and experiment with the sport's rules, endorsing the New York rules even as the New England game remained popular among soldiers. In 1863, a national sporting weekly edited by a George Wilkes, *Wilkes' Spirit of the Times*, grandly proclaimed, "The National Association game has won for itself the almost unanimous approval of all who take any interest in the sport; and the clubs who adopt any other style of playing are every day, becoming 'small by degrees, and beautifully less.'"

The most striking evidence of baseball's capacity to flourish amid the adversity of war was the first invasion of Philadelphia players into the New York City area, in 1862. When a select "nine" competed before about 15,000 spectators in a series of games against Newark, New York, and Brooklyn teams, *Wilkes' Spirit* reported that the Philadelphia challenges awakened in New York "the old *furore* for the game that marked the years 1857–8 and 9." The paper noted that the victory of the guests over a New York team at Hoboken did more to create interest in the game in that city than five ordinary seasons' play would have done. Teams from Brooklyn and New York returned the visit later in the summer, generating excitement in their contests with the local teams: the Olympics, Adriatics, Athletics, and Keystones. The following year the Athletics won two of six games against tough opponents and established themselves as contenders for baseball's championship. By the end of the war, trips by Brooklyn, New York, and New Jersey clubs to Philadelphia were commonplace. Some of the matches were arranged to benefit the U.S. Sanitary Commission.

The tours succeeded despite the atmosphere of crisis that pervaded the entire region so near to the seat of war. In most cases, the war did not detract from the excitement of the contests, and there is little evidence that citizens disapproved of men who played ball instead of serving in the army. Understandably, though, military news sometimes completely overshadowed baseball. When Brooklyn's crack Atlantics swept a series in Philadelphia in August 1864, few fans attended, and there was little additional interest. The *Clipper* explained that the local citizens "were absorbed in the important subject of resisting the rebel invasion of the State, and this and

... Voices from the Stands

After the Civil War, the veterans returned to Hendricks County, Indiana, just west of Indianapolis, taking with them a new game they called townball. My great-grandfather, Jesse Thompson, had had five sons born before he left for the war. Upon his return, a sixth son was born—my grandfather, William. These six boys became the nucleus of Danville's team, the Browns. In 1884, a scout from Detroit visited the area to see one of these boys, Cyrus, play ball. The scout, however, became enamored with the ability of Cyrus's brother, Sam, who was only playing that day because the team agreed to pay him $2.50, the same amount he would have made building a roof.

The scout enlisted Sam as a player for Evansville in the Western League, and his professional career began. The next year he was playing in Indianapolis, and by July 1885, he was a member of the Detroit Wolverines. That was just the start. By the time he ended his career as a member of the Philadelphia Phillies in 1898, he had amassed hitting records that took decades to break. Sam Thompson, who died in 1922, was elected to the National Baseball Hall of Fame in 1974.

Don A. Thompson
Mesa, Arizona

The Battle of Gettysburg was like a game in the World Series. In order to win the championship, the undefeated Rebels once again had to defeat the Yankees. The Rebels were confident, even though the Yankees had home-field advantage this time. The game ended in a tie, but the Yankees viewed it as a victory, and the Rebels could no longer be considered unbeatable. But it is not who wins or loses that matters. It is how the game—or the war—is played, and the Rebels played very well against all odds.

Laura Race
Penn Yan, New York

Born in the decades before the Civil War, baseball spread like wildfire during the war. Union boys in the Midwest learned it from the boys of the East, and Yankees from the North taught it to their Confederate captors. Enthusiasm for the game reached all regions, all classes. What had once been the province of city merchants and professionals, the gentlemen of the day, became a game for the people. The Civil War democratized American society, including baseball, our national pastime.

Tom William Odom
Lake Worth, Florida

Not so much a metaphor of shared experience, the connection between baseball and the Civil War seems more deeply rooted in a return to that which once was. The need to get on with things may be eclipsed by a yearning to reconnect with patterns of life that disappeared on a thousand battlefields. Baseball may have enabled former soldiers to regain a portion of their lost innocence. They would agree that the game of baseball, with its simple message of competition, fair play, and male bonding, is as much a quest for innocence as it is a celebration of the strength of America—South and North—and a lasting epitaph to the courageous energy of that era.

Rich Hill
Metuchen, New Jersey

the preparations to respond to the Governor's call for 30,000 militia, materially interfered with the sensation their visit would otherwise have created." Most of the Philadelphia clubs could not play many of their best men, the journal reported, because they had responded "to the call of duty."

The return of peace to the United States in 1865 ignited a new baseball boom, prompting the *Newark Daily Advertiser* to announce that the sport "is

rightfully called the National Game of America." Veterans played a key role in spreading the sport around the nation after the war. "When soldiers were off duty," declared the *Clipper* in 1865, "base ball was naturalized in nearly every state in the Union, and thus extended in popularity."

Regional rivalries, tours by prominent clubs, and intersectional matches helped smooth relations between North and South immediately after the Civil

War. "Maryland [was] fast being reconstructed on this base-is," punned the *Clipper* in 1865. The game was even taking hold in Richmond, Virginia, the former capital of the Confederacy. "Base ball fever," the *Clipper* reported, "is rapidly assuming the form of an epidemic among the constructed and reconstructed denizens of the former stronghold of the extinct Davisocracy." But the journal followed up this news with a rebuke of the Richmond club for refusing the challenge of that city's Union team, made up mostly of businessmen and federal officials. "We regret to learn of such petty feeling and sectional animosity being evinced by any party of Southern gentlemen calling themselves ball players," the journal opined. "Our national game is intended to be national in every sense of the word, and, until this example was set by the 'Richmond club,' nothing of a sectional character has emanated from a single club in the country."

Northern and Southern journalists believed the tours of the great Eastern ball clubs would help heal the bitter wounds of war. When the Nationals of Washington, D.C., visited Brooklyn in July 1866, the Excelsiors treated them to a lavish dinner, even though a National Association of Base Ball Players rule prohibited expensive entertainment. The *Clipper* argued that the Brooklynites' extravagance showed Southerners that "the ball players' 'policy of reconstruction' is one marked by true fraternal regard, irrespective of all political opinions or sectional feelings, the National Association knowing . . . 'no North, no South, no East, no West,' but simply the interest and welfare of the game itself, and the cultivation of kindly feelings between the different clubs." When the Nationals stopped at Louisville in 1867, however, *Wilkes' Spirit* reported, "a crowd of the most unruly partisan boors and rowdy boys" extended the so-called invading Yankees a greeting "not at all in accordance with the reputation for chivalric sentiments which the Southern cities have hitherto claimed." The journal singled out the women spectators for special criticism and urged that sectional feelings be kept out of the game. "The Nationals . . . though from the shores of

... Voices from the Stands

In baseball, you don't have to hate your opponent while the action plays out, and after the contest is over, the camaraderie becomes part of the game. Though death was often the outcome in battle, there was little hatred involved; they were just trying to win. Abner Doubleday would probably have been happier throwing a baseball than lobbing a cannonball from Fort Sumter, but he no doubt noted the similarities.

Roy E. Triebel
Wantagh, New York

Americans are passionate about both the Civil War and baseball because there are not any two things that are more American. The mythical feats of the great generals and players stimulate the passions and imaginations of both the historian and the fan. Robert E. Lee's boldness in dividing his army at Chancellorsville and Babe Ruth's in calling his shot in the 1932 World Series are the stories of legend. While their triumphs are out of reach of the normal man, we can all envision ourselves as bit players.

David F. Nolan
Richmond Hill, Georgia

Baseball played a vital role for the soldiers in camp, relieving them of the horrors of war. After the war they took the game home and created a baseball boom, truly nationalizing the game. But the real story is the game itself. Were it not so much fun to play and watch, baseball would have gone the way of its parents, rounders and cricket, and become just a footnote in American history.

William Gump
Kent, Ohio

Both the war and the game evoke feelings of pride and serve as a testament to the indomitable spirit of man. Americans rally to protect battlefields such as Gettysburg and Antietam to remember forever the heroic deeds of a bygone era. The same sense of maintaining continuity with the past surrounds the desire of many to preserve the pristine nature of the nation's ballparks. So long as the country relishes its past, there will always be someone willing to learn about the great war or relive the epic game seven.

Keith M. Finley
Hammond, Louisiana

Baseball and the Civil War share a common core. In the war, both sides felt that blacks were incapable of independence without support of their white "fathers." In 1863 Abraham Lincoln freed the slaves. Some of them became soldiers, but they were led by white officers. Later, in baseball, blacks were prevented from playing the game with whites until 1947, when Branch Rickey, owner of the Brooklyn Dodgers, enlisted Jackie Robinson for his team. It is now 51 years later, and the game's leadership remains white. Blacks still hold no real power.

Milton Pascaner
Decatur, Georgia

the Potomac, had too much of the North about them apparently to merit the favor of Southern women," the journal remarked.

During the summer of 1868, the Philadelphia Athletics received a warmer reception in Louisville. For Philadelphia's part, the Pennsylvania city's *Sunday Mercury* defended the Louisville players' gray uniforms, which "had been help up to scorn, and those who wear it denounced as rebels." The paper reported that the choice of uni-

form color did not necessarily indicate the players had sided with the South in the war, and even if it did, it "has got nothing to do with our National Game." The article's author concluded, "If Jefferson Davis . . . was to meet me on the ball field, and salute me as a gentleman, I would endeavor to prove to him that I was one." When a New Orleans newspaper announced the upcoming trip of its Southern Club to Memphis and St. Louis with players who had organized while prisoners of war at Johnson's Island, its editor wondered, along with his Northern counterparts, "would it not be pleasant to see the hatchet buried in the great national game, 'spite of the efforts of politicians to keep up ill feeling between the sections?" *Wilkes' Spirit*, reporting on the New York Mutual Club's December 1869 excursion to New Orleans, observed: "This National Game seems destined to close the National Wounds opened by the late war. It is no idle pastime which draws young men, separated by two thousand miles, together to contest in friendship, upon

fields but lately crimsoned with their brothers' blood in mortal combat."

Of course baseball alone could not heal the wounds of the Civil War, but it did help reunite the nation, establishing itself as a popular institution in the social and cultural worlds of the American people. Publicists relished the sport's success and promoted it as a democratic game that offered all classes and ethnic groups an opportunity to play, if not in a stadium, then at least on a sandlot. Baseball had become the national pastime, and the stage was set for the

game's glory years—and the glory years of the nation itself.

George B. Kirsch, a professor of history at Manhattan College, adapted this article from portions of his book The Creation of American Team Sports: Baseball and Cricket, 1838–72 (*University of Illinois Press, 1989*).

America's Rites of Passage

The Author of **Play for a Kingdom** *discovers America—and himself—in our war and our game*

Thomas Dyja

ON A SUMMER'S DAY SIX YEARS AGO NOW, I CAME across a story that would change my life. It was in sports patriarch Albert G. Spalding's 1911 book *Base Ball: America's National Game*, and though it was only a rumor, it deserved to be true. "It is said," the passage read, "that in Virginia, in the long campaign before Richmond, at periods when active hostilities were in abeyance, a series of games was played between picked nines from Federal and Confederate forces." What a rumor—a sort of North-South baseball tournament in the climactic period of the Civil War! Having resolved many years earlier that my first novel would be something different from all the coming-of-age tales I'd read (and written) over the years, I fell on Spalding's story and began work on what would eventually become *Play for a Kingdom*, a historical novel that I was determined would be anything but autobiographical.

The god of first novels, though, had the last laugh. Wanting to approach the war fresh, I tried to put away all my preconceptions when I began, all the

things I believed I knew. But one morning, as I was writing the bloody battle scene of the first day of the Wilderness, my mind flashed back more than 20 years to my childhood in Chicago and the days I had spent re-creating the Battle of Lookout Mountain on my dresser top using scores of Britain's soldiers, and an illustrated edition of Bruce Catton's *This Hallowed Ground* as a guide. I suddenly remembered all my visits to the Grand Army of the Republic museum in the Chicago Public Library, a drive out to Grant's home in Galena, summer vacation trips to Springfield and "Lincolnland." Bound to my boyhood memories of Wrigley Field, White Sox owner Bill Veeck, and striking out with a regularity usually associated in that place and time with Mayor Daley's garbage crews, *Play for a Kingdom* became a very personal book, a way of revisiting who I once was, who I was becoming, and who I wanted to be. The internal struggles of my characters as they learned to be husbands, fathers, friends, and Americans were all born of the questions I was asking myself as I came

of age during those years of writing. And so, despite my best efforts, my first novel ended up a novel of identity.

But it is not just a novel of *my* identity; *Play for a Kingdom* was always meant to be an imagined moment from the creation of the American identity. The Civil War marked this nation's coming of age, and baseball, as promoted by men such as sportswriter Henry Chadwick, took hold as our American game at the same time. Since those pivotal years when America became truly one and baseball beat out cricket for the hearts of American sportsmen, the Civil War and baseball have been linked. That the two are so linked is not coincidence or confluence, but a case of a nation and an organized sport forged together in one furnace by a certain people and their time. The citizens of Grant's and Lincoln's new industrial democracy were the first to pay to watch baseball, and were the first to be paid to play it. What seemed to be a meritocracy of sport developed in the 1860s: the talented, no matter where they came from, would be paid to do their best. The quality of the game improved, and baseball's days as the pastime of a Jeffersonian citizen elite were sacrificed to a greater good, to a form of play for all Americans.

Or so it seemed. There was, for a while, a Freedman's Bureau, and the gifted black catcher Fleet Walker played on the same teams with white men. But the bureau's promised "40 acres and a mule" and all they stood for never showed up, and when Chicago's towering slugger Cap Anson refused to step onto a field with Walker in the 1880s, organized baseball lined right up behind him. The tolerant curiosity of Reconstruction yielded to a sense of threat, and as victory in the Civil War was awarded to those who'd originally lost, a new and very white elite took hold again of baseball with a grip that we've only recently begun to loosen.

And so the dance continues. The all-American sport is still a monopoly, still a boy's club, yet with all the worst excesses of a free market gone mad. Baseball today exists in a business atmosphere where second-best seems fine as long as the money's right. We find ourselves tangled up in debates about designated hitter rules that let pitchers delegate their turn at bat to men who don't play in the field, and playoffs that can send a "wild card" team to the World Series even if it didn't win its division title. Bigger baseball is better baseball, right? Why not Super Size it? Have a monster home run off a third-rate pitcher who made it into the majors only because of overexpansion. These changes in the game, these debates and dissatisfactions, express the nature of America today and the continual, small vibrations in the tension between the individual and the group which both baseball and the Civil War embody.

Baseball and the Civil War have other things in common, things that make them of eternal interest to us. Both are feasts of details, full of the minutiae that make for wonderful hobbies. There's always something more to learn, some statistic or oddity that reconfirms and justifies our fascination. For many of us, our interests become passions, even escapes. Indeed, arcane battle plans and batting averages are much easier to master than everyday life, but hobbies and courses of interest do release some better part of ourselves that we believe has no place in our offices and stations. The challenge to those of us who split our time between office, home, and either battlefield park or ballpark is to bring that better—and, we hope, happier—part back with us, to turn the facts we uncover into explanations for why we are who we are today and how we can be better as a nation.

Baseball and the Civil War are also both very much about community. Even in these days of free agency and of team owners begging and threatening their cities for bigger and better stadiums, our baseball teams still represent our communities, like it or not, just as most Civil War regiments were made up of citizen-soldiers and represented their communities of origin. After the war, following the fortunes of our regiments blurred easily into following the fortunes of our teams, and even now millions of us use baseball and the Civil War as ways to define our communities, and to define ourselves within them. It's important to move past the scores and troop movements and remember these communities, to reenact not just a soldier, but a man from a place. Imagine his place, his time, and learn to see your own place and time from where he stands. Don't just examine baseball and watch baseball, but play baseball with your neighbors and your kids.

The Civil War and baseball are not essential to understanding America; they *are* America, and every journey into the game or the war is a journey of identity for any American. Instead of building battle dioramas and picking over statistical bones, let's use our passions for the Civil War and baseball as ways to learn about ourselves. That is the very information we need for the daily necessity of recreating our nation.

Thomas Dyja is the author of the novel Play for a Kingdom, *published by Harcourt Brace. The book recently won the Casey Award for Best Baseball Book. Dyja lives with his wife and two children in New York City.*

The New View of Reconstruction

Whatever you were taught or thought you knew about the post–Civil War era is probably wrong in the light of recent study

Eric Foner

Eric Foner is Professor of History at Columbia University and author of Nothing but Freedom: Emancipation and Its Legacy.

In the past twenty years, no period of American history has been the subject of a more thoroughgoing reevaluation than Reconstruction—the violent, dramatic, and still controversial era following the Civil War. Race relations, politics, social life, and economic change during Reconstruction have all been reinterpreted in the light of changed attitudes toward the place of blacks within American society. If historians have not yet forged a fully satisfying portrait of Reconstruction as a whole, the traditional interpretation that dominated historical writing for much of this century has irrevocably been laid to rest.

Anyone who attended high school before 1960 learned that Reconstruction was a era of unrelieved sordidness in American political and social life. The martyred Lincoln, according to this view, had planned a quick and painless readmission of the Southern states as equal members of the national family. President Andrew Johnson, his successor, attempted to carry out Lincoln's policies but was foiled by the Radical Republicans (also known as Vindictives or Jacobins). Motivated by an irrational hatred of Rebels or by ties with Northern capitalists out to plunder the South,

the Radicals swept aside Johnson's lenient program and fastened black supremacy upon the defeated Confederacy. An orgy of corruption followed, presided over by unscrupulous carpetbaggers (Northerners who ventured south to reap the spoils of office), traitorous scalawags (Southern whites who cooperated with the new governments for personal gain), and the ignorant and childlike freedmen, who were incapable of properly exercising the political power that had been thrust upon them. After much needless suffering, the white community of the South banded together to overthrow these "black" governments and restore home rule (their euphemism for white supremacy). All told, Reconstruction was just about the darkest page in the American saga.

Originating in anti-Reconstruction propaganda of Southern Democrats during the 1870s, this traditional interpretation achieved scholarly legitimacy around the turn of the century through the work of William Dunning and his students at Columbia University. It reached the larger public through films like *Birth of a Nation* and *Gone With the Wind* and that best-selling work of myth-making masquerading as history, *The Tragic Era* by Claude G. Bowers. In language as exaggerated as it was colorful, Bowers told how Andrew Johnson "fought the bravest battle for constitutional liberty and for the preservation of

our institutions ever waged by an Executive" but was overwhelmed by the "poisonous propaganda" of the Radicals. Southern whites, as a result, "literally were put to the torture" by "emissaries of hate" who manipulated the "simple-minded" freedmen, inflaming the negroes' "egotism" and even inspiring "lustful assaults" by blacks upon white womanhood.

In a discipline that sometimes seems to pride itself on the rapid rise and fall of historical interpretations, this traditional portrait of Reconstruction enjoyed remarkable staying power. The long reign of the old interpretation is not difficult to explain. It presented a set of easily identifiable heroes and villains. It enjoyed the imprimatur of the nation's leading scholars. And it accorded with the political and social realities of the first half of this century. This image of Reconstruction helped freeze the mind of the white South in unalterable opposition to any movement for breaching the ascendancy of the Democratic party, eliminating segregation, or readmitting disfranchised blacks to the vote.

Nevertheless, the demise of the traditional interpretation was inevitable, for it ignored the testimony of the central participant in the drama of Reconstruction—the black freedman. Furthermore, it was grounded in the conviction that blacks were unfit to share in political power. As Dunning's Columbia colleague John W. Burgess put it, "A black skin means membership in a race of men which has never of itself succeeded in subjecting passion to reason, has never, therefore, created any civilization of any kind." Once objective scholarship and modern experience rendered that assumption untenable, the entire edifice was bound to fall.

The work of "revising" the history of Reconstruction began with the writings of a handful of survivors of the era, such as John R. Lynch, who had served as a black congressman from Mississippi af-

> *Black initiative established as many schools as did Northern religious societies and the Freedmen's Bureau. The right to vote was not simply thrust upon them by meddling outsiders, since blacks began agitating for the suffrage as soon as they were freed.*

ter the Civil War. In the 1930s white scholars like Francis Simkins and Robert Woody carried the task forward. Then, in 1935, the black historian and activist W. E. B. Du Bois produced *Black Reconstruction in America,* a monumental revaluation that closed with an irrefutable indictment of a historical profession that had sacrificed scholarly objectivity on the altar of racial bias. "One fact and one alone," he wrote, "explains the attitude of most recent writers toward Reconstruction; they cannot conceive of Negroes as men." Du Bois's work, however, was ignored by most historians.

It was not until the 1960s that the full force of the revisionist wave broke over the field. Then, in rapid succession, virtu-

ally every assumption of the traditional viewpoint was systematically dismantled. A drastically different portrait emerged to take its place. President Lincoln did not have a coherent "plan" for Reconstruction, but at the time of his assassination he had been cautiously contemplating black suffrage. Andrew Johnson was a stubborn, racist politician who lacked the ability to compromise. By isolating himself from the broad currents of public opinion that had nourished Lincoln's career, Johnson created an impasse with Congress that Lincoln would certainly have avoided, thus throwing away his political power and destroying his own plans for reconstructing the South.

The Radicals in Congress were acquitted of both vindictive motives and the charge of serving as the stalking-horses of Northern capitalism. They emerged instead as idealists in the best nineteenth-century reform tradition. Radical leaders like Charles Sumner and Thaddeus Stevens had worked for the rights of blacks long before any conceivable political advantage flowed from such a commitment. Stevens refused to sign the Pennsylvania Constitution of 1838 because it disfranchised the state's black citizens; Sumner led a fight in the 1850s to integrate Boston's public schools. Their Reconstruction policies were based on principle, not petty po-

litical advantage, for the central issue dividing Johnson and these Radical Republicans was the civil rights of freedmen. Studies of congressional policy-making, such as Eric L. McKitrick's *Andrew Johnson and Reconstruction,* also revealed that Reconstruction legislation, ranging from the Civil Rights Act of 1866 to the Fourteenth and Fifteenth Amendments, enjoyed broad support from moderate and conservative Republicans. It was not simply the work of a narrow radical faction.

Even more startling was the revised portrait of Reconstruction in the South itself. Imbued with the spirit of the civil rights movement and rejecting entirely the racial assumptions that had underpinned the traditional interpretation, these historians evaluated Reconstruction from the black point of view. Works like Joel Williamson's *After Slavery* portrayed the period as a time of extraordinary political, social, and economic progress for blacks. The establishment of public school systems, the granting of equal citizenship to blacks, the effort to restore the devastated Southern economy, the attempt to construct an interracial political democracy from the ashes of slavery, all these were commendable achievements, not the elements of Bowers's "tragic era."

Until recently, Thaddeus Stevens had been viewed as motivated by irrational hatred of the Rebels (left). Now he has emerged as an idealist in the best reform tradition.

NEW YORK PUBLIC LIBRARY, PRINT ROOM

LIBRARY OF CONGRESS

EDWARD S. ELLIS. *The History of Our Country.* **VOL. 5, 1900**

Reconstruction governments were portrayed as disastrous failures because elected blacks were ignorant or corrupt. In fact, postwar corruption cannot be blamed on former slaves.

SCHOMBERG CENTER, NEW YORK PUBLIC LIBRARY

Unlike earlier writers, the revisionists stressed the active role of the freedmen in shaping Reconstruction. Black initiative established as many schools as did Northern religious societies and the Freedmen's Bureau. The right to vote was not simply thrust upon them by meddling outsiders, since blacks began agitating for the suffrage as soon as they were freed. In 1865 black conventions throughout the South issued eloquent, though unheeded, appeals for equal civil and political rights.

With the advent of Radical Reconstruction in 1867, the freedmen did enjoy a real measure of political power. But black supremacy never existed. In most states blacks held only a small fraction of political offices, and even in South Carolina, where they comprised a majority of the state legislature's lower house, effective power remained in white hands. As for corruption, moral standards in both government and private enterprise were at low ebb throughout the nation in the postwar years—the era of Boss Tweed, the Credit Mobilier scandal, and the Whiskey Ring. Southern corruption could hardly be blamed on former slaves.

Other actors in the Reconstruction drama also came in for reevaluation. Most carpetbaggers were former Union soldiers seeking economic opportunity in the postwar South, not unscrupulous adventurers. Their motives, a typically American amalgam of humanitarianism and the pursuit of profit, were no more insidious than those of Western pioneers. Scalawags, previously seen as traitors to the white race, now emerged as "Old Line" Whig Unionists who had

opposed secession in the first place or as poor whites who had long resented planters' domination of Southern life and who saw in Reconstruction a chance to recast Southern society along more democratic lines. Strongholds of Southern white Republicanism like east Tennessee and western North Carolina had been the scene of resistance to Confederate rule throughout the civil War; now,

Under slavery most blacks had lived in nuclear family units, although they faced the constant threat of separation from loved ones by sale. Reconstruction provided the opportunity for blacks to solidify their preexisting family ties.

as one scalawag newspaper put it, the choice was "between salvation at the hand of the Negro or destruction at the hand of the rebels."

At the same time, the Ku Klux Klan and kindred groups, whose campaign of violence against black and white Repub-

licans had been minimized or excused in older writings, were portrayed as they really were. Earlier scholars had conveyed the impression that the Klan intimidated blacks mainly by dressing as ghosts and playing on the freedmen's superstitions. In fact, black fears were all too real: the Klan was a terrorist organization that beat and killed its political opponents to deprive blacks of their newly won rights. The complicity of the Democratic party and the silence of prominent whites in the face of such outrages stood as an indictment of the moral code the South had inherited from the days of slavery.

By the end of the 1960s, then, the old interpretation had been completely reversed. Southern freedmen were the heroes, the "Redeemers" who overthrew Reconstruction were the villains, and if the era was "tragic," it was because change did not go far enough. Reconstruction had been a time of real progress and its failure a lost opportunity for the South and the nation. But the legacy of Reconstruction—the Fourteenth and Fifteenth Amendments—endured to inspire future efforts for civil rights. As Kenneth Stampp wrote in *The Era of Reconstruction,* a superb summary of revisionist findings published in 1965, "if it was worth four years of civil war to save the Union, it was worth a few years of radical reconstruction to give the American Negro the ultimate promise of equal civil and political rights."

As Stampp's statement suggests, the reevaluation of the first Reconstruction was inspired in large measure by the impact of the second—the modern civil rights movement. And with the waning of that movement in recent years, writing on Reconstruction has undergone still another transformation. Instead of seeing the Civil War and its aftermath as a second American Revolution (as Charles Beard had), a regression into barbarism (as Bowers argued), or a golden opportunity squandered (as the revisionists saw it), recent writers argue that Radical Reconstruction was not really very radical. Since land was not distributed to the former slaves, the remained economically dependent upon their former owners. The planter class survived both the war and Reconstruction with its property (apart from slaves) and prestige more or less intact.

Not only changing times but also the changing concerns of historians have contributed to this latest reassessment of Reconstruction. The hallmark of the pst decade's historical writing has been an emphasis upon "social history"—the evocation of the past lives of ordinary Americans—and the downplaying of strictly political events. When applied to Reconstruction, this concern with the "social" suggested that black suffrage and officeholding, once seen as the most radical departures of the Reconstruction era, were relatively insignificant.

Recent historians have focused their investigations not upon the politics of Reconstruction but upon the social and economic aspects of the transition from slavery to freedom. Herbert Gutman's influential study of the black family during and after slavery found little change in family structure or relations between men and women resulting from emancipation. Under slavery most blacks had lived in nuclear family units, although they faced the constant threat of separation from loved ones by sale. Reconstruction provided the opportunity for blacks to solidify their preexisting family ties. Conflicts over whether black women should work in the cotton fields (planters said yes, many black families said no) and over white attempts to "apprentice" black children revealed that the autonomy of family life was a major preoccupation of the freedmen. Indeed, whether manifested in their withdrawal from churches controlled by whites, in the blossoming of black fraternal, benevolent, and self-improvement organizations, or in the demise of the slave quarters and their replacement by small tenant farms occupied by individual families, the quest for independence from white authority and control over their own day-to-day lives shaped the black response to emancipation.

In the post–Civil War South the surest guarantee of economic autonomy, blacks believed, was land. To the freedmen the justice of a claim to land based on their years of unrequited labor appeared self-evident. As an Alabama black convention put it, "The property which they [the planters] hold was nearly all earned by the sweat of *our* brows." As Leon Litwack showed in *Been in the Storm So Long,* a Pultizer Prize–winning account of the black response to emancipation, many freedmen in 1865 and 1866 refused to sign labor contracts, expecting the federal government to give them land. In some localities, as one Alabama overseer reported, they "set up claims to the plantation and all on it."

The Civil War raised the decisive questions of American's national existence: the relations between local and national authority, the definition of citizenship, the balance between force and consent in generating obedience to authority.

In the end, of course, the vast majority of Southern blacks remained propertyless and poor. But exactly why the South, and especially its black population, suffered from dire poverty and economic retardation in the decades following the Civil War is a matter of much dispute. In *One Kind of Freedom* economists Roger Ransom and Richard Sutch indicted country merchants for monopolizing credit and charging usurious interest rates, forcing black tenants into debt and locking the South into a dependence on cotton production that impoverished the entire region. But Jonathan Wiener, in his study of postwar Alabama, argued that planters used their political power to compel blacks to remain on the plantations. Planters succeeded in stabilizing the plantation system, but only by blocking the growth of alternative enterprises, like factories, that might draw off black laborers, thus locking the region into a pattern of economic backwardness.

If the trust of recent writing has emphasized the social and economic aspects of Reconstruction, politics has not been entirely neglected. But political studies have also reflected the postrevisionist mood summarized by C. Vann Woodward when he observed "how essentially nonrevolutionary and conservative Reconstruction really was." Recent writers, unlike their revisionist predecessors, have found little to praise in federal policy toward the emancipated blacks.

A new sensitivity to the strength of prejudice and laissez-faire ideas in the nineteenth-century North has led many historians to doubt whether the Republican party ever made a genuine commitment to racial justice in the South. The granting of black suffrage was an alternative to a long-term federal responsibility for protecting the rights of the former slaves. Once enfranchised, blacks could be left to fend for themselves. With the exception of a few Radicals like Thaddeus Stevens, nearly all Northern policy-makers and educators are criticized today for assuming that, so long as the unfettered operations of the marketplace afforded blacks the opportunity to advance through diligent labor, federal efforts to assist them in acquiring land were unnecessary.

Probably the most innovative recent writing on Reconstruction politics has centered on a broad reassessment of black Republicanism, largely undertaken by a new generation of black historians. Scholars like Thomas Holt and

Some scholars exalted the motives of the Ku Klux Klan (left). Actually, its members were part of a terrorist organization that beat and killed its political opponents to deprive blacks of their rights.

Nell Painter insist that Reconstruction was not simply a matter of black and white. Conflicts within the black community, no less than divisions among whites, shaped Reconstruction politics. Where revisionist scholars, both black and white, had celebrated the accomplishments of black political leaders, Holt, Painter, and others charge that they failed to address the economic plight of the black masses. Painter criticized "representative colored men," as national black leaders were called, for failing to provide ordinary freedmen with effective political leadership. Holt found that black officeholders in South Carolina most emerged from the old free mulatto class of Charleston, which shared many assumptions with prominent whites. "Basically bourgeois in their origins and orientation," he wrote, they "failed to act in the interest of black peasants."

In emphasizing the persistence from slavery of divisions between free blacks and slaves, these writers reflect the increasing concern with continuity and conservatism in Reconstruction. Their work reflects a startling extension of revisionist premises. If, as has been argued for the past twenty years, blacks were active agents rather than mere victims of manipulation, then they could not be absolved of blame for the ultimate failure of Reconstruction.

Despite the excellence of recent writings and the continual expansion of our knowledge of the period, historians of Reconstruction today face a unique dilemma. An old interpretation has been overthrown, but a coherent new synthesis has yet to take its place. The revisionists of the 1960s effectively established a series of negative points: the Reconstruction governments were not as bad as had been portrayed, black supremacy was a myth, the Radicals were not cynical manipulators of the freedmen. Yet no convincing overall portrait of the quality of political and social life emerged from their writings. More recent historians have rightly pointed to elements of continuity that spanned the nineteenth-century Southern experience, especially the survival, in modified form, of the plantation system. Nevertheless, by denying the real changes that did occur, they have failed to provide a convincing portrait of an era characterized above all by drama, turmoil, and social change.

Building upon the findings of the past twenty years of scholarship, a new portrait of Reconstruction ought to begin by viewing it not as a specific time period, bounded by the years 1865 and 1877, but as an episode in a prolonged historical process—American society's adjustment to the consequences of the Civil War and emancipation. The Civil War, of course, raised the decisive questions of America's national existence: the relations between local and national authority, the definition of citizenship, the balance between force and consent in generating obedience to authority. The war and Reconstruction, as Allan Nevins observed over fifty years ago, marked the "emergence of modern America." This was the era of the completion of the national railroad network, the creation of the modern steel industry, the conquest of the West and final subduing of the Indians, and the expansion of the mining frontier. Lincoln's America—the world of the small farm and artisan shop—gave way to a rapidly industrializing economy. The issues that galvanized postwar Northern politics—from the question of the greenback currency to the mode of paying holders of the national debt—arose from the economic changes unleased by the Civil War.

Above all, the war irrevocably abolished slavery. Since 1619, when "twenty negars" disembarked from a Dutch ship in Virginia, racial injustice had haunted American life, mocking its professed ideals even as tobacco and cotton, the products of slave labor, helped finance the nation's economic development. Now the implications of the black presence could no longer be ignored. The Civil War resolved the problem of slavery but, as the Philadelphia diarist Sydney George Fisher observed in June 1865, it opened an even more intractable problem: "What shall we do with the Negro?" Indeed, he went on, this was a problem "*incapable*" of any solution that will satisfy both North and South."

As Fisher realized, the focal point of Reconstruction was the social revolution known as emancipation. Plantation slavery was simultaneously a system of labor, a form of racial domination, and the foundation upon which arose a distinctive ruling class within the South. Its demise threw open the most fundamental questions of economy, society, and politics. A new system of labor, social, racial, and political relations had to be created to replace slavery.

The United States was not the only nation to experience emancipation in the nineteenth century. Neither plantation slavery nor abolition were unique to the United States. But Reconstruction was. In a comparative perspective Radical Reconstruction stands as a remarkable experiment, the only effort of a society experiencing abolition to bring the former slaves within the umbrella of equal citizenship. Because the Radicals did not achieve everything they wanted, historians have lately tended to play down the stunning departure represented by black suffrage and officeholding. Former slaves, most fewer than two years removed from bondage, debated the fundamental questions of the polity: what is a republican form of government? Should the state provide equal education for all? How could political equality be reconciled with a society in which property was so unequally distributed? There was something inspiring in the way such men met the challenge of Reconstruction. "I knew nothing more than to obey my master," James K. Greene, an Alabama black politician later recalled. "But the tocsin of freedom sounded and knocked at the door and we walked out like free men and we met the exigencies as they grew up, and shouldered the responsibilities."

You never saw a people more excited on the subject of politics than are the negroes of the south," one planter observed in 1867. And there were more than a few Southern whites as well who in these years shook off the prejudices of the past to embrace the revision of a new South dedicated to the principles of equal citizenship and social justice. One ordinary South Carolinian expressed the new sense of possibility in 1868 to the Republican governor of the state: "I am sorry that I cannot write an elegant stiled letter to your excellency. But I rejoice to think that God almighty has given to the poor of S.C. a Gov. to hear to feel to protect the humble poor without distinction to race or color. . . . I am a native borned S.C. a poor man never owned a Negro in my life nor my father before me. . . . Remember the true and loyal are the poor of the whites and blacks, outside of these you can find none loyal."

Few modern scholars believe the Reconstruction governments established in the South in 1867 and 1868 fulfilled the aspirations of their humble constituents. While their achievements in such realms as education, civil rights, and the economic rebuilding of the South are now widely appreciated, historians today believe they failed to affect either the economic plight of the emancipated slave or the ongoing transformation of independent white farmers into cotton tenants. Yet their opponents did perceive the Reconstruction governments in precisely this way—as representatives of a revolution that had put the bottom rail, both racial and economic, on top. This perception helps explain the ferocity of the attacks leveled against them and the pervasiveness of violence in the post-emancipation South.

The spectacle of black men voting and holding office was anathema to large numbers of Southern whites. Even more disturbing, at least in the view of those who still controlled the plantation regions of the South, was the emergence of local officials, black and white, who sympathized with the plight of the black laborer. Alabama's vagrancy law was a "dead letter" in 1870, "because those who are charged with its enforcement are indebted to the vagrant vote for their offices and emoluments." Political debates over the level and incidence of taxation, the control of crops, and the resolution of contract disputes revealed that a primary issue of Reconstruction was the role of government in a plantation society. During presidential Reconstruction, and after "Redemption," with planters and their allies in control of politics, the law emerged as a means of stabilizing and promoting the plantation system. If Radical Reconstruction failed to redistribute the land of the South, the ouster of the planter class from control of politics as least ensured that the sanctions of the criminal law would not be employed to discipline the black labor force.

An understanding of this fundamental conflict over the relation between government and society helps explain the pervasive complaints concerning corruption and "extravagance" during Radical Reconstruction. Corruption there was aplenty; tax rates did rise sharply. More significant than the rate of taxation, however, was the change in its incidence. For the first time, planters and white farmers had to pay a significant portion of their income to the government, while propertyless blacks often escaped scot-free. Several states, moreover, enacted heavy taxes on uncultivated land to discourage land speculation and force land onto the market, benefiting, it was hoped, the freedmen.

In the end neither the abolition of slavery nor Reconstruction succeeded in resolving the debate over the meaning of freedom in American life.

As time passed, complaints about the "extravagance" and corruption of Southern governments found a sympathetic audience among influential Northerners. The Democratic charge that universal suffrage in the South was responsible for high taxes and governmental extravagance coincided with a rising conviction among the urban middle classes of the North that city government had to be taken out o the hands of the immigrant poor and returned to the "best men"—the educated, professional, financially independent citizens unable to exert much political influence at a time of mass parties and machine politics. Increasingly the "respectable" middle classes began to retreat from the very notion of universal suffrage. The poor were not longer perceived as honest producers, the backbone of the social order; now they became the "dangerous classes," the "mob." As the historian Francis Parkman put it, too much power rested with "masses of imported ignorance and hereditary ineptitude." To Parkman the Irish of the Northern cities and the blacks of the South were equally incapable of utilizing the ballot: "Witness the municipal corruptions of New York, and the monstrosities of negro rule in South Carolina." Such attitudes helped to justify Northern inaction as, one by one, the Reconstruction regimes of the South were overthrown by political violence.

In the end, then, neither the abolition of slavery nor Reconstruction succeeded in resolving the debate over the meaning of freedom in American life. Twenty years before the American Civil War, writing about the prospect of abolition in France's colonies, Alexis de Tocqueville had written, "If the Negroes have the right to become free, the [planters] have the incontestable right not to be ruined by the Negroes' freedom." And in the United States, as in nearly every plantation society that experienced the end of slavery, a rigid social and political dichotomy between former master and former slave, an ideology of racism, and a dependent labor force with limited economic opportunities all survived abolition. Unless one means by freedom the simple fact of not being a slave, emancipation thrust blacks into a kind of no-man's land, a partial freedom that made a mockery of the American ideal of equal citizenship.

Yet by the same token the ultimate outcome underscores the uniqueness of Reconstruction itself. Alone among the societies that abolished slavery in the nineteenth century, the United States, for a moment, offered the freedmen a measure of political control over their own destinies. However brief its sway, Reconstruction allowed scope for a remarkable political and social mobilization of the black community. It opened doors of opportunity that could never be completely closed. Reconstruction transformed the lives of Southern blacks in ways unmeasurable by statistics and unreachable by law. It raised their expectations and aspirations, redefined their status in relation to the larger society, and allowed space for the creation of institutions that enabled them to survive the repression that followed. And it established constitutional principles of civil and political equality that, while flagrantly violated after Redemption, planted the seeds of future struggle.

Certainly, it terms of the sense of possibility with which it opened, Reconstruction failed. But as Du Bois observed, it was a "splendid failure." For its animating vision—a society in which social advancement would be open to all on the basis of individual merit, not inherited caste distinctions—is as old as America itself and remains relevant to a nation still grappling with the unresolved legacy of emancipation.

Test Your Knowledge Form

We encourage you to photocopy and use this page as a tool to assess how the articles in **Annual Editions** expand on the information in your textbook. By reflecting on the articles you will gain enhanced text information. You can also access this useful form on a product's book support Web site at **http://www.dushkin.com/ online/.**

NAME: _____ DATE: _____

TITLE AND NUMBER OF ARTICLE: _____

BRIEFLY STATE THE MAIN IDEA OF THIS ARTICLE: _____

LIST THREE IMPORTANT FACTS THAT THE AUTHOR USES TO SUPPORT THE MAIN IDEA:

WHAT INFORMATION OR IDEAS DISCUSSED IN THIS ARTICLE ARE ALSO DISCUSSED IN YOUR TEXTBOOK OR OTHER READINGS THAT YOU HAVE DONE? LIST THE TEXTBOOK CHAPTERS AND PAGE NUMBERS:

LIST ANY EXAMPLES OF BIAS OR FAULTY REASONING THAT YOU FOUND IN THE ARTICLE:

LIST ANY NEW TERMS/CONCEPTS THAT WERE DISCUSSED IN THE ARTICLE, AND WRITE A SHORT DEFINITION:

ANNUAL EDITIONS revisions depend on two major opinion sources: one is our Advisory Board, listed in the front of this volume, which works with us in scanning the thousands of articles published in the public press each year; the other is you—the person actually using the book. Please help us and the users of the next edition by completing the prepaid article rating form on this page and returning it to us. Thank you for your help!

ANNUAL EDITIONS: American History, Volume 1
Pre-Colonial through Reconstruction, 16th Edition

ARTICLE RATING FORM

Here is an opportunity for you to have direct input into the next revision of this volume. We would like you to rate each of the 34 articles listed below, using the following scale:

1. Excellent: should definitely be retained
2. Above average: should probably be retained
3. Below average: should probably be deleted
4. Poor: should definitely be deleted

Your ratings will play a vital part in the next revision.
So please mail this prepaid form to us just as soon as you complete it.
Thanks for your help!

We Want Your Advice

RATING

ARTICLE

1. The Americas
2. Columbus Meets Pocahontas in the American South
3. A "Newfounde Lande"
4. Laboring in the Fields of the Lord
5. The Missing Women of Martin's Hundred
6. Bearing the Burden? Puritan Wives
7. Penning a Legacy
8. The Right to Marry: Loving v. Virginia
9. Flora MacDonald
10. Jefferson's Secret Life
11. Making Sense of the Fourth of July
12. George Washington, Spymaster
13. The Canton War
14. . . . by the Unanimous Consent of the States
15. The Founding Fathers, Conditional Antislavery, and the Nonradicalism of the American Revolution
16. The Greatness of George Washington
17. Order vs. Liberty
18. Lewis and Clark: Trailblazers Who Opened the Continent

RATING

ARTICLE

19. Chief Justice Marshall Takes the Law in Hand
20. The Florida Quagmire
21. "All We Want Is Make Us Free!"
22. "All Men & Women Are Created Equal"
23. James K. Polk and the Expansionist Spirit
24. The Lives of Slave Women
25. Eden Ravished
26. Assault in the Senate
27. "The Doom of Slavery": Ulysses S. Grant, War Aims, and Emancipation, 1861–1863
28. Pride and Prejudice in the American Civil War
29. The Struggle for Black Freedom before Emancipation
30. Lee's Greatest Victory
31. A Yankee Scarlett O'Hara in Atlanta
32. Sherman's War
33. Bats, Balls, and Bullets: Baseball and the Civil War
34. The New View of Reconstruction

(Continued on next page)

ANNUAL EDITIONS: AMERICAN HISTORY, Volume 1, 16th Edition

BUSINESS REPLY MAIL
FIRST-CLASS MAIL PERMIT NO. 84 GUILFORD CT

POSTAGE WILL BE PAID BY ADDRESSEE

McGraw-Hill/Dushkin
530 Old Whitfield Street
Guilford, CT 06437-9989

ABOUT YOU

Name

Date

Are you a teacher? ☐ A student? ☐

Your school's name

Department

Address

City

State

Zip

School telephone #

YOUR COMMENTS ARE IMPORTANT TO US !

Please fill in the following information:
For which course did you use this book?

Did you use a text with this *ANNUAL EDITION*? ☐ yes ☐ no
What was the title of the text?

What are your general reactions to the *Annual Editions* concept?

Have you read any particular articles recently that you think should be included in the next edition?

Are there any articles you feel should be replaced in the next edition? Why?

Are there any World Wide Web sites you feel should be included in the next edition? Please annotate.

May we contact you for editorial input? ☐ yes ☐ no
May we quote your comments? ☐ yes ☐ no